Understanding Adorno, Understanding Modernism

UNDERSTANDING PHILOSOPHY, UNDERSTANDING MODERNISM

The aim of each volume in **Understanding Philosophy, Understanding Modernism** is to understand a philosophical thinker more fully through literary and cultural modernism and consequently to understand literary modernism better through a key philosophical figure. In this way, the series also rethinks the limits of modernism, calling attention to lacunae in modernist studies and sometimes in the philosophical work under examination.

Series Editors

Paul Ardoin, S. E. Gontarski, and Laci Mattison

Volumes in the Series

Understanding Bergson, Understanding Modernism
Edited by Paul Ardoin, S. E. Gontarski, and Laci Mattison

Understanding Deleuze, Understanding Modernism
Edited by S. E. Gontarski, Paul Ardoin, and Laci Mattison

Understanding Wittgenstein, Understanding Modernism
Edited by Anat Matar

Understanding Foucault, Understanding Modernism
Edited by David Scott

Understanding James, Understanding Modernism
Edited by David H. Evans

Understanding Rancière, Understanding Modernism
Edited by Patrick M. Bray

Understanding Blanchot, Understanding Modernism
Edited by Christopher Langlois

Understanding Merleau-Ponty, Understanding Modernism
Edited by Ariane Mildenberg

Understanding Nietzsche, Understanding Modernism
Edited by Douglas Burnham and Brian Pines

Understanding Derrida, Understanding Modernism
Edited by Jean-Michel Rabaté

Understanding Adorno, Understanding Modernism
Edited by Robin Truth Goodman

Understanding Cavell, Understanding Modernism (forthcoming)
Edited by Paola Marrati

Understanding Flusser, Understanding Modernism (forthcoming)
Edited by Aaron Jaffe, Rodrigo Martini, and Michael F. Miller

Understanding Marx, Understanding Modernism (forthcoming)
Edited by Mark Steven

Understanding Adorno, Understanding Modernism

Edited by Robin Truth Goodman

BLOOMSBURY ACADEMIC
NEW YORK • LONDON • OXFORD • NEW DELHI • SYDNEY

BLOOMSBURY ACADEMIC
Bloomsbury Publishing Inc
1385 Broadway, New York, NY 10018, USA
50 Bedford Square, London, WC1B 3DP

BLOOMSBURY, BLOOMSBURY ACADEMIC and the Diana logo are trademarks of
Bloomsbury Publishing Plc

First published in the United States of America 2020
This paperback edition published 2022

Copyright © Robin Truth Goodman and Contributors, 2020

Cover design by Louise Dugdale and Eleanor Rose
Cover Image: Lebbeus Woods, Shard House, from San Francisco: Inhabiting the Quake, 1995. Courtesy San Francisco Museum of Modern Art © Estate of Lebbeus Woods. Photograph: Don Ross

For legal purposes the Acknowledgments on p. ix constitute an extension of this copyright page.

All rights reserved. No part of this publication may be reproduced or transmitted in any form or by any means, electronic or mechanical, including photocopying, recording, or any information storage or retrieval system, without prior permission in writing from the publishers.

Bloomsbury Publishing Inc does not have any control over, or responsibility for, any third-party websites referred to or in this book. All internet addresses given in this book were correct at the time of going to press. The author and publisher regret any inconvenience caused if addresses have changed or sites have ceased to exist, but can accept no responsibility for any such changes.

Library of Congress Cataloging-in-Publication Data
Names: Goodman, Robin Truth, 1966- editor.
Title: Understanding Adorno, understanding modernism / edited by Robin Truth Goodman.
Description: New York: Bloomsbury Academic, 2020. | Series: Understanding philosophy, understanding modernism | Includes bibliographical references and index. | Summary: "Explores and illuminates Adorno's profound impact on our understanding of literary modernism"– Provided by publisher.
Identifiers: LCCN 2020029927 (print) | LCCN 2020029928 (ebook) | ISBN 9781501342950 (hb) | ISBN 9781501370311 (paperback) | ISBN 9781501342967 (ebook) | ISBN 9781501342974 (epdf)
Subjects: LCSH: Adorno, Theodor W., 1903-1969. | Adorno, Theodor W., 1903-1969–Influence. | Modernism (Literature) | Literature–Philosophy.
Classification: LCC B3199.A34 U53 2020 (print) | LCC B3199.A34 (ebook) | DDC 193–dc23
LC record available at https://lccn.loc.gov/2020029927
LC ebook record available at https://lccn.loc.gov/2020029928

ISBN: HB: 978-1-5013-4295-0
ISBN: PB: 978-1-5013-7031-1
ePDF: 978-1-5013-4297-4
eBook: 978-1-5013-4296-7

Series: Understanding Philosophy, Understanding Modernism

Typeset by Deanta Global Publishing Services, Chennai, India

To find out more about our authors and books visit www.bloomsbury.com and sign up for our newsletters.

SERIES PREFACE

Sometime in the late twentieth century, modernism, like philosophy itself, underwent something of an unmooring from (at least) linear literary history in favor of the multi-perspectival history implicit in "new historicism" or, say, varieties of "presentism." Amid current reassessments of modernism and modernity, critics have posited various "new" or alternative modernisms—postcolonial, cosmopolitan, transatlantic, transnational, geomodernism, or even "bad" modernisms. In doing so, they have not only reassessed modernism as a category but also, more broadly, rethought epistemology and ontology, aesthetics, metaphysics, materialism, history, and being itself, opening possibilities of rethinking not only which texts we read as modernist but also how we read those texts. Much of this new conversation constitutes something of a critique of the periodization of modernism or modernist studies in favor of modernism as mode (or mode of production) or concept. *Understanding Philosophy, Understanding Modernism* situates itself amid the plurality of discourses, offering collections focused on key philosophical thinkers influential both to the moment of modernism and to our current understanding of that moment's genealogy, archaeology, and becomings. Such critiques of modernism(s) and modernity afford opportunities to rethink and reassess the overlaps, folds, interrelationships, interleavings, or cross-pollinations of modernism and philosophy. Our goal in each volume of the series is to understand literary modernism better through philosophy as we also better understand a philosopher through literary modernism. The first two volumes of the series, those on Henri Bergson and Gilles Deleuze, have established a tripartite structure that serves to offer accessibility to both the philosopher's principal texts and current new research. Each volume opens with a section focused on "conceptualizing" the philosopher through close readings of seminal texts in the thinker's oeuvre. A second section, on aesthetics, maps connections between modernist works and the philosophical figure, often surveying key modernist trends and shedding new light on authors and texts. The final section of each volume serves as an extended glossary of principal terms in the philosopher's work, each treated at length, allowing a fuller engagement with and examination of the many, sometimes contradictory, ways terms are deployed. The series is thus designed both to introduce philosophers and to rethink their relationship to modernist studies, revising our understandings of both modernism and philosophy, and offering resources that will be of use across disciplines, from philosophy, theory, and literature, to religion, the visual and performing arts, and often to the sciences as well.

CONTENTS

Series Preface v
Acknowledgments ix

Introduction: Understanding Adorno, Understanding Modernism *Robin Truth Goodman* 1

PART ONE Adorno's Keywords 5

1 Adorno and Beyond: The Modern as Critique of Modernism *Max Paddison* 7

2 Under the Skin of Modernity: The Subcutaneous *Birgit Antonia Hofstätter* 21

3 Mimesis unto Death *Robin Truth Goodman* 36

PART TWO Adorno's Aesthetics 55

4 Adorno on Vinyl *Jeffrey R. Di Leo* 57

5 Critique, Complexity, Content: Adorno and Musical Modernism since 1970 *Larson Powell* 80

6 Between the Culture Industry and Art: Adorno's Approach to Film *Stefanie Baumann* 94

7 How It Is (after Auschwitz): Adorno and Beckett *Jean-Michel Rabaté* 108

8 Thinking through and beyond Modernism: Adorno and Contemporary Performance *Sabine Wilke* 126

9   Rereading Adorno's Reading of Eichendorff in the Context of 1957 *Christian P. Weber* 141

10 Adorno and the Ethics of Camp *Heidi Schlipphacke* 160

PART THREE Adorno's Constellations 179

11 Art and Animals in Adorno *Camilla Flodin* 181

12 The Art of Dehumanization: Adorno's Animals *Natalie Lozinski-Veach* 195

13 Social Labor and the Work of Art, According to Adorno *Ulrich Plass* 214

14 Conspiracy against Theory: Superagents, Conspirators, and the Educational Legacies of Positivism *Kenneth J. Saltman* 232

15 Aspects of Adorno's Critical Theory of Culture *Stefan Müller-Doohm and Trans. Daniel Steuer* 247

Notes on Contributors 263
Index 267

ACKNOWLEDGMENTS

I owe a deep gratitude to the series editors of *Understanding Philosophy, Understanding Modernism*: Paul Ardoin, S. E. Gontarski, and Laci Mattison. Not only were they enormously helpful in conceiving the idea and working through some of the snags involved in including Adorno in the series, but they also continued to provide inspiration, criticism, and encouragement throughout the long process. In this vein, I also thank Haaris Naqvi and the folks at Bloomsbury for both material and spiritual support.

At the top of the list of acknowledgments is, of course, Theodor W. Adorno, but also the writers who continue to think with him, to think about history and politics in the tradition of his philosophical insights, and to continue to feel the urgency of the philosophical, historical, and political crisis that he identified. In this category, I include the writers in this volume, who continue to apply Adorno's aesthetic reasoning to the momentous needs of our present. I appreciate in particular how Adorno makes culture and interpretation centrally relevant to political and philosophical inquiry.

I also thank Jeffrey Di Leo and Aaron Jaffe for collaborating with me on the Society of Critical Exchange's Winter Theory Institute's annual conference in 2019 on "Control," held at Florida State University in Tallahassee. This conference gave me the opportunity to present and discuss some of my own contributions to this volume. Additionally, I thank Martin Jay, Shierry Weber Nicholson, and Henry Pickford for their suggestions.

Introduction

Understanding Adorno, Understanding Modernism

Robin Truth Goodman

Understanding Adorno, Understanding Modernism is an excellent fit for a book series that focuses on philosophical contributions to modernist practices as well as modernist contributions to philosophical practices. In fact, Adorno is so central to our current understanding of modernism that his inclusion is almost too obvious, too well-done, and too pat. Yet, what a reconsideration of Adorno's thinking on modernism may still offer is some keys to highlighting the innovations modernist aesthetics granted to social thought.

Having studied philosophy at a time when its traditions were being seriously uprooted by the atrocities of the Second World War, Theodor Adorno had an enormous impact on thinking about aesthetics at a transitional historical moment when the philosophy of science and leftist politics were looking for new ground. His interest in aesthetics—not only its philosophical traditions but also its traditions in music, art, and literature—makes artistic practices an integral part to his critique; Adorno fishes into the history of aesthetics, and particularly of modernist aesthetics, to develop ideas of autonomy, transience, sensuality, objectivity, and mimetic representation, for example, that are all key to his critique of philosophy, his political frameworks, and the workings of his dialectic. As he says in his lectures on aesthetics,

> [A]rt is indeed largely the area whose substance includes those very impulses, forms of behavior, feelings or whatever else that otherwise fall victim to the progressive control over nature and to the rationality that progresses together with it. Art, then, cannot simply be subsumed under the concepts of reason or rationality but is, rather, this rationality itself, only in the form of its otherness, in the form—if you will—of a particular resistance against it. (9)

Though Adorno rejects Benjamin's optimism that promised revolutionary results in art's technological evolution, aesthetic theory supplied Adorno with possibilities of utopian hope, non-domination, and freedom from within the total instrumentalization of history and reason that the administered society would enact.

Moreover, with his focus on the rise of commercial culture and its effects on identity construction, Adorno can be said to have reinvigorated modernist concerns by introducing the prevailing terms in our contemporary versions of cultural politics and cultural studies. As Fredric Jameson says of Adorno in a book that analyzes his relation to modernism, through reviving some "old-fashioned" philosophical motifs Adorno "may well turn out to have been the analyst of our own period" (5). Though Adorno contributed to our thinking about a range of artistic practices, what underlies Jameson's claim is his sense of Adorno as a social philosopher. Indeed, Adorno's reading of art as a mediation between the universal and the particular that cannot be reconciled becomes the basis for his analysis of capitalism as an objective and total system, based in the domination of nature, that at the same time is challenged by its own fetishes. Modernism's construction of the autonomy of the art object furnishes Adorno's model for resistance to the totally administered society. As Adorno himself remarks in *Aesthetic Theory*, "The artistic subject is inherently social. . . . [W]atching over the artist's shoulder is a collective subject that has yet to be realized" (231). And more:

> In artworks, the forces of production are not themselves different from social productive forces except by their constitutive absenting from real society. Scarcely anything is done or produced in artworks that does not have its model, however latently, in social production. (236)

In art, objectified thought sedimented in the art object—an art object, that is, in line with exchange society—at the same time is unsettled by the aesthetic spirit. As the negation of the real, art for Adorno embodies critique, and there can be no constituted sociological fact that is not already embattled by its critique as part of its factuality: art, as such, exemplifies "a theory that does not stand in abstract opposition to the facts with which it is connected" (*Philosophical Elements*, 23). Adorno's interpretation of the aesthetic as the de-instrumentalization of the Concept and its technologies informs, as well, his critique of fascism. His ideas about artistic autonomy are necessary to his formulation of alienation as a socially embedded reaction to the abstractions of traditional social sciences and the exploitations of the commodity form. What a volume on Adorno adds to this Bloomsbury series is thus an inquiry into modernism's reimagining of the aesthetic in terms of how it frames social critique in our day. Not only do the contributors consider Adorno in relation to art, literature, film, and music, but they also see Adorno as relevant for thinking about animal studies, queer theory, educational policy, and postcolonial trauma.

The volume traces Adorno's social, philosophical, and aesthetic ideas as they appear and reappear in his corpus. Adorno's thinking travels between works. Certain of his themes and constellations of thoughts appear within multiple contexts, arguments, and processes, and his reasoning is applied in various narrative settings. Whereas his great tomes—*Dialectic of Enlightenment*, *Negative Dialectics*, *Aesthetic Theory*, and *Minima Moralia*, for example—have become classics and touchstones of continental philosophy and its appearances in modernist works, Adorno's less critically acknowledged and more recently published lectures provide, perhaps, more accessible treatments of related interventions.

This volume has three parts. The first, "Adorno's keywords," is organized by the aesthetic terms around which Adorno's philosophy circulates. Reflections on "keywords" present accessible explanations and illustrations of Adorno's aesthetic ideas traced through focal points in his oeuvre. For Adorno, words are opposed by—or, nonidentical to—their definitions because they, like artworks, are alive in history, borrowing pieces of social development and historical facts even while repressing prior stages. This volume, then, focuses on some "keywords" of Adorno's aesthetic philosophy and approach to modernism as they are multiply charged for his particular brand of dialectical sociology. Aesthetic terms important to Adorno include but are not limited to autonomy, the culture industry, non-instrumentalism, the nonidentical, nature, reconciliation, mimesis, dissonance, repression, fetishism (reification), commitment, alienation, lyric, mediation, myth, the sublime, the sensual (and the non-sensual), utopia, domination, the crisis in representation, semblance, and appearance. This volume covers some of these in this first part, though the terms themselves appear throughout the volume as they underlie the whole of Adorno's thinking.

The second part is devoted to "Adorno's aesthetics." Not only have Adorno's philosophical viewpoints influenced modernism's evolution into the twenty-first, but also the history of modernist aesthetics has shaped his philosophical approaches. Adorno's move toward social philosophy was triggered by his readings of artworks: Samuel Beckett, James Joyce, Franz Kafka, Marcel Proust, Thomas Mann, Bertolt Brecht, Charles Baudelaire, Gustave Flaubert, Honoré de Balzac, Arnold Schoenberg, Igor Stravinski, Paul Klee, Pablo Picasso, surrealism, tragedy, the sublime, realism, and romanticism, for example. Rather than tracing artistic lineages, influences, and progressive patterns, Adorno discusses these antecedents as they flash up at moments when they can be recognized to illuminate the breakages in the present, the moments when the future shines through.

The third part is called "Adorno's constellations." Since the "Concept" is a philosophical problem for Adorno, a mode of domination that fetishizes its objects, constellations unlock the traditional Concept, unsealing it by coming to know "the [social] process stored in the object" (*Negative Dialectics*, 163). In other words, unlike linear causalities, systems, or external classifications, constellations are combinations that are nonidentical to the unity of the philosophical concept and reveal the context of the social object's coming to be in relation to the nonconceptual, the antagonistic subjective substance submerged but bursting from inside the social object. Adorno's methods of describing the social thus invoke aesthetic mediations, like composing, sensing, and suffering. This section discusses how aesthetic form in Adorno's thinking underlies the terms of his social analysis. For example, Adorno worried greatly over the disappearance of the individual, the fading of subjectivity under the eclipse of a dominating objectivity, the fall of reason, the constitution of the fact as wrenched out of its social foundations by positivist empiricism, disenchantment, conformity, the administered society, and the problem of freedom. Reconsidering Adorno's modernist aesthetics allows us to reconsider, at a historical moment of increasing cynicism and sometimes despair, how modernism has helped to identify not only the cultural factors of domination but also the utopian impulses in the social world, the social imaginings that can "bring forth another world, one opposed to the empirical world" (1), as Adorno suggests at the very beginning of his posthumously published *Aesthetic Theory*.

This format emphasizes a crucial but underappreciated linking between the history of art and social theory, a linking that seems to contradict modernism's assertion of autonomy while—according to Adorno—fully informing it. In addition, the format makes this book amenable to both research and teaching, offering scholars new insights while giving advanced undergraduate and graduate students pathways to learn about Adorno's thought.

Works Cited

Adorno, Theodor W. *Aesthetics 1958/59*. Trans. Wieland Hoban and Ed. Eberhard Ortland. Cambridge, UK and Malden, MA: Polity, 2018.

Adorno, Theodor W. *Aesthetic Theory*. Trans. and Ed. Robert Hullot-Kentor. Minneapolis, MN: University of Minnesota Press, 1977.

Adorno, Theodor W. *Negative Dialectics*. Trans. E. B. Ashton. London and New York: Routledge, 1973.

Adorno, Theodor W. *Philosophical Elements of a Theory of Society*. Ed. Tobias ten Brink and Marc Phillip Nogueira and Trans. Wieland Hoban. Cambridge, UK and Malden, MA: Polity, 2019.

Jameson, Fredric. *Late Marxism: Adorno or the Persistence of the Dialectic*. London and New York: Verso, 1990.

PART ONE

Adorno's Keywords

1

Adorno and Beyond

The Modern as Critique of Modernism

Max Paddison

Adorno is often regarded as the protagonist of modernism, even though this is based on a misunderstanding. Adorno's focus was on a different concept—"the modern," and on how Enlightenment rationality and the process of rationalization (with its association with "modernization") had ended up serving irrational ends. The aim of this chapter is to explore the relationship between these connected but often blurred concepts in the context of Adorno's thinking and in key debates around the experience of modernity and "the modern" in critical aesthetics, cultural theory, and the arts that emerged in the decades following his death in 1969.

Adorno's concept of "the modern" in art can be understood, on the one hand, as a range of different and frequently conflicting responses to a fundamental predicament: an experience of instability, uncertainty, and alienation in the face of constant change and the threat to survival. On the other hand, "the modern" also needs to be seen as presenting a *critical* position in relation to the concept of modernism, and indeed to the concept of art itself. This raises issues of terminology, problems of ideology, and questions of the modern's relation to modernism, as well as to the avant-garde and the New. It also raises questions regarding art's relation to the repressed and unresolved contradictions of our experience of modernity. Underlying this argument is the issue that emerges clearly only toward the end: whether the art of "the modern" has been able to address Adorno's famous injunctions regarding the survival of art after Auschwitz.

Concepts of Modernism and the Modern

The first concern is with the problem of terminology, given the general confusion around the terms "modernism," "modernity," "the modern," and, for good measure, "modernization." In fact, the word *Modernismus* rarely appears in Adorno's writings. A quick search of the DVD (Suhrkamp DB097) containing the entire twenty volumes of Adorno's collected writings in German, as published in the Suhrkamp *Gesammelte Schriften*, shows that the word occurs in total only fifteen times.[1] It crops up far more frequently in English translations of Adorno, however, because translators have usually chosen to render *die Moderne* either as "modernism" or as "modernity."[2] To confuse matters even further, "the modern" can sometimes embrace both these concepts as an umbrella concept. What is clear, nevertheless, is that Adorno favors the concept of "the modern," which in German includes a broader and more far-reaching set of concerns than is implied by the more limited (and mainly Anglophone) term "modernism," with its connotations of being an art movement, or at least a portmanteau term for the whole range of modern art tendencies and styles that he calls "the -isms" (*die Ismen*). The concepts of "modernism," "the modern," and "modernity" also overlap, and a degree of fuzziness pervades attempts at clarification, not helped by the fact that Adorno himself seldom provided clear definitions of the concepts he employed. In view of this I want first to attempt a preliminary differentiation among these related but often opposed concepts, and consider the position of "modern art" within this context, before tackling in more detail how Adorno uses these terms.

In general academic usage, the concepts of "the modern" and of "modernity" are often taken as coterminous, to the extent that they are used to embrace the historical, cultural, social, economic, technological, and political dimensions of modern life. Both terms suggest a *process* (dynamic and ongoing) and a *condition* (experiential and existential), rather than something fixed, like a single historical period, specific style, an artistic movement, or pertaining to a particular geographical location. At the same time "modernity" also has an association with the application of reason and the process of rationalization, in which respect it connects with the concept of modernization, even though its rationality may be directed toward irrational ends. "The modern," on the other hand, as well as meaning "up-to-date," in tune with the present time, and in conflict with tradition, implies an imperative, in that it calls up Rimbaud's famous exhortation: *il faut être absolument moderne*.[3] To be "modern" in this sense is to push the boundaries of experience, expression, and the latest technical means.

The experience of being "modern" is characterized by extremes, all-embracing and inescapable and at the same time fragmentary and without bounds. Much of this is implied in Marshall Berman's account, when he writes,

> To be modern is to find ourselves in an environment that promises us adventure, power, joy, growth, transformation of ourselves and the world—and, at the same time that threatens to destroy everything we have, everything we know, everything we are. . . . To be modern is to be part of a universe in which, as Marx said, "all that is solid melts into air." (Berman 15)

Viewed historically, modernity can be said to have a beginning (the eighteenth-century Enlightenment, perhaps?—or maybe the early modern era going back to the Renaissance in the period from the fifteenth to the early seventeenth centuries, when the word "modern" first began to be used to refer to "now," the "present time" in contrast to antiquity?). But modernity appears to have no end (or at least, none is currently conceivable—the advocates of postmodernity notwithstanding). The American sociologist Peter Berger has argued that two things are fundamental to modernity and belong to "the normative assumptions about it" (Berger 10): one is the founding myth of modernity, which is that of continuous *progress*, and the other is that, in spite of appearances to the contrary, modernity is *historical*.

Modernity and the experience of the modern acquired an affinity with the experience of the *sublime* that is also historical. It involves the shift from the concept of the beautiful in nature and in art, to the experience of the sublime in nature, via the experience of the sublime in art, toward the experience of modernity as sublime—that is, modern urban society has come to appear as opaque and impenetrable to those who live in it. It was the appearance of the "unboundedness" of modernity and the impossibility of grasping the experience of the modern as a totality, to put it in Kantian terms, which led Jean-François Lyotard to claim that "the sublime is perhaps the only mode of artistic sensibility to characterize the modern" (Lyotard 93). But Lyotard owes this insight as much to Adorno as to Kant. In *Ästhetische Theorie* (*Aesthetic Theory*) Adorno writes, "The more decisively that empirical reality shut itself off from it, the more art was funneled toward the sublime; subtly understood, it was the sublime alone among the traditional ideas of aesthetics that remained for the modern after the fall of formal beauty" (Adorno GS7, 293–4, my trans.). But Kant points to a further requirement for the experience of the sublime (as opposed to the direct threat posed to one's existence by the perils of real life): he says in §28 of the *Critique of the Power of Judgment* that we can only experience it as the sublime (*das Erhabene*) "as long as we find ourselves in safety" (Kant 2000, 144; Kant 1957, 348). The immediate experience of modernity, however, does not always allow for a safe place from which to measure ourselves against the overwhelming experience of the tumultuous complexity of modern life. "Modern art" (not to be confused with "modern life") might therefore be seen as a mediated and parallel sphere of activity, a kind of "safe place" in and from which to contemplate such experiences. Its autonomous forms can be seen as what Umberto Eco called "*complements* of the world" (Eco 1997, 50, my trans.),[4] but not the world directly. This remains the case, however much modern art—including the New and the avant-garde—attempts either to extend or to break down the boundaries between art and life, or to claim that art has escaped from its parallel sphere into the real world.

The concept of "modernization," on the other hand, is associated particularly with the social sciences, where it applies to the shift from traditional semifeudal rural societies to modern industrialized urban societies driven by capitalism. By extension the term can also be defined as the forms taken by rationalization, as organization, as bureaucratic, political, and cultural control, to attempt to shape modernity toward particular ends. I shall not discuss the experience of modernization as "an adventure" in positive and developmental terms, as Marshall Berman does when he concludes: "The process of modernization, even as it torments and exploits us, brings our energies and imaginations to life, drives us to grasp and confront the world that modernization makes, and to strive to make it our own" (Berman 348). On the contrary, I see modernization (*Modernisierung*) as a euphemism for rationalization (*Rationalisierung*) in the sense in which Max Weber uses the term in *Wirtschaft und Gesellschaft* (*Economy and Society*), as political and cultural control through bureaucratization that leads to alienation. This is also emphasized by S. N. Eisenstadt, who writes,

> Both political and cultural processes attendant on modernization have paradoxically enough created, through the very drawing in of broader groups to the center, the potential for alienation of wide groups from the central political and social system, for the development of feelings of anonymity and anomic estrangement from their societies, which became stronger as their expectation of participation in the center . . . grew. (Eisenstadt 21–2)

This wide concept of modernization as drawing everything toward the center, and in the process creating feelings of estrangement from the center as well as relegating traditions to the margins, has a further contradictory manifestation in the arts. It creates powerful urban centers of elite culture and at the same time creates the conditions for the reification of "the New" by the bourgeois cultural institutions that control the arts. These same conditions lead to the constant and continuing revolt by art against reification and institutionalization.

This brings us back to the concept of "modernism," so widely used in the English-speaking world, but in a more limited way elsewhere. While in a very general sense the term "modernism" can be said to refer to the manifestation of modernity in the aesthetic sphere, particularly during the first half of the twentieth century in the West (in which sense it overlaps with the concept of "the modern"), it is nevertheless most often used in a very specific sense to imply a style (e.g., in architecture), or a movement or tendency (e.g., in literature). The most obvious case is the academic study of literature in the English language, which has employed the label "modernism" to refer particularly to the experimental use of language and narrative in Anglo-American and Irish writers like Yeats, Woolf, Eliot, Pound, and Joyce in the period 1890–1950.

The term "modernism" is intrinsically plural, as represented by the "-isms" of which it is constituted (impressionism, symbolism, expressionism, cubism, neoclassicism, and so on), and it has to be admitted that it is a cause of confusion when it is used both as a label for one movement among others in the arts and as the overarching concept that embraces all these movements. Talking of "modernisms" (or maybe "modern-isms") in the plural could enable us to recognize the continuing transformations of art in relation to the process of permanent change brought about by the ongoing crises in culture, society, and the capitalist economy. In view of all this, I suggest that "modernism" can be said to refer to a changing set of artistic practices and aesthetic discourses that are inextricably part of what Habermas calls "the unfinished project of the modern" as a response to the condition of modernity. It is precisely because of its relative autonomy that this artistic and aesthetic response finds itself in perpetual conflict with, on the one hand, the process of modernization and, on the other hand, nostalgia for tradition and the dream of an imagined past. I suggest that these are the tensions that characterize all "modernisms." Adorno, however, goes further: he not only sees "modernism" (including the plurality of its "-isms") as a subset of "the modern" but also makes a critical distinction between them.

In 1955 Adorno caused controversy by publishing an article entitled "Das Altern der neuen Musik" (The Aging of the New Music) in the periodical *Der Monat*, which also appeared in revised form the following year in his essay collection *Dissonanzen* (Adorno GS14, 143–67). In it Adorno argued that the highly rationalized developments in the New Music of the first half of the 1950s later known as "multiple serialism" had led to the total reification of the musical material itself, to the extent that it had now become stultified and defunct. In 1957 Adorno went on to give a lecture at the New Music festival in Kranichstein with the title "Kriterien der neuen Musik" (Criteria of New Music, later published in his essay collection *Klangfiguren* in 1959) in which he took up the case he had made in "The Aging of the New Music" to argue, "As soon as the highly-cultivated [musical] material removes from the [composer] the effort required to construct the substance of the music, modernism begins to establish itself as a style that betrays the habitus of the avant-garde that [the composer] has turned into a stylistic trait" (Adorno GS16, 209, my trans.).

A version of this argument, first elaborated in the context of the New Music and the avant-garde, is developed by Adorno in relation to the literature of "the modern," especially that of Beckett and Kafka. In 1961 in his essay on Beckett's play *Endgame*, "Versuch, das Endspiel zu verstehen" (Adorno *GS*11), Adorno writes of "modernism as what is outdated in the modern" (Adorno *GS*11, 281, my trans.).[5] Ideas generated by modernism and its "-isms," argues Adorno, are used by Beckett as a kind of "second-order material," as part of the cultural and historical trash and detritus that becomes the material of his plays and novels. He writes, "[Beckett] uses thoughts...as clichés, fragmentary materials...the reified residues of culture" (Adorno 1991, 243; see Adorno *GS*11, 281). In brief, Adorno understands "the modern" as critique of "modernisms." That is to say, "modernism" and its "-isms" and the chatter around them rapidly become historically dated and trivialized, so that they themselves turn into fragmented material for "the modern." This suggests that for Adorno "the modern" cannot be pinned down, rather like the concept of art itself, because it is in a process of constant redefinition and negation of its own concept. To this extent "the modern" initially appeared to coincide for Adorno with the concept of "the New," as in *neue Kunst* and *neue Musik*. However, as we have seen, the New also grows old, and degenerates to an "-ism," in the process betraying the aspirations of the avant-garde which for Adorno still seemed to suggest the latest manifestation of "the modern" at any particular time.

Critiques of Modernism and the Modern

The critique of "modernism" from the perspective of "the modern" nevertheless comes with a cautionary warning from Adorno. In *Aesthetic Theory* he writes,

> But the reduction of modernism to the attitudes and opinions of the camp-followers of the genuinely modern is not valid, because without the subjective attitudes and opinions stimulated by the New the objectively modern would not be crystallized. In truth the distinction [between modernism and the modern] is demagogic: those who complain about modernism mean the modern, just as when the camp-followers are attacked it is always the protagonists of the modern who are the real target. (Adorno GS7, 45, my trans.)

What is clear, therefore, is that a distinction needs to be made between "the modern" and "modernism" along the lines I have tried to sketch earlier, but that for Adorno this distinction, which is not fixed, is governed in part by the historical process of reification and in part by what he sees as resistance to the conformist critics of the New and the avant-garde. This takes me to a consideration of critiques of modernism and the modern after Adorno, and to the ideological aspects of the canonization of what has often been called "classic modernism."

The problem with the term "modernism" is that it has been categorized, like "modernity" and, indeed, "the modern" itself, as signifying a historically limited movement in the rewriting of history that has been the key feature of the ideological case made for *post*modernism, *post*modernity, and the *post*modern in the period following Adorno's death. One of those responsible for lending this view of history powerful support has been Jean-François Lyotard, particularly in his influential *La condition postmoderne* (1979). Lyotard, like Adorno, talks of modernity (*modernité*) and the modern (*la moderne*), rather than of "modernism," even though translations often obscure this distinction. By the late 1980s, however, Lyotard had rewritten his case yet again, in a paper that went through several versions between 1986 and 1988 called "Rewriting Modernity," where he now argued that the attempt to distinguish "modernity" and "postmodernity" as separate entities is pointless. He now wrote that "neither modernity nor so-called postmodernity can be identified and defined as clearly circumscribed historical entities, of which the latter would always come 'after' the former" (Lyotard 1991, 25). He continued: "Rather we have to say that the postmodern is always implied in the modern because of the fact that modernity, modern temporality, comprises in itself an impulsion to exceed itself into a state other than itself" (Lyotard 25). In other words, modernity is in a process of constant transformation and transition, giving birth to new versions of itself, and therefore has no need for a concept of what comes "after" because, by Lyotard's own admission, it is already implicit within modernity itself. But we already have concepts for this: they are the "New" and the innovatory that constitute the constant renewal of the modern. Lyotard's rather convoluted attempt to retain the concept of "postmodernity" and "the postmodern" has served as a distraction from the more important issues he raises, which sociologically concern the ongoing technological transformation of modern society, and culturally and aesthetically our changing experience of living in such a society. What is remarkable is how Lyotard, via the circuitous route of his notion of the "postmodern," arrives back at a concept of the modern as persisting in a process of perpetual redefinition and movement beyond itself that closely resembles Adorno's concept of "the modern."

Other attempts to justify the continuing use of the concept of the postmodern, or to salvage something from it, seem equally diversionary and circuitous. The case put forward by Wolfgang Welsch in *Unsere Postmoderne Moderne* (1987) that "the postmodern is the forward-looking form taken by the transformation of the modern" (Welsch 107, my trans.) is an example of the elaborate detours required of those seeking to relate to the concept of the postmodern while arguing that it is either a transformation of the modern itself or a reaction against it—or, indeed, that it is both. They simply end up demonstrating the validity of Habermas's attack on the ideology of the postmodern and the underlying conservatism of its proponents. In his Adorno Prize lecture of 1980 Habermas had argued for the continuing incompleteness of the modern as an historical project, against the attempt of the theorists of a reactionary postmodernity to shut it down (see Habermas 3–15).[6]

Part of the problem has also been the institutional impulse to canonize the more historically limited version of the modern as artistic modernism, and to move it from the margins to the center in the process of lending it classic status. Raymond Williams has argued that the canonization of "Modernism" as an historical movement (with significant initial capital), in which he emphasizes academic art historians and literary theorists have been complicit, has served ideologically to fix its works as classics at the center of the bourgeois museum culture, so claiming to bring the process of the modern to a halt—together with the art "movement" called Modernism. What then follows has to claim to be *post*modern. Williams writes,

> After Modernism is canonized, however, by the post-war settlement and its accompanying, complicit academic endorsements, there is then the presumption that since Modernism is *here* in this specific phase or period, there is nothing beyond it. The marginal or rejected artists become classics of organized teaching and of travelling exhibitions in the great galleries of the metropolitan cities. "Modernism" is confined to this highly selective field and denied to everything else in an act of pure ideology, whose first, unconscious irony is that, absurdly, it stops history dead. Modernism being the terminus, everything afterwards is counted out of development. It is *after*; stuck in the post. (Williams 34–5)

Williams makes the point that "[Modernism's] isolated, estranged images of alienation and loss, the narrative discontinuities, have become the easy iconography of the commercials, and the lonely, bitter, sardonic and sceptical hero takes his ready-made place as star of the thriller" (Williams 35).

Appropriation of features of modernism and its techniques by the entertainment industry is one aspect of art's relation to modernity in the process of reification. Another aspect of the relationship is the sublimation and repression of the experience of modernity through art. Adorno insists that the actuality of aesthetic experience and artistic practice in relation to the continuing crisis of modernity is characterized by sublimation, which, he argues, is also what Freud meant by the term "repression." Art's attraction toward what has been repressed and to bringing it to expression has been its dominant feature since the emphasis on the New, the strange, and the fantastic that characterized the beginnings of romanticism in the early nineteenth century. Transformations of this feature persist today in relation to the self-evident upheaval and instability that are the reality of our own period. In these terms, Adorno sought to answer the critics of "the modern" and the New in art, writing in *Aesthetic Theory*,

> What the enemies of [the new] art [*neue Kunst*], with a better instinct than its anxious apologists, call its negativity is the epitome of what established culture has repressed and that toward which art is drawn. In its pleasure in the repressed, art at the same time takes into itself the disaster, the principle of repression, rather than merely protesting hopelessly against it. (Adorno 1997, 19; Adorno *GS7*, 35)

I suggest that it is this feature—the bringing-to-experience of that which is socially repressed—that distinguishes repression in the art of the modern from repression as a form of denial in everyday life. At the same time, the ways in which this might manifest in art can no longer follow modernist models like expressionism, long ago pressed into service by the film industry and now part of the cultural detritus of exhausted expressive means. Adorno's comment in the 1961 essay on *Endgame* that "Beckett's trashcans are emblems of the culture rebuilt after Auschwitz" (Adorno 1991, 266–7; Adorno *GS11*, 311) is taken up and amplified in *Negative Dialektik* (*Negative Dialectics*, 1966), where Adorno writes, "All culture after Auschwitz, together with the urgent critique of it, is garbage" (Adorno *GS6*, 359, my trans.).

The Art of the Modern after Auschwitz

My final concern is the longer-term effect of Adorno's conception of the art of the modern after the Holocaust. For Adorno, Auschwitz is the horrific consequence of repression, the dark underside of unreflective Enlightenment positivity, where rational means come to serve irrational ends. Underlying a strand of serious-minded, self-reflective Austro-German art that stretches from the immediate aftermath of the Second World War to the first decades of the twenty-first century, I suggest that we cannot help but sense responses to Adorno's famous statement of 1951 (which had its earliest airing in a paper of 1949) about the impossibility of writing poetry after Auschwitz. But clearly, poetry continued to be written, music composed, and art created; so are we to understand this as yet another case of Adorno using exaggeration to make a rhetorical point? Any attempt to answer this requires consideration of what Adorno means by *Kulturkritik* (culture criticism).

The dominant feature of Adorno's conception of a critical cultural theory is that purely aesthetic issues cannot be isolated from the historical, political, and cultural conditions of modern society. This involves the contradictory, or at very least paradoxical character of modernity, with its powerful tendencies toward rationalization and reification and, through this, toward what Adorno saw as the danger of regression to barbarism. These are the key themes of his joint book with Max Horkheimer *Dialektik der Aufklärung* (*Dialectic of Enlightenment*, 1944). Adorno makes these concerns clear in the following passage from his essay "Culture Critique and Society," and reading the often cited quotation on Auschwitz and the impossibility of poetry in context make his intentions more apparent. He writes,

> The more total society becomes, the more reified the mind (*Geist*) also becomes and the more paradoxical its attempt to escape reification through its own efforts. Even the most extreme awareness of doom threatens to degenerate into tittle-tattle. Culture critique is faced with the final stage of the dialectic of culture and barbarism: after Auschwitz to write a poem is barbaric, and this even eats into the knowledge that gives voice to the reason why it has become impossible to write poems today. (Adorno *GS*10.1, 30, my trans.)

The focus in this passage is on the problem of cultural theory after Auschwitz faced with a situation where both art and theoretical reflection upon it are rendered futile. The attempt to create art commensurate to such a catastrophe descends by comparison into crassness and triviality. By the early 1960s, however, Adorno argues that although the art of the modern is doomed to fail, its failure may also bear witness as a form of what he calls "the unconscious writing of history." In his 1962 essay "Jene zwanziger Jahre" (Those Nineteen Twenties,) we find the following development in his thinking on culture in the shadow of Auschwitz:

> The concept of a culture arising after Auschwitz is illusory and unthinkable, and for this reason any form of it that does arise has to pay the bitter price. Precisely because the world has survived its own downfall it also has need of art as its unconscious writing of history. The authentic artists of the present are those in whose works there shudders the most extreme horror. (Adorno *GS*10.2, 506, my trans.)

For Adorno, the most potent image of art after Auschwitz was the gesture of "falling silent" (*verstummen*). In one of the fragments collected together as "Paralipomena" at the end of his unfinished *Aesthetic Theory* he wrote of the Romanian poet Paul Celan—a concentration camp survivor who was a German-language poet and whose poem "Todesfuge" (Death-fugue) had been published to acclaim in 1946—that "[his] poems want to speak of the most extreme horror through silence. . . . It is that of the dead speaking of stones and stars" (Adorno 1997, 322; Adorno *GS*7, 477). This image of silence does not mean a form of quietism, a disengagement from active involvement and a retreat into the ivory tower; the image presented by Celan's poem is rather that of someone wishing to speak, but unable to do so, having been struck dumb. It is the struggle to speak while being prevented from speaking, and all that can be offered are ciphers without syntax and without a key. It is an image that emerges in much contemporary music—not "silence" as the absence of sound, as in John Cage's famous silent piece *4' 33''* (1952), but rather sound striving to articulate, in the absence of words or semantic meaning, but that appears to speak without us knowing what it is that is being said. Further still, there is the image of sound unable to sound because it is prevented from sounding.

In the light of Adorno's critical concept of "the modern" and the challenge to art after Auschwitz, I now want to turn by way of conclusion to a consideration of the German artist Joseph Beuys (1921–86). Although Beuys, who first came to public attention in the 1960s, was probably unknown to Adorno (at least, I can find no mention of him in the *Gesammelte Schriften*), his work, perhaps more than that of any other artist of the post-1945 period, made an oblique but unwavering attempt in a wide range of media (drawing, installations, and performance) toward rendering the silence after Auschwitz articulate. I want briefly to comment on one work—his sculpture/installation *Infiltration Homogen für Konzertflügel* (*Homogeneous Infiltration for Piano*, 1966), now in the Georges Pompidou Centre, Paris. This consists of a concert grand piano completely encased in a thick "skin" of grey felt and leather that would stifle any sound made by the instrument, were it capable of being played under such conditions. The resulting object (the insignia of the International Red Cross on its side) has the unsettling presence of a large wounded and bandaged animal, like an elephant or hippopotamus, but headless, immobile, and mute. The piece arouses a sense of suppressed tragedy and melancholy absurdity. Hanging from a hook on the wall beside the piano is another felt "skin," likewise with Red Cross insignia, the dull grey of the felt bringing to mind the grey of the Second World War German army greatcoat. Beuys said of this piece:

> The sound of the piano is trapped inside the felt skin. Normally, a piano is an instrument used to produce sounds. When it is not in use, it retains its sonorous potential. Here no sound is possible, and the piano is condemned to silence. (Beuys, cited in Duplaix 347)

Beuys was accused in 1980 by the art critic Benjamin Buchloh of drawing on the mythology, symbolism, and nature mysticism of the Third Reich in his art, and of self-mythologizing his own past in the Luftwaffe (Beuys had been a radio operator in a Stuka dive bomber on the Russian Front in 1944) as a form of denial and repression of the truth of his participation in the war. Buchloh wrote of the Beuys retrospective exhibition of 1979/80 at the

Guggenheim Museum in New York: "But of course, the repressed returns with ever-increasing strength, and the very negation of Beuys' origin in a historic period of German fascism affirms every aspect of his work as being totally dependent on, and deriving from, that period" (Buchloh 203). It is undeniable that Beuys's work draws on what he claims were his own experiences during the Second World War, and also that it is certain that he made these the stuff of a personal mythology. Peter Bürger points out that "Beuys creates a sort of alphabet for himself out of the materials. It is one which does not consist of phonemes but of complex concepts" (Bürger 156). These concepts depend on a system of symbols related to his materials that are in turn derived from the "foundational myth" of his plane crash in the Crimea.

But what if the foundational moment from which Beuys constructed his personal mythology and the symbolism he attaches to the materials that he returned to again and again (fat, fur, felt) was not as he claims—or perhaps was simply not true? It has to be acknowledged that considerable doubt has been cast on the factual basis of Beuys's own account of his wartime experiences, and in particular the plane crash during a blizzard in the Crimea and his claim that he was rescued by nomadic Tartars who saved his life by covering him with fat and wrapping him in felt and furs to conserve his body heat in subzero temperatures. A recently discovered letter written by Beuys in 1944 giving an account of the plane crash shortly after it occurred contradicts much of the artist's later mythologizing of the event and its aftermath. (The letter was published in full in an article in *Der Spiegel* in 2013.)[7]

I propose that another interpretation of Beuys's work is possible: that through his sculptures, installations, and *Aktionen*, and the personal mythology he constructed (no matter whether strictly true or fabricated) Beuys mimetically reenacted elements of a collective German past that could neither be directly expressed nor rationally recovered and conceptualized. One might say that in this respect Beuys also counters the postmodern relation to the past which, as Umberto Eco formulates it, "consists of recognizing that the past, since it cannot really be destroyed, because its destruction leads to silence, must be revisited, but with irony, not innocently" (Eco 1994, 67). To invert Eco's formulation, we might say that Beuys does revisit the past, but with innocence, not ironically, and in doing so makes the silence eloquent. The kind of silence presented by the object *Homogeneous Infiltration for Piano* speaks powerfully as the embodiment of repressed suffering and guilt that is thereby only to be expressed through being objectified and externalized, innocently and even naively, by someone who cannot directly look at what has been repressed for fear of being destroyed by it. In externalizing and objectifying suffering, Beuys embodies it and at the same time illuminates it. In this way it could be seen as one response to Adorno's challenge concerning the possibility of art after Auschwitz, and a potent example of the "unconscious writing of history."

Notes

1. This figure does not include the Nachlass writings from the T. W. Adorno Archive edited and published since the publication of the *Gesammelte Schriften*.
2. To maintain the distinctions between "the modern," "modernism," and "modernity," I have chosen to do my own translations where necessary.
3. Arthur Rimbaud, *Une saison en enfer* (*A Season in Hell*, 1873).
4. "Art, rather than *knowing* the world, *produces complements* of the world: it creates autonomous forms adding to those that exist, and possessing a life and laws of their own" (my trans.). Umberto Eco, "La poetica dell'opera aperta" (1959), in *Opera aperta* (Milan: Bompiani, 1997), p. 50. The passage in question also appears in the French translation (1965). It is inexplicably omitted from the English translation, "The Poetics of the Open Work," trans. Bruce Merry, in *The Role of the Reader: Explorations in the Semiotics of Texts* (London: Hutchinson, 1981), pp. 47–66.
5. "Modernismus als das Veraltete an Moderne." Shierry Weber Nicholsen translates this as "modernism as what is obsolete in modernity" (Adorno, "Trying to understand *Endgame*," *Notes to Literature* Vol. I (New York: Columbia University Press, 1991), 241. While "modernity" and "the modern" can sometimes be taken as coterminous, in this instance Adorno is making an important distinction between them.
6. The lecture delivered by Habermas on being awarded the T. W. Adorno Prize in 1980 had the title "Das unvollendete Projekt der *Moderne*." The English translation of the lecture by Seyla Ben-Habib appeared in *Postmodern Culture*, ed. Hal Foster (London: Pluto Press, 1985), 3–15, translated as "*Modernity*—an Incomplete Project."
7. See Knöfel 118–23.

Works Cited

Adorno, Theodor W. *Aesthetic Theory*. Trans. Robert Hullot-Kentor. London: Athlone Press, 1997.

Adorno, Theodor W. *Ästhetische Theorie*. *Gesammelte Schriften* [hereafter *GS*], vol. 7. Ed. Rolf Tiedemann and Gretel Adorno. Frankfurt am Main: Suhrkamp Verlag, 1970.

Adorno, Theodor W. "Das Altern der neuen Musik" (1956). *Dissonanzen*. *GS*14, ed. Rolf Tiedemann. Frankfurt am Main: Suhrkamp Verlag, 1973, pp. 143–67.

Adorno, Theodor W. "Engagement" (1962). *Noten zur Literatur III*. *GS*11. Ed. Rolf Tiedemann. Frankfurt am Main: Suhrkamp Verlag, 1974, pp. 409–30.

Adorno, Theodor W. "Jene zwanziger Jahre" (1962). *Eingriffe. Kulturkritik und Gesellschaft* I/II. *GS*10.2. Ed. Rolf Tiedemann. Frankfurt am Main: Suhrkamp Verlag, 1977, pp. 499–506.

Adorno, Theodor W. "Kriterien der neuen Musik" (1959). *Klangfiguren*. *GS*16, ed. Rolf iedemann. Frankfurt am Main: Suhrkamp Verlag, 1978, pp. 170–228.

Adorno, Theodor W. "Kulturkritik und Gesellschaft" (1951). *Prismen. Kulturkritik und Gesellschaft* I/II. *GS*10.1. Ed. Rolf Tiedemann. Frankfurt am Main: Suhrkamp Verlag, 1977, pp. 11–30.
Adorno, Theodor W. *Negative Dialektik* (1966). *GS*6, ed. Rolf Tiedemann. Frankfurt am Main: Suhrkamp Verlag, 1977.
Adorno, Theodor W. "Trying to Understand *Endgame*." In *Notes to Literature*, Vol. 1. Trans. Shierry Weber Nicholsen. New York: Columbia University Press, 1991, pp. 241–75.
Adorno, Theodor W. "Versuch, das Endspiel zu verstehen" (1961). In *Noten zur Literatur II* (1961), *GS*11. Ed. Rolf Tiedemann. Frankfurt am Main: Suhrkamp Verlag, 1974, pp. 281–321.
Adorno, Theodor W. and Horkheimer, Max. *Dialektik der Aufklärung* (1944). *GS*3, ed. Rolf Tiedemann. Frankfurt am Main: Suhrkamp Verlag, 1981.
Berger, Peter L. *Facing Up to Modernity*. Harmondsworth: Penguin, 1979.
Berman, Marshall. *All That Is Solid Melts into Air: The Experience of Modernity*. London and New York: Verso, 2010.
Buchloh, Benjamin H. D. "Beuys: The Twilight of the Idol—Preliminary Notes for a Critique" (1980). Reprinted in *Joseph Beuys: Mapping the Legacy*. Ed. Gene Ray. New York: D.A.P, 2001, pp. 199–211.
Bürger, Peter. *The Decline of Modernism*. Trans. Nicholas Walker. Cambridge: Polity Press, 1992.
Duplaix, Sonia. *Sons et Lumières: Une histoire du son dans l'art du XX siècle*. Paris: Éditions du Centre Pompidou, 2004.
Eco, Umberto. "La poetica dell'opera aperta" (1959). In *Opera aperta*. Milan: Bompiani, 1997.
Eco, Umberto. *Reflections on the Name of the Rose*. Trans. William Weaver. London: Random House/ Minerva Editions, 1994.
Eisenstadt, S. N. *Modernization: Protest and Change*. Englewood Cliffs, NJ: Prentice-Hall, 1966.
Habermas, Jürgen. "Modernity—An Incomplete Project." In *Postmodern Culture*. Ed. Hal Foster. London: Pluto Press, 1983, pp. 3–15.
Kant, Immanuel. *Critique of the Power of Judgment* (1790). Trans. Paul Guyer and Eric Matthews. Cambridge and New York: Cambridge University Press, 2000.
Kant, Immanuel. *Kritik der Urteilskraft*, in *Werke* V. Ed. Wilhelm Weischedel. Wiesbaden: Insel Verlag, 1957.
Knöfel, Ulrike. "Flug in die Ewigkeit." *Der Spiegel* 28 (2013): 118–23.
Lyotard, Jean-François. *The Inhuman: Reflections on Time*. Trans. Geoffrey Bennington and Rachel Bowlby. Cambridge: Polity Press, 1991.
Lyotard, Jean-Francois. *La Condition Postmoderne*. Paris: Les Editions de Minuit, 1979.
Weber, Max. *Wirtschaft und Gesellschaft*. Tübingen: JCB Mohr, 1922.
Welsch, Wolfgang. *Unsere Postmoderne Moderne*. Berlin: Akademie Verlag, 1987.
Williams, Raymond. "When Was Modernism?" *Politics of Modernism: Against the New Conformists*. London: Verso, 1989, pp. 34–5.

2

Under the Skin of Modernity

The Subcutaneous

Birgit Antonia Hofstätter

Introduction

The term "subcutaneous"—*das Subkutane* or *subkutan*—is an unusual keyword.[1] Readers of Adorno's works on literature might have paused and wondered when coming across the notion of the subcutaneous in the essays on Helms or Hölderlin; its most common terrain, however, are Adorno's writings on music. While Adorno's work on music is increasingly moving into the focus of scholarship, it is still not uncommon for readers of his philosophy to shy away from this aspect of his thinking.[2] This is not particularly surprising. After all, those of us who are not versed musicologists or trained musicians take the risk that the spontaneously and truly rewarding experience of thinking along with Adorno's musical writings with a "speculative ear," as it were, turns into a feeling of despair—that we find ourselves abandoned in the intricacies of musical analyses with only our *Halbbildung* to chew on. And yet it is here, saturated with aesthetic experience, that Adorno's thinking crystallizes in an almost unrivalled wealth and precision, indeed, that much of his thought comes to life. In other words, it is a risk worth taking.

In this exciting, frustrating, half-lit territory, we come across the subcutaneous. While its prominent cousins—"semblance," "identity thinking," "reification," and all the other terms that no introductory lecture on Adorno can do without—have been in the focus of scholarship for many decades, the subcutaneous can claim no such manifest significance.[3] Yet, the subcutaneous does not simply stand in the shadow of others, but as its literal meaning—"under the skin"—already indicates, it points itself to the world of shadows, to the silent and hidden processes of phenomena. And it is precisely by respecting this hidden radius, in fact, by taking its soundings, that I want to approach the subcutaneous in the present chapter. I will thus focus less on what the subcutaneous *is* than on teasing out its sometimes latent, sometimes open entwinement with Adorno's philosophy of history, in particular his thinking on modernism and tradition.[4] The subcutaneous and the particular historical moment in which it surfaces is a small but powerful nodal point in Adorno's oeuvre. In opening it up, I seek to trace the intricate historical and philosophical calibrations in which it stands and, ultimately, to throw light on how we might understand Adorno's modernism.

Adorno was both a child in modernity and a child of modernity; yet, to him, being modern, no matter in what time or what place, is not an option, but an "imperative" that calls upon art and philosophy alike: "Rimbaud's *il faut être absolument moderne*, itself modern, remains normative," he writes in *Aesthetic Theory* (192). While the imperative of being modern goes beyond the narrower historical concept of modernity or modernism—the German term *die Moderne* covers both concepts—it is nevertheless modeled on a specific form of comportment, which we can call with Adorno, Benjamin, and, ultimately, Baudelaire, heroic modernism. In Adorno's philosophy of music, we can grasp this heroic moment in terms of music's desire to become mature: "Music wanted finally to do justice to the Kantian precept that nothing sensuous is sublime, and the more the market debases music into a childish game, the more emphatically true music presses toward maturity through spiritualization" ("The Aging of the New Music," 188). Music's heroic moment, its striving for maturity at a time in which the ever-same of late capitalism increasingly swallows up its space, can be defined negatively as its emancipation from its pre-given categories of form, in other words, in terms of its breaking with its traditional idiom, with tonality. Another way of framing this moment would be as the breaking through of music's *subcutaneous* fabric.

The notion of the subcutaneous is borrowed from Schönberg. As Adorno writes in "Das Erbe und die neue Musik,"

> In his last book, Schönberg [...] at one point speaks about the "subcutaneous," about an irregularity that takes place underneath the skin of the regular. I believe that the notion of subcutaneous configuration [*Gestaltung*, A. H.] applies to any music of true distinction in all of its aspects. I mean by this precisely the ability to develop all sensual moments of the here and now as moments of a unified meaning [*Sinn*, A. H.] that adheres to its own logic. (688–9)

For Adorno, the web of relations that defines the meaning of a musical work as the unifying articulation of its distinct elements is crucial both to modern and traditional music—and by "traditional music" Adorno means the music of the approved German-Austrian tradition of roughly the last 300 years.[5] Yet, while in traditional music the subcutaneous fabric was hidden underneath the mediations and greater architecture of tonality, at the height of modernity, at what Adorno sometimes calls the "event" of Schönberg, the latent fabric breaks through the conventional musical surface and becomes manifest ("Understanding Schoenberg," 634). We will explore this in more detail later on; for now, it suffices to say that what music registers at its heroic point is what the experience of modernity confirms: that tradition—the "pregiven, unreflective and binding existence of social forms—the actuality of the past," as Adorno puts it—is irretrievably lost ("On Tradition," 75). What must not be lost, however, as readers of early critical theory know well, are the hopes of the past. In Adorno's Schönberg, empowered by the demystifying force of modernity, we encounter a critical historical consciousness that turns the forces of tradition against itself: in the critique of the past, the new becomes answerable to the hopes of the past. The thinking of a latent, subcutaneous current which surfaces in the negation of tradition as the voice of its unfulfilled promises, becomes the model for Adorno's rethinking of tradition at the very moment at which it is put into question.

The Scene of Modernity

To awaken the notion of the subcutaneous from its slumber, I suggest we begin not in Vienna or Frankfurt or even Pacific Palisades but in higher altitudes: in a sanatorium in the Swiss mountains, the setting for Thomas Mann's *The Magic Mountain*, the eminently modern novel, which was written and rewritten in the shadows of the First World War. In the thin air of historical speculation, there emerges a compelling correspondence between Mann's novel and Adorno's philosophy of music, a correspondence which shines its light on those aspects of the subcutaneous that appear to be hidden to our current sensibilities. Let us take a look at the following episode from Mann's novel: in the basement of the sanatorium, Hans Castorp, the modern protagonist, attends to a procedure that from today's perspective appears rather unremarkable, but which brought to consciousness something uncanny—the taking of an x-ray.[6]

> And Hans Castorp saw, precisely what he must have expected, but what it is hardly permitted man to see, and what he had never thought it would be vouchsafed him to see: he looked into his own grave. The process of decay was forestalled by the powers of the light ray, the flesh in which

> he walked disintegrated, annihilated, dissolved in vacant mist, and there within it was the finely turned skeleton of his own hand, the seal ring he had inherited from his grandfather hanging loose and black on the joint of his ringfinger—a hard, metal object, with which man adorns the body that is fated to melt away beneath it, when it passes on to another flesh that can wear it for yet a little while. (218)

The light rays that penetrate Hans Castorp's skin reveal the secret known to all, but hidden by the vital surface of the body: "[F]or the first time in his life he understood that he will die" (218). The process of decay that is anticipated by the light rays of the medical apparatus, the mortification of what is alive for the sake of the preservation of life, appears as an allegory of the modern condition as one in which the forces of rationalization penetrate to the bone. Indeed, the apparatus illuminates the patient's body as mortal through and through. In the skeleton as projected onto the screen, the forces of progress meet with the forces of disenchantment and in a strange reversal, the procedure itself, its magic powers of vision, come to appear mystical. *Spukhaft*, "ghostly," the *Hofrat*, operating the machine, calls it. But then it was over: "He closed off the current. The floor ceased to vibrate, the lightnings to play, the magic window was quenched in darkness" (219).

While the scene in the basement of the sanatorium has drawn to a close, the curtain has fallen, the *Spuk* of modernity continues. Indeed, it is no secret that entwined with the movement of modernity, of progressive rationalization if you like, is a movement of decay, of disintegration, of death. The ghostly character of modernity, if we were to pin it down, consists in the living on of what has been outlived. *Fortwesen*, Adorno likes to call it as a neologism whose resonance with the German word *Verwesen*, the material decomposition of bodies, forms a counterpoint to the prefix *fort-* , its persistence. "The backbone of spirit has been broken," Adorno writes in "The Aging of the New Music," "and anyone who pays no attention to this and acts as though nothing has happened, must crawl like an insect, not walk upright" (200). What Adorno claims here with reference to the ultimate trauma of modernity, the Holocaust, is preceded for him by a lesser trauma, but a trauma nevertheless, which determines the life of modern thought and culture as always already an afterlife: the broken promise of human emancipation. The experiences of modernity put an end to the narrative of progress and affirmation; the unfulfilled hopes of the Enlightenment, however, form the latent force of negativity that compels spirit to think against all negativity. The first sentence of *Negative Dialectics* hardly bears repeating anymore: "Philosophy, which once seemed obsolete, lives on because the moment to realize it was missed" (3). This applies no less to Adorno's thinking on art and music. If modern culture begins with the mute crack of its own spine, it survives (itself) as critique.[7]

A Subcutaneous Critique of Classicism

Hans Castorp's encounter with his subcutaneous predicament in *The Magic Mountain* can serve as our working model for aesthetic modernism as the critique of the musical tradition, in particular of classicism. Indeed, if the model for classic and romantic aesthetics is that of the "perfected, beautiful individual," as theorized in terms of the artistic symbol, the skeleton or, as in Benjamin's writing, the torso, the skull, the corpse, the emblem of allegory is its antagonist (*Tragic Drama*, 160).[8] "The music in which we are still immediately living—and it does begin with Bach, after all—labors from its inception under an internal difficulty, a contradiction," Adorno writes, "[o]n the one hand it is tied into a system, the system of triads, keys, and their relationships. On the other hand, the subject is trying to express itself in it; instead of every norm that is merely imposed externally, it wants to generate the regularities from within" ("Understanding Schoenberg," 633). The antagonistic dynamic between these two poles, which is later revealed as resistant to mediation and sketched by Adorno in terms of a manifest and subcutaneous layer, is precisely what gives the classical work, laboring toward the resolution of this tension, its force. As Adorno puts it in "Klassik, Romantik, neue Musik,"

> It is an essential aspect of classicism [. . .] that its impulses do not pour themselves submissively into given, so-called objective forms, but that the forms are co-construed by the unruly subjectivity that opposes them. They become binding only where objectivity of form, handed down and alienated from consciousness, is saturated with critical subjectivity[.] (130)

At the height of tonality—the Viennese Classicism of Beethoven, Mozart, or Haydn—the tension between this "objectivity of form" and "unruly subjectivity" appears successfully resolved in the individual works. Indeed, for Adorno, it was the outstanding achievement of the middle Beethoven to out-Hegel Hegel, as it were, and to have redeemed the "objective" tonal norms through the force of a unified compositional subject. In affirmatively enacting the reconciliation of subject and object, the works of Viennese Classicism express the hope of the bourgeois age that the objective course of history and the free development of its subjects ultimately coincide.

If the classical artwork lays claim to the identity of essence and appearance, subject and object, the skeleton that is presented by the x-ray apparatus, in contrast, reveals the nonidentity of the subject, the work with itself. In making visible what remains most incommensurable with the perceived universality of consciousness or form—namely, the irrefutable and irrefutably melancholic insight that, to speak with Adorno, the subject is "itself a piece of nature" and, hence, like everything that is alive, it must perish—the x-ray apparatus secularizes the *Gestalt* in a gesture of critique: it disempowers the appearance of universality by revealing the transience that is not only the work's destiny but also its hidden condition of possibility. In other words, it appears as a variant of the "immersive gaze [*Tiefblick*, A. H.] of allegory," which Adorno, crediting Benjamin, regards as "perhaps the model for the philosophical gaze as such" (*History and Freedom*, 134; trans. mod.). Akin to the scene in the sanatorium, when Hans Castorp saw his own death in the here and now, allegory is the form of signification which expresses death or transience as its very presupposition: as "other discourse," it reveals the constitution of meaning as necessarily always also an act of decay. In disempowering the semblance of organic reconciliation, of life, the allegorical gaze coincides, emphatically, with the demystifying force of critique: "critique," for Benjamin, "is the mortification of works" (*Tragic Drama*, 182).

Indeed, "every penetrating analysis of an artwork turns up fictions in its claim to aesthetic unity," Adorno writes in *Aesthetic Theory* (105). The penetrating *Tiefblick* reveals the reconciliatory claim of the past works as chimerical: in puncturing its vibrant sensual appearance, it lays bare the work's inner process as one in which its parts do not spontaneously cohere: it attends to the work's inner transience. The promise of classicism that the particular is fully and concretely expressed in the totality of the work collides with the dominance of form, which always already compromises the integrity of the particular.

> Though in classicism the subject rises up aesthetically, violence is done to it, to that eloquent particular that opposes the mute universal. In the much admired universality of the classical work the pernicious universality of myth—the inescapability of the spell—is perpetuated as the norm of the process of formation. (*Aesthetic Theory*, 162; trans. mod.)

In drawing out the social and historical mediations of the artwork, the allegorical *Tiefblick*, in turn, reveals within these mediations the persistence of myth, of natural deterioration. As in bourgeois society, the equilibrium of subject and object to which the classical artwork is committed, proves ultimately unattainable. Its staging involves concealment—Adorno speaks of "polish and balance" by means of "tact" (*Aesthetic Theory*, 109). Just as tactfulness coincides with an element of self-censorship and "renunciation," as Adorno puts it in *Minima Moralia*, the work passes over those elements that dissent from the collective agreement that the totality expresses and which only comes to shine in relation to what it silences (36). "[I]nternal to everything in art that can justly be called harmonious there survives something desperate and mutually contradictory," Adorno writes, "[. . .]. Dissonance is the truth about harmony" (*Aesthetic Theory*, 109–10).

Revealed by the allegorical *Tiefblick* is the broken promise of the bourgeoisie as the broken promise of classicism: that the aspired to emancipation of humankind terminated in its semblance is the trauma that haunts the history of modernity and, with it, the musical tradition.

The Critical Decomposition of the Musical Tradition

The critical *Tiefblick*, which disempowers the semblance of the unified organic whole by making visible the transience that lies at its heart, is not randomly imposed on the artwork. Rather, it answers the process of decay and disintegration that the tonal paradigm undergoes in modernity and in which the individual works lay bare the aporia intrinsic to their form.

The desideratum of the classical work to seamlessly reconcile subject and object in the compositional subject irrevocably shatters in the very exercise of this tension: indeed, the immanent decay of traditional music sets in at the very moment at which it is effectively consummated. The more strictly the artwork commits to the ideal of the appearing essence, in other words, the more incorruptly it attends to the particular musical events from which it ought to derive—its subcutaneous fabric—the more it gives way to a disintegrating pull that answers to the unfulfilled demands of the particular. "The utmost integration is utmost semblance and this causes the former's reversal" (*Aesthetic Theory*, 45). The trauma of modern music leads to an ever-widening splitting into a conscious surface phenomenon and a latent, subcutaneous fabric. Compositional subjectivity, sworn to fully expressing itself in all aspects and relations of the work, begins to distance itself from the forms it can no longer fill; the vacated manifest forms, in turn, lose their force of necessity and degenerate into empty conventions: they become heteronomous to the work. In fact, the familiar and soothing sounds of the traditional facade blend into the ever-same of the culture industry. "The aspect of commonality in the tonal language increasingly emerged as one of the comparability of everything with everything, of levelling and convention," Adorno writes in "Difficulties,"

> [t]he simplest sign of this is the way the principle chords of the tonal system can be inserted at innumerable points, as a kind of form of equivalence, in which something that is always identical stands in for something that is always different, without, themselves, having to be modified. This comparability of the aspect of musical language increasingly put itself at the disposal of the consumer character, as its vehicle. [. . .] Gradually [. . .] the consumer character spread itself over the entire language

of music. This became unendurable; what had once been language, in music, turned into clatter. (665)

What could once be brought into a precarious tactful balance is now separated by an unbreachable abyss. With the aging and commodification of the tonal paradigm, semblance has become decisively ideological. Indeed, the affirmation of reconciliation that each work pretends to accomplish aesthetically has become intolerable "in proportion as reality, through the universal, accords the particular less and less of what the latter has been promised and promises itself," Adorno writes in "Difficulties." "Aesthetic ties are a lie because the real ties have become a lie" (669).

The critical decomposition of the traditional paradigm in modernity—its consummation until the given forms and normed relations are hollowed out, begin to clatter and reveal their contingent and repressive nature—retroactively lays bare the innermost untruth of the classical law of form: "The concrete transience of the classical [. . .] exposes the transience of its concept and the norms deriving from it," as Adorno puts it in *Aesthetic Theory* (161). The history of decay of traditional music is the history of its stripping bare its semblance character. In the revelation of its broken promise, however, the promise itself comes to be remembered.

The "Event" of the Subcutaneous

It is the plight of the modern subject, coerced into false identity with the universal, that ultimately explodes the already brittle affirmative facade, soothing in its familiarity and order, yet essentially deceptive and violent in character. For Adorno, Schönberg's "spontaneous productive power" puts an end to the manifest *Fortwesen*: he "executed an objective historical verdict—he liberated the latent structure while disposing of the manifest one" ("Arnold Schoenberg," 156). The eruption of music's inner life devours the hollow continuities on its surface—akin to the anti-traditional maelstrom of which Adorno, reminiscent of Benjamin's notion of origin, speaks in *Aesthetic Theory* (23)—and, with it, challenges the legitimacy of tradition itself:

> The concept of modernism [*die Moderne*, A. H.] is privative; since its origins it is more the negation of what not ought to be than a positive slogan. It does not, however, negate previous artistic practices, as styles have done throughout the ages, but rather tradition itself[.] (*Aesthetic Theory*, 21; trans. mod.)

Tradition is irrevocably lost to the modern consciousness; nothing is gained from preserving it. And it is at this point of no return, of having to let go of what is familiar, that the redemptive historical force of the subcutaneous makes itself known.

While Schönberg's music might have sounded like extraterrestrial noise to the ears of the Viennese audience of the early twentieth century, the shocking force of the supposedly unheard sounds—which Adorno attributes to their "disturbing and disturbed quality"—did not come from outer space ("Aging," 181; trans. mod.). If anything, outer space might be its utopian destination and not its point of departure. If we listen to a Beethoven piece in a culinary manner (to use one of Adorno's slightly acidic terms), we indeed already *know* the subcutaneous, in the same way as we *know* something that is repressed: the subcutaneous is that which ultimately makes musical sense of, but is not identical with, the by now (in)famous *da, da, da, dumm*. The surfacing of the subcutaneous in Schönberg's compositions is thus the reappearance of something not wholly unfamiliar. While the force of its disturbance might thus be owed to the uncanny nature of its re-cognition, for Adorno, it has also been nurtured in the sheltered twilight of latency. Indeed, Adorno, as Benjamin before him, recognizes with Freud the dialectical aspects of repression or forgetting (see Benjamin "Baudelaire," 162–3): impressions are kept alive not where they can be accessed by conscious recollection—"precisely where [memories] become controllable and objectified [. . .] [they] fade like delicate wallpapers in bright sunlight," Adorno writes in *Minima Moralia*—but rather where they are shielded from conscious exposure in subcutaneous depth, awaiting recovery (166). The subcutaneous, as the secret substratum of the musical tradition, is its innermost and inconspicuous momentum of resistance: both a product of the totality and beyond its reach, it emerges from its latent depths to defend the autonomous will of the tradition against the ever-same into which the tradition itself has turned.

This sheds light on Adorno's rethinking of tradition at the brink of its impossibility: "The fact that tradition cannot be conjured up corresponds to Freud's great insight that it is the return of the repressed. This does not occur under the gaze of conscious memory; rather, tradition would be sheltered [*geborgen*, A. H.] in involuntary memory alone," Adorno writes in his piece on tradition in *Dissonanzen* (132). The surfacing of the subcutaneous in modernity is imagined by Adorno as both the return of the repressed, conditioned by the trauma that lies at its origin, and as an instance of a Proustian *memoire involontaire*. The ambiguity of this moment of remembrance is as apparent as it is exemplary for Adorno's dialectical aesthetics: while the uncanny character of the conflicting and dissonant sounds might appear "disturbing and disturbed," it is also saturated with the bliss of remembrance, that is, with the happiness of giving voice to what had previously been unheard (see *Ästhetik 1958/59*: 66–7). Indeed, the memory of suffering discloses a broken utopian horizon.

Redeeming the Hopes of the Past

The breaking through of the subcutaneous in modernity sets into motion the distinction between life and death: the spiritualizing move toward greater "abstraction" from the surface, from what appears immediately catchy or stimulating to the senses—that is, from what appears, deceptively, alive—coincides with an opening up to a latent spectrum of wealth that bears the mark of transience, to "what has not been socially approved and preformed," as Adorno puts it in *Aesthetic Theory* (93). In following the urge of the subcutaneous to be fully and concretely realized in the work—which is but the desire of the work to be fully and concretely realized in itself—Adorno's Schönberg answers to the broken promise of the musical tradition by honoring its intention. It is worth reminding ourselves with a quote from "Klassik, Romantik, neue Musik":

> The postulate of an objectivity that passes through the subject itself, is mediated by the subject and, in turn, receives the subject within itself, which Viennese Classicism hoped to satisfy, still persists. What the great composers of the Viennese School—from Haydn to Schubert—desired, namely a music that is fully conjoined within itself, entirely right, entirely binding and yet at every moment subject, actually emancipated humankind, has not been able to find its voice yet. Still, it endures as the task of anticipating the image of a society in which the common interest would truly coincide with the interest of each individual, a society without violence and oppression. (141)

In Schönberg, the urge of the uncensored particular to be realized in the composition meets with a will to form—indeed, to domination—that ensures its objectivation: Adorno likes to capture this dynamic with Schönberg's phrase *Triebleben der Klänge* (roughly, the libidinal life of sounds), which he juxtaposes with "an ego strong enough not to have to deny the drives" ("Arnold Schoenberg," 149; trans. mod.). Out of the free play of drives, in Freud's words, "awesome in their indeterminateness," ought to emerge a compositional subject which is highly differentiated and determinate in all of its aspects (Freud 529).

> By virtue of being called by its name, hence by being expressed immediately, the emancipated aesthetic subject is to be intensified into its own objectivity, out of itself, in the course of articulating what, in truth, it is. This [. . .] requires a powerful and self-controlled intensification of those impulses which the average bourgeois standards have sanctioned with a taboo. ("Klassik, Romantik," 143)

Concretely, this means that each distinct element of the musical totality is the carrier of a unified compositional meaning (*Sinn*) and that the musical meaning, in turn, emerges as the very articulation or, indeed, intensification of its differentiated elements through motivic-thematic work: "[W]hat is crucial is the variegated alternation of distinct and contrasting figures with the general unity of motivic-thematic relations," Adorno writes in *Prisms* (154). The totality is not seamlessly accomplished; it does not collapse into a static image, as it were. Rather, it emerges in the open playing out of its compositional labor that attempts "the strict unity of an abundant manifold," which crucially testifies to the social antagonism that it reflects ("Das Erbe," 691). The aim is to make its "irreconcilability determinate," to speak with Adorno in *Aesthetic Theory*: "Paradoxically, art must testify to the unreconciled and at the same time envision its reconciliation" (168).

The decisive difference between traditional music and modern music is that, in modern music, the reconciliation between essence and appearance is not presented as accomplished, the universal and particular do not break even: rather, the establishment of the totality is precisely what constitutes the problem of the composition. While in traditional music the resolution of the tension between subject and object in their identity appears ultimately guaranteed by the surface schema, in new music the totality is, without resolve, each time to be openly established out of the untamed subcutaneous fabric itself: "It is music of identity in nonidentity" ("Arnold Schoenberg," 154).

The negation of tradition through its subcutaneous substratum also has retroactive force: it opens up the possibility of thinking the new not only as redeeming the hopes of the past but also as releasing the latent promise in past works themselves. In fact, in Schönberg's attempt to answer the promises that the tradition raised and that it could not fulfill, the past works, in turn, are revealed as incomplete, indeed, as awaiting their future realization. Not unlike the experience of trauma, which is defined, in Cathy Caruth's words, less by "the forgetting of a reality that can hence never be fully known, than by an inherent latency within the experience itself," the surfacing of the subcutaneous in modernity, the return of the repressed, retroactively reveals the silent temporal nucleus within the past works themselves (Caruth 7–8; see also Richter 10). Adorno, in his draft on musical reproduction, turns to Benjamin's account of translation to explore this point:

> One can apply what Benjamin remarks concerning the relationship between literature and translation, where he develops the idea of the "original," to music: "[. . .] in living on, which would be a meaningless phrase if it were not a transformation and a renewal of something alive, the original changes." [. . .] The newer works shed light on the older ones[.] (*Musical Reproduction*, 545–6)

The experience of Schönberg changes the experience of Beethoven and vice versa. For musical reproduction, this means that the freeing of the subcutaneous in modernity ultimately motivates a mode of interpretation that lays bare the hidden processual character of traditional works. When Adorno, in this context, speaks about musical reproduction as the x-ray image of the work—and here we meet again with our original metaphor—he means that the latent subcutaneous fabric must be articulated down to the subtlest of its nuances and effectively reintegrate the schematic elements into the fabric of meaning (see *Musical Reproduction* §1). In other words, in drawing out the latent intention of form, musical interpretation, as it were, must "actualise its [the work's A. H.] force-field": "That is, not *only* playing the dissonances and dropping the consonances, but also realizing the *tension* between the two according to the compositional sense" (*Musical Reproduction*, §50, trans. mod.). Musical reproduction that lends voice to the subcutaneous dialectically attends to the split between latent and manifest layer in such a way that the labor of its antagonism becomes audible and the work as a whole comes to life in the articulation of its progression. The negation of schema by the subcutaneous in every act of interpretation is its ever-belated gesture of rescue.

Schönberg's compositions do not fulfill the outstanding promise of the musical tradition but keep its memory alive in the paradoxical act of reconciliation that testifies to the irreconciled; similarly, interpretation does not once and for all mend the trauma of past works. However, "the dead are our children," Adorno writes in his "Marginalia to Mahler," and it is perhaps in the re-cognition of like and like across the sea of history that a glimmer of hope still persists (612; trans. mod.).

Conclusion

The music in which Adorno was at home—the works of Bach, Beethoven, Mahler, or Schönberg—demands a form of comportment in which the fleeting moment of the present is realized in relation to what has passed and to what shall follow and, indeed, to what coexists: "Highly organised music always means the presence of the non-present, i.e. remembrance and anticipation," Adorno noted (*Musical Reproduction*, § 70; trans. mod.). In musical modernism, this temporal dedication—which is always the labor of negation and integration (and never one without the other)—is heightened to a condition of possibility: while traditional music, by virtue of its familiar schematic elements, tolerates a passive attitude, new music, "because it is more specific and more articulated in all of its events," upsets the false agreement between work and listener in which the work itself is misrecognized—"one cannot swim along in it" ("Difficulties," 672). New music, then, at its heroic moment, calls upon the receptive subject to establish relations across time and truly divergent elements and to hold open the force field that emerges.[9]

> New music, as a whole, postulates—as consciousness of tension— experience, the dimension of happiness and suffering, the capacity for the

extreme, for what has not already been pre-formed, in order, as it were, to salvage what is being destroyed by the apparatus of the administered world. (673)

This capacity for the extreme, for happiness and suffering, for what has not already been preformed coincides with the capacity for remembrance: with the ability to give voice to what is silenced. The history of modernity as the history of decay is a story of loss and broken promises; *therefore*, it is the time of critique. In setting free what resides in the subcutaneous depths of phenomena, critique attends to the unfulfilled hopes of the past and opens them up to a possible future. No sentence captures better what is at stake than the following one from *Negative Dialectics*: "Only if what is can be changed, is that which is not all there is" (398; trans. mod.). Its urgency remains unchanged today.

Notes

1 I would like to thank Daniel Steuer for his insightful and encouraging comments on a draft version of this piece. I am also grateful to my mother, Petra Hofstätter, for reminding me of the x-ray passage in *The Magic Mountain*. Where I cite directly from the German original, the translations are mine.

2 The increasing interest in Adorno's musical writings is not least due to the (relatively) recent publication of a collection of translations of musical texts in the volume *Essays on Music* in 2002 and, more recently, *Night Music: Essays on Music 1928–1962*. And, of course, much is owed of the work of Lydia Goehr, Robert Hullot-Kentor, Max Paddison, Shierry Weber Nicholsen, and other "pioneers" in the field of Adorno's philosophy of music.

3 While occasionally mentioned, the notion of the subcutaneous has to my knowledge, not been the subject of a more extensive exploration in the context of Adorno's work. In her article on "Listening as the Work of Co-composing," however, Shierry Weber Nicholsen discusses the subcutaneous in the context of Adorno's thoughts on listening and musical reproduction, with which this article shares some common themes. In an earlier publication, I develop an aspect of the subcutaneous in relationship to the philosophical comportment of *Selbstbesinnung* in Adorno's work (see Hofstätter 155–70).

4 In fact, in this contribution, I choose a rather specific angle to explore the notion of the subcutaneous, which means that some other crucial aspects remain only hinted at, such as its entwinement with Adorno's notion of aesthetic meaning (*Sinn*) or its relationship to the notion of language character. For reasons of space, the wider relationship between Adorno's philosophy and Schönberg's music remains also unexplored. For a brilliant account thereof see Lydia Goehr's piece on "Adorno, Schoenberg, and the Totentanz der Prinzipien."

5 For a concrete and detailed account of the subcutaneous, as it is operative in new and traditional music, see "Das Erbe und die neue Musik." For the

notion of aesthetic meaning (*Sinn*), with which the notion of the subcutaneous entwines, see the section on "Coherence and Meaning," in *Aesthetic Theory* (136–63).

6   Inspired by the notion of subcutaneous, the metaphor of the x-ray is crucial to Adorno's work on musical reproduction, on which I will touch briefly in the later part of this chapter: "True reproduction is the x-ray image of the work" (*Reproduction*, § 1).

7   In his inspiring piece "Lager, Nach-Welt, Überleben," Irving Wohlfarth unfolds this dynamic in Adorno's work in great detail. For a contextualization of Adorno's work in the wider discourse of modernity as the inherently "belated" age, see Gerhard Richter's book on *afterness*.

8   Indeed, for Benjamin the corpse becomes the emblem of modernity and modernity crucially the age of allegory. Something very similar is going on in Adorno's philosophy of music, as we shall see. Unfortunately, I am unable to discuss the decisive influence of Benjamin's conceptualization of modernity on Adorno's work in any detail in this piece.

9   For a more developed account of the relationship between new music and emancipatory subjectivity, see again Weber Nicholsen's piece on listening.

Works Cited

Adorno, Theodor W. *Aesthetic Theory*. Trans. Robert Hullot-Kentor. London: Continuum, 2004.
Adorno, Theodor W. "Arnold Schoenberg: 1874-1951." In *Prisms*. Trans. Shierry and Samuel Weber. Cambridge, MA: MIT Press, 1981, pp. 147–72.
Adorno, Theodor W. *Ästhetik (1958/59). Nachgelassene Schriften*, div. IV, vol. 3. Ed. Eberhard Ortland. Frankfurt am Main: Suhrkamp Verlag, 2009.
Adorno, Theodor W. "Das Erbe und die neue Musik." In *Gesammelte Schriften*, vol. 18. Ed. Rolf Tiedemann. Frankfurt am Main: Suhrkamp Verlag, 1984, pp. 684–94.
Adorno, Theodor W. "Difficulties." In *Essays on Music*. Ed. Richard Leppert. Berkeley and Los Angeles: University of California Press, 2002, pp. 644–80.
Adorno, Theodor W. *History and Freedom*. Ed. Rolf Tiedemann. Trans. Rodney Livingstone. Cambridge: Polity, 2006.
Adorno, Theodor W. "Klassik, Romantik, neue Musik." In *Gesammelte Schriften*, vol. 16. Ed. Rolf Tiedemann. Frankfurt am Main: Suhrkamp Verlag, 1978, pp. 126–44.
Adorno, Theodor W. "Marginalia on Mahler" In *Essays on Music*. Ed. Richard Leppert. Berkeley and Los Angeles: University of California Press, 2002, pp. 612–18.
Adorno, Theodor W. *Minima Moralia: Reflections on a Damaged Life*. Trans. E. F. N. Jephcott. London: Verso Books, 2005.
Adorno, Theodor W. *Negative Dialectics*. Trans. E.B. Ashton. London: Continuum, 1973.
Adorno, Theodor W. *Night Music: Essays on Music 1928-1962*. Trans. Wieland Hoban, New York: Columbia University Press, 2009.
Adorno, Theodor W. "On Tradition." *Telos*, vol. 94 (1992): 75–82.

Adorno, Theodor W. "The Aging of the New Music." In *Essays on Music*. Ed. Richard Leppert. Berkeley and Los Angeles: University of California Press, 2002, pp. 181-203.
Adorno, Theodor W. "Toward an Understanding of Schönberg." In *Essays on Music*. Ed. Richard Leppert. Berkeley and Los Angeles: University of California Press, pp. 627-43.
Adorno, Theodor W. *Towards a Theory of Musical Reproduction: Notes, a Draft and Two Schemata*. Edited by Henry Lonitz. Translated by Wieland Hoban, Cambridge: Polity Press, 2006. Open eBook.
Adorno, Theodor W. "Tradition." In *Gesammelte Schriften*, vol. 14. Ed. Rolf Tiedemann. Frankfurt am Main: Suhrkamp Verlag, 1973, pp. 127-42.
Benjamin, Walter. "On Some Motifs in Baudelaire." In *Illuminations*. Ed. Hannah Arendt. London: Fontana Books, 1973, pp. 157-202.
Benjamin, Walter. *The Origin of the German Tragic Drama*. Trans. John Osborne. London: Verso Books, 1998.
Caruth, Cathy. "Introduction." In *Trauma: Explorations in Memory*. Ed. Cathy Caruth. Baltimore and London: John Hopkins University Press, 1995, pp. 3-12.
Freud, Sigmund. "Neue Folge der Vorlesungen zur Einführung in die Psychoanalyse." In *Studienausgabe*, vol. 1. Ed. Alexander Mitscherlich, Angela Richards, James Strachey, 4th ed., Frankfurt am Main: S. Fischer Verlag, 1969, pp. 448-608.
Goehr, Lydia. "Adorno, Schoenberg, and the Totentanz der Prinzipien—In Thirteen Steps." *Journal of the American Musicological Society* 56, no. 3 (2003): 595-636.
Hofstätter, Birgit A. "Adorno and Performance: Thinking with the Movement of Language." In *Adorno and Performance*. Ed. Will Daddario and Karoline Gritzner. Basingstoke: Palgrave, 2014, pp. 155-70.
Mann, Thomas. *The Magic Mountain*. Trans. H. T. Lowe-Porter, London: Secker & Warburg, 1965.
Richter, Gerhard. *Afterness: Figures of Following in Modern Thought and Aesthetics*. New York: Columbia University Press, 2011.
Weber Nicholsen, Shierry. "Listening as the Work of Co-Composing: A Note on the Actuality of Adorno's Musical Thought." *Zeitschrift für kritische Theorie* 42/43 (2016): 41-56.
Wohlfarth, Irving. "Lager, Nach-Welt, Überleben." In *Wozu Adorno? Beiträge zur Kritik und zum Fortbestand einer Schlüsseltheorie des 20. Jahrhunderts*. Ed. Georg Kohler and Stefan Müller-Doohm. Weilerswist: Velbrück Wissenschaft, 2008, pp. 155-98.

3

Mimesis unto Death

Robin Truth Goodman

The first killer I interviewed took me to a riverbank where he helped kill 10,500 people, and asked us to take a picture of him and his fellow death-squad leader, giving a thumbs up and making the victory sign. This was in February 2004. In April 2004, pictures of American soldiers in Abu Ghraib, giving the victory sign while torturing people, were all over the news. I made this film contemporaneously with an evolving nightmare in my own country in which political leaders were celebrating torture, and torturers were getting their methods from watching Jack Bauer in 24.
—JOSHUA OPPENHEIMER

The roots must be sought in the persecutors, not in the victims who are murdered under the paltriest of pretenses. . . . One must come to know the mechanisms that render people capable of such deeds, must reveal these mechanisms to them, and strive, by awakening a general awareness of those mechanisms, to prevent people from becoming so again.
—THEODOR ADORNO, "EDUCATION AFTER AUSCHWITZ"

The Act of Killing is about mass death. Directed by Joshua Oppenheimer (quoted above) in 2013, and produced by Werner Herzog and Errol Morris, nominated for an Academy Award for Best Documentary in 2014 and winner of the BAFTA award (and a number of others) in that same year, this film is a retelling of the 1965–66 massacres in Indonesia ordered by the soon-to-be dictator Suharto—the September 30 Movement.[1] On September 30, 1965, a group of army officers linked to then general Suharto staged a one-day coup against the anti-imperialist president Sukarno, kidnapping and killing six senior generals and one lieutenant and holding Sukarno hostage. The event was blamed (without evidence) on the Indonesian Communist Party (PKI), then the largest Communist Party in the world outside China and Russia,[2] and Suharto called on paramilitaries and gangsters to exterminate them. The estimated deaths from the following six months (some of them may have been communists, but most of them were union members, landless farmers, intellectuals, and ethnic Chinese) range from 78,500 to 3 million, though as Geoffrey Robinson concludes in his study of the killings, "[t]here is a broad consensus among scholars . . . that something like half a million people were killed."[3] The alleged threat of communism and the strong-armed clampdown catapulted Suharto to power in 1966, when he forced Sukarno to step down with United States and United Kingdom backing, and continued to justify his 32-year reign until the Asian financial crisis brought him down in 1998.

The film proceeds through a series of reenactments of the killings. Oppenheimer originally went to Indonesia to advise unions on how to make films for organizing. While he was filming the family members and communities of the victims of the repression, the army would step in to stop production. The victims told him that the perpetrators, still supported by the state and still proud, would happily appear on film. Early on, Oppenheimer captured on film one of the perpetrators describing with laughter, in front of his young daughter, how he cut the throats of his victims and held them upside down as he crushed their skulls with his foot (*The Globalization Tapes* 2003).

The Act of Killing gives the perpetrators the opportunity to boast about the murders by making a gangster film in the guise of a Hollywood classic: a film within a film. Before the Sukarno regime had banned foreign films, the perpetrators had been aficionados of classical Hollywood genre cinema (what Adorno might call "the culture industry" or the "commodity form," whose link to authoritarianism he notes in the earlier citation) and were enticed by the chance to make a film that would tell their own story. In one scene, the killers Anwar (the central character) and Herman (his sidekick), reminiscing on Elvis, joyfully dance from the now boarded-up movie theater across the street to the paramilitary office where they strangled their victims with chicken wire. Having pushed his way past the aisles piled with cheap pink plastic handbags and backpacks decorated with cartoon figures in the store that now occupies his former office, Anwar there admits to the presence of ghosts.

By showing a politics of domination transpiring through commodity enactments,[4] Oppenheimer's film brings up questions about violence and representation, about authoritarianism and our reconciliation (or identification) with it, that harken back to the Frankfurt School's critique of the commodity and that haunt us still. Adorno's famous quarrel with Walter Benjamin was over whether a collective impulse was immanent in film and its technologies as a resistance to commodification's repetitions, to bureaucratic calculation, or to an authoritarian incitement of the masses to fall into lockstep. Adorno's attitude toward film barely changed from his work in the 1940s on the culture industry and his 1947 book with Hanns Eisler on film music, *Composing for the Films*, to his reevaluation in his 1966 "Transparencies on Film," where he writes, the culture industry, and especially film, is "the projection of the will of those in control over their victims" (205). As Miriam Hansen points out, his analysis of film conformed to his critique of the culture industry as the system of total exchangeability, but it was never clear whether Adorno's critique was that film production was controlled by the profit motives of the studio/industrial system or whether the indexical nature of the film medium itself meant that film could be nothing but a repetition of the "what is" through representation (215). "The last emergence of film," says Adorno in "Transparencies . . .," "makes it difficult to distinguish between technique and technology" (200). Since film is a modern art form, it does not, like music, says Adorno, have a history before technological reproducibility. Yet, in contrast to the realist theories of Siegfried Kracauer, who saw political potential in film's ability to focus on objects to animate a sociology of everyday life,[5] Adorno does locate film's promise in its ability to produce subjective movements where, he says, through the discontinuities the subject brings out in the image, "film may become art" ("Transparencies . . .," 201).

Adorno's critics very rarely address the efficacity of film, that is, how it mobilizes such subjective breaks with the industry whose technology constitutes subjects through identification.[6] In Adorno's version of the commodified world, subjectivities reflect the object-world under the control of production. In *Brave New World*, for example, Adorno says, men themselves are "products of the corporations' absolute power" (98), sacrificed to standardization, collectivization, and compliance "even down to biological constitution" (99) by participating in multisensory cinematic events. At the same time, commodification gives rise to its own undoing in the aesthetic play which Adorno calls "mimesis," though Adorno never makes clear if mimesis is an inevitable outcome of dialectical movement in time or if the artwork as artwork in its essence subverts the objectifying tendencies of modernity. In fact, in his discussions of mimesis, Adorno gives no indications of how mimesis moves from its primitive play in sacrifice and denunciation toward the next phase of history in myth and the next in industrialization and exchange.[7]

On the other hand, *The Act of Killing*—as Oppenheimer said in multiple interviews[8]—shows how cinematic technique elicits the unraveling psychology of a murderer as his subjectivity is absorbed into cinema's commodification, effectively exposing the regime's rottenness and envisioning a world of difference.[9] The point for Oppenheimer is not solely to criticize cultural imperialism or to push out the boundaries of documentary realism;[10] also, he studies the commodity's power to hail authoritarian identifications in order to expose and animate its limit. Adorno believed that the limits to the commodity were in the waning resistance of the individual subject, the human element that was never completely absorbed into its objective context despite the near totality of perfect exchangeability that commodity society authorizes. *The Act of Killing* is able to show a film forcing the commodity's irreconcilability to create effects, that is, that the aesthetic moment in the commodity is not dormant in the dialectical (or mimetic) nature of thought but is, rather, an intervention by mimetic action. What Stuart Jeffries characterizes as "impotence" (19) in Adorno's thinking about activism—or "a principled withdrawal into a fortress of thought" (19)—Oppenheimer interprets as an active element in art.

For Oppenheimer, acts of identification allow the repressed to appear from just below the surface as expressions of nonidentity and non-reconciliation with the commodity's repetitions. Like the film Oppenheimer produced earlier, *The Globalization Tapes*, *The Act of Killing* uses montage and other experimental techniques developed from the early twentieth-century Russian avant-garde, the mid-century French avant-garde, and Third Cinema to give expression to social antagonism. Like in Octavio Getino and Fernando Solanas's 1968 canonical film *La hora de los hornos* (*The Hour of the Furnaces*), for example, in *The Globalization Tapes* moving flashes of block lettering interrupt the image, stock footage is inserted cut with other stock footage, and a collage of cut-up commercials breaks in like bullets, while terrible scenes of exploitation and pesticide poisoning contradict a background soundtrack of happy American pop.[11] Likewise in *The Act of Killing*, montage and "fever dream" intensify as the film proceeds, particularly in its jarring cuts between brutal carnage and colorful, synchronized musical numbers, chorus girls dancing in front of a restaurant building in the shape of a giant fish; or when Herman cross-dressed in the kitschy feathered outfit of a daemon-god aggressively cuts, beheads, and dismembers a rubber mask; or when Anwar is buried in mud up to his neck as the cross-dressed Herman feeds him pieces of raw and bloody flesh, alleging the flesh is his penis and rotten. Indicatively, Anwar sometimes also loses control of his body: on the roof of the paramilitary office, most notably, the camera holds on Anwar as he is overtaken by coughs and sputters, or when Oppenheimer screens for him the scene of him playing his own victim, inner turmoil appears to be trying to escape through his face in seemingly uncontrollable grimaces,[12] wrinkles, and then tears—Anwar's tics, twitches, dry heaves, and chokes are the convulsions of irrationality bubbling up from inside the rationally constructed world, "the result of the antagonistic forces driving the process that takes place within it" (Adorno 141). The twitches and grimaces[13] are evidence of the nonidentity of Anwar's body with its capture by the Hollywood character replaying the Hollywood plot.[14] For Adorno, these violent guttural and gestural rebellions of Anwar's interiority would be intimations of repressed history,[15] like the history of social labor buried in the commodity.

The Act of Killing often suggests a *something else* or a *something different* hovering on the frame—an outside that is the unrepresentable inside of the image. As Adorno explains in his 1958–59 lectures on aesthetics, "it is the task of art to give a voice to mutilated nature, meaning nature in the respective form in which it exists through its historical mediations at a particular stage of history" (77).[16] At the end of the film, for example, Anwar disappears out of the old storefront that used to be the paramilitary office, and the camera lingers on the doorway, refusing to follow him: the film ends on an irreconcilable edge, suppressing the picture of Anwar on the other side.[17] In Adorno's terms, the task of *The Act of Killing* "is almost entirely to express what has been damaged" in order to give "a voice to what has been muted or suppressed—not necessarily destroyed—in the process of the progressive control of nature" (54), or "to express the powerless and oppressed parts of humans" (54), that is, to give repressed, unseen, and unheard nature a voice *as objective history*.[18] In between scenes of violence, the film sometimes hesitates for minutes in scenes of startling stillness—empty streets, birds in the distance flying in formation, a lighted window framing a conversing couple, a faraway worker climbing a poll—suggesting in the silence, according to Melis Behlil, "the vanished masses" (26), or, as Oppenheimer himself invokes, "the sense of something just below the surface, something that must come out" (29) or "the miasmic horror [that] slips between the frames" (28).

When Oppenheimer started making the film in the early aughts, the perpetrators still held power; in fact, he likened his experience in Indonesia to returning to Germany (from where his parents had fled) forty years after the Second World War if the Nazis were still ruling.[19] Oppenheimer encourages us to read his two films as one project: *The Act of Killing* along with his subsequent 2015 film *The Look of Silence*[20]—also nominated for an Academy Award—where Oppenheimer's Indonesian directorial partner for *The Act of Killing*, Adi Rukun, directly confronts the perpetrators and their families with evidence of their involvement in the torture and murder of his brother, hoping for their acknowledgment. In numerous interviews, Oppenheimer lists two intentions in making the films: (1) to allow Indonesians to begin a conversation about an experience that has been buried under continuing fear, with victims living right next door to killers;[21] and (2) to educate US citizens who may not know of their government's involvement. On the one hand, the truth-revelations of the crime would allow for truth and reconciliation, even the forgiveness of the Cold War rifts absorbed into Indonesian society. On the other hand, *The Act of Killing* is about constructing an afterlife of the commodified world in the failures of its reconciliation.

Mimesis

The Act of Killing and its companion film *The Look of Silence* both understand rituals of political repression as constitutive of subjective misidentification. "If we didn't drink human blood, we'd go crazy," boasts Inong, leader of the village death squad whom Adi Rukun interviews in *The Look of Silence* while performing the seemingly banal task of fitting him for glasses. "Drink your victims' blood, or go crazy. . . . But if you drink your victim's blood, you can do anything!" "I know from experience," he continues, "—if you cut off a woman's breast, it looks like a coconut milk filter. Full of holes." Such irrational brutality breaks through the documentary realism with a sense of emergency: snippets of everyday situations expose the violence beneath things: "The venerable belief in sacrifice is probably itself a behavior pattern drilled into the subjugated," Horkheimer and Adorno reflect, "by which they reenact against themselves the wrong done to them in order to be able to bear it" (41). In *Dialectic of Enlightenment*, ritual sacrifice is absorbed and repressed within scientific, political, and economic rationalization: ritual sacrifice overcomes the fear of nature's immediacy. Thought distances itself from nature in order to control it, but in distancing itself, thought becomes nature-like in its very brutality.

A colonialist reading might interpret this sacrificial practice of the killings as an archaic, primitive, tribal event integral to the local culture in Indonesia.[22] Even so, as an irrational act intended to rationalize Indonesian society, sacrifice in *The Act of Killing* is, like Horkheimer and Adorno argue, a way of treating nature as though shaped according to the logic of exchange and calculation—you give something and you get back an abstract equivalent: for sacrifice to take place, nature seems to be put there, in the image of human consciousness, for human consumption, in the interests of self-preservation. *The Globalization Tapes* starts off with a montage of rain forest trees cut with stock market ticker tape buzzing aloud the headlines from the financial press, followed by another montage of advertisements for palm oil products (e.g., vegetable oil, lipstick, skin cream, soap, mascara, canned soup, and potato chips) against shots of workers and their children chopping down the palm trees for less than $1.14 per day, the voice-over dialogue explaining that large corporations and banks like HSBC and Citibank capitalize the raw product with the help of loans from the World Bank. Turning human nature into a means to an end, the commodity's sacrificial rationale here parallels the perpetrators' rationale in *The Act of Killing*, where nature is imbued with ready-made thoughts and tidbits of human nature whose power can, through ritual sacrifice, be appropriated and instrumentalized for warding off perceived threats to survival.

Mimesis is the process of producing the idea of nature as a threat to culture in order to appropriate its power and control it. For Adorno, the nature/culture split that presents nature as culture's binary opposite only comes into play once nature can be seen as something outside of industry so it can serve, internalized, as its raw material. In this, mimesis is Enlightenment's version of sacrifice: it marks the moment when animated nature comes under the control of the commodity form in rituals that objectify nature. Adorno's theory of mimesis is based on the Freudian death drive, Roger Callois's theory of psychasthenia, and Benjamin's essays on "The Mimetic Faculty" and "The Doctrine of the Similar." Though, says Benjamin, the mimetic production of "non-sensuous similarities" "liquidated . . . magic" (336) (or rather, repressed nature's expressiveness), such similarities still "flit past" as "flashes" (335) of history in the present.[23] Scrutinizing mimesis as an evolutionary strategy where animals under threat take on the characteristics of their environment in camouflage, Callois figures mimesis as a trading-off of animate (natural) for inanimate (reified) features and functions, requiring a reduction of *élan vital* to inertia in *an instinct for renunciation* (32) at "the expense of the individual" (31). Linked to the Kantian sublime, where the subject assumes the power of terrifying nature in order to dominate it, Adorno's version of mimesis includes magic and calculating reason. By taking on the characteristics of what they repress and control in a deathlike stillness of the object-form, these mimetic rituals allow the history of terrifying nature to resurface. "The chaotically regular flight reactions of the lower animals, the patterns of swarming crowds, the convulsive gestures of the tortured—all these express what wretched life can never quite control: the mimetic impulse. In the death throes of the creature, at the furthest extreme from freedom, freedom itself irresistibly shines forth as the thwarted destiny of matter" (*Dialectic*, 151). Rather than condemning the culture industry in toto for "subordinating all branches of intellectual production equally to the single purpose of imposing on the senses of human beings, from the time they leave the factory in the evening to the time they clock on in the morning, the imprint of the work routine" (104), the theory of mimesis carries with it, as well, an internal resistance.

In various scenes, *The Act of Killing* makes clear that the main purpose of the sacrificial acts is to enable the reification and control of nature in commodity form. Most prevalently, one of the paramilitary leaders and businessmen, Haji Anif, owns a nature preserve which he acquired, he proudly boasts, by scaring the inhabitants to give him the land: the dead animals mounted on the walls are the only remaining original inhabitants of the land. Resembling a museum and a mausoleum at once, the home displays kitschy crystal sculptures, like mass-produced items sold in airports, in the shape of roses and elephants, as Anif boasts of their distinction. He then shows the film crew elaborate panoramas of taxidermied wild beasts, some eerily wrapped in Saran wrap, the camera lingering on selected animal heads in mortuary-like reverence: deer, bears, wolves, and moose all colorfully glowing, when the sacred-like tune of *Born Free* suddenly crashes in. Next appear monkeys in cages, chewing—a scene that anticipates a later one where Anwar is playing a headless victim buried under branches in the woods, with monkeys all around him swinging on trees and chewing a red flower that makes their mouths look as though they are dripping Anwar's blood. As dead nature, the nature preserve foreshadows Anwar's own ritualistic renunciation, his becoming nature through imitating it in death, becoming culture's showcase as the vines and greenery crawl over him in a fiery fever dream and the voracious monkeys move in as consumers.

Replicating magical rituals to control the nature they refer to, the commodity is, then, a developed form of mimetic practice, demanding conformity to its environment through renunciation. Using the praying mantis as an example of psychic form, Callois summarizes, where space—like the commodity—is the environmental context, "I know where I am, but I do not feel as though I'm at the spot where I find myself. . . . To these dispossessed souls, space seems to be a devouring force. Space pursues them, encircles them, digests them." (30): life is absorbed in the commodified environment. "In technology," Horkheimer and Adorno similarly note, "the adaptation to lifelessness in the service of self-preservation is no longer accomplished, as in magic, by bodily imitation of external nature, but by automating mental processes, turning them into blind sequences" (149). Fascism, then, appropriates the rituals of the commodity: "The purpose of the fascist cult of formulae, the ritualized discipline, the uniforms, and the whole allegedly irrational apparatus, is to make possible mimetic behavior" (152).The paranoia manipulated by the fascist regime, where the terrors of internal nature are projected onto the externalized world for purposes of control, underlies the modern subject's tendencies to camouflage by repeating itself within the world of objects, to identify with the forces of domination for self-preservation.

The Act of Killing locates the repressive power of the regime within the subjectivities of those who thus act on its behalf through ritualistic sacrifice and camouflage. Indeed, Anwar is backed by the continued growth of the Pancasila Youth Movement (with three million members, men and women)—a paramilitary arm of the state with both legal and illegal status. Wearing uniforms of orange-and-black camouflage, the Pancasila denizens appear at various moments performing synchronized dances, group prayers, venerations of pop singers, or hailing authority as the leaders—on giant screens, in front of mass audiences who laugh and clap—praise the death squads and torturers. The camouflage outfits are designed to replicate the doubletoned green familiar to guerrilla warfare, where the soldier melts into the natural environment. As Horkheimer and Adorno explain, "Protection as petrified terror is a form of camouflage. These numb human reactions are archaic patterns of self-preservation: the tribute life pays for its continued existence is adaptation to death" (148). Yet, the uniforms shine in bright kitschy orange, making their attempts to dissolve into the background the very basis of their standing out.

The traumatized subject of *The Act of Killing* is not, as in Freud's telling, a buried kernel of terror that defines the interior subject but rather, as in Adorno, the objectified world of the commodity as it appears in subjectivity. In Fredric Jameson's reading of mimesis, the gangster (for Adorno, in the form of Odesseus, for example), in his view, is quintessentially the mimetic subject—the modern gangster inherits an older tradition of the peasant "reintegrated into a larger market strategy" (69) and transformed by Hollywood. Like the rebel, the gangster's practice of dissidence for Horkheimer and Adorno, says Jameson, "can be accommodated as a style or an eccentricity" as it has been "registered and classified by the culture industry" (69). "Anyone who resists," Horkheimer and Adorno specify, "can survive only by being incorporated" (104),[24] and by this logic of the culture industry, the rebel becomes the entrepreneur.

The Act of Killing also indicates that the state gains its power by appropriating the ritualistic power of the gangsters that the state itself has made powerful. As Pancasila leader and vice president of Indonesia, Jusuf Kalla, remarks in the film, the system of governing incorporates Anwar and his band of criminals as the anti-systemic elements that the system needs to exercise power. As he gives a rousing speech in his orange-and-black camouflage uniform, melting into the wallpaper behind him that sports the same colors and designs, he praises the gangsters as "free men":[25] "If everyone worked for the government," he laments, pointing his finger accusingly at the laughing crowd of Pancasila leaders, "we'd be a nation of bureaucrats. We'd get nothing done. We need gangsters to get things done. Free, private men who get things done. We need gangsters—who are willing to take risks in business." The film situates the critique of the state inside the state itself, allowing the state to become the principal source of anti-statist unregulated lawlessness. Whereas Adorno reads the industrial production of the commodity as threatening the individual, Oppenheimer interprets the logic of the commodity as producing neoliberal social relations based in transferring public power into individualizing private-power identifications—the state encourages its citizens to identify with the gangster-outlaw-entrepreneur in order to better demand their conformity, submission, and obedience to rule.

Adorno thus offers a way of understanding the constitution of contemporary subjectivity and its identifications that does not depend on the deep structure of the psyche as in psychoanalysis but rather on the logic of the camouflage and mimesis, where the subject assimilates by melting into the categories it creates in its environment for knowing objects. In addition, however, mimesis is the flitting by of natural history as it resurfaces in the image. The presence of natural history in the commodity means that the mimetic identification with the environment is never completely in control but is disrupted by the speaking of human suffering inside of it, that is, its aesthetic content.

Art is what allows for this human suffering to be expressed because of its irreconcilability with the world as it is. "One could say," Adorno resumes, "that every dissonance is a small remembrance of the suffering which the control over nature, and ultimately a society of domination as such, inflicts on nature, and only in the form of this suffering, only in the form of yearning—and dissonance is always substantially yearning and suffering—only thus can suppressed nature find its voice at all" (39). As Robert Hullot-Kentor notes in his "Translator's Introduction" to Adorno's *Aesthetic Theory*, "Aesthetic concepts would become the memory of nature sedimented in art, which for Adorno takes shape in *Aesthetic Theory* as the unconscious, mimetically written history of human suffering against which enlightenment elsewhere seals itself off" (xiii). True, Adorno knew that suffering is difficult to disassociate from other conventions and tropes, as we recognize it in sentimental, sensational, criminal, or victimization commercial narratives, for example. However, for Adorno, there is a part of human suffering that cannot be reduced to its administered, calculable, predictable form: "Suffering remains foreign to knowledge; though knowledge can subordinate it conceptually and provide means for its amelioration, knowledge can scarcely express it through its own means of experience without itself becoming irrational" (*Aesthetic Theory*, 18). Mimesis, for Adorno, is the subject that suffers, expressed in dissonance.

The dissonance of nature—or, spirit—*is* for Adorno the subjective voices of dead labor speaking from inside the material of dead objects constituting history. These subjective voices get their life, for Adorno, from the history of aesthetics, in particular, at the points where aesthetic history makes its mark inside the philosophy of history. The individual subject in Kant's account of the sublime, says Adorno, ultimately gains distance and control over the nature that it fears by assuming nature's power for himself. Hegel reworks this control over nature into the idealist subject of history as it comes to dominate objects in the world, the products of social labor. The sublime— or idealist History—erases by imitating the social labor that makes the objects in the world it encounters as itself but still retains within itself the voice of nature "sublated and preserved in the work though now in the form of that dissonance" (38). "It is only this brutality of coercion," writes Adorno in his lectures on Hegel's aesthetics, "that creates the semblance of reconciliation in the doctrine of an identity that has been produced" (20). "The philosopher's labor," Adorno goes on, "actually aims solely at helping to express what is active in the material itself" (22). This might be said, as well, for the filmmaker.

Oppenheimer shares with Adorno this view that what guards against the anesthetization of politics (e.g., the reification and instrumentalism of art for political purposes) is the irreconcilability of History, the voices of the dead speaking through it. In particular, *The Act of Killing* demonstrates how the act of (artistic) production activates this resistance in apparently dead nature, bringing it to life against the authority of its object-form. Toward the end of *The Act of Killing*, Oppenheimer replays for Anwar some of the clips of the gangster film they are making together. After the scene where they are performing *Born Free* in front of a waterfall—where Anwar delights in "how the waterfall expresses such deep feelings!" as the actors playing the dead communist victims rise up to thank him and offer him a medal for sending them to heaven—Anwar scrutinizes another scene where he is playing his own torture victim. Anwar asks Oppenheimer, "Did the people I tortured feel that way I do here?" He goes on: "All the terror suddenly possessed my body," he says, arching his arms around and flexing his fingers as though crushing something. When Oppenheimer—off-screen—tells him that actually he is different than his victims because they know they are being killed while he knows he is acting, Anwar loses composure and starts to cry. Framed by fake crystal bowls, a porcelain vase depicting mythological war scenes, a chairback with curlicues of plastic flowers, and other ridiculous furnishings, Anwar is made to confront the demons of his own dead victims as they come at him through his own artful imitation. This cuts into the scene of Anwar retching on the rooftop where he had strangled his victims with chicken wire.

Commodity

Oppenheimer has been criticized for not pointing his finger directly at the United States for its support of the Suharto regime in *The Act of Killing*. Behlil, for example, asks, "While *The Act of Killing* has been widely praised, it was also criticized for leaving out the role of American complicity" (30). Oppenheimer responds, "Those criticisms are answered in *The Look of Silence*, which shows the complicity of a multinational U.S. Corporation and mentions the complicity of the U.S. government" (ibid.). He goes on: "I think that it's almost more important to show the complicity of a multinational corporation and the U.S. media" (Behlil 30).[26] An overwhelming presence of commodities invades the film. Behind the opening explanatory titles, a modern building looms up in the dusk. The set is lifeless and almost still. Yet, in the corner of the frame, a cube spins with shiny, golden advertisements on every side, celebrating rum and fruit juice. Where the dominant visual emphasizes darkness, functionality, and geometric regularities etched in horizontal lines, the repeating kitschy promises of thirst-quenching happiness on the cube's billboards split the screen.

The eerie, deathlike stillness of the commodity form is recurrent. In the scene where Adi Zukaldy, Anwar's partner in the killings, visits the mall with his family, the revolving door spins onto flattened block-images of tomb-like storefronts, glass cases and shelves (reminiscent of the cases of ornaments in the nature preserve), and well-lit aisles strewn with rows of objects for sale: watches, workout cycles, and refrigerators. The salespeople stand about completing rows of flattened cardboard signs as though they, too, are objects on offer. While Adi Zukaldy passes with his wife and daughter through the eerily vacant shops and perfume counters, Adi's disassociated voice-over announces gruesome commentary from an unseen loudspeaker, as though announcing promotions and discounts: "We crushed their necks with wood. We hung them," he details, as he and his family cross in front of the silent lighted advertisements of cosmetics, underwear, corporate logos, and electric razors. The disembodied, isolated voice projects as the repressed voice of the commodity, its afterlife.

At the same time, *The Look of Silence* explicitly links subjective constitution to commodity production. Shots of Adi Rukun gazing at the television screen are intercut with a 1967 NBC news report about Goodyear reaping profits from Indonesia's rich natural rubber reserves. A gunshot-like blast and military drums sound from the set, with a cut to the TV screen revealing US tanks coming over a hill, the voice-over boasting that Indonesia has accomplished the most decisive victory over communism in the world. A native from Bali tells the NBC reporter that Bali is more beautiful now that it has been cleansed of communists who, anyways, asked to be killed. "In some camps they are starved to death," we hear the reporter openly bragging to its US news audience, "or released periodically to be killed by the local citizens." The voice-over explains that the former union workers now have to work under gunpoint. Like the perpetrators, Goodyear and NBC brag of US-sponsored deaths and the institution of slave labor for corporate profits. Contrasted with shots of Adi Rukun in still but disturbed contemplation, the news footage almost seems to be glowing forth from Adi's head. The TV reporter claims national satisfaction after the final communist repression and the liquidation of their families. Another cut shows a still and silent night scene, where a solitary worker—for the lengthy extent of sixteen seconds—uses a duster to clean the windows of a furniture store which now seems eerily to sit, unsettled, on top of the dead, as a mausoleum.

The claims to objective happiness promoted by the classic gangster films and by the spectacle of victory over communism that NBC celebrates reveal the inadequacy of objectified happiness to satisfy the basic subjective needs which are, therefore, antagonistic. Goodyear in the film resembles Wrigley's gum in Adorno's analysis of Aldous Huxley, where the profits made from chewing gum "have their roots in the social function of reconciling people to bad conditions and thus diverting them from criticism" ("Aldous Huxley," 109). *The Act of Killing* ends with a bright musical number, *Born Free*, happily frolicking in brightness as the communists rise from the dead to thank Anwar for killing them, hanging a medal around his neck as the chorus line swings its hips in pink fluffy skirts in the background. The totalitarian state, says Adorno, promotes a promise of reconciliation through accepting the commodity's terms, its narratives of lawless adventure, and entrepreneurial profiteering overlying its domination of nature. Yet, the commodity in its petrified refuge at the same time antagonizes objective history from within, turning everything into an imitation of itself by imitating, in the commodity, irreconcilable suffering. As the dancing women shiver uncontrollably under the chilling spray from the waterfall, subjectivity screams out from within its objectification.

Adorno proclaimed that the main goal for criticism and for education is to ensure that Auschwitz never happens again. Since, he wrote, "the possibility of changing the objective—namely societal and political—conditions is extremely limited today" (192), the task is to change subjectivity by redirecting identifications toward "not cooperating" (195). *The Act of Killing* is about the propensity of the commodified world toward authoritarian brutality and the inability of the subject to reconcile. The question that both Oppenheimer and Adorno leave for us is how we will lay claim to that resistance without falling into the logic of fear and self-preservation that forces us back into the totalitarianism of the exchange imperative that currently undergirds our political life.

Notes

1 Benedict Anderson laid out with precision the evidence that Suharto was responsible and, ultimately, planned the coup to fail in order "to create an anti-communist hysteria" (9) and to justify his own draconian rule. The evidence suggests that Suharto instructed his army allies to stage the coup and then afterward labeled them as communists and initiated an offensive against them. Talking about the seeming incompetence of the movement's decisions, Anderson writes that "the suspicion naturally arises that this string was deliberately arranged to ensure the Movement's failure" (14).
2 The PKI had a membership of 3.5 million plus 23.5 million affiliates, mostly composed of workers, farmers, and women's groups.
3 Robinson 315.
4 For Nicholsen, Adornian mimesis entails "an assimilation of the self to the other" which she calls "enactment"; a practice of mimesis that is archaic but in modernity still resides in language as its last refuge; in art and aesthetics, an act of assimilating the self to the other as a mode of expression as well as the artwork as a form of objectivity of expression; a technique of objectivication;

and lastly, the language character of art (62). Nicholsen sees "enactment" inside both the production and reception of every work of art, which requires assimilation to the other to form the subject.

5   Keya Ganguly remarks on how the Frankfurt School's version of modernity is indebted to Third World film production, particularly through Kracauer's interest in Satyajit Ray's films: "Films like the Apu trilogy enabled Kracauer to clinch his arguments about the medium's expansive capacities and . . . what he derived from Ray . . . is the prospect of a mode of expression that could capture the continuities between art and life without mystifying them" (182).

6   In *Composing for the Films*, for example, Eisler and Adorno start by pointing out the importance of the film industry in determining film content, but then also call attention to how technological development is out of sync with film's rules of standardization, creating contradictions. Hansen, along with Philip Rosen, has detected parts of Adorno's analysis, outside of the condemnation of the culture industry, that redeem film's potential for autonomy and critique: Rosen, for example, underscores the gap between the two-dimensionality of the image and the three-dimensionality of the score (173) resulting in a tension between image and sound, while Hansen reads in "Transparencies . . ." Adorno's sense that film is capable of recreating subjective experience lost to modernity, the technological aspect dominating experience through its domination of nature, and, at the same time, letting it speak through "the potential of technology, albeit under transformed relations of production, to develop a mimetic solidarity with nature" (230).

7   Mimesis, for Hulatt, is incapable "of driving its own development" (139): Adorno's theory of mimesis does not, for him, explain how mimesis is repressed in its first phase of immediacy to nature, moves into magical ritual, and then inhabits the logic of the commodity and rationalization.

8   See, for example, the interview with Amy Goodman on *Democracy Now!* (July 19, 2013).

9   In the first book-length study of Oppenheimer's Indonesian films (which places Oppenheimer in a documentary tradition from Werner Herzog to Lucien Castaing-Taylor), Baxstrom and Meyers lambaste the film as a film "of collusion" (49). They allege that Oppenheimer portrays his characters as traumatic subjects, universalizing the shame and trauma that they experience as a result of the atrocities they commit and thereby, in a sense, letting the killers off the hook for their particular crimes. Assuming that these horrors are beyond representation, Oppenheimer, they say, turns the killers' guilt into an existential guilt based in an animal nature that we all share: "Anwar's shame is displayed as a particularly virulent example of everyone's shame, . . . nullifying the very question of justice" (66). The universalizing of guilt, they continue, means that there can be only one response: "the director's anticipation of his audience's 'correct' attitude toward his material is, in our estimation, the most vile aspect of Oppenheimer's display" (60). What they omit from their account is any mention of politics or, indeed, capital. The freedom of the killers in the political and military system that supports them is a reality that Oppenheimer openly and explicitly critiques, and this freedom is installed on the back of

the commodity form. The guilt that the film may want us to accept (if any) is not an existential or a psychoanalytic guilt but rather one related to the stakes in our participation in the commodity's world. Anwar's apprehension, arrest, trial, or punishment would not fix the problem but would just, as catharsis, make us more comfortable with it.

10 Bill Nichols faults the film for its lack of "moral compass": "the film withholds the independent, non-ironic perspective we anticipate and desire so that we may distinguish the honorable from the appalling, the deluded from the sober, the fantasmatic from its surrounding social reality" (28).

11 Oppenheimer's other films—for example, *The Places We Learned to Call Home* (1996) and *The Entire History of the Louisiana Purchase* (1998)—similarly construct a paranoid aesthetics of images disassociated from sound—clips of sci-fi B movies with robots wrestling dinosaurs and women with baby carriages dancing in barren landscapes interspersed with blazing fires on chairs—to explore disturbed psychologies of militias, gun enthusiasts, religious fanatics, and killers (in *The Entire History* . . . , a woman nukes her baby in a microwave oven, claiming she was impregnated by space aliens working for the Antichrist).

12 Errol Morris (along with others) questions whether Anwar is really expressing emotion or whether he is still acting for his film. "[A]t the end of the film," he tells Oppenheimer in an interview, "I actually do not know who this man is . . . Yes. The vomiting—whether the vomiting is one more performance for himself and for us." Oppenheimer is more convinced by the performance. Baxstrom and Meyers comment, "[C]ritics suggest that this scene 'seems staged,' but that is the point—all confessions are staged, collaborations between interrogators and suspects" (65).

13 Horkheimer and Adorno note, "The grimace seems like play-acting because, instead of performing serious work, it prefers to portray displeasure. It appears to evade the seriousness of life by admitting it without restraint. . . . . It is always overdone, no matter how heartfelt it may be, because, as in each work of art, the whole world seems contained in every plaintive sound" (150).

14 Oppenheimer has spoken about such moments in the film as "pure poetry," as a "surreal fever dream," or as a "sort of danse macabre at the edge of the abyss" (Lusztig), as the film mixes genres and, as the documentary critic Bill Nichols argues, dislodges signifiers from "what they stand to signify" (28), making uncertain the realist conventions of representing history.

15 "Through the medium of aesthetics questions concerning the philosophy of history and even metaphysics become legible" (125). "[A]rt always tries at the same time to do justice to that element of suppressed nature" (41).

16 Martin Jay sees mimesis as the utopian aspect of Adorno's theory, since it allows for particularity, irreconcilability, and nonconformity, a refuge for the sensual within the systematization of the concept for self-preservation: "[B]y refusing to imitate, or be assimilated entirely to, a bad external reality—by paradoxically honoring, one might say, the Jewish taboo on graven images—works of art hold out the hope for a more benign version of mimesis in a future world beyond domination and reification" (35). Molnar

and Molnar also see the utopian aspect of mimesis, particularly in music: Adorno's theory of mimesis, they write, "always bore the marks of these two poles: the mythological, which may discover much more in nature than the 'mathematical natural sciences' can, and the lyrical, which may revive in us the memory of the unity of subject and object, or primordial oneness with nature" (66).

17 Baxstrom and Meyers interpret this differently: "He slowly exits the roof and the building, the camera continuing to linger on him as he goes. Only when he makes his exit does the camera stop. He is still a murderer, but he is free to go" (65). I see a ghostlike or expectant quality in the excessive amount of time that the camera lingers in the dark doorway, as though something is about to speak through the emptiness.

18 *The Act of Killing* lends itself to a psychological story line in some interpretations. "[T]hese constructions make meaning," Janet Walker, for example, asserts, ". . . according to the paradoxical logic of traumatic testimony" (16). Such an interpretation would not be Adorno's, who would see the psychoanalytic subject as socially mediated.

19 "I had the feeling that I'd wandered into Germany forty years after the Holocaust only to find the Nazis still in power" (Behlil 27).

20 "I knew from the outset that there should be two films. There should be one about the genres of the perpetrators' boasting, the shared scripts, lies, fantasies, and stories they would tell to escape the reality of what they did . . . But I knew equally that there was another film to be made that was just as urgent, one about what it means for human beings to have to rebuild their lives and continue to live in this haunted rubble, side by side with the people who killed their relatives . . . I hope that people will stop seeing the two films as separate, directing criticism at one and praise at the other. I think they are two parts of a greater work" (Behlil 27–30).

21 See, for example, Behlil (2015): *The Act of Killing* "asks viewers to approach the perpetrators through my intimacy with them, and ultimately to empathize, if not necessarily sympathize, with them. The film asks viewers to feel the enormous consequences of mass violence, impunity, and guilt on an entire society" (30). Indonesian screenings of *The Act of Killing* ranged from small, secret theaters to audiences of 600 people. The film had a big effect on Indonesian audiences, and many—including Oppenheimer—considered it to have influenced the outcome of the 2019 national elections that brought Joko Widodo to power on a reformist platform, beating out his opponent Prabowo Subianto, who was Suharto's son-in-law. President Joko Widodo made some gestures toward investigating the massacres, but the army threatened his regime if he pursued these efforts, and so they were not pursued.

22 Though his theory of mimesis borrowed from anthropology, particularly as inflected through Freud, Adorno was inexplicit about the relation of his philosophy to imperialism. References to specific headlines show that Adorno thought of violence in the imperialized world as a repetition of Europe's transition toward the Enlightenment, similarly carrying forward the spirit

of history (or exchange). In his 1964–5 lectures on *History and Freedom*, Adorno comments on recent events in the Congo: "If you read the newspapers and are able to imagine what is involved in the events in the Congo, you can reflect on the balance of horror between the atrocities committed by the natives and those committed by the forces of civilization by way of revenge. ... The cheers that greeted the liberation of Stanleyville by the [Belgian] paras are just as revolting as the mendacious claims by the Eastern camp that liberating Stanleyville from the natives and their atrocities was manifestly an instance of European imperialism" (93–4). Anthropologist Michael Taussig calls Horkheimer and Adorno's mimesis the "colonial mirror of production" which is not illustrative of "the violence of the colonial frontier" but rather of the "blow-up within modern European civilization itself" (66). What Taussig sees as distinctive for anthropology in Horkheimer and Adorno's analysis of mimesis is that "racism is seen as a manifestation of what is essential to modern civilization's cultural apparatus, namely continuous mimetic repression" (68)—that is, the "organized control of mimesis" (68) is the European practice of attributing magical powers to "the primitive" in order to appropriate such power as the repressed Other.

23 Richard Wolin notes that even though Adorno thinks "commodity fetishism cannot be resolved—only mystified—by being transposed to the world of dreams" (111), he still embraced some surrealist techniques in *Aesthetic Theory*, like montage and shock in particular, for defetishizing: "exploding the pretense of a rationalized capitalist life world to being natural and eternal" (116). Susan Gillespie's book *The Challenge of Surrealism* makes the case through Adorno's letters that Adorno had more affinities with surrealism than he has been credited with having.

24 "Once registered as diverging from the culture industry, they belong to it as the land reformer does to capitalism. Realistic indignation is the trademark of those with a new idea to sell" (*Dialectic*, 104).

25 The first part of the movie returns many times to the etymological theme that the word "gangster" means "free man."

26 He explains, "I suppose the reason I didn't talk about how I would be addressing these things in *The Look of Silence* while releasing *The Act of Killing* was that I felt *The Act of Killing* didn't need excuses made for it. What *The Act of Killing* shows is something I entirely stand by. It asks viewers to approach the perpetrators through my intimacy with them, ... and to recognize that we're all closer to perpetrators than we'd like to think" (30).

Works Cited

Adorno, Theodor W. *Aesthetics 1958/59*. Trans. Wieland Hoban. Ed. Eberhard Ortland. Cambridge, UK and Medford, MA: Polity, 2018.

Adorno, Theodor W. *Aesthetic Theory*. Ed. Gretel Adorno and Rolf Tiedemann. Trans. Robert Hullot-Kentor. Minneapolis, MN: University of Minnesota Press, 1997.

Adorno, Theodor W. *An Introduction to Dialectics (1958)*. Trans. Nicholas Walker. Ed. Christoph Ziermann. Cambridge, UK and Malden, MA: Polity, 2017.

Adorno, Theodor W. "Aldous Huxley and Utopia." In *Prisms*. Trans. Samuel and Shierry Weber. Cambridge, MA: The MIT Press, 1967, pp. 95-117.

Adorno, Theodor W. "Education after Auschwitz." In *Critical Models: Interventions and Catchwords*. Trans. Henry W. Pickford. New York: Columbia University Press, 1998, pp. 191-204.

Adorno, Theodor W. *Hegel: Three Studies*. Trans. Sheirry Weber Nicholsen. Cambridge, MA and London: The MIT Press, 1993.

Adorno, Theodor W. *History and Freedom Lectures 1964-1965*. Trans. Rodney Livingstone. Ed. Rolf Tiedemann. Cambridge, UK and Malden, MA: Polity, 2006.

Adorno, Theodor W. "Transparencies of Film." Trans. Thomas Y. Levin. *New German Critique* 24/25 (Autumn 1981-Winter 1982): 199-205.

Adorno, Theodor, and Eisler, Hanns. *Composing for the Films*. London and Atlantic Highlands: The Athlone Press, 1994.

Anderson, Benedict. "Petrus Dadi Ratu." *New Left Review* 3 (May-June 2000): 7-15.

Baxstrom, Richard and Meyers, Todd. *Violence's Fabled Experiment: Kleine Edition 27*. Berlin: August Verlag, 2018.

Behlil, Melis, Oppenheimer, Joshua, and Cashill, Robert. "The Act of Killing: An Interview with Joshua Oppenheimer." *Cinéaste* 38, no. 3 (Summer 2013): 26-30.

Behlil, Melis, Oppenheimer, Joshua, and Rukun, Adi. "The Look of Silence: An Interview with Joshua Oppenheimer and Adi Rukun." *Cinéaste* 40, no. 3 (Summer 2015): 26-31.

Benjamin, Walter. "The Mimetic Faculty." In *Reflections: Essays, Aphorisms, Autobiographical Writings*. Ed. Peter Demetz. Trans. Edmund Jephcott. New York: Shoken Books, 1978.

Buck-Morss. Susan. *The Origin of Negative Dialectics: Theodor W. Adorno, Walter Benjamin, and the Frankfurt Institute*. New York: The Free Press, 1977.

Callois, Roger. "Mimicry and Legendary Psychasthenia." Trans. John Shepley. *October* 31 (Winter 1984): 16-32.

Ganguly, Keya. *Cinema, Emergence, and the Films of Satyajit Ray*. Berkeley, CA: University of California Press, 2010.

Gillespie, Susan H., Ed. and Trans. *The Challenge of Surrealism: The Correspondence of Theodor W. Adorno and Elisabeth Lenk*. Minneapolis, MN and London: University of Minnesota Press, 2015.

Goodman, Amy. "'The Act of Killing' New Film Shows U.S.-Backed Indonesian Death Squad Leaders Re-enacting Massacres." *Democracy Now!* (19 July 2013). https://www.democracynow.org/2013/7/19/the_act_of_killing_new:film. Accessed 11 June 2018.

Hansen, Miriam Bratu. *Cinema and Experience: Siegfried Kracauer, Walter Benjamin, and Theodor W. Adorno*. Berkeley, CA: University of California Press, 2012.

Horkheimer, Max, and Adorno, Theodor. *The Dialectic of Enlightenment: Philosophical Fragments*. Trans. Edmund Jephcott and Ed. Gunzelin Schmid Noerr. Stanford, CA: Stanford University Press, 2002.

Hulatt, Owen. "Reason, Mimesis, and Self-Preservation in Adorno." *Journal of the History of Philosophy* 54, no. 1 (January 2016): 135–51.
Hullot-Kentor, Robert. "Translator's Introduction." In *Aesthetic Theory*. By Theodor Adorno. Ed. Gretel Adorno and Rolf Tiedemann. Trans. Robert Hullot-Kentor. Minneapolis: University of Minnesota Press, 1997, pp. xi–xxi.
Jameson, Fredric. *Late Marxism: Adorno, or, the Persistence of the Dialectic*. London and New York: Verso, 1990.
Jay, Martin. "Mimesis and Mimetology: Adorno and Lacoue-Labarthe." In *The Semblance of Subjectivity: Essays in Adorno's Aesthetic Theory*. Ed. Tom Huhn and Lambert Zuidervaart. Cambridge, MA and London: The MIT Press, 1997, pp. 29–55.
Jeffries, Stuart. *Grand Hotel Abyss: The Lives of the Frankfurt School*. New York: Verso, 2016.
Lusztig, Irene. "The Fever Dream of Documentary: A Conversation with Joshua Oppenheimer." *Film Quarterly* 67, no. 2 (Winter 2013): 50–6.
Molnar, Dragana Jeremic and Molnar, Aleksandar. "Adorno, Schubert, and Mimesis." *19th-Century Music* 38, no. 1 (Summer 2014): 53–78.
Morris, Errol. "The Murders of Gonzago." *Slate* (10 July 2013). http://www.slate.com/articles/arts/history/2013/07/the_act_of_killing_essay_how:indonesia_s_mass_killings_could_have_slowed.html. Accessed 15 June 2018.
Nichols, Bill. "Irony, Cruelty, Evil (and a Wink) in *The Act of Killing*." *Film Quarterly* 67, no. 2 (Winter 2013): 25–9.
Nicholsen, Shierry Weber. "*Aesthetic Theory*'s Mimesis of Walter Benjamin." *The Semblance of Subjectivity: Essays in Adorno's Aesthetic Theory*. Ed. Tom Huhn and Lambert Zuidervaart. Cambridge, MA and London: The MIT Press, 1997, pp. 55–91.
Robinson, Geoffrey. *The Killing Season: A History of the Indonesian Massacres, 1965-66*. Princeton, NJ and Oxford, UK: Princeton University Press, 2018.
Rosen, Philip. "Adorno and Film Music: Theoretical Notes on *Composing for the Films*." *Yale French Studies* 60 (1980): 157–82.
Taussig, Michael. *Mimesis and Alterity: A Particular History of the Senses*. New York and London: Routledge, 1993.
Walker, Janet. "Referred Pain: *The Act of Killing* and the Production of a Crime Scene." *Film Quarterly* 67, no. 2 (Winter 2013): 14–20.
Wolin, Richard. "Benjamin, Adorno, Surrealism." In *The Semblance of Subjectivity: Essays in Adorno's Aesthetic Theory*. Ed. Tom Huhn and Lambert Zuidervaart. Cambridge, MA and London: The MIT Press, 1997, pp. 93–122.

PART TWO

Adorno's Aesthetics

4

Adorno on Vinyl

Jeffrey R. Di Leo

The preservation of music in records reminds one of canned food.
—THEODOR W. ADORNO, "THE RADIO VOICE [1939]," 349

The phonograph was patented by Thomas Edison in 1877. Still, it would not be until the second decade of the twentieth century that it would be technically feasible to produce music on phonographic records. Prior to 1910, the phonograph was primarily viewed as "an archival apparatus for exemplary words" (Attali, *Noise*, 92). Moreover, it was not until 1914 that the first symphony was put to record: Beethoven's *Fifth Symphony* conducted by Artur Nikish (Attali, *Noise*, 92).

In short, no one foresaw during the late nineteenth and early twentieth century the mass production of music on vinyl. Edison even went so far as to oppose the use of the phonograph in jukeboxes because it would make "it appear as though it were nothing more than a toy" (Attali, *Noise*, 93; citing Edison). It would not be until 1898, over twenty-two years after patenting his invention, that Edison "realized the commercial potential for recorded music" (Attali, *Noise*, 94).

Igor Stravinsky was one of the first composers in the twentieth century to embrace the potential of the phonograph. Around 1928–29, Stravinsky signed a contract with the Columbia Gramophone Company to record his work as a pianist and composer. "This work greatly interested me," wrote Stravinsky in his autobiography completed in 1934, "for here, far better than with piano rolls, I was able to express all my intentions with real exactitude" (Stravinsky, *Autobiography*, 150). Not only did the composer find in the phonograph an ideal way to archive his own interpretations of his music, he also regarded musical recording for the phonograph as a way to supplement his own income (Chanan 117).

Still, in spite of touting its benefits for musical composers, he also had some doubts about those who use the phonograph to listen to music: "the evil of this so-called progress lies" in the "lack of necessity for any effort" that the gramophone requires of the listener. Stravinsky writes, "anyone, living no matter where, has only to turn a knob or put on a record to hear what he likes," the ease of which leads some to then "listen without hearing" (Stravinsky, *Autobiography*, 152).[1]

Perhaps though there was no more outspoken opponent of the gramophone during this early period of sound reproduction than the young Theodor W. Adorno, who began his published criticism of it in the last 1920s—and would continue right through his death in the late 1960s. For him, the gramophone encapsulated well the negative dialectics of modernity: the capacity to capture sound on vinyl was at once one of modernity's most remarkable technical achievements and also one of the music world's most disappointing developments. For Adorno, the invention of the gramophone paved the way for the commodification of music through the phonographic record. Moreover, the music that came to be commodified (or "canned" as Adorno says in our epigraph) was mass art that resisted musical innovation. It was music that did not require "listening," or in Adorno's terms, was "popular music" wherein "[t]he composition hears for the listener" (Adorno, "On Popular Music," 442). The music that resisted "commodification" and "canning" was the autonomous art or "serious music" that was unsuited to the technical capacities of the phonograph.

Adorno's writing on the topic of the phonograph primarily focused on the negative aspects of music's adaptation to reproduction. He repeatedly insisted that the technical capacities of musical recording and sound reproduction were simply insufficient to meet the needs of the music he critically championed, namely, "serious music," from Beethoven to Berg—even though musical recording and sound reproduction in the age of vinyl was more than sufficient to serve the ends of the "popular music" he loathed. To put an even finer point on this distinction, we might alternately say that the phonograph for Adorno was more than capable of meeting the demands of "music which accepts its character as a commodity, thus becoming identical with the machinations of the culture industry itself," but did not meet the demands of "self-reflexive music which critically opposes its fate as a commodity, and thus ends up by alienating itself from present society by becoming unacceptable to it" (Paddison, "The Critique Criticized," 204).

It should be noted though that Adorno does not completely lay blame for "popular music" on the phonograph and the music industry that grew from it. For him, the kind of music produced by the culture industry through the phonograph "probably" preexisted its invention—at least in rudimentary form:

> The stagnation of the culture industry is probably not the result of monopolization, but was a property of so-called entertainment from the first. Kitsch is composed of that structure of invariables which the philosophical lie ascribes to its solemn designs. On principle, nothing in them must change, since the whole mischief is intended to hammer into men that nothing must change. (Adorno, *Minima Moralia*, 147)

But, as we shall see, Adorno's reflections on the phonographic record extended well beyond just the general character of the music put to vinyl and the record as a product of the culture industry. These topics as well as the listening habits of those who played records were of course discussed by him—and are certainly interesting and debatable ones.

However, in addition to these "sociological" observations on vinyl, Adorno also contributed a much deeper "philosophical" and "phenomenological" set of reflections, most of which were completed well before the advent of the "long-playing" record and the electric phonograph. To be sure, Adorno's *major* philosophical reflections on the phonograph were completed in the age of the "short-playing" record and the spring-driven nonelectric gramophone.

My thesis here is that these deep philosophical reflections of the young Adorno coming to terms with the "mechanized sound" of the gramophone coupled with the fact that composers such as Stravinsky—whose style of musical modernism he found reactionary[2]—*embraced* mechanical music and the phonographic record contributed along with other factors to a lifelong disparagement of the phonograph. This disparagement would continue unchanged even after major "improvements" were made to phonographic technology—a position he seemed to establish *in advance* of later changes in the technology. Finally, after a lifetime of sociological and philosophical dismissal of vinyl, he published a statement in the same year that he died that would mark a surprising change in attitude regarding vinyl. But let's not get too ahead of ourselves.

The Words of a Composer

In the twenty-volume German collected edition of his work, over 4,000 of its roughly 10,000 pages are given to the topic of music. Principal among this work are his books, *Philosophy of Modern Music* (1949), *In Search of Wagner* (1952), *Dissonanzen* (1956), *Sound Figures* (1959), *Mahler: A Musical Physiognomy* (1960), *Introduction to the Sociology of Music*

(1962), *Der getreue Korrepetitor* (1963), *Quasi una fantasia: Essays on Modern Music* (1963), *Moments musicaux* (1964), *Alban Berg: Master of the Smallest Link* (1968), and *Impromptus* (1968), which all appeared during his lifetime, as well as *Beethoven: The Philosophy of Music* (1993), *Theory of Musical Reproduction* (2006), and *Current of Music* (2009), which were published posthumously.

In these works and many others, he writes about nearly every aspect of the world of music: composers from Bach and Beethoven to Berg and Boulez; compositions ranging from chamber and orchestral music to opera; compositional procedure; conductors and conducting; musical form; musical listening; musical nationalism; musical pedagogy; musical performances; new music; popular and light music; jazz; kitsch; radio music; recording technology; the role of the critic in music; and so on. To be sure, no other twentieth-century philosopher has written as much about music or covered so many specific aspects of it as Adorno.

But it should not be forgotten too that Adorno was not only a philosopher of music and a music critic but also a respectable music composer himself. In his youth, he entertained the idea of becoming a composer and concert pianist, and even took piano lessons with Bernhard Sekles, who was also the teacher of the composer Paul Hindemith. In 1925, when he was only twenty-two years old, Adorno moved to Vienna where he became a composition student of Alban Berg and took piano lessons from Eduard Steuermann (Leppert, "Introduction," 4), who along with Berg was a member of Arnold Schoenberg's circle.[3] Of Adorno's *First String Quartet*, composed during this period, Berg wrote to Schoenberg that it is "very good and I believe would meet with your approval" (Berg and Schoenberg 355; cited by Leppert ["Introduction," 14]). Adorno would go on to compose music for most of his adult life, including an unfinished opera based on the writings of Mark Twain.[4]

However, of these one million words about music, only three very short essays are devoted to the principal means of its mechanical or technological reproduction in the twentieth century: the phonograph and the phonographic record. Two were written very early in his career—the first when he was in his mid-twenties and the second in his early thirties—and the last was published in the year of his death. This means that the philosopher who famously introduced (along with Max Horkheimer) the world to "the culture industry"[5] and discussed "[a]musement under late capitalism" (Horkheimer and Adorno 137) in *Dialectic of Enlightenment* in 1944, and whose work was dominated by the critical analysis of music, largely ignored *directly* addressing not only the phonographic record and the technology of phonographic recording but also the industry built upon these technologies, namely the record industry. This, however, is not to say that he did not write extensively about the music that was put to record; nor is it to say that he did not extensively speculate on other technologies of music reproduction such as radio. Rather, it is to say that his work, by and large, dismissed early both the record as a *viable* means of music reproduction and the record industry as a *legitimate* source for "serious" music.[6]

This lack creates a strange void in his work on music—albeit one that can perhaps only be understood by examining his approach to and reflections on the phonograph and the phonographic record as stated in these three remarkable essays, which form his aesthetic triptych on the phonograph. On the one hand, no critical thinker has more extensively examined the composition and development of modern music in the twentieth century than Adorno; on the other hand, while he identifies a role for music under late capitalism, his examination of its political economy vis-à-vis twentieth-century advances in the technology of its reproduction is arguably severely underdeveloped, especially when compared, for example, to the work of Jacques Attali, one of his successors, who used the development of sound recording in the twentieth century to situate the record album at the center of the emerging new economy, late capitalism.[7]

Adorno, however, as we shall see, does not take his own reflections on the record as far as Attali. Though the advent and growth of phonographic recording plays a large role in determining how we consume music, and the impact of the phonograph on musical consumption also affects the production of music, Adorno stops far short of Attali's conclusion that the invention of the phonograph brought about a *new* form of political economy. Rather, for Adorno, while "music underwrote the principle of consumerism during the early heyday of the Industrial Revolution that anchored commonplace understanding of the very nature of modernity" (Leppert, "Commentary," 232), its reproduction on vinyl did not, as Attali argues, usher in postmodernity and a new form of political economy, namely, what has come to be known as "neoliberalism" or "late capitalism."

Records and the industry that produces them, for Adorno, function as a species of "amusement" *under* late capitalism:

> Amusement under late capitalism is the prolongation of work. It is sought after as an escape from the mechanized work process, and to recruit strength in order to be able to cope with it again. But at the same time mechanization has such power over man's leisure and happiness, and so profoundly determines the manufacture of amusement goods, that his experiences are inevitably afterimages of the work process itself. (Horkheimer and Adorno 137)

That Adorno will early on regard the phonograph as the *mechanization* of music or "mechanical music" only contributes to the later disdain he has toward the phonographic record.

As an example, though, of how the phonograph "underwrote the principle of consumerism during the early heyday of the Industrial Revolution,"

Adorno commentator Richard Leppert asks us to consider "the history of piano design, manufacture, and distribution in the course of the nineteenth century," which he regards as a "perfect metaphor of capitalist economic principles in operation" and "an agent of capitalism's political, economic, and ideological success":

> Manufactured on a massive scale for a seemingly insatiable audience of consumers, the domestic piano bespoke a principal contradiction on nineteenth-century bourgeois society. High-caste pianos with elaborately decorated cases virtually fetishized conspicuous materialism; at the same time the music to be played on the instrument was valorized precisely because of its immateriality, to the nineteenth century the sine qua non of music's supposedly socially transcendent autonomy. Whatever its aesthetic correlates, the piano was a consumer product whose presence helped to define familial prestige akin to that of today's family-room "entertainment centers," not for nothing so-named, in advertising lingo that teaches us to focus our eyes on the screen and ears on the speakers to learn what's for sale, in exchange for the shows and music that come along as loss leaders. (Leppert, "Commentary," 232)

It is in much the same way that Adorno came to view the phonograph and the phonographic record: namely, as metaphor for capitalist economic principles in operation—and not, with Attali, as determinant of a *new* form of political economy.

In short, for Adorno, the phonograph and the phonographic record not only underwrote the principle of consumerism that anchored the commonplace understanding of the very nature of modernity; it was also typical of the kind of amusement functioning under late capitalism. Let's now look at each of Adorno's three essays on the phonograph in turn, and see his thoughts on the technology that made music into a commodity.

The Curves of a Needle

When Adorno went to Vienna in 1925 to study composition with Alban Berg, he was just twenty-two years old. In the same year, he started to contribute essays on music to *Musikblätter des Anbruch*, an avant-garde music journal founded in Vienna in 1919. Berg was the first editor of the journal, and presumably established his student's connection with the journal. It was here that he first began to work out in print his thoughts on music, culture, and technology.

In 1929, after four years as a frequent contributor to the journal, he was put on its editorial board. One of his first contributions was to change the title to simply *Anbruch*. At the same time, he also initiated an attack on the reactionary forces in the music world and broadened the scope of the journal to include "light music" and kitsch. In fact, one of the first issues of *Anbruch* was entirely devoted to the subject of "light music." Its contributors included Ernst Bloch, Ernst Krenek, Kurt Weill, and Adorno, who wrote an essay on three popular hit tunes of the day. Other topics covered in the issue included operettas, film music, salon orchestras, and radio (Levin 27n13).

Adorno early on recognized the importance of studying the complete range of musical production, and not just the so-called serious music. In "Zum *Anbruch*: Exposé," an unpublished manuscript from 1928, he writes,

> In conjunction with sociological analyses there is also an entire field of music—previously denied any serious study whatsoever—which ought to be incorporated into the domain of *Anbruch*; namely, the entire realm of "light music," of kitsch, not only jazz but also the European operetta, the hit tune, etc. In doing so, one ought to adopt a very particular kind of approach that ought to be circumscribed in two senses. On the one hand, one must abandon the arrogance characteristic of an understanding of "serious" music which believes it can completely ignore the music which today constitutes the only musical material consumed by the vast majority of people. Kitsch must be played out and defended against everything that is merely elevated mediocre art, against the now rotten ideals of personality, culture, etc. On the other hand, however, one must not fall prey to the tendency—all too fashionable these days, above all in Berlin—to simply glorify kitsch and consider it the true art of the epoch merely because of its popularity. (Adorno, "Zum *Anbruch*," 601–2; cited and trans., Levin 27–8)

So, well before his work with Horkheimer on "the culture industry," Adorno was grappling on his own with aspects of this later critique. Here kitsch is both defended against immediate dismissal, but at the same time not simply glorified because of its popularity.

But he also recognized in this early work that consideration of the technologies of music cannot be disregarded in the study of music. To this end, he proposed that *Anbruch* include a section dedicated to the subject of music and machines, namely "Mechanische Music." In its previous incarnation as *Musikblätter des Anbruch*, the journal used to have a feature oriented toward "the *producers* of mechanical music, i.e., the record industry, the gramophone manufacturers, etc., in hopes of attracting advertising" (Levin 28), but because the manufacturers had their own trade journals, the revenue from advertisement never materialized, and so the journal dropped the feature. Adorno writes,

> The purpose of the rubric on mechanical [music] is not merely to trace journalistically a conspicuous trend in current musical life. Rather, it

will attempt to shed light on the meaning of mechanization, will weigh the different tendencies of mechanization against each other and will try to have an influence on the politics of programming. All of this grows out of the conviction that the mechanical presentation of music today is of contemporary relevance in a deeper sense than merely being currently available as a new technological means. To put it another way, this position arises out of the conviction that the availability of means corresponds to an availability of consciousness and that the current historical state of the works themselves to a large extent requires them to be presented mechanically. (Adorno, "Zum *Anbruch*," 607; cited and trans., Levin 29)

For Adorno, the category of mechanical music is a "trend" that includes radio broadcasts, phonographic records, and film scores for both silent film and sound film. Thus, this *Ansbruch* forum on "mechanical music" was directed toward providing *consumers* of these various sound media technical and musicological advice on its usage—albeit, and most importantly, not as an "advertising stooge" for the gramophone industry (like a "trade" journal).

It is within this context of widening the scope of music considered to include popular music, and suggesting that technological trends were an important part of music criticism, that Adorno engages in the first of his three major expositions on the gramophone.

The essay "Nadelkurven," translated as "The Curves of the Needle," was written in 1927, and first published in *Musikblätter des Anbruch* in February 1928, well before he joined its editorial board (Adorno, "Nadelkurven" [1928], 47–50). It was again reprinted in *Phono: Internationale Schallplatten-Zeitschrift* in 1965 though with slight revisions, and this important note from Adorno:

It goes without saying that over the course of forty years, insights into a technological medium become outdated. On the other hand, even at that time there was already a recognition of aspects of the transformed character of experience which, even as it was caused by technology, also had an effect on that very same technology. The motifs have been retained unchanged and with no attempt to cover up the temporal distance; the author made changes in the language to the extent that he deemed it necessary. (Adorno, "Nadelkurven" [1965], 123; cited in Adorno, "The Curves of the Needle," 49)

In many ways, this note is the place to begin regarding Adorno's thoughts on this technological medium because in it he admits that for the most part his views on the phonograph and phonographic recordings have remained the same over the course of the forty years since he wrote the essay. While the technology of the medium has changed over the years, the motifs he related to the phonograph in 1927 (and then again a few years later) remain unchanged in 1965. What then are these "motifs"? I will identify what I take to be the major ones found in this particular essay here—and then in the next two sections identify the additional ones found in the other two essays.

1. The phonographic record is comparable to the photograph. According to Adorno, in the early stages of photographic technology (e.g., the daguerreotype), it "had the power to penetrate rationally the reigning artistic practice." However, as soon as one "attempts to improve these early technologies through an emphasis on concrete fidelity, the exactness one has ascribed to them is exposed as an illusion by the very technology itself" (Adorno, "The Curves of the Needle," 49). He believes that the same holds for the phonograph: the more "recordings become more perfect in terms of plasticity and volume, the subtlety of color and the authenticity of vocal sound declines as if the singer were being distanced more and more from the apparatus" (Adorno, "The Curves of the Needle," 49). For Adorno, "the transition from artisanal to industrial production transforms not only the technology of distribution but also that which is distributed" (Adorno, "The Curves of the Needle," 49). In short, as technology works to "improve" sound fidelity, sound "authenticity" declines proportionally. Adorno was not interested in accounting for the changes in sound recording technology over the forty-year span of the republication of his essay because he believed such advances only further confirmed what he said in 1927: that is, records were on the decline ever since the invention of the "talking machine."

Today it is difficult not to read Adorno's comments here through the lens of Walter Benjamin's 1936 essay, "The Work of Art in the Age of Mechanical Reproduction,"[8] especially since Adorno was Benjamin's "first and only disciple" (Arendt 2). But unlike Benjamin who bemoans the loss of "aura" in the mechanical reproduction of art, Adorno seems to be saying something a bit different here, namely, that advances in photographic and phonographic technology only serve to deteriorate the "indexical" relationship among the sign, its object, and its interpreter. As recording technology improves, the indexical relationship between the music performed (the object) and its recording (the representamen) degenerates for its listeners (the interpretant).[9]

Later, however, he literally mimics the voice of Benjamin, commenting in 1940:

> Now, we believe that *this* authenticity, or aura, is vanishing in music because of mechanical reproduction. The phonograph record destroys the "now" of the live performance and, in a way, its "here" as well. (Adorno, "Radio Physiognomics [1940]," 36)

Nevertheless, regardless of how you theoretically formalize Adorno's remarks here, his message is the same: technological progress in phonograph sound reproduction is inversely proportional to the quality of the listening experience.

2. *The relevance of talking machines is debatable.* This line is so important that Adorno repeats it verbatim twice in "Nadelkurven." He views the phonograph as a "utensil of the private life that regulates the consumption of art" (Adorno, "The Curves of the Needle," 50). Key to this "regulation" is that some music reproduces better on the phonograph than other music. "For the time being, Beethoven defies the gramophone," comments Adorno. "The diffuse and atmospheric comfort of the small but bright gramophone sound corresponds to the humming gaslight and is not entirely foreign to the whistling teakettle of bygone literature" (Adorno, "The Curves of the Needle," 50). In other words, because the range of music that can be "authentically" reproduced on the phonograph is limited—it can reproduce "popular music," for example "light music," kitsch, jazz, the hit tune, and so on, authentically but not "serious music," for example, Beethoven—its "relevance" is debatable.

3. *The phonograph has become a status symbol.* Just as the piano was transformed "from a musical instrument to a piece bourgeois furniture" (Adorno, "The Curves of the Needle," 51), so too has the phonograph been transformed but only "in an extraordinarily more rapid fashion" (Adorno, "The Curves of the Needle," 51). "In the functional salon, the gramophone stands innocuously as a little mahogany cabinet on little rococo legs," reports Adorno. "Its cover provides a space for the artistic photograph of the divorced wife with the baby," he cleverly continues, drawing our attention back to the similarities between the fate of the photograph and that of the phonograph. He mocks those who as "the expert examines all the needles and chooses the best one," while others who cannot afford to own their own phonograph, let alone a high-end phonograph, "just drops in his dime [into the jukebox]," saying that "the sound that responds to both [the actions of the expert and the jukebox user] may well be the same" (Adorno, "The Curves of the Needle," 52). Here the social status of owning an expensive phonograph is undermined by his assertion that even those who cannot afford this luxury can still experience the same sound fidelity albeit for a fraction of the cost. In short, again, Adorno sees in the phonograph a metaphor for *capitalist* economic principles in operation—not serious *musical* ones.

4. *Records allow us to hear ourselves.* Adorno speaks of the "primordial affect which the gramophone stimulated and which perhaps even gave rise to the gramophone in the first place" (Adorno, "The Curves of the Needle," 54). This "primordial affect," which he refers to as "the mirror function of the gramophone" (Adorno, "The Curves of the Needle," 54), is its ability to allow the listener to hear himself. "What the gramophone listener actually wants to hear is himself," writes Adorno. The musical artist offers to the listener through the phonograph record "a substitute for the sounding

image of his own person." As such, when records perform this "mirror function," they become "virtual photographs of their owners, flattering photographs—ideologies." Even if the primary function of records is to archive sound or sound images of musical art, their "primordial affect" is *to preserve their listeners*. Records are valuable to their listeners because they are a means for the listeners to "possess" or own themselves. Thus, when we safeguard records, we are safeguarding ourselves. "The only reason that he [the possessor of a record] accords the record such value is because he himself could also be just as well preserved" (Adorno, "The Curves of the Needle," 54).[10]

This, of course, is an obvious nod to Jacques Lacan's well-known "mirror stage," where the child gains its first sense of identity. But, as with Benjamin's famous essay noted earlier, Lacan's "The Mirror State as Formative of the I Function as Revealed in Psychoanalytic Experience" was also published well after Adorno's work here—in 1949, over twenty years later (Lacan). So too is Adorno's mention of the record's connection with the "ideologies" of their listeners a nod to Lacan, for as one of psychoanalyst's commentators put it, "the mirror stage is our initial imaginary gateway to the ongoing operations of normativity that help put the 'I' in ideology and keep ideology in the 'I'" (Thomas 577). Adorno thinks that the HMV record logo where the dog "Nipper" is seen listening to his master's voice through the gramophone horn is the "right emblem" for the mirroring function of records. Presumably, just as we can hear our own sound image in our records, so too can our dog, who primarily communicates with us through our sound images. Needless to say, the mirroring function of records only works *if* there are sound images available on vinyl that are representative of the listener's ideology. But what happens when these sound images are *not* available on record?

5. *The mechanical reproduction of sound is limited*. The technology of the phonograph, though, is limited in its ability to perform the mirror function. Adorno comments, "What is best reproduced gramophonically is the singing voice" (Adorno, "The Curves of the Needle," 54). However, "[m]ale voices can be reproduced better than female voices" (Adorno, "The Curves of the Needle," 54). By "best" Adorno means "most faithful to the natural ur-image and not at all most appropriate to the mechanical from the outset" (Adorno, "The Curves of the Needle," 54). Thus, on the one hand, the gramophone gives "every female voice a sound that is needy and incomplete," while on the other hand, the capacities of gramophonic technology explain "Caruso's uncontested dominance" (Adorno, "The Curves of the Needle," 54). But just as there are limits to vocal reproduction by the gramophone, so too does "absolute pitch run into difficulties" (Adorno, "The Curves of the Needle," 54). "It is almost impossible," by listening to a record, "to guess the actual pitch if it deviates from the original one" (Adorno, "The Curves of the Needle," 54). As such, "the original pitch becomes confused with that of the phonographic reproduction" (Adorno, "The Curves of the Needle," 54).

These mechanical limitations negatively impact both the "relevance" of the phonograph and its ability to perform widely the "mirror function." A very limited vehicle of mechanical sound reproduction, Adorno's phenomenological assessment of the phonograph here leaves very little room for it to have a positive impact on either listeners or music appreciation.

6. *Records are like empty clay pots.* Adorno compares the turntable to the potter's wheel as both produce a *Ton-Masse* (Adorno, "The Curves of the Needle," 55). The German word for "clay" is *Ton*. But it is also the word for "tone" or "sound." This word, *Ton-Masse*, thus allows Adorno to bring together the spinning motion of both tables in one compound word. Thus, in the final analysis of the young Adorno, the "turntable of the talking machines is comparable to the potter's wheel," which begins by spinning a "clay mass" (Adorno, "The Curves of the Needle," 55). When "finished," the clay container that is produced is "empty" until it is filled by a user. The same goes for records: the turntable begins by spinning a "sound mass" or "tone mass," that is, a record. However, the record, like the clay container produced by the potter's wheel, is empty until it is "filled by the hearer."

In sum, each these six motifs are the heart of the young composer's reflections on the phonograph. And each, of course, just touch the surface of deeper and more complex sets of issues he has with phonographic records in general. What is clear, though, from this initial set of motifs is that Adorno is not very impressed with the mechanization of sound reproduction via the phonograph—and that this early work sets the stage well for a lifetime of negative comments about the phonograph.

The Form of a Record

Adorno would not write another piece explicitly on the phonograph record for another seven years—and even then, it would be published under a pseudonym. The essay "Die Form der Schallplatte," translated as "The Form of the Phonographic Record," was published in 1934 in the journal *23: Eine Wiener Musikzeitschrift*, which was founded a few years earlier in 1932. The journal takes its title from paragraph 23 of Austrian journalism law, which guarantees the right to force publication of corrections to falsely published information. While established to provide rigorous music criticism as a "corrective" to unrigorous music criticism, it quickly widened its scope beyond just music criticism (Levin 31n20). Presumably, given the controversial nature of the journal, Adorno opted to publish his essay under the name "Hektor Rottweiler."[11]

While some of the motifs addressed in "The Curves of the Needle" are again taken up in "The Form of the Phonograph Record," for example, the comparisons of the phonograph to photography and the limits of the mechanical reproduction of sound, not only are some new ones taken up, but there is a distinctly different approach to this later essay.

As for the similarities, there are again comparisons of the photograph to phonographic recording but with a slightly different emphasis. Here, Adorno comments that because phonograph records were "spared the artisanal transfiguration of artistic specificity," they have remained "nothing more than the acoustic photographs that the dog [viz., the dog "Nipper" in the HMV record logo who is seen listening to his master's voice through the gramophone horn] so happily recognizes" (Adorno, "The Form of the Phonograph Record," 57). Moreover, record collecting is compared to photograph collecting:

> records are possessed like photographs; the nineteenth century had good reasons for coming up with phonograph record albums alongside photographic and postage-stamp albums, all of them herbaria of artificial life that are present in the smallest space and ready to conjure up every recollection that would otherwise be mercilessly shredded between the haste and hum-drum of private life. (Adorno, "The Form of the Phonograph Record," 58)

The comment that records have been "spared the artisanal transfiguration of artistic specificity" refers to the claim that, as of 1934, "[t]here has been no development of phonographic composers" and there "has never been any gramophone-specific music" (Adorno, "The Form of the Phonograph Record," 57). Specifically, he calls out Stravinsky in this context, saying "despite all his good will towards the electric piano, [he] has not made any effort in this direction." Consequently, because the phonograph has not played any role in musical *composition*, "the phonograph record is not good for much more than reproducing and storing a music deprived of its best dimension, a music, namely, that was already in existence before the phonograph record and is not significantly altered by it" (Adorno, "The Form of the Phonograph Record," 57).

Adorno calls out Stravinsky because of his long-standing interest in mechanical music, wherein, he in fact even wrote in 1917 a specific piece of music for the pianola, and in 1923 signed a six-year contract to record his entire corpus on pianola rolls (Adorno, "The Form of the Phonograph Record," 57n3)—and, as mentioned earlier, a few years later signed another contract to put his entire oeuvre on phonograph record. It should be noted that the "Pianola," later called the "player piano," was patented in 1897. The "Pianola" was a cabinet with wooden "fingers" projecting from it that was stationed in front of an ordinary piano. A paper roll activated the "fingers" to play the "recorded" music. This technology still exists with digital memory replacing the paper rolls.

In the early twentieth century, these pianolas could "reproduce" performances by Claude Debussy, Sergey Rachmaninoff, Artur Rubenstein, and George Gershwin. Later versions could even capture nuances of playing such as tempo change, crescendos, and other dynamics. They would come to be called "reproducing pianos." Player piano technology developed more or less simultaneously with phonograph technology. Early development of the player piano was roughly contemporaneous with the early development of the phonograph, and dates back to Frechman Henri Fourneaux's invention of the "pianista" in 1863.[12]

Later, in 1930, four years before Adorno's essay, Stravinsky wrote in "My Position on the Phonograph Record," "it would be of the greatest interest to produce music specifically for phonographic reproduction, a music which would only attain its true image—its original sound—through the mechanical production." "This," he continues, "is probably the ultimate goal for the gramophonic composer of the future" (Stravinsky [1930]; cited and trans., Adorno ["The Form of the Phonograph Record," 57n3]). But the expectation of using the phonograph as an artisanal element in music composition is more Adorno "the composer" speaking rather than Adorno "the philosopher," as the same comment could be made for all mechanisms of sound reproduction from radio transmission to digital reproduction.

As to the limits of sound reproduction, he goes nowhere into the depth of the earlier article, but does note that "the inevitable brevity dictated by the size of the vinyl plate" makes it "too sparse for the first movement of the Eroica [viz., Beethoven's Third Symphony] to be allowed to unfold without interruption" (Adorno, "The Form of the Phonograph Record," 58). Much later, as we shall see later, the capacity to put lengthier pieces of music on one side of a record, more than anything else, leads Adorno to reverse course on his general opinion of phonograph records. But in the earlier context of the "shorter-playing" records of the early 1930s, this comment is developed within the context of a set of remarks about the "thingness" of records—a motif not developed in the earlier essay.

7. *The phonographic record allows us for the first time to possess music like a thing.* But Adorno is clear that the need or desire to possess music like a thing is one that had to be developed, and is not a "human requirement" or "human need." "[O]nce the thing [i.e., the phonographic record] already exists and is spinning in its own orbit," the "need" for it "is initially produced by advertisement" (Adorno, "The Form of the Phonograph Record," 56). In other words, though advertising has convinced us that we *need* to possess music like a thing, we don't really need records. Phonographic recordings may be a technological marvel, but they are not a response to human needs. It is here that Adorno establishes the role of modernity and modernization in the development of the phonographic record.

8. *The phonographic record is a product of modernity, not human need.* For Adorno, the record is one of the first of the technological artistic

inventions of modernity. It "stems from an era that cynically acknowledges the dominance of things over people through the emancipation of technology from human requirements and human needs through the presentation of achievements whose significance is not primarily humane" (Adorno, "The Form of the Phonograph Record," 56).

For him, the technological prehistory of the phonograph is to be found in mechanical musical instruments like the barrel organ. With these mechanical musical instruments, which now includes the phonograph, "*time* gains a new approach to music" (Adorno, "The Form of the Phonograph Record," 58). This new approach "is not the time in which music happens, nor is it the time which music monumentalizes by means of its 'style'"; rather it is "time as evanescence, enduring in mute music" (Adorno, "The Form of the Phonograph Record," 58). "If the 'modernity' of all mechanical instruments gives music an age old appearance—as if, in the rigidity of its repetitions, it had existed for ever, having been submitted to the pitiless eternity of the clockwork—then the evanescence and recollection that is associated with the barrel organ as a mere sound in a compelling yet indeterminate way has become tangible and manifest through the gramophone records" (Adorno, "The Form of the Phonograph Record," 58).

9. *The phonographic record is a form of writing.* The phonographic record, observes Adorno, "is covered with curves, a delicately scribbled, utterly illegible writing" (Adorno, "The Form of the Phonograph Record," 56). And it is in its connection with writing that Adorno locates the "most profound justification" for the phonographic record in this second essay.

> There is no doubt that, as music is removed by the phonograph record from the realm of live production and from the imperative of artistic creativity and becomes petrified, it absorbs into itself, in this process of petrification, the very life that would otherwise vanish. The dead art rescues the ephemeral and perishing art as the only one alive. Therein may lie the phonograph record's most profound justification, which cannot be impugned by an aesthetic objection to its reification. For this justification reestablishes by the very means of reification an age-old, submerged and yet warranted relationship: that between music and *writing*. (Adorno, "The Form of the Phonograph Record," 59)

Adorno sees in musical notation an earlier effort to convey music by writing that is limited because this form of musical writing (notation) is only understandable to a limited audience. With the advent of the "writing" of the phonographic record comes Adorno's "hope that . . . it will some day become as readable as the 'last remaining universal language since the construction of the tower'" (Adorno, "The Form of the Phonograph Record," 59).[13] Thus, a surprising reversal by Adorno after so much negativity about the record: it holds out the promise of becoming a universal language which was once merely "conveyed by writing," but now "suddenly itself turns into writing" (Adorno, "The Form of the Phonograph Record," 59). Adorno writes, "through the curves of the needle on the phonographic record, music approaches decisively its true character as writing" (Adorno, "The Form of the Phonograph Record," 59).

Opera without Wigs

The final panel in Adorno's essayistic triptych on the phonograph was published a few months before his death in August of 1969. "'Die Oper Ueberwintert auf der Langspeilplatte': Theodor W. Adorno über die Revolution der Schallplatte," first appeared in the news magazine *Der Spiegel* (169). The essay is important because it is largely a retraction of some of Adorno's earlier comments on the phonograph. Hence, it introduces a new albeit late motif regarding the phonographic record.

10. *The long-playing record is revolutionary.* Adorno says that when he wrote his earlier essays, "it still had to be claimed that, as a form, the phonograph record had not given rise to anything unique to it" (Adorno, "Opera and the Long-Playing Record," 63). In part, this was because when he was writing these essays in the 1920s and early 1930s, there were no long-playing records available.

Though the long-playing record was introduced by RCA in 1931, it was only for use in radio, wherein it "provided a means of transcription that allowed material to be prerecorded and exchanged between different stations" (Chanan 92). It would not be until 1948, long after Adorno's opinions on the phonograph were set, that the 33 1/3 r.p.m. microgroove LP record was launched by Columbia in the United States. Instead of changing the record every three or four minutes as one did with the 78 r.p.m. record about which Adorno had been writing, the 33 1/3 r.p.m. LP allowed for a much longer listening time before having to switch out the record. Particularly in the "classical market," the LP was a rapid success (Chanan 93).[14]

The advent of LP records radically changed his opinion of the phonograph record. Adorno now says "the term 'revolution' is hardly an exaggeration with regard to the long-playing record" (Adorno, "Opera and the Long-Playing Record," 63). "The entire musical literature could now become available in quite-authentic form to listeners desirous of auditioning and studying such works at a time convenient to them" (Adorno, "Opera and the Long-Playing Record," 63). Ironically, though, the technology that changed Adorno's position on the record was introduced to the market for *financial* reasons, namely, to allow the record industry to better compete with the emerging television industry (just as years earlier the talking-movie was introduced in part to better compete with the emerging radio industry) (Chanan 92).

In particular, this "revolution" is linked to the ability of long-playing records to present operas "[s]horn of phony hoopla," "powdered ladies and gentlemen," and "the Germanic beards in the *Ring*" (Adorno, "Opera and the Long-Playing Record," 64). Long-playing records allow listeners "to recapture some of the force and intensity that had been worn threadbare in the opera houses" through the limitations of staging and costuming. Whether one uses period staging, which in case of Mozart's *Figaro* "resembles the praline box," or uses "the practices of contemporary dance, dressed in sweat suits or even timeless outfits, one cannot avoid asking, What's the point?" (Adorno, "Opera and the Long-Playing Record," 64). The LP allows one "to spare Mozart [and other operatic composers] from this," and focus our attention on what is important in opera: the music.

The "short-playing records of yesteryear—acoustic daguerreotypes that are already now hard to play in a way that produces a satisfying sound due to the lack of proper apparatuses—unconsciously also corresponded to their epoch: the desire for highbrow diversion, the salon pieces, favorite arias, and the Neopolitan semihits" (Adorno, "Opera and the Long-Playing Record," 65). For Adorno, the advent of the LP record marked a close to "this sphere of music," for "there is now only music of the highest standards and obvious kitsch, with nothing in between" (Adorno, "Opera and the Long-Playing Record," 65). "The LP expresses this historical change rather precisely" (Adorno, "Opera and the Long-Playing Record," 65). Thus, he sees in the development of the phonographic record a pattern not uncommon in the history of music, namely, "it is not all that rare for technological inventions to gain significance only long after their inception" (Adorno, "Opera and the Long-Playing Record," 62).

So, in this late essay, Adorno does a complete 180 degree turn regarding the significance of the phonographic record to music: whereas earlier he viewed it as a flawed musical development of modernity, he now understands it as a welcome technological invention that allows us to more perfectly appreciate opera. Still, the LP record is not without its deficiencies. Chief among them are the "rather steep prices" of LP records, "the manipulation of the sound" by the recording engineers, and the making of cuts within an operatic act. Withstanding these relatively minor mechanical and economic issues, the LP record "might well be able to help resurrect opera in a decisive way at a time when it has become anachronistic in its own loci" (Adorno, "Opera and the Long-Playing Record," 66). So, the distance of phonographic records from the live performance of music becomes a benefit not a limit in the case of opera in the late 1960s. "LPs provide the opportunity—more perfectly than the supposedly live performances—to recreate without disturbance the temporal dimension essential to operas" (Adorno, "Opera and the Long-Playing Record," 65). Thus, circa 1969, the "relevance of the talking machine," one of his earlier motifs, is no longer debatable for Adorno—at least when it comes to the importance of records to operatic music.

Conclusion

Adorno's early impressions of the phonograph record were not favorable ones. He saw this technology as an imperfect "trend" that contributed little if nothing to the advancement of music—even though phonograph records held the potential as a form of writing to be become a "universal language."

It was only in the last year of his life that he came to recognize a major value for the phonograph record—albeit at the expense of the theatrical elements of opera. Still, there are signs that his transformation in attitude toward the phonographic record was not simply a "death bed conversion" in 1969.

In the winter term of 1961–62, Adorno delivered a series of lectures on music at Frankfurt University, with parts of them also broadcast over North German Radio. They were published in 1962 under the title *Einleitung in die Musiksoziologie*, and later translated into English as *Introduction to the Sociology of Music*. Though this volume only contains a few brief statements about phonographic records, they are significant ones as they provide a good bridge between his early pessimism and later optimism.

He comments here that records give listeners the opportunity through repeated listening to acquaint themselves with and become more educated about music. "In principle, the medium of the record," Adorno comments,

> would enable us today to make all of musical literature available to all of those willing to hear, and this potential abolition of educational privilege in music should outweigh the disadvantages which hoarding records as a hobby of an audience of consumers involves under present conditions. (Adorno, *Introduction to the Sociology of Music*, 134)

Adorno also notes that records "technically have now been vastly perfected, especially since LP recording broke the time barrier that limited older discs to short pieces and often to genre music, excluding the great symphonic forms and making records the musical counterpart of bric-à-brac" (Adorno, *Introduction to the Sociology of Music*, 134). Years earlier, he had commented that when we listen "to a recorded symphony the interruptions always remind the listener of the separation between the record and the live performance and destroy the music continuum" (Adorno, "Radio Physiognomics [1940]," 75). This now takes us to possibly the central reason that Adorno had for so long been pessimistic about phonograph records: the music that he preferred was not well represented on vinyl.

The ensuing comments from his *Introduction to the Sociology of Music* begin to confirm this point. He writes,

> Thus the phonographic record, which might accomplish a productive change in musical consciousness, reproduces every dubious side of

current judgment. One would need a catalog of what is missing: to this day, for instance, only a small part of Schönberg's oeuvre is accessible in Germany. (Adorno, *Introduction to the Sociology of Music*, 134)

And, as in the case of another member of the Schoenberg school, even though recordings were available, they might be bad ones: "the first recordings of Berg operas were caricatures bound to reinforce the social prejudice against things modern" (Adorno, *Introduction to the Sociology of Music*, 135). This is all complicated further by the difficulties of purchasing quality records in shops which did not normally stock them: "Outside of New York it could quite recently happen that a record shop would refuse to order a serious modern disc because ordering a single one did not pay" (Adorno, *Introduction to the Sociology of Music*, 135).

As his work from the 1960s indicates, there is hope for records because their form now allows for the distribution of the kind of music that Adorno prefers: "serious music," or what is called more popularly and crassly "classical music." When Adorno was forming his early thoughts on the phonograph, the technology had not yet caught up with his musical preferences. It simply was either not listenable on the gramophone or not available on record. Yet, when it starts to become available, that is, in the late 1950s and early 1960s, one can see him start to shift to a more positive attitude toward the phonograph record. While his early work struggled to philosophically understand a key feature of modernity, namely, the ability to write sound, his later works came to find a decisive role for it in society.

Adorno's modernist perceptions of the phonograph record were formed relatively early in his life *and* its life. The ability to put symphonic music to record was still in its infancy, and the kinds of music that Adorno wanted to hear on record either were not yet available or sounded bad. For him, the phonograph had more in common with the world of the barrel organ and the potter's wheel than that of hi-fidelity and stereophonic sound. Which leads one to wonder: would he have regarded today's 180 gram vinyl as "canned food"? Would he have viewed the curves of the needle differently if they were tracing the path of a studio recording of his *First String Quartet* or his opera *Der Schatz des Indianer-Joe*? Adorno *on* vinyl might have changed everything for this music-obsessed philosopher-composer.[15]

Notes

1 For Stravinsky, the ease of listening to the gramophone is even more apparent when compared to what Bach had to do to hear his own work: "In John Sebastian Bach's day it was necessary for him to walk ten miles to a neighboring town to hear Buxtenhude play his works" (Stravinsky, *Autobiography*, 152).

2   The poles of musical modernism were developed by Adorno most famously in his *Philosophy of Modern Music* (1949), with Stravinsky on one end of the spectrum and Schoenberg on the other.

3   Arnold Schoenberg lived and taught in Vienna between 1903 and 1925. The "circle" refers to the group of composers, conductors, and musicians who studied with him during this period. This "Second Vienna School" included Alban Berg, Anton Webern, Ernst Krenek, Heinrich Jalowetz, Erwin Stein, Egon Wellesz, Eduard Steuermann, Hanns Eisler, Roberto Gerhard, Norbert von Hannenheim, Rudolf Kolisch, Paul A. Pisk, Karl Rankl, Josef Rufer, Nikos Skalkottas, Viktor Ullmann, and Winfried Zillig (see Leibowitz). "Like Bach," writes Leibowitz, "Schoenberg succeeded in a great renewal; for just as the death of the modal system brought life to the tonal system, which was definitely constituted in the work of Bach, even so the classic tonal system, dead since Wagner, is transmuted, in Schoenberg's work, into [a] system" studied and practiced by the students in his "school" (286).

4   Adorno's opera was entitled *Der Schatz des Indianer-Joe* (*The Treasure of Indian-Joe*) (Gordon and Rehding 2).

5   See Horkheimer and Adorno.

6   My claim there is only further amplified by the recent reconstruction of his extensive work from 1939 to 1941 on radio, published in *Current of Music: Elements of a Radio Theory* (2009). In short, radio as a means of musical reproduction was worthy of extensive investigation, whereas the phonograph only in passing (largely dismissive) comment and a few brief early essays.

7   I think this becomes particularly evident when Adorno's work on the phonographic record is played *backward* against the work of Attali, who in his book, *Bruits: essai sur l'économie de la musique* (1977), published eight years after Adorno's death, shows how the invention of the phonograph brought about a new form of political economy, one he calls "repetition," but which we call today "neoliberal" political economy. However, this discussion will be left for another occasion, and focus here is placed on establishing Adorno's position on vinyl. For my thoughts on Attali on vinyl, see Di Leo, "Late Capitalism on Vinyl."

8   This work first appeared in *Zeitschrift für Sozialforschung*, V, 1, 1936. Reprinted and trans. in Walter Benjamin, *Illuminations* (217–52).

9   I'm using here the triadic semiotics of Charles Peirce because of the way it formalizes the phenomenology of indexical experience in Adorno's description. Peirce describes the "hic et nunc" ("here and now") of indexical experience that arise through his phenomenological category of "secondness." However, there are of course other senses of indexicality. See Di Leo, "The Semiotics of Indexical Experience," for an overview of Peirce's work here.

10 It should also be noted that early phonographs could both record sound and play it back.

11 Adorno also published his controversial essay, "Über Jazz," under the same pseudonym, albeit in a different journal, *Zeitschrift für Sozialforschung* 2 (1936): 235–59.

12 See "Player piano," www.britannica.com.
13 Here Adorno is quoting Walter Benjamin, *The Origin of German Tragic Drama* (1928), his *Habilitation* for the University of Frankfurt in 1925. It was submitted to the university by Benjamin but later withdrawn.
14 It should also be noted that the 45 r.p.m. record was introduced by RCA Victor in 1949, a technology that unlike the 33 1/3 LP would not be immune to Adorno's early criticisms of the phonographic record.
15 Starting in the 1950s, polyvinyl chloride became a common material in record production. Thus, the term "vinyl" came to be short for "vinyl phonographic records."

Works Cited

Adorno, Theodor W. *Current of Music: Elements of a Radio Theory*. Ed. Robert Hullot-Kentor. Malden, MA: Polity, 2009.
Adorno, Theodor W. "Die Form der Schallplatte." In *23: Eine Wiener Musikzeitschrift* 17–19 (15 December 1934): 35–9. Signed "Hektor Rottweiler."
Adorno, Theodor W. "'Die Oper Ueberwintert auf der Langspeilplatte': Theodor W. Adorno über die Revolution der Schallplatte." *Der Spiegel* 23 (March 24, 1969): 169.
Adorno, Theodor W. *Einleitung in die Musiksoziologie*. Frankfurt-am-Main: Suhrkamp Verlag, 1962.
Adorno, Theodor W. *Introduction to the Sociology of Music* [1962]. Trans. E. B. Ashton. New York: The Seabury Press, 1976.
Adorno, Theodor W. *Minima Moralia: Reflections from a Damaged Life* [1951]. Trans. E. F. N. Jephcott. New York: Verso, 1994.
Adorno, Theodor W. "Nadelkurven." *Musikblätter des Anbruch* 10 (February 1928): 47–50.
Adorno, Theodor W. "Nadelkurven." *Phono: Internationale Schallplatten-Zeitschrift* 6 (July-August 1965): 123–4.
Adorno, Theodor W. "On Popular Music [1941], with the Assistance of George Simpson." In Theodor W. Adorno, *Essays on Music: Selected, with Introduction, Commentary, and Notes*. Ed. Richard Leppert. Berkeley: University of California Press, 2002, pp. 437–69.
Adorno, Theodor W. "Opera and the Long-Playing Record." Trans. Thomas Y. Levin. *October* 55 (Winter 1990): 62–6.
Adorno, Theodor W. *Philosophy of Modern Music* [1949]. Trans. Anne G. Mitchell and Wesley V. Blomster. New York: Continuum, 1985.
Adorno, Theodor W. "Radio Physiognomics [1940]." In *Current of Music: Elements of a Radio Theory*. Ed. Robert Hullot-Kentor. Malden, MA: Polity, 2009, pp. 41–132.
Adorno, Theodor W. "The Curves of the Needle." Trans. Thomas Y. Levin. *October* 55 (Winter 1990): 49–55.
Adorno, Theodor W. "The Form of the Phonograph Record." Trans. Thomas Y. Levin. *October* 55 (Winter 1990): 56–61.

Adorno, Theodor W. "The Radio Voice [1939]." In *Current of Music: Elements of a Radio Theory*. Ed. Robert Hullot-Kentor. Malden, MA: Polity, 2009, pp. 345–91.

Adorno, Theodor W. "Über Jazz." *Zeitschrift für Sozialforschung* 2 (1936): 235–59.

Adorno, Theodor W. "Zum *Anbruch*: Exposé." *Gesammelte Schriften*, 20 volumes in 23. Ed. Rolf Tiedemann. Frankfurt am Main: Suhrkamp, 1970–1986. 19: 601–2.

Adorno, Theodor W. "Zum Jahrgang 1929 des *Anbruch*." *Gesammelte Schriften*, 20 volumes in 23. Ed. Rolf Tiedemann. Frankfurt am Main: Suhrkamp, 1970–1986. 19: 605–8.

Arendt, Hannah. "Introduction: Walter Benjamin, 1892–1940." In Walter Benjamin, *Illuminations*. Ed. Hannah Arendt. Trans. Harry Zohn. New York: Schocken Books, 1968, pp. 1–58.

Attali, Jacques. *Bruits: essai sur l'économie politique de la musique*. Paris: Presses Universitaires de France, 1977.

Attali, Jacques. *Noise: The Political Economy of Music* [1977]. Trans. Brian Massumi. Minneapolis: University of Minnesota Press, 1985.

Benjamin, Walter. *The Origin of German Tragic Drama* [1928]. Trans. John Osborne. London and New York: Verso, 2009.

Benjamin, Walter. "The Work of Art in the Age of Mechanical Reproduction [1936]." In Walter Benjamin, *Illuminations*. Ed. Hannah Arendt. Trans. Harry Zohn. New York: Schocken Books, 1968, pp. 217–52.

Berg, Alban, and Arnold Schoenberg. *The Berg-Schoenberg Correspondence: Selected Letters*. Ed. Juliane Brand, Christopher Hailey, and Donald Harris. Trans. Juliane Brand and Christopher Hailey. New York: Norton, 1987.

Chanan, Michael. *Repeated Takes: A Short History of Recording and Its Effects on Music*. London and New York: Verso, 1995.

Di Leo, Jeffrey R. "Late Capitalism on Vinyl: Neoliberalism, Biopolitics, and Music." *CR: The New Centennial Review* 18, no. 2 (2018): 107–34.

Di Leo, Jeffrey R. "The Semiotics of Indexical Experience." *Semiotics 1989*. Ed. John Deely, Terry Prewitt, and Karen Haworth. New York and London: University Press of America, 1990, pp. 10–15.

Gordon, Peter E. and Alex Rehding. "Editor's Introduction: Adorno, Music, Modernity." *New German Critique* 43 (2016): 1–4.

Horkheimer, Max and Theordor W. Adorno. "The Culture Industry: Enlightenment as Mass Deception [1944]." In *Dialectic of Enlightenment*. By Max Horkheimer and Theordor W. Adorno. Trans. John Cumming. New York: Seabury Press, 1972, pp. 120–67.

Lacan, Jacques. "The Mirror State as Formative of the I Function as Revealed in Psychoanalytic Experience [1949]." *Écrits: A Selection*. Trans. Bruce Fink. New York: Norton, 2002, pp. 3–9.

Leibowitz, René. *Schoenberg and His School: The Contemporary Stage of the Language of Music*. Trans. Dika Newlin. New York: Philosophical Library, 1949.

Leppert, Richard. "Commentary: Culture, Technology, and Listening." In *Essays on Music: Selected, with Introduction, Commentary, and Notes*. Ed. Richard Leppert. Berkeley: University of California Press, 2002, pp. 213–50.

Leppert, Richard. "Introduction." In Theodor W. Adorno, *Essays on Music: Selected, with Introduction, Commentary, and Notes*. Ed. Richard Leppert. Berkeley: University of California Press, 2002, pp. 1–84.

Levin, Thomas Y. "For the Record: Adorno on Music in the Age of Its Technological Reproducibility." *October* 55 (Winter 1990): 22–47.

Paddison, Max. "The Critique Criticized: Adorno and Popular Music." *Popular Music* 2 (1982): 201–18.

Stravinsky, Igor. *An Autobiography* [1936]. New York: W. W. Norton & Company, 1962.

Stravinsky, Igor. "Meine Stellung zur Schallplatte." *Kulture und Schallplatte* 1 (March 1930): 65.

Thomas, Calvin. "Mirror Stage." In *The Bloomsbury Handbook of Literary and Cultural Theory*. Ed. Jeffrey R. Di Leo. London and New York: Bloomsbury, 2018, pp. 576–7.

5

Critique, Complexity, Content

Adorno and Musical Modernism since 1970

Larson Powell

Adorno after Postmodernism

Although Adorno's influence on aesthetics seemed to be waning during the brief heyday of postmodernism in the 1980s and early 1990s (due both to influential revisions of his perspective and to its outright rejection or misunderstanding by the populism of American New Musicology),[1] there has been a fresh rethinking of his work beginning in Germany in the late 1990s and continuing to the present. This current has, while reinterpreting some aspects of Adorno's work (in particular, his Hegelian philosophy of history), sought to extend his crucial insights about the nature of modernism into new areas, including composers on whom he never wrote, or into new sociological and analytic dimensions, or dialogue with French thinkers like Lacan or Derrida. Thus Gunnar Hindrichs's recent work *Die Autonomie des Klangs* (2013) continues to work with many central Adornian ideas (like the "tendencies of the material"); philosopher Harry Lehmann's *Die flüchtige Wahrheit der Kunst* (2005) brought Adorno into contrastive dialogue with Niklas Luhmann. We can find Adornian concerns in the philosophical work of British musicologists like Michael Spitzer (2006) as well. Moreover, Adorno never ceased to be a strong presence for European composers, whether in the political "negative aesthetics" of

Helmut Lachenmann (b. 1934), the resolutely modernist works of Klaus Huber (1924–2017), or even younger New Complexity composers like Claus-Steffen Mahnkopf (b. 1962), who is also a theorist of music and whose many publications centrally refer to Adorno (as is evident in titles like *Kritik der neuen Musik* [1998] or *Kritische Theorie der Musik* [2006]). The reception of Adorno's aesthetics was arguably a belated one, not only in the English-speaking world (due to poor or delayed translations) but even in German musicology (where his work was often criticized in his lifetime by Carl Dahlhaus and others). What follows will develop what Adorno's work has continued to offer to compositional thought and practice since his death, especially in terms of how to reevaluate the legacy of modernism after the waning of the post.[2]

No philosopher has ever written about music with the depth of understanding of Adorno, which explains his ongoing influence on modernist composers. Nonetheless, Adorno's work could not be taken as a positive program to follow out or realize; his own deliberate avoidance of a normative aesthetic already forbade this. Yet several key concepts of his have remained present in musical debates. Among them is the idea that art, including music, could have a critical function in modern society; another is the notion of aesthetic autonomy, inherited from German idealism, but given new formulation in Adorno's work. These two central ideas stand in a productive tension not only within Adorno's thought but also in the work and writing of many of the most important composers who have continued the modernist tradition since Adorno's death. Broadly speaking, one can see an alternation between these two ideas of critique and autonomy during the decades since 1970, with critique occupying a central place in the work of Helmut Lachenmann and autonomy in the "new complexity" associated with the work of Brian Ferneyhough (b. 1943) and his students since the 1980s, and most recently a renewed concern with what music might refer to outside itself, now formulated not in terms of critique but of *Gehalt* or social content, on the part of Claus-Steffen Mahnkopf and others.

Art's Social Content: Lachenmann

Although this is often missed by uninformed readings of his work, Adorno was very clear that autonomy is only half the story of art's social content:

> Art perceived strictly aesthetically is art aesthetically misperceived. Only when art's other is sensed as one of the primary layers in the experience of art does it become possible to sublimate this layer, to dissolve the material bonds, without the autonomy of the artwork becoming a matter of indifference. (*Ästhetische Theorie*, 6; *Aesthetic Theory*, 17)

The philosophical dignity of modernist music, as put forward in the *Philosophy of Modern Music*, was inseparable from just this reference outside of itself, namely to the negativity of modern society, which music of value echoes in its internal formal laws and tensions. Schoenberg's work was seen as a paradigm of a critique of illusion and play, of the unitary work of art, of ornament, or of large extended forms. In this, art acquires the capacity to know and not merely reproduce society:

> In the act of knowing that art carries out, its form criticizes the contradiction by indicating the possibility of its reconciliation.... For this reason, the form also becomes the element in which the act of knowledge comes to a halt [*innehält*].... New art leaves the contradiction standing and exposes the barren bedrock of its categories of judgement: the form. ... Only in the fragmentary work, renouncing itself, is the critical content [*Gehalt*] liberated. (*Philosophy of New Music*, 47; *Philosophie der neuen Musik*, 112)

Many of the motifs we will find again in the work of late twentieth- and early twenty-first-century composers are contained in this quote. The idea of critique is central to the work of Helmut Lachenmann (b. 1935), who had studied with Luigi Nono (1924–90), one of the few Darmstadt composers who sought to link modernist musical language with overt political content. Unlike his teacher (and like Adorno), Lachenmann was skeptical about the possibility of direct political engagement, even though he set to music texts by the British Marxist Christopher Caudwell and by Gudrun Ensslin (in *Salut für Caudwell* [1977] and the opera *Das Mädchen mit den Schwefelhölzern* [1996] respectively); rather, he believed (again like Adorno) that the composer's contest with society had to take place within the language of music—its technique—and not in its overt message (93). Lachenmann developed his distinctive compositional technique, which he calls *musique concrète instrumentale*,[3] in the later 1960s, in works like *Air* (1968–9) for solo percussion and orchestra, *Pression* for solo cello (1969–70), and *Kontrakadenz* for orchestra (1970–1). All these pieces incorporated noisy and unconventional means of playing classical instruments: clicking woodwind keys without blowing, playing string instruments below the bridge, or bowing gongs and cymbals, and even a small bathtub with water and ping-pong balls (in *Kontrakadenz*); yet unlike Maurizio Kagel, another composer active in the 1960s, Lachenmann did not do this in a spirit of theatrical or neo-Dadaist provocation, but actually sought to integrate these new sounds into a coherent structure. Unlike the deliberate randomness of Cage or other composers of graphic scores, Lachenmann always carefully and painstakingly spells out in his scores how violin bodies are to be struck with the bow or how a water-filled French horn is still to be played; there is a traditional (perhaps "German") element of artisanal craft in his scores that marks them off from any mere dilettantish play or "do-it-yourself."

Of the "critical" moments previously listed in Adorno, Lachenmann thus moderates the critique of the closed artwork by preserving the idea of aesthetic cohesion. Nor does he abandon longer forms, the way the Second Viennese School (especially Webern) did in its expressionist phase: many of his pieces (*Ausklang*, 1985; *Serynade*, 1998; *Nun*, 1999) are between a half hour and fifty minutes long. Where Lachenmann's critique is chiefly located is in another central Adornian concept, namely the musical material. For Adorno, the Marxist historical necessity of atonality and then of twelve-tone composition were grounded in what he saw as the "tendencies of the material"—a view of late-romantic harmony that owed something to Ernst Kurth's (1886–1946) energetic conception of Wagner's music (for Kurth's context, see Rothfarb). In this view, the push toward atonality found in Schoenberg's compositions circa 1908 was only the logical outcome of a tendency to chromatic harmony found in all music after Beethoven (or at least all German and Austrian music). A comparable moment in the evolution of modern painting might be cubism's emergence from the tendency in late Cézanne to break the picture plane up into a mosaic of equal brushstrokes. Such a view of modernism's necessity was also promulgated, in cognate form, by the Darmstadt composers, especially Boulez and Stockhausen. Lachenmann's conception of musical material, however, encompasses far more than merely harmony alone. He calls it "the aesthetic apparatus," and it constitutes "a system of tonally anchored laws, cadential extensions, definitions of dissonance, homophonic and polyphonic writing techniques of all kinds, melodic, thematic and rhythmic schemata and variants oriented to them, all the way to the familiar traditional instrumental and instrumentational techniques, and all the expressive formulae resulting from them."[4] So large and encompassing a notion of "material" could hardly be subject to the same historical necessity as Adorno's harmony; even though the development of European art music since Beethoven had included an increasing interest in tone color (from Berlioz to Wagner and Debussy and then the use of percussion in Varèse, Boulez, and others), Lachenmann's inclusion of nontraditional instrumental techniques had to represent a historical break, a "knight's move" (in Viktor Shklovsky's sense) away from the streamlined functionalism and structuralism that had dominated modernist musical thought in the 1950s.

The consequences, for Lachenmann's thought and his musical practice, of this turn to sound (*Klang*) and its production as a structural element are immense. Where the Viennese, and Boulez and Stockhausen after them, had seen their work as merely following out the possibilities implied in their harmonic (and rhythmic) materials—so that the composer, in Adorno's reading of this, "is no creator," (*Philosophie der neuen Musik*, 42; *Philosophy of New Music*, 33), but only the executor of the music's impersonal will—Lachenmann sees the material as, in Hegel's sense, *ein Gewordenes*: "something which has become" a product of history hardened into second nature. His own response to the material has thus something of Stravinsky's ironic detachment about it, and not Schoenberg's obsessive and organic sinking into the material; when Nonnenmann (226) refers to Lachenmann's "attempt to negate music with music," one is reminded of Adorno's characterization of Stravinsky's work as "music about music," or music at one remove (Adorno, *Philosophie der neuen Musik*, 166; *Philosophy of New Music*, 137). This also explains the frequent presence of humor in Lachenmann's music—a matter linking him more to Stravinsky than Schoenberg. Yet the last Nonnenmann quote on "negating music with music" continues: "in order, in this way, to write a music that wants to be nothing other than the occasion of a new and intensified perceptual and communicational experience." Lachenmann is no mere Stravinskyan cynic, but still shares very much in the old Utopian perspective of modernism: the hope of an emancipated listening that would contribute, however indirectly, to an emancipated society.

All of the central contradictions of Lachenmann's work are contained in this paradoxical combination of negating musical habit in favor of a newer form of music. For he has, in order to suggest this, to try to find a way to combine his anarchic noises into a form or structure. This is, strictly speaking, impossible: there is no organized "scale" of noise comparable to the chromatic scale (which is why Western music had to exclude noise when it began to organize itself rationally in the Middle Ages) (Weber). In fact, Lachenmann's material splits into two diametrically opposed and irreconcilable aspects: one, what he calls "the auratic," meaning the historically accumulated or sedimented cultural semantics of classical music, and the other, the raw material of sheer sound, which is sometimes referred to as "sound-energetic." Adorno had already detected a tendency to viewing sound as pure nature in late Webern, and one could find this in Stockhausen's work as well, or indeed in Cage's Zen mysticism. Lachenmann, however, is more socially conscious than either of his great predecessors, and wants to mediate (in Hegelian, or dialectical terms) between these aspects of material. To do so, he tried to classify different types of sound but ended up inventing oxymoronic formulations like *Strukturklang* or "structure-sound" (Lachenmann 36). As Mahnkopf has noted (in a piece of sympathetic criticism), this is incoherent: sound and structure are two different things, and Lachenmann, despite his continued fidelity to serial organization of his pitch material (Cavalotti 2005), is no structuralist. (Structuralism in musical modernity would correspond, unsurprisingly, with Boulez's austere *Structures I* of 1951–2, a musical Writing Degree Zero.) As Mahnkopf ("Zwei Versuche zu Helmut Lachenmann," 17–18) puts it, "Lachenmann is a genius of sounds, of their interaction, their ramification, their internal differentiation. . . . Lachenmann is a sound-improviser. . . . The technical problem of Lachenmann's sound art is that sounds, in and of themselves, do not offer any formal strategies. . . . [Yet] Lachenmann does something that is actually not possible: he creates forms." He does so by finding similarities between sounds produced by different instruments or gestural connections between them, and even still tries to compose movements based on this type of material. It is, however, by no means easy for a listener to follow these forms (although it is certainly not more difficult than following the forms of serialism or of New Complexity).

Moreover, Lachenmann's unleashing of the noise-element in sound results in a number of terminological and perceptual confusions. First, it is unclear what sort of ideological message—what social content (*Gehalt*)—this move entails. Nonnenmann, one of the composer's most careful exegetes, oscillates between an array of different and conflicting terms: "sound realism" (14, 37, 51, 55), "resistance" (81), emancipation of noise or sound from its supposed "repression" (45, 53, 59, 60), or admission of the "everyday" into music (43–4, 76). This sort of politicized interpretation of music was common in the 1960s, not least in the work of the influential popularizer Heinz-Klaus Metzger (1932–2009), a one-time rival to Adorno for the title of musical modernism's most widely read critic. Yet these concepts often make no sense in musical terms. Music has never been a "realistic" art, so that to speak of "sound realism" is nonsense.[5] Writing of Lachenmann's clarinet "anti-concerto" *Accanto* (1975–6), a work ironically based on Mozart's canonical concerto for the same instrument (K. 622), Nonnenmann notes that the later piece produces "a quasi naturalistic sound language, which gives expression to the repression of the bodily through a normative aesthetic" (271). But Western classical music did not simply "repress" the bodily; it sublimated it, and this makes all the difference in the world (Adorno, *Versuch über Wagner*, 32).

Most serious, however, is that a number of admirers of Lachenmann's music have admitted that they simply cannot hear the "critique" or negation his compositional technique is meant to have as its social content (Brinkmann; a contrasting view is given by Wellmer). Lachenmann's own work testifies to this uncertainty, as his development since the 1980s has been to develop an ever more luxuriant richness of tone in his writing, even integrating remnants of former tonal harmony within it. (This is done, however, without any directly restorative intent: Lachenmann is no neotonalist. It is also carried out without any diminishing of the composer's ostensible political intentions: the opera *Das Mädchen mit den Schwefelhölzern* [1988–96], which uses texts by Ulrike Meinhof, is also one of his most sensuously beautiful scores.) Even in his earlier work, he had argued for a rehabilitation of the idea of musical beauty, as a legitimate human need; in this, he might resemble the later Brecht, who recognized a need for pleasure and entertainment in the theater, and therefore moved away from the austerity of his earlier *Lehrstücke*.

These contradictions are not, however, symptoms of the composer's failure but rather, following Adorno, a sign of historical authenticity. Like the contradictions between mimesis and construction, or general and particular, such aporias "cannot be eliminated"; it is precisely an index of Lachenmann's truthfulness that his work has generated them and labors to contain them. "For the technique of a work is constituted by its problems, by the aporetic task that it objectively poses to itself" (Adorno, *Philosophy of New Music*, 54, 213; *Philosophie der neuen Musik*, 87, 317). One could apply to Lachenmann Adorno's judgment on Brecht: "His whole oeuvre is a Sisyphean labor to reconcile his highly cultivated and subtle taste with the crudely heteronomous demands which he desperately imposed on himself" (Adorno, "Engagement," 422).

Autonomy Reaffirmed: Ferneyhough

The music of Lachenmann's slightly younger contemporary Brian Ferneyhough (b. 1943), while sounding quite different on the surface, shares with Lachenmann some of this concentration on contradictions, as also a concern with musical material. (A link between the two composers has been made by Feller and Hockings.) Both composers strove to get beyond the serialist paradigm developed by the postwar Darmstadt generation (of Boulez and Stockhausen), while avoiding any simplistic returns to the past (like the New Simplicity [*Neue Einfachkeit*] or neo-romanticism of the 1970s). Like Lachenmann, Ferneyhough was well aware of Adorno's work (455), although he insisted that his compositions were in no way illustrations of any extant theories (97). Unlike Lachenmann, however, Ferneyhough tilts his work decidedly away from the pole of overt critique and toward that of autonomy (248, 327). Although he rejects the aestheticizing opposition of *l'art pour l'art* and political commitment ("I can't write just music"; "sound is never just sound") (250, 282), for many of his works have been inspired by and thus refer to visual art, he recognizes that his work, especially since the mid-1970s, has been increasingly concerned with "the immediate world of reference offered by the music itself" (326). The development of Ferneyhough's work made him the leading figure in what has come to be known as New Complexity, a loose grouping of composers emerging in the 1980s and sometimes linked to the music school of Freiburg-im-Breisgau, where Ferneyhough taught from 1973 to 1986 (Toop). As its name implies, complexism in music is tied to an often extreme density and difficulty of writing, to the point where it becomes impossible for any performer to realize all the notes on the score. (Ferneyhough has composed many pieces for one performer, such as cello or flute, written on multiple staves at once.) This deliberately vertiginous overload of information would in fact link Ferneyhough's practice more to the systems theory of Niklas Luhmann (1927–98) or (as we will see) to Deleuze as much as to Adorno; Ferneyhough himself—one of the most well-read and reflective of modern composers—has consciously linked his work to "complexity and chaos" (419) and to what Habermas (1985) called *die neue Unübersichtlichkeit*, meaning the late-capitalist growth of social complexity to the point where it was no longer graspable in older terms of democratic political initiative or critique, and his actual compositional practice would support this, since it includes the use of what he calls "random funnel" computer programs to introduce randomized variation into musical material (on this see Feller). The sonorous surface of a work like *La Terre est un Homme* (1979) certainly conveys the sense of overwhelming density to the point of chaos: such works are a challenge to the listener's comprehension as much as to the performer's virtuosity. It might be hasty to dub Ferneyhough a postmodernist, though (as Feller has done), for he is very clear in his unwillingness to abandon central modernist concepts or attitudes such as a responsibility to history or a belief in the necessity of the subject and the unity of personal musical style (this comes out most clearly in the essay "Parallel Universes" [76–83]).

It is in Ferneyhough's idea of musical material that we can best grasp where he stands relative to Adorno's conception of modernism. Lois Fitch (2005) has suggested a proximity between the composer's idea of material and Adorno's; and indeed there are many formulations in Ferneyhough's writings and interviews that suggest his awareness of the historicity of musical material as a determining factor in musical creation.[6] Yet a closer look at how he thinks about musical material shows that he is closer to Deleuze (whose work he refers to) than to Adorno. In *Philosophy of New Music*, Adorno had, as earlier noted, argued that modernism's historical necessity was grounded in inherent "tendencies of the material" toward both the emancipation of dissonance and its subsequent rationalization; similar arguments were made by Boulez and others in the 1950s.[7] This conception depended on a transposition of a Marxist materialist dialectic into music, where subject and object corresponded to composer and material, and Lachenmann continued this, albeit with a greatly expanded concept of material, including noise and timbre and not only harmony. It is just this dialectic that Ferneyhough's concept, and his practice, sidestep.

Adorno had seen the compositional practice of German music from Beethoven to Schoenberg as kin to Hegel's positing (*Setzen*) of a concept. The positing of a musical idea (*Einfall*) would be followed by the exhaustive deduction of all of its inner implications, according to an organic and logical model of form. Thus the opening of a work by Beethoven stated not only a theme but also the harmonic and rhythmic parameters within which the rest of the movement would operate. Similarly, the positing of a twelve-tone row predetermined the possibilities that any work based on that material could unfold. In the early phases of dodecaphony, the row might be identical with a theme in the traditional sense, as it was in Schoenberg's Op. 25 or his last two string quartets; postwar serialists, taking Webern's athematicism as their point of departure, broke up the series into smaller cells (as in Boulez's *Second Piano Sonata*) or groups (as in Stockhausen's *Klavierstücke I-IV*) which could then be subject to more flexible manipulation, as in Boulez's technique of multiplication of series by themselves (Boulez; Koblyakov). The fundamental idea of serialism remained, however, the notion of derivation of all materials from one series (or several); Stockhausen's later practice of formula-composition (in *Mantra*, *Inori*, and *Licht*) continued this organicist model, to the point where an entire operatic cycle of some twenty-nine hours was based on one "superformula" (Conen). Even Lachenmann, despite his averred wish to get beyond the paradigm of serialism, remained true to this underlying compositional structure.

Ferneyhough, however, explicitly rejects this kind of constructive procedure, which he calls "tautological" (228; see also 253). "It seems to me fundamentally wrong to reveal the basic essence of a work, and then multiply it. This is Boulez' idea, but not mine. My idea is to start with the multiplied mass, and gradually through various processes focus down to the given" (264). This rejection of deductive logic means also that the processes worked through in Ferneyhough's music are less linear or conclusive than in that of his predecessors.[8] Instead of deriving his individual melodic and rhythmic shapes from an underlying basic material, Ferneyhough prefers to work with a more fluid relation between what he calls gesture and figure, sometimes contrasting them with a third term, texture. The definitions of these terms are not hard and fast: "While these terms do not correspond precisely to foreground-middleground-background categories, there *are* discernable intuitive parallels" (414, author's emphasis). Gesture is, for Ferneyhough, a *Gestalt* or shape (Courtot 63), and figure designates the parametric components of that shape: "The thing that distinguishes the figural way of constructing or observing a gesture . . . is that one is attempting to realize the totality of the gesture in terms of its possible deconstruction into parametric tendencies" (285).[9]

One might thus be tempted to see figure as occupying the place formerly held by Adorno's material, but this would not be accurate; rather, Ferneyhough is seeking to escape precisely the traditional dual opposition of form and content, or figure and ground, implied by that idea. The figure is not a "substrate" in the same way that material was in Adorno's Marxist thinking. It represents rather a kind of energetic or virtual potential of the gesture. Here is where Ferneyhough is indeed closer to Deleuze's peculiar variant of "materialism" than to Adorno's. In his critique of Freud's idea of compulsion to repeat, Deleuze singles out Freud's dependency on an older duality of representation and represented, of spirit and matter: Freud's repetitions are

> considered to be only the conscious or unconscious, latent or manifest, repressed or repressing *representations* of the subject. The whole theory

of repetition is thereby subordinated to the requirements of simple representation, from the standpoint of its realism, materialism and subjectivism. (Deleuze 104)

Ferneyhough similarly rejects the idea that the individual gesture or *Gestalt* is merely a "representation" of an underlying material. Another way of putting this would be in terms of Deleuze's rejection of Hegelian dialectics, which depend on a certain understanding of negativity as motive force (Haynes 8). Thus for Adorno, the material of music represented a negative force for compositional subjectivity, which had to "subject itself" to the material's objective demands. Ferneyhough does not see the composer's relation to musical material in such antagonistic terms but rather as one of equal "conversation partners": "There is little point in one of the involved parties—either the language, expression, or the composing will or volition—predominating" (155).

What this means, concretely, is that Ferneyhough's pieces can take as their point of departure not a total disposition of the material which predetermines everything that will happen but rather an individual gesture, as in the beginning of the *Second String Quartet* (an analysis is in Melchiorre). The individuality of the gesture is thus not subordinated ab initio to the anonymous collective instance of the material, but can generate the work's material out of itself. This process on the level of the individual work mirrors Ferneyhough's larger belief that, given the absence of any one binding musical language in the present, a composer must himself or herself create such a language (or material) through the diachronic unfolding of a larger oeuvre. As opposed to Adorno's retrospective model of musical determination, where the sedimentation of the past in the musical material constricts the composer's choice, Ferneyhough's model is oriented toward the future, toward musical becoming: he conceives of his musical gesture as, precisely, such a future potential (27, 32, 132). This also helps to explain his fondness for Deleuzian terms like "energy" or "lines of force": gestures or figures exist less in themselves than as possibilities or points of departure. Thus the opening statement of *Lemma-Icon-Epigram* is virtually random, in itself insignificant (Melchiorre 81; Toop 56); what matters is its subsequent development, which is however anything but rigidly logical in Adorno's sense, for the piece is, in the composer's eyes, a deliberate failure in formal terms—which, despite its very un-Adornian conception of its material, would nonetheless make it valid for Adorno, who praised Beckett and Mahler precisely for their readiness to fail at producing conventionally coherent artworks.

The Turn to Substance Aesthetics: Mahnkopf

While Lachenmann sought to escape what he saw as the formalism of post-Webernist serial composing by developing a new ear for sonorous material and Ferneyhough rejected the totalizing, deductive aspect of serial thinking in favor of a more inductive mode of composing, Claus-Steffen Mahnkopf (b.1962) is in some ways a synthesis of these predecessors' works. Thus we can find in Mahnkopf's music the critical extension of musical material—in exemplary form in his works for oboe, where he has developed and systematically explored new techniques of multiphonics or overblowing, as in *Gorgoneion* (1990) or *Medusa* (1990–2)—and an extremely dense complexity like that found in the work of his teacher Ferneyhough. But it is in his recent development of aesthetics of "substance" or "purport"—in German *Gehalt*, a term also from Adorno—that he goes beyond his models. *Gehalt* is not the same as *Inhalt*, which was opposed to form in traditional aesthetics.[10]

Mahnkopf has indeed hit on a key aspect of Adorno's influence: it was precisely Adorno's conferral of social content (*Gehalt*) onto modernist music, namely music as critique and negation of a false world, that gave that music its prestige after 1945, and it is the loss of this content—of classical music's representative status—that makes musical modernism now seem irrelevant, at best an official academic enterprise. Mahnkopf's appeal to a renewal of *Gehalt* is thus an attempt to escape the dead end of musical formalism which complexity and material progress have become. This has taken concrete form in his *void* cycle of works reflecting on catastrophes of modernity (the Holocaust in particular). He believes that "an artist—a primary producer—can . . . base a work process, as with a working hypothesis, on a substance that is aimed for"—but immediately adds, "This does not guarantee that the substance interpreted afterwards will correspond to the artist's personal intention, but at least the artist has a program guiding the concretion of the work's genesis" ("What Is the Meaning of Musical Substance?"18).

The difficulty encountered here is that, for Adorno, art's social content lay not in any specific historical reference but in the negation of meaning or traditional formal closure, perceived as *analogous* to social critique. Can a listener unacquainted with Mahnkopf's intentions actually hear the reference to the Holocaust in his extremely abstract work? Like Lachenmann and Ferneyhough, Mahnkopf must struggle with an unresolved contradiction here. It is in this confrontation, more than in conventional artistic "success," that his work is still indebted to Adorno.

Notes

1 For one revision, see Huyssen. New Musicology would be associated with the name of Susan McClary, who, although she acknowledges a debt to Adorno, has often arrived at conclusions diametrically opposed to his (for a critical view of her work, see Savage).

2   A fresh imagining of what modernism might still be, with reference to Adorno, is offered in Jameson.

3   This is a rather confusing name, for *musique concrète* was a type of electronic music developed by Pierre Schaeffer in Paris in the 1940s, using everyday sounds; as Nonnenmann (33) shows, Lachenmann's conception has less to do with Schaeffer than with the practices of Concrete Poetry.

4   "ein System aus tonal verankerten Gesetzmäßigkeiten, Kadenzerweiterungen, Dissonanzbestimmungen, homophonen und polyphonen Satztechniken aller Art, melodischen, thematischen und rhythmischen Schemata und daran orientierten Varianten, bis hin zu den bekannten traditionellen Instrumentalund Instrumentationstechniken, und aus all diesem resultierenden expressiven Formeln" (Lachenmann 23–4, my translation).

5   "Musik kann zwar ihre eigene Überlieferung, die Form- und Gattungstraditionen, von denen sie zehrt, und die Regeln des kompositorischen Metiers verleugnen oder als ausgehöhlt und hinfällig zeigen. Aber sie kann, da sie Wirklichkeit weder abbildet noch auf sie verweist, sondern in sich selbst beruht und eingeschlossen ist, nicht ein Stück Realität als absurd kenntlich machen" (Dahlhaus 257).

6   "Solutions already latent in the material," Ferneyhough 31; composer as "constantly in dialogue with one's means," 155.

7   This argument runs together Max Weber's two ideas of instrumental rationality and value-rationality: the following out of technical (instrumental) reason in music produces, for Adorno, the (political and ethical) value of social critique.

8   Boulez's technique of "proliferation" of his material and Stockhausen's "moment form" were already nonlinear; but the idea of an exhaustive treatment of materials remained central for both composers (see Griffiths 49; on proliferation, Misch 57–79).

9   "Parameters" are the different components of music: pitch, rhythm, register, or tone color; analysis into music's parameters was developed by the serialists (especially Boulez), and thus represents part of Ferneyhough's inheritance from them.

10 *Gehalt* means something more like "social content," as opposed to *Inhalt*, which is the traditional notion of "content as different from form"; thus Lambert Zuidervaart (38, 183) translates *Gehalt* as "import." The philosopher Harry Lehmann (2016) has also developed this idea, with different conclusions than Mahnkopf's.

Works Cited

Adorno, Theodor W. *Aesthetic Theory*. Trans. R. Hullot-Kentor. New York: Continuum, 1997d.

Adorno, Theodor W. *Ästhetische Theorie* (*Gesammelte Schriften* 7). Frankfurt: Suhrkamp, 1997a.

Adorno, Theodor W. "Engagement." *Noten zur Literatur*. (Gesammelte Schriften 11), Frankfurt: Suhrkamp, 1997e, pp. 409–30.
Adorno, Theodor W. *Philosophie der neuen Musik*. (*Gesammelte Schriften* 12). Frankfurt: Suhrkamp, 1997b.
Adorno, Theodor W. *Philosophy of New Music*. Trans. R. Hullot-Kentor. Minneapolis: University of Minnesota Press, 2006.
Adorno, Theodor W. *Versuch über Wagner*. (*Gesammelte Schriften* 13). Frankfurt: Suhrkamp, 1997c.
Boulez, Pierre. *Penser la musique aujourd'hui*. Geneva: Gonthier, 1964.
Brinkmann, Reinhold. "Der Autor als sein Exeget: Fragen an Werk und Ästhetik Helmut Lachenmanns." In *Nachgedachte Musik: Studien zum Werk von Helmut Lachenmann*. Ed. Jörn Peter Hiekel and Siegfried Mauser. Saarbrücken: Pfau Verlag, 2006, pp. 116–27.
Cavalotti, Pietro. "Präformation des Materials und kreative Freiheit: Die Funktion des Strukturnetzes am Beispiel von 'Mouvement (-vor der Erstarrung)' von Helmut Lachenmann." In *Nachgedachte Musik: Studien zur Musik Helmut Lachenmanns*. Ed. J. P .Hiekel and S. Mauser. Saarbrücken: Pfau, 2005, pp. 145–70.
Conen, Hermann. *Formel-Komposition: zu Stockhausens Musik der siebziger Jahre*. Mainz: Schott, 1991.
Courtot, Francis. *Brian Ferneyhough, figures et dialogues*. Paris: L'Harmattan, 2009.
Dahlhaus, Carl. "Über Sinn und Sinnlosigkeit in der Musik." In *Gesammelte Schriften in 10 Bänden*, vol. 8. Laaber: Laaber Verlag, 2005, pp. 252–62.
Deleuze, Gilles. *Difference and Repetition*. Trans. Paul Patton. New York: Columbia University Press, 1994.
Feller, Ross. "Random Funnels in Brian Ferneyhough's *Trittico per Gertrude Stein*." *Mitteilungen der Paul Sacher Stiftung* 10, March 1997, pp. 32–8.
Feller, Ross. "Resistant Strains of Postmodernism: The Music of Helmut Lachenmann and Brian Ferneyhough." In *Postmodern Music/Postmodern Thought*. Ed. Joseph Auner and Judy Lockhead. London and New York: Routledge, 2002, pp. 249–62.
Ferneyhough, Brian. *Collected Writings*. Ed. James Boros and Richard Toop. Amsterdam: Harwood, 1995.
Fitch, Lois. "Brian Ferneyhough: The Logic of the Figure," Durham theses, Durham University, 2005. Available at Durham E-Theses Online. http://etheses.dur.ac.uk/1770/
Griffiths, Paul. *Boulez*. London: Oxford University Press, 1978.
Habermas, Jürgen. *Die neue Unübersichtlichkeit*. Frankfurt: Suhrkamp, 1985.
Haynes, Patrice. *Immanent Transcendence: Reconfiguring Materialism in Continental Philosophy*. New York: Continuum, 2012.
Hindrichs, Gunnar. *Die Autonomie des Klangs*. Berlin: Suhrkamp, 2013.
Hockings, Elke. "Helmut Lachenmann's Concept of Rejection." *Tempo* 193, 1995, pp. 4–74.
Huyssen, Andreas. *After the Great Divide*. Bloomington: Indiana University Press, 1987.
Jameson, Fredric. *A Singular Modernity: Essay on the Ontology of the Present*. London: Verso, 2002.

Koblyakov, Lev. *Pierre Boulez: A World of Harmony.* Chur: Harwood, 1990.
Kurth, Ernst. *Romantische Harmonik und ihre Krise in Wagners 'Tristan.'* Berlin: Hesse, 1920.
Lachenmann, Helmut. *Musik als existentielle Erfahrung: Schriften 1966–1995.* Ed. Josef Häusler. Wiesbaden: Breitkopf und Härtel, 1996.
Lehmann, Harry. *Die flüchtige Wahrheit der Kunst.* Munich: Wilhelm Fink, 2005.
Lehmann, Harry. *Gehaltsästhetik.* Munich: Fink, 2016.
Luhmann, Niklas. *Art as a Social System.* Trans. Eva Knodt. Stanford: Stanford University Press, 2000.
Luhmann, Niklas. *Die Kunst der Gesellschaft.* Frankfurt: Suhrkamp, 1995.
Mahnkopf. Claus-Steffen. *Kritik der neuen Musik.* Kassel: Bärenreiter, 1998.
Mahnkopf, Claus-Steffen. *Kritische Theorie der Musik.* Weilerswist: Velbrück, 2006.
Mahnkopf, Claus-Steffen. "What Is the Meaning of Musical Substance?" In *Substance and Content in Music Today.* Ed. Claus-Steffen Mahnkopf, Frank Cox and Wolfram Schurig. Hofheim: Wolke, 2014, pp. 9–21.
Mahnkopf. Claus-Steffen. "Zwei Versuche zu Helmut Lachenmann." In *auf- und zuhören: 14 essayistische Reflexionen über die Musik und die Person Helmut Lachenmann.* Ed. Hans-Peter Jahn. Hofheim: Wolke, 2005, pp. 17–18.
Melchiorre, Alessandro. "Les Labyrinthes de Ferneyhough. À propos du *2e Quatuor* et de *Lemma-Icon-Epigram*." *Entretemps* 3, February 1987, pp. 69–88.
Misch, Imke. "Musikalische Wucherungen. Zu Pierre Boulez, *Notations*." In *Kompositorische Stationen des 20. Jahrhundertes.* Ed. Christoph von Blumröder. Münster: Lit, 2004, pp. 57–79.
Nonnenmann, Raine4. *Angebot durch Verweigerung. Die Ästhetik instrumentalkonkreten Klangkomponierens in Helmut Lachenmanns frühen Orchesterwerken.* Mainz: Schott, 2000.
Rothfarb, Lee. *Ernst Kurth as Theorist and Analyst.* Philadelphia: University of Pennsylvania Press, 1988.
Savage, Roger W. H. *Hermeneutics and Music Criticism.* New York: Routledge, 2010.
Spitzer, Michael. *Music as Philosophy: Adorno and Beethoven's Late Style.* Bloomington: Indiana University Press, 2006.
Toop, Richard. "Brian Ferneyhough's *Lemma-Icon-Epigram*." *Perspectives of New Music* 28, no. 2 (Summer 1990): 52–100.
Toop, Richard. "Four Facets of the 'New Complexity.'" *Contact,* no. 32 (1988): 4–8.
Weber, Max. *The Rational and Social Foundations of Music.* Trans. Don Martindale, Johannes Riedel, and Gertrud Neuwirth. Carbondale: Southern Illinois University Press, 1958.
Wellmer, Albrecht. "Uber Negativitat, Autonomie und Welthaftigkeit oder Musik als existenzielle Erfahrung." In *Der Atem des Wanderers.* Ed. Hans-Klaus Jungheinrich. Mainz: Schott, 2006, pp. 131–52.
Zuidervaart, Lambert. *Adorno's Aesthetic Theory: The Redemption of Illusion.* Cambridge: MIT Press, 1991.

6

Between the Culture Industry and Art

Adorno's Approach to Film

Stefanie Baumann

Film was certainly not Theodor W. Adorno's preferred medium. While he had an acute sensitivity to the subversive agency of modernism in the traditional arts, he took on a primarily critical stance when it came to the motion picture, this art form that stems from modernity itself. What made him suspicious was that film, especially in form of commercial cinema, fits all too well in the capitalistic society in which it flourished most. Both its general mode of production and the product itself are predicated on advanced capitalism: the film industry, a highly lucrative business, depends on powerful and costly technological devices and a production system based on the division of labor, and the movies themselves are "complete[ly] subordinat[ed] to the producers' idea of the effect it will make on the public" (*Composing*, 56), and thus subjected to the same market criteria as any other commodity. Consequently, Adorno considered film to be the principal agent and "most characteristic medium" (*Composing*, li) of the culture industry.

Already in 1936, Adorno's scathing verdict on the current state of the film world and its entanglement with the capitalist society led to a fierce controversy with his philosophical friend Walter Benjamin. According to the latter, the technological apparatus wipes out the aura of images, making them appear in a different light through the shock-effects produced by montage (cf. *Work of Art*, 119–20). Thus, Benjamin believed that film would prepare the public for coping with the conditions of reality in a critical manner, by establishing a "reflexive relation with modernity and modernization" (Hansen, *Mass Production*, 69). Adorno did not share his friend's optimism regarding this new medium. He refuted Benjamin's assertion that a transformative potential would inhere the camera technology itself. He particularly contested that technological images were per se devoid of aura. On the contrary, he observed that commercial Hollywood movies especially were infused with auratic effects through and through (cf. *Letters to Walter Benjamin*, 123). What is more, given the conventional, consumer-friendly, and predictable shape of the majority of the films shown in movie theaters, he also called into question that the motion picture was a priori progressive. Thus, Adorno accused Benjamin of overrating the inherent forces of the medium and overlooking its actual appearance in society, which showed that film was part of the problem of the modern society rather than a means to overcome its current state. While Benjamin was convinced that film could be released from the hegemony of capital and appropriated by the masses (cf. *Work of Art*, 115), Adorno not only doubted that such a liberation was possible; he also remained pessimistic about both the capacity and the desire of spectators to emancipate themselves from the dominating power structures of society.

Adorno's judgment on the imbrication of film with the culture industry, however, did not come out of nowhere. Nor, as it is sometimes claimed, is it simply a by-product of his alleged elitist perspective on the popular arts. In fact, although he did not write profusely on film, and although he was certainly not as engaged in the aesthetics of cinema as he was in that of music or literature, he was still familiar with it. During his American exile, he even gained some direct insights into the modus operandi of the film industry. While living in Los Angeles, he was not only in contact with important Hollywood figures such as Charlie Chaplin and Fritz Lang, but he even participated in the development of an (albeit unrealized) experimental film, entitled *Below the Surface*, in the framework of a research project on anti-Semitism conducted by the Institute of Social Research (cf. Jeneman, chapter 3, 105–47). What is more, he wrote together with Hanns Eisler a comprehensive book on film scores which referred explicitly to the conditions of cinema production in Hollywood. All these experiences confirmed what he had already brought forward against Benjamin's optimism in 1936: that the culture industry relies on strategic calculations of the masses as target audience and thus objectifies the spectators rather than addressing them as a subject, and that the criteria applied to film were based on its market value rather than on intrinsically aesthetic qualities.

Nonetheless, Adorno never denied that film could eventually become a veritable art form. However pessimistic his account of commercial cinema might have been, and however critical he was about the inherent revolutionary force of its technology, he neither condemned the medium as such nor excluded it once and for all from the sphere of genuine art. He approached this sphere through the dimension of its historical development and in a dialectical relation with the society from which it stems and which it challenges. Hence, he claimed in *Aesthetic Theory*:

> Posed from on high, the question whether something such as film is or is no longer art leads nowhere. Because art is what it has become, its concept refers to what it does not contain. [. . .] Art can be understood only by its laws of movement, not according to any set of invariants. It is defined by its relation to what it is not. The specifically artistic in art must be derived concretely from its other; that alone would fulfill the demands of a materialistic-dialectical aesthetics. (3)

Rather than relating the aesthetic agency of art to a particular media, to normative criteria or eternal forms, Adorno understood genuine artworks as the unassimilable other of society; a counterpart that disrupts society's appearance as an overarching totality by rescuing that which it excludes and represses, the nonidentical. Consequently, the artistic quality of film, just as the aesthetic potential of any art form, depends on its capacity of establishing an antagonistic relation with society through its subversive configuration rather than on its technological condition or the intention of the filmmaker.

Instead of taking a categorical position, Adorno approached film dialectically by relating a critique of its actual position in the current society to the medium's intrinsic forces able to challenge this very reality. Already in *Composing for the Film* (first published in 1947 under Eisler's name alone), he wrote that "[a] discussion of industrialized culture must show the interaction of these two factors: the aesthetic potentialities of mass art in the future, and its ideological character in the present" (liii). A few years later, in the 1960s, Adorno would even mention some examples of films that he considered to bear genuinely artistic dimensions: De Sica's *Bicycle Thieves* (1948), for instance, or Michelangelo Antonioni's *La Notte* (1961). In the latter, he saw an expression of the impossibility of intact relationships transpiring through the film's "static character" (*Transparencies*, 180). The particularly slow rhythm of the film introduces "a sort of hollow space in the normal course of the stream of consciousness" (*Podiumsgespräch*, 44, translation by the author). Moreover, Adorno defended the aesthetic autonomy of Fritz Lang's approach to cinema (cf. Claussen 172), and, in the wake of the *Oberhausen Manifesto*, encouraged the critical endeavors of the filmmakers from the *New German Cinema* (including his friend Alexander Kluge), who claimed the facilitation of economic and political conditions for an independent, alternative, experimental cinema beyond conventional motion pictures. Adorno's text "Transparencies on Film" refers directly to this young generation of filmmakers. Dragging out filmic images from their superficial immediacy, reflecting critically on the persuasive effects of the photographic material, considering the collective dimension in the film's composition—these are, for Adorno, critical attempts by the new cinema to disrupt its seemingly direct relation with the real which allow for the development of a genuine filmic art. This chapter aims to unfold the particular field of tension in which film operates according to Adorno, and carve out the conditions for the deployment of its potential as art form in its own right.

Art in the Age of the Culture Industry

In order to grasp the double-edged position that film takes on in modern society, according to Adorno, it is first of all important to understand what he means when he writes about the culture industry. Admittedly, this famous concept codeveloped with Max Horkheimer in the 1940s overstates the situation. Yet, as Adorno claims in a different context, "only exaggeration per se today can be the medium of truth" (*Meaning of Working through the Past*, 89). And indeed, the overemphasis on the systemic character of culture industrial production allows Adorno to outline a new quality in the capitalist infiltration of society: besides its complete seizure of the sphere of material goods, it also literally usurps the cultural realm by "transfer[ring] the profit motive naked onto cultural forms" (*Culture Industry Reconsidered*, 99). Rather than responding to a sincere interest, the pretended orientation on the concerns and demands of the public is yet another manipulative sales strategy. For "[t]he masses are not the measure but the ideology of the culture industry" (*Culture Industry Reconsidered*, 99). They are barely taken into consideration as potential consumers. Hence, production by the culture industry differs fundamentally from popular art forms that emerge spontaneously from the people themselves and thereby express a certain resistance to subjection. Instead, the products of the culture industry are strategically planned from above and deliberately designed for the market. Consequently, they are also antipodal to veritable art in an Adornian sense. While genuine artworks unfold their critical potential precisely by sustaining a critical distance from the social reality from which they stem, the products of the culture industry are perfectly in line with the reigning power structure based on advanced capitalism. Manufactured in order to be widely consumed, they are effect-oriented rather than original. For the sake of profitability, they always (re)produce the same stereotypes, rigid identities, and fixed values. Genuinely artistic qualities are but secondary concerns. Nevertheless, the influence of the culture industry is not limited to those artifacts that are deliberately designed for the market such as commercial cinema. It also gets hold of folkloristic creations and formerly autonomous artworks. For the culture industry tends to slickly integrate any cultural production into the circuit of the market and turn them into commodities. Subsumed under the same commercial logic, the only relevant difference between serious art, entertainment formats, and popular forms of expression lies in their target audiences. Hence, genuine artworks inevitably lose their particularity and their transgressive force when they are absorbed by the sphere of consumption and reduced to their exchange-value. A modernistic painting in the cabinet of a dentist, a Beethoven symphony as background music in a supermarket, or an extract of a play by Beckett employed as a slogan are products of the culture industry just as catchy hit songs, crime novels, Westerns, or mainstream television series are. They turn into clichés in the same way as the glossy and hackneyed images produced in the studios of Hollywood.

This conditioning of perception through the corruption of the culture industry is a particularly objectionable aspect for Adorno. By normalizing the forms and formats, the products of the culture industry, especially those that rely on visual media such as film, sway the perception of reality. They eradicate the singularity of things by converting them into clichés, for the products of the culture industry are "infecting everything with sameness" (*Dialectic of Enlightenment*, 94). As Eric L. Krakauer puts it, "By mediating everything, giving everything the appearance of similarity, culture envelops or covers over what it seems to discover, expose, master" (40). Through their association with specific moods, stereotypical features or frozen genres, the objects and situations mediated by the products of the culture industry get deprived of their uniqueness, become reducible to generalized cyphers and substitutable by fairly identical others. As Adorno writes in "Culture Industry Reconsidered," "The colour film demolishes the genial old tavern to a greater extent than bombs ever could: the film exterminates its imago. No homeland can survive being processed by the films which celebrate it, and which thereby turn the unique character on which it thrives into an interchangeable sameness" (103). Annihilating the differences and subsuming every particularity under familiar types, the culture industry's products transform that which is singular into characteristic features without leaving any place for otherness. This is how a normative imagery worms its way into collective consciousness and establishes a biased, uniform way of looking at reality. The overpowering presence of the products of the culture industry shapes a perception of the world in which singularity is immediately obliterated and superseded by commonplaces. Images become patterns, because the associations triggered by omnipresent clichés cultivate reflex reactions in perception.

Adorno would certainly not assert that every product created in the age of capitalism, not even every Hollywood film, adopts the same features and incorporates the market-based principles of the culture industry in the same absolute manner. His hyperbolic formulation is aimed at pointing at a particular scheme recurrent in late capitalism, which not only reduces cultural goods to their exchange-value but also engenders a standardized perception. Concealing the persisting antagonisms of reality under an ideological veil of coherence, the average products of the culture industry keep on advertising the world as it is instead of seriously problematizing the conditions of modern life in the disenchanted, rationalized world and producing a critical awareness. The culture industry's colonialization of the sensuous world makes society appear to be a hermetic, unchangeable structure, and thereby perpetually endorses a homogenized imagery of the status quo. This situation also constitutes a particular challenge for modern art. What has art become in a world in which the products of the culture industry submerge everyday life and overdetermine the perception of reality? How can an artwork oppose its integration into the logics of the market, its becoming decorative, and the standardization of forms? How can art still constitute society's subversive counterpart, its utopian outside capable of deflecting its appearance as a hermetic totality?

According to Adorno, modern artworks withdraw from representation so as to avoid their immediate assimilation and to resist signification according to the benchmarks of the culture industry. For only by eluding integration into the established codes of capitalist society, only by undermining the conventional modes of apprehending reality, do they maintain their subversive force. Hence, while the visual images of the culture industry are illustrative and refer to empirical elements which are associated with a specific meaning, artworks, as "imageless images" (*Aesthetic Theory*, 379), transcend the appearance of things by following their own material rather than a preestablished structure of meaning. Rather than encompassing a meaning to deduce through logical reasoning and identity thinking, they foreshadow a hitherto unassimilable alterity. Hence, they generate a fundamentally different subject-object relation than that constituted by signs. While a sign designates an object as a specific case subordinate to established categories, which makes it accessible for intellectual appropriation by a detached subject, a genuine image, as Adorno understands it, suspends this hierarchical subject-object relation that permeates society through and through. For those images constituted by artworks are not copies of the empirical world. They are complex configurations in which the elements are interconnected and mediated one through the other in manifold ways. In these images, the object is not subsumable: it appears in its irreducible otherness. It transcends the underlying structure of the social reality and alludes to a fundamentally different mode of existence. This is what manifests art's indissolubly enigmatic character and its inherently utopian aspiration. It is not devoid of meaning, but its meaning remains elusive and does not exhaust itself through discursive means. Hence, it constitutes the dialectical counterpart to that which signifies in society: "the meaning of an artwork is at the same time the essence that conceals itself in the factual; meaning summons into appearance what appearance otherwise obstructs" (*Aesthetic Theory*, 145).

Yet, if artworks, as genuine images, renounce representation in order to signify differently, if their force lies in the subversion of the logic of signs in order to open up a divergent approach of reality, if they are "imageless images" beyond the visual appearance of the empirical world, then how can film, whose very material is indexical images, become a veritable art form?

The Representational Character of Filmic Material

According to Adorno, filmic material confronts artists and their critics with a particular problem: it is of a substantially different nature than traditional art forms. Photographic images are a priori visual copies of that which is captured by the camera. Purely mechanical, the technological device registers anything that appears in front of the lens. While painters, musicians, sculptors, and writers dispose of a material that only becomes expressive through construction, through their subjective mediation, filmmakers deal with technical images that stick to the empirical reality and cannot be fully appropriated by an artistic subject. "Even where film dissolves and modifies its objects as much as it can, the disintegration is never complete," writes Adorno in *Transparencies of Film*. "Consequently, it does not permit absolute construction: its elements, however abstract, always retain something representational; they are never purely aesthetic values" (182). Given this particularity of filmic material, modernistic innovations such as abstraction cannot be regarded in the same way as in traditional art forms. In traditional art forms, formal abstraction, as sedimented content, is an expression of the reified social relations that characterize modernity. ("New art is as abstract as social relations have in truth become," writes Adorno in *Aesthetic Theory*, 42.) In comparison, abstraction in film is but an artificial, decorative ornamentation resulting from an empty analogy that does not contain any serious truth content. "Seeking to translate modernist norms into the medium of film, abstract film ends up disavowing the (photographic) character of its material and the immanent aesthetic principles that might be derived of it" (Hansen, *Cinema and Experience*, 217). Rather than imposing formal principles to the film that proved their expressive agency in other art forms, a genuinely filmic aesthetics should emanate from the material itself. Yet, the photographed images produced and set in motion by a technical apparatus are devoid of any determinate meaning to disclose: they are simply the result of an automatic recording. What makes them meaningful comes after, through montage, their juxtaposition with sound and music, their rhythm, and so on.

The problem lies in the fact that these artistic strategies are delicate. When the indexicality of filmic images is taken uncritically in its immediacy, those strategies are likely to be put in the service of communication of an extra-artistic content. Non-intentional and seemingly objective, the images incline themselves to any imposed meaning or explicit message, while their visual similarity with the depicted objects seems to confirm the degree of reality and thus the validity of the imposed signification. This is one of the reasons why propaganda movies are so efficient, and why the commercial productions of the culture industry have such a strong impact on the collective perception of reality: because of their visual likeness with the empirical world, and because of their "inherent tendency to adopt the tone of the factual report" (*Dialectic of Enlightenment*, 118), they appear as immediate duplication of the reality. Blurring the differences between life and its representation until reality itself appears as a series of images, those films form the perception of society in a particularly persuasive way, and the associated identification scheme and logic of signification smoothly worm their way into the consciousness of the masses. For "[f]ar more strongly than in the theatre of illusion, film denies its audience any dimension in which they might roam freely in imagination—contained by the film's framework but unsupervised by its precise actualities—without losing the threat; thus it trains those exposed to it to identify film directly with reality" (*Dialectic of Enlightenment*, 99–100).

The problem of an externally introduced meaning into an artwork—which for Adorno discredits it as such—is not limited to totalitarian propaganda films and the "pseudo-realism of the culture industry" (*Minima Moralia*, 141). The same criticism applies to any other form of artistic realism, including the diverging conceptions of Georg Lukács and Bertolt Brecht. Lukács's Marxist-Leninist conception is based on the theory of reflection, according to which the realism based on the model of nineteenth-century literature is the only artistic method able to represent the relevant dialectical forces at work in reality. Brecht's openly committed realism, in contrast, relies on modernist forms in order to mobilize the public. But even if their ideas about the adequate representation of reality differ profoundly in many respects, they converge in their aim to break the ideological surface appearance of things in order to reveal the underlying power structures of reality, and thus to counter the glossy, ideological appearance of reality through the products of the culture industry. Yet—and this is Adorno's criticism—all these conceptions of realism have an element in common with the "pseudo-realism of the culture industry": both use an artistic form for the communication of a particular, premeditated meaning which does not emanate from the artistic material itself (cf. *Engagement, Reconciliation*). According to Adorno, however, the very idea of inducing a meaning from the outside to an aesthetic material, of instrumentalizing artworks for intentional purposes and inflecting them through an extra-aesthetic content, is a corruption of the particular force of art. For the latter consists precisely in its resistance against the societal logic and schemes of signification. By contrast, the very idea of communication through an artwork, be it for ideological or emancipatory purposes, turns it into a social product like any other. Consequently, Adorno argues, "Art does not provide knowledge of reality by reflecting it photographically or 'from a particular perspective' but by revealing whatever is veiled by the empirical form assumed by reality, and this is possible only by virtue of art's own autonomous status" (*Reconciliation*, 162). Art's particular force and expressive agency thus lies in the form, not in a transmitted topical message. As he writes in *Aesthetic Theory*, "In all art that is still possible, social critique must be raised to the level of form, to the point that it wipes out all manifestly social content [*Inhalt*]" (339).

How can a film be thought in terms of a particular, autonomous form, while its very material is a visual copy of reality and therefore appears as its immediate reflection rather than as an artistic mediation? Is it possible, through filmic means, to produce subversive forms that are neither purely contingent (and thus devoid of any subjective mediation) nor artificial products of an intentional subject (and thus ideological constructions that do not take the specificity of the filmic material into account)? In *Minima Moralia*, Adorno addresses this dilemma specifically:

> Radical naturalism, to which the technique of film lends itself, would dissolve all surface coherence of meaning and finish up as the antithesis of familiar realism. The film would turn into an associative stream of images, deriving its form from their pure, immanent construction. Yet if, for commercial reasons, or even with some disinterested intention, it strives to choose words and gestures in a way that relates them to an idea conferring meaning, this perhaps inevitable attempt finds itself in equally inevitable contradiction with the presupposition of naturalism. The less dense reproduction of reality in naturalist literature left room for intentions: in the unbroken duplication achieved by the technical apparatus of film every intention, even that of truth, becomes a lie. (93)

The challenge of a genuine filmic aesthetics which appears to Adorno in the 1940s as an aporia lies in the difficulty to generate artistic forms that neither betray the representational character of the photographic material nor uncritically consider it as hermetic copy of the real. But is it possible to disrupt the seemingly seamless photographic depiction of reality without imposing an external sense? Can a film be representative *and* reflexive, close to the empirical world, and still critical of its own appearance as immediate? In *Minima Moralia*, Adorno remained skeptical: "One is trapped," he continues the aforementioned quotation, "conformism is produced a priori by meaning in itself, no matter what the concrete meaning may be, while it is only by meaning something that conformism, the respectful reiteration of the factual, could be shaken" (93).

However, already in his text *Composing for the Film* written with Eisler during the same period as *Minima Moralia*, Adorno considered montage as the potential means to deflect the images from their apparent immediacy. While this early text does not address the problem of images themselves, but rather discusses their interference by antagonistic music scores, it still alludes to the possibility of subverting the representational character of filmic images through their contrapuntal juxtaposition. Against the tendency in mainstream cinema to produce familiar moods or strong affects through the harmonization of sound and image, the two authors plead for a subversive employment of music. Rather than merely accompanying the visuals so as to amplify the intended effects, they think of the soundtrack as a constitutive part of the film, as a relatively autonomous element of the construction of the whole, which disrupts the visuals and deflects them from their immediate appearance. Thus, the relation between music and images, their montage, "is not one of similarity, but, as a rule, one of question and answer, affirmation and negation, appearance and essence" (70). As a dialectical other to the visuals, that sort of music composition interrupts the commonsensical perception and adds a subversive dimension that unfolds through their concomitant presence.

Dialectics of Montage

In the 1960s, Adorno thought the representational character of film anew, especially its indexical and naturalistic injunction. Revisiting the genuine material of film, Adorno discovered in *Transparencies* that despite their technological nature, film images are eventually, as things for themselves, able to express subjective experiences. They do so not by producing specific affects but through the discontinuity of their movement which resembles associative streams of consciousness: "Such movement of interior images may be to film what the visible world is to painting or the acoustic world to music. As the objectifying recreation of this type of experience, film may become art" (*Transparencies*, 180). In a world in which motion pictures have become a constitutive element of reality itself, film expresses the inner organization of perceptions in modern society, itself shaped by the omnipresence of all kinds of indexical images, and their afterlife in human consciousness. The expression of this kind of experience requires a thorough organization of the material so as to carve out its collective dimension. It is this genuine collectivity of the filmic medium—the fact that a film's images are capable of embodying collective imagery rather than an artificial construction imposed by the capitalistic machinery—that leads Adorno finally to consider it as a potential art form. Hence, in the same text, he further writes that it is precisely that which differentiates the film from the traditional art forms, its technical neutrality and closeness to the objective world, that bears a particular artistic potential.

In the same text, Adorno also discerned that a dimension of mediation already inheres in photographic images, and this dimension touches precisely the collectivity of the medium. However, it does not lie in the indexicality of the medium as such, nor in the subjective manipulation of images. Rather, it resides in that which is pictured in a disinterested way: the represented objects and situations themselves. Echoing Walter Benjamin's idea of the optical unconsciousness, according to which photographic images grant access to that which has been captured objectively by the camera—sometimes despite the intentions of the photographer (cf. *Little History*, 512)—Adorno claims that the neutrality of the medium permits the disclosure of something that is hidden behind the ideological veil of modern society when the immediacy of representation is critically reflected through the form. Through the disinterestedness of the camera eye, there "emerges something of the essence [*Wesen*] or the curse [*Unwesen*] of this world which allows the humans to eventually understand what comes out of their self-inflicted incapacitation" (*Podiumsgespräch*, 40, translation by the author). What transpires through the indexical images is social reality in its historical state of development, for "[t]hat which is irreducible about the objects in film is itself a mark of society, prior to the aesthetic realization of an intention" (*Transparencies*, 182). This societal imprint inscribed in the appearance of reality can be carved out, artistically mediated, and critically deflected through filmic means.

This conjuncture is not revealed directly, however, as factual evidence or representation. Rather, it potentially shines *through* the images if they are arranged in an unconventional way that does not fall into the familiar signification scheme of the current society. As the latter appears, by dint of its ubiquity, as obvious and inevitable, it has to be disrupted in its flux in order to grant access for a divergent approach. To construct a new meaning through filmic means presupposes, first and foremost, a *deconstruction* of the seemingly evident appearance of reality. Hence, Adorno argued, "The liberated film would have to wrest its a priori collectivity from the mechanisms of unconscious and irrational influence and enlist this collectivity in the service of emancipatory intentions" (*Transparencies*, 183). Such a film would penetrate into the seemingly hermetic imagery of reality by generating a critical distance to it, and thus burst open the smooth surface appearance of the image that reality has become. Reflexive in its indexicality and representational stance, it would expose the clichéd canons of the culture industry as such, deflect their ideological embedding, and disrupt standardized perception. Such a reflexivity has to be produced through montage: a montage "which does not interfere with things but rather arranges them in a constellation akin to that of writing" (*Transparencies*, 182). Only as such a constellation, a film potentially acquires an image character as does the figure of the constellation, so dear to Adorno, which neither corrupts its elements nor aligns them in order to produce a unilateral meaning. As Adorno wrote in a different context, "Constellation is not system. Everything does not become resolved, everything does not come out even; rather, one moment sheds light on the other, and the figures that the individual moments form together are specific signs and a legible script" (*Hegel*, 109). This opening generated by the constellation and produced by a thorough montage, at the same time, puts heterogeneous elements in a multitude of relations and keeps the antagonistic tensions between them alive. Such an opening confers a genuinely aesthetic force to a film, for this type of montage "goes beyond photography immanently without infiltrating it with a facile sorcery, but also without sanctioning as a norm its status as a thing: It is photography's self-correction" (*Aesthetic Theory*, 211).

However, montage has its limits and is not to be taken as a universal principle allowing a priori for subversion. Its agency depends, once again, on the historical development of society and the perceptual habits it generates. The shock-effects produced by montage that Benjamin still praised for their challenging ability, for instance, wore away quickly with habit. Today, the fast cuts-only editing of music clips or big Hollywood productions have become the norm: rather than disrupting the conventional mode of perception, they constitute its standard. Just as any other formal principle, the different forms of montage are not immune against their absorption by the ideological sphere of the culture industrial clichés. Once again, the problem lies in the condition of possibility for producing a divergent sensuous experience of society, countering the commonsensical perception of reality, and dragging the images out of their stereotypical standardization. How can a critical awareness be raised through artistic forms? Which forms are able to penetrate into the seemingly harmonious appearance of reality and disrupt its ostensible universality? How can filmic images avoid turning into clichés? These questions cannot be answered once and for all, but need to be addressed each time anew with regards to the social reality in question.

Adorno considered film, this genuinely modern invention conceived for the masses, as an inherently collective medium: the images set in motion are the images of the collective. As such, it bears a particular subversive potential: its images, rhythms, and forms grant access to collective experience in relation to the social reality from which they emerge. While cinema is certainly more social fact than autonomous form—to the point that its collective dimension becomes primary—it is nevertheless not completely devoid of artistic autonomy. That much was true for Adorno: one cannot ignore the ideological power of film and should not refrain from criticizing its instrumentalization. On the other hand, nor should one disregard its critical potential as a form able to penetrate into the standardized representation that capitalist society disseminates through the products of the culture industry. In the service of the culture industry, film takes part in the construction of the ideological veil that hides the antagonisms of reality under a glossy, falsely harmonized imagery—but it is also through filmic means that this veil can be pierced and problematized in its impacts on society.

Works Cited

Adorno, Theodor W. *Aesthetic Theory*. Trans. Robert Hullot-Kentor. Minneapolis, MN and London: University of Minnesota Press, 1997.
Adorno, Theodor W. "Commitment." In *Aesthetics and Politics*. By Ernst Bloch, Georg Lukács, Bertolt Brecht, Walter Benjamin, Theodor Adorno. Trans. Francis McDonagh. London: Verso, 1980, pp. 177–95.
Adorno, Theodor W. "Culture Industry Reconsidered." In *The Culture Industry: Selected Essays on Mass Culture*. Ed. J. M. Bernstein. London and New York: Routledge Classics, 2001, pp. 98–106.
Adorno, Theodor W. *Hegel. Three Studies*. Trans. Shierry Weber Nicholsen. Cambridge, MA and London: The MIT Press, 1993.
Adorno, Theodor W. "Letters to Walter Benjamin." In *Aesthetics and Politics*. By Ernst Bloch, Georg Lukács, Bertolt Brecht, Walter Benjamin, Theodor Adorno. London: Verso, 1980, pp. 110–33.
Adorno, Theodor W. *Minima Moralia: Reflections from Damaged Life*. Trans. E. F. N. Jephcott. London and New York: Verso, 2005.
Adorno, Theodor W. "Reconciliation Under Duress." In *Aesthetics and Politics*. By Ernst Bloch, Georg Lukács, Bertolt Brecht, Walter Benjamin, Theodor Adorno. Trans. Rodney Livingstone. London: Verso, 1980, pp. 151–76.
Adorno, Theodor W. "The Meaning of Working Through the Past." In *Critical Models*. Trans. Henry W. Pickford. New York: Columbia University Press, 2005, pp. 89–103.
Adorno, Theodor W. "Transparencies on Film." In *The Culture Industry. Selected Essays on Mass Culture*. Ed. J. M. Bernstein. New York and London: Routledge Classics, 2001, pp. 178–86.
Adorno, Theodor W., and Hanns Eisler. *Composing for the Films*. London, Atlantic Highlands, NJ: Athlone Press, 1994.
Adorno, Theodor W., and Max Horkheimer. *Dialectic of Enlightenment: Philosophical Fragments*. Ed. G. S. Noerr. Trans. E. Jephcott. Stanford, CA: Stanford University Press, 2002.
Adorno Theodor W. , Joseph Rovan, Alexander Kluge, Edgar Reitz, Hans Rolf Strobel and Haro Senft. "Podiumsgespräch mit der 'Gruppe junger deutscher Film' zum Thema 'Forderungen an den Film' während der 'Internationalen Filmwoche Mannheim 1962.'" In *Provokation der Wirklichkeit. Das Oberhauser Manifest und die Folgen*. Ed. Ralph Eue and Lars Henrik Gass. Munich: edition text + kritik, 2012, pp. 27–47.
Benjamin, Walter. "Little History of Photography." In *Selected Writings Volume 2, part 2 1931-1934*. Ed. Michael W. Jennings, Howard Eiland, and Gary Smith. Trans. Rodney Livingstone, Ben Brewster, Edmund Jephcott, Harry Zohn, Kingsley Shorter, Anna Bostock, Thomas Y. Levin, Michael Jennings and

Howard Eiland. Cambridge, MA and London: The Belknap Press of Harvard University Press, 2005. pp. 507-30.
Benjamin, Walter. "The Work of Art in the Age of Its Technological Reproducibility (Second Version)." In *Selected Writings Volume 3, 1935-1938*. Trans, Edmund Jephcott, Howard Eiland, and others. Ed. Howard Eiland and Michael W. Jennings. Cambridge, MA and London: The Belknap Press of Harvard University Press, 2006, pp. 101-33.
Claussen, Detlev. *Theodor W. Adorno: One Last Genius*. Trans. Rodney Livingstone. Cambrige, MA and London: The Belknap Press of Harvard University Press, 2008.
Hansen, Miriam Bratu. *Cinema and Experience. Siegfried Kracauer, Walter Benjamin, and Theodor W. Adorno*. Berkeley, CA: University of California Press, 2012.
Hansen, Miriam Bratu. "The Mass Production of the Senses: Classical Cinema as Vernacular Modernism." *Modernism/Modernity* 6, no. 2 (1999): 59-77.
Jenemann, David. *Adorno in America*. Minneapolis, MN and London: University of Minnesota Press, 2007.
Krakauer, Eric. *The Disposition of the Subject: Reading Adorno's Dialectic of Technology*. Evanston, IL: Northwestern University Press, 1998.

7

How It Is (after Auschwitz)

Adorno and Beckett

Jean-Michel Rabaté

Beginning in the mid-fifties, Adorno reflected on Beckett's work, reading his texts closely and drawing important lessons from them. Beckett provided a paradigm of cultural negativity that could be harnessed for a systematic theory of responsible art. In Adorno's reading, the writings of Beckett tackled a central problem, namely the possibility of creating art after Auschwitz. What is more, Adorno understood how much Beckett aimed at simplifying the issues of art, life, politics, and ethics, issues that would be reduced to a few basic images, and his solution was that these images would have to be rethought dialectically. While developing his dialectical synthesis, Adorno was not above making slight mistakes or imposing "strong" readings, going at times against the author's resistance. In the end, Beckett provided new tasks for his negative dialectics and as a response Adorno brought a host of original readings, which contributed to the philosophical scholarship growing around the Irish writer.

Beckett's works are strong enough to welcome new theoretical frameworks, even if Beckett was impatient or ironical facing what he called the "profundities" coming from Adorno concerning his plays.[1] Adorno historicized Beckett in his production and reception, fashioning for him a role on par with Proust, Joyce, Kafka, Schönberg, and Berg—artists whose works were so progressive that they divided the cultural history of Western thought in a before and an after. Adorno assumed that some knowledge of Beckett's oeuvre was indispensable if one wanted to understand the evolution of twentieth-century art, arguing that his work's impact changed our attitudes in matters of ethics, politics, epistemology, let alone metaphysical questions about the value of life.

Adorno engaged with Beckett relatively late in his career; he was fifty-five when he met Beckett who was three years younger. Recounting his discovery to Horkheimer, he mentions having chanced upon a different negativity.[2] Beckett's work would provide an important step in his confrontation with Heidegger. Adorno's encounter with Beckett forced him to develop a sharper critique of French existentialism and of Stalinist Marxism while making him account more solidly for the autonomy of aesthetics. However, Adorno never used Beckett to highlight the kind of mystical autonomy of art that one finds in Maurice Blanchot, for instance, because his interpretive procedures were always buttressed on careful exercises in close reading: first with *Endgame* and later with *The Unnamable*. I first focus on Adorno's essay on *Endgame*, and then will sketch his evolution in the 1960s.

How to Understand Adorno Understanding *Endgame*

As a sign of deference, Adorno dedicated his essay on Beckett to Beckett himself in English: "To S.B. in memory of Paris, Fall 1958." The Americanism of "Fall" reminds us that Adorno spent several years in the United States while suggesting something like a "Fall Beckett" (in German). There would be a "Beckett case," which would be furthered by the knowledge that he teaches us not only to fall but also to "fall better."

Adorno's involved essay on *Endgame* begins abruptly: "Beckett's oeuvre has many things in common with Parisian existentialism" (Adorno 241). Indeed, Paris had to be foregrounded because this is where Beckett and Adorno met for the first time. This was in November 1958, when Adorno went to Paris to give lectures at the Sorbonne, and when existentialism was still very much in the air. While Beckett belonged to the "nouveaux romanciers," a distant participant in a cohort including Alain Robbe-Grillet, Michel Butor, and Nathalie Sarraute, the dominant philosophical discourse in France was existentialism. Sartre would get the Nobel Prize in 1964 (and decline it), five years before it would be Beckett's turn. Camus's Nobel Prize in 1957 did nothing to dispel the animosity that had erupted earlier between him and Sartre, when the former friends quarreled bitterly about issues of ethics and politics. As for Beckett, his fame had come less from his novels than from the success of plays like *Waiting for Godot* (1953), *Fin de Partie* (1957), and *Krapp's Last Tape* (1958). Adorno who had seen *Endgame* in Vienna in April 1958, and wrote to Horkheimer expressing his admiration, considered Beckett as a playwright first before discovering the prose writer (Müller-Doohm 357).

Adorno had arranged the Paris meeting through the intervention of Peter Suhrkamp. He and Beckett had a conversation on *Godot* and *Endgame* at the Coupole and later in Beckett's favorite restaurant, Les Îles Marquises. Adorno jotted down statements that gave him prompts and keys for his own reading. Perhaps surprised by the fact that Beckett's favorite German novel was *Effi Briest* by Fondane, he also heard him make unspecified "reproaches" against Kafka, which may have tempered his decision to develop a systematic comparison between the two writers. Earlier Beckett had voiced objections against Kafka, accusing him of not being experimental enough. The modernist questioning of form, Beckett felt, was an element lagging behind in Kafka. He told Israel Shenker in 1956, "You notice how Kafka's form is classic, it goes on like a steamroller—almost serene. It seems to be threatened the whole time—but the consternation is in the form. In my work there is consternation behind the form, not in the form" (Graver and Fedferman 228). "Consternation" is a term that Adorno might have used, while suggesting Beckett's own wish to push further the links between form and content. On this point, Adorno understood him perfectly.

When Adorno took more notes on *Endgame* during the holidays following their meeting, he wrote down, "NB Beckett's criticism of Kafka" (Adorno 159). He remained convinced of the affinity between their methods while being aware of a certain gap, of an inversion in the methods, as we see in a note on the next page: "Beckett relates to Kafka the way the serial composers relate to Schönberg. His criticism of Kafka contains the same problem as the integral composition in its relation to the antagonistic one" (Adorno 159–60). The assessment was more circumspect in the final version of the essay on *Endgame*, in a passage in which a similar lack of freedom is observed in Beckett's and Kafka's characters: "In this too Beckett's play is heir to Kafka's novels. His relationship to Kafka is analogous to that of the serial composers to Schönberg: he provides Kafka with a further self-reflection (*er reflektiert ihn nochmals in sich*) and turns him upside down (*krempelt ihn*) by totalizing his principle" (Adorno 262).[3]

This sentence is condensed and almost opaque—happily Adorno unpacks it, and makes sense of the musical analogy by offering a brilliant statement about the status of the theater in Beckett's play:

> The same thing that militates against the dramatization of Kafka's novels becomes Beckett's subject-matter. The dramatic constituents put in a posthumous appearance. Exposition, complication, plot, peripetia and catastrophe return in decomposed form as participants in an examination of the dramaturgical corpse. [. . .] Those constituents have collapsed, along with meaning, to which drama once served as an invitation. *Endgame* performs a test-tube study on the drama of the age, a drama that no longer tolerates any of its constituents. (Adorno 260)

Here is the main thesis on the play: Beckett has not only absorbed Kafka's lessons but redoubled them by "self-reflection" in an inverted totalization, which means that nothing escapes from this generalized parody. All that pertains to thought and meaning is taken to task in a farce that destroys the very possibility of the theater. Of course, philosophy is not spared in this debunking process, which has certain consequences for existentialism. Indeed, parallels between Beckett and existentialism used to be taken as a privileged handle to discuss Beckett, who at the time was regularly classified as an "absurdist." Adorno's second collection of essays on literature with his reading of *Endgame* was published in 1961, the same year as the influential *The Theater of the Absurd* by Martin Esslin, who listed Samuel Beckett, Arthur Adamov, Eugene Ionesco, Jean Genet, and Harold Pinter as contributing representations of the absurdity of life.

When Adorno highlights "Parisian existentialism," he refers to Sartre. Common themes are listed: the absurd, the situation, and the impossibility of decision-making processes. However, what distinguishes Sartre from Beckett is form: Sartre's plays remain conventional "pièces à these," whereas Beckett, the heir of Joyce and Kafka, debunks this old-fashioned model: "Impulsive ideas (*Impulse*) (Adorno 188) are raised to the level of the most advanced artistic techniques, those of Joyce and Kafka" (Adorno 241, modified). Beckett adds to the combined influence of Joyce and Kafka not only universal parody but the practice of subtraction, which can be understood as an almost mathematical principle. One revealing note of Adorno is this: "Beckett (after Godot). Not abstraction but subtraction" (Tiedemann 25).

Adorno saw how Beckett reduced philosophy to a string of meaningless clichés, criticizing the "existentialist jargon" that would offer a mystified image of the human condition. If existentialism essentializes life in a "process of abstraction that is not aware of itself," then Beckett subtracts all he can from such an abstract vision: "To this kind of unacknowledged process of abstraction, Beckett poses the decisive antithesis: an avowed process of subtraction" (Adorno 246). This is a sort of phenomenological reduction without any phenomenology.

Targeting existentialism, Adorno was looking beyond Sartre at Heidegger, whom he was to attack with virulence in *The Jargon of Authenticity* in 1963–4. Beckett's "subtraction" thus destroys the "abstraction" of thinkers who negate concrete life and its historical determinations. The process of subtraction works with a reduced subject, who sends off abstractions of existentialism in laughable caricatures. Beckett derides philosophical abstraction by exhibiting its dead end—an end from which one can be saved by regressive and unsparing laughter.

The names of Kierkegaard and Jaspers are mentioned along with Heidegger, whose *Being and Time* is quoted. What Kierkegaard, Jaspers, Heidegger, and Sartre have in common is an overestimation of the individual's power, its substantiality, and absoluteness. Adorno mentions Sartre's conceit that the freedom of a prisoner is enhanced in jail, and rightly concludes that *Endgame* "destroys such illusions" (Adorno 249). Adorno criticizes Heidegger for underscoring such illusions: "Dragged out of the sphere of inwardness, Heidegger's *Befindlichkeiten* (states of being) and Jaspers' situations become materialist" (Adorno 252). Heidegger's *Befindlichkeit* refers to existence defined as "being in a given mood." *Befindlichkeit* defines the aspect of *Dasein* (being there or existence) through the fact of having moods, feelings, or affects. The term evokes "disposedness" as a "state of mind." For Adorno, "disposedness" is caught up in a dialectical relationship, for in *Being and Time*, moods do not come from the inside or the outside but are generated by the structure of being in the world. Affective phenomena like depression or enthusiasm thus acquire a social and ontological value.

Adorno understands that even Heidegger's dialectics of existence and ontology presuppose the unity of consciousness in *Dasein*. The unity of the existent being is negated by Beckett, whose debunking and clowning strategies point to "the dissociation of the unity of consciousness into disparate elements, into non-identity" (Adorno 252). The subjects of *Endgame* are "no longer unquestionably identical" with themselves. In the end, "situations of inwardness become those of *physis*, of physical reality" (Adorno 252). Beckett's combination of materialistic reduction to the body and of constant clowning evokes the catatonic reactions to a catastrophe, that is a desperate reaction to what Karl Jaspers had called "limit-situations" (*Grenzsituationen*) (Adorno 252, modified).

What would Beckett's response to French existentialism, to Jaspers's or Heidegger's phenomenology, be predicated on? A first answer proposed by Adorno is history—in history, abstraction is destroyed: "French existentialism had tackled the problem of history. In Beckett, history swallows up existentialism. In *Endgame*, a historical moment unfolds, namely the experience captured in the title of one of the culture industry's cheap novels, *Kaputt*" (Adorno 244). Here, we catch Adorno being rather condescending toward Kurzio Malaparte's novel *Kaputt* (1944), which is one of the most chilling and unforgettable accounts of human cruelty during the Second World War. Malaparte zoomed in on the frenzy of destructiveness that seized the German armies on the western front. However, Adorno had a point when suggesting that immediate and gripping evocations of sadism function as a prelude to what we discover in *Endgame*: "After the Second World War, everything, including a resurrected culture, has been destroyed without realizing it; humankind continues to vegetate, creeping along after events that even the survivors cannot really survive" (Adorno 244).

However, in what looks like the most blatant contradiction of the essay, Adorno asserts close to the end that even history fails to save Beckett, for with him as with Walter Benjamin, one remains caught in dialectics at a standstill: "Rather, what is eternal and enduring for Beckett is the infinite catastrophe; [. . .] Prehistory lives on; the fantasm of eternity is its curse" (Adorno 273). Here might be why the only unmistakable historical allusion found in *Endgame* is to the city of Sedan (Adorno 266). The reference reminds us of the double defeat of the French army, first in 1870, when Napoleon III was taken prisoner and his empire collapsed, then in 1940, when the French armies were beaten to a pulp by the Blitzkrieg of the superior German army. Sedan is sufficient to call up Marx's insight that history repeats itself as a farce, here a rather sinister farce:

NAGG: Do you remember—
NELL: No.
NAGG: When we crashed on our tandem and lost our shanks.
 [They laugh heartily.]
NELL: It was in the Ardennes.
 [They laugh less heartily.]
NAGG: On the road to Sedan.
 [They laugh less heartily.] (Beckett 1958, 16)

For Adorno, these lines sound like parodies of Benjamin: *Theses of the Philosophy of History*. Debunking any sense of messianism, even a "weak" messianism, Beckett has Hamm respond to Clov, who is asking whether he believes in the "life to come": "Mine was always that" (quoted Adorno 274). As Adorno notes, all these one-liners seem to offer a "test of Benjamin's idea that a single cell of reality . . . counterbalances the rest of the world" (Adorno 272).

However, the coupling of Benjamin and Beckett produces a perfect war machine to attack and destroy Georg Lukács's position. Lukács's mistake had been to criticize Beckett's negativity by reclaiming its opposite, that is, the concept of a full life considered from the point of view of totality:

> True to official optimism, Lukács complains that in Beckett human beings are reduced to their animal qualities. [. . .] Just as it is ridiculous to impute an abstract subjectivist ontology to Beckett and then put that ontology on some index of degenerate art, as Lukács does, on the basis of its wordlessness and infantilism, so it would be ridiculous to put Beckett on the stand as a star political witness. (Adorno 247–8)

When he had completed his essay on Beckett, Adorno announced that it would present a perfect refutation of Lukács's wooden Marxism. The famous critic was attacking an "absurdist" theater deemed to be nothing but "pettybourgeois nihilism." For Adorno, on the contrary, Beckett's alleged apolitical stance was highly political: Beckett exposed both the disingenuousness of

Marxist humanism and the sterility of Heidegger's ontological essentialism. Adorno is ferocious: "Adherents of totalitarianism like Lukács, who wax indignant about the decadence of this truly *terrible simplificateur*, are not ill-advised by the interest of their bosses. What they hate in Beckett is what they betrayed" (Adorno 243). One follows the transformation from an apolitical Beckett to a figure of resistance to totalitarianism of any kind, and of salutary cynicism facing the complacent illusions of the bourgeoisie about living well without a purpose.

In order to achieve a reconciliation of sorts with his old friend Benjamin, Adorno made a curious detour via a philosopher one would not expect to find mentioned here, Heinrich Rickert, whose posthumously published book *Immediacy and the Interpretation of Meaning* (1939) is quoted at some length. Rickert had been a disciple of Wilhelm Windelband, whose compendium on philosophy was a major source of inspiration for Beckett in the thirties—did Adorno know this? In fact, Rickert had supervised not only Heidegger but also Benjamin; he was a neo-Kantian who kept open a dialogue with Husserl's phenomenology. As Benjamin declared to Adorno in 1940, "I am myself a student of Rickert."[4] Rickert's approach to meaning and interpretation impressed Benjamin whose essay "The Image of Proust" defines the image by way of physiognomy: "The image of Proust is the highest physiognomic expression which the irresistibly growing discrepancy between literature and life was able to assume."[5] Benjamin's essay "The Image of Proust" was published in 1929, one year before Beckett's own *Proust* monograph was published in 1930.

Benjamin's conception of the dialectical image relates two distinct spheres, while registering their discrepancy; for him, images exhibit a non-synthetic holding together of opposites that function moreover like a physiognomy in the allegorical portrait of a given period. This was one of the crucial concepts launched in section N of the *Arcades Project*. In a parallel manner, Rickert's *Unmittelbarkeit und Sinndeutung* has a footnote quoting an essay by Ernst Robert Curtius on Proust dating from 1925. Curtius presents Proust as a materialist phenomenologist who rejects Cartesian dualism predicated on the difference between res cogitans and res extensa for he did not "recognize the division between thinking substance and extended substance" (Rickert 133, note). Underlining the word *seelig* (meaning "spiritual" or "mental") in the expression "psychic fluid" used by Curtius, Rickert argued that one had to go beyond the formulas inherited from psychology: "In fact, one can learn from Proust's novels that what matters in art is to question not only the old opposition between the psychic and the physical, but also the distinction between sensuous perception and supra-sensible intellection. Should thus poetry precede science and show the way?" (Rickert 134, note). Adorno quotes Rickert quoting Curtius about the disappearance of the concept of the psychological, and its possible replacement by the "physiognomy of objective expression" (Adorno 254). Thus, as with Kafka, Beckett goes further than Proust who located this sensuous physiognomy in the process of involuntary memory:

> Proust continues to cling affirmatively to that physiognomy, derived from a buried mystical tradition, as though involuntary memory revealed the secret language of things; in Beckett this becomes the physiognomy of what is no longer human. His situations are the counter-images of the inextinguishable substance conjured up in Proust's, wrested from the tide of schizophrenia, against which terrified health defends itself by crying bloody murder. (Adorno 254, modified)

The demonstration of this analysis is provided by the passage of *Endgame* in which Hamm speaks about a madman who refused to believe that there was any life left in the world; he would look at fields, at the sea, and only saw ashes and death. As Adorno sees it, this is a mirror image of the situation Clov finds himself in; his task it is to look outside the house through a telescope, and he sees only death and destruction—up to a last reversal at the end, when he sees a boy outside.

Beckett often worked by developing a strong visual image, and in this respect, Adorno provides a surprising key to the play. He quotes a personal memory offered by Beckett himself, when sketching one memory-image that led Beckett to write the play: "Sticking in Beckett's memory is something like an apoplectic middle-aged man taking his midday nap with a cloth over his eyes to protect them from light or flies. The cloth makes him unrecognizable" (Adorno 254). No Beckett scholar has ever mentioned this echo of the conversation in Paris. This image is the first thing we perceive when the play opens; the memory explains why a blind man like Hamm needs to protect his face with a bloody handkerchief when he cannot perceive differences of light and darkness. Adorno alludes to the anecdote to argue that the horror in this case derives from the dehumanized state of the character: Hamm may be alive still but already looks like a corpse.

Less unexpected than the reference to Rickert is an allusion to Heidegger and Husserl's former student, Günther Anders. Anders saw Adorno regularly in California during the war. His book *Die Antiquiertheit des Menschen* (Munich, Beck, 1956) left an impact on Adorno's reading of Beckett. The philosopher and essayist who had been Hannah Arendt's first husband, also a cousin of Walter Benjamin, had written an excellent essay on *Waiting for Godot*.[6] Like Adorno, Anders rejected any allegorical or religious interpretation of Beckett's play. For him, Beckett's negative parable stages characters who are swallowed by an absence of meaning, but this absence would be wrongly interpreted as the "absurd."

Indeed, Didi and Gogo no longer share a coherent world. They have no "world" at their disposal and thus renounce action entirely: there is nothing to do, even if they keep on living pointlessly. As Anders argues, they believe that, by dint of waiting, they will prove that they were waiting for something. This turns them, as Anders insists, into "metaphysicians" in Heidegger's sense: they believe in meaning, even if it is a meaning to come, an always future and deferred meaning. Even this will be questioned more radically in *Endgame*: Hamm and Clove are aware that there is no way that they might "mean" (*signifier*, in Beckett's French original) anything at all, and they know that there is nothing to wait for.

Anders sees no "absurd" in *Waiting for Godot* even if indeed Didi and Gogo live outside nature, time, and history. In fact, they just embody "Being without time," and killing time with antics that satirize Heidegger's philosophy of time. Then Anders analyzes the irruption of the second couple, Lucky and Pozzo, in terms of the Hegelian dialectics of the master and the slave: "The Hegelian dialectic of master and servant, which Anders discussed in relation to *Godot*, is not 'given form' in accordance with the tenets of traditional aesthetics so much as ridiculed" (Adorno 269). In *Endgame* the couple of Hamm and Clov replays the interaction between Lucky and Pozzo (they were the exact same actors in the first French production).

In *Godot*, their sudden entrance on the stage is read as an interruption and an interpretation: thus, Pozzo and Lucky play a "deciphering function."[7] They march on as a second "pseudo-couple" (Beckett's coining to refer to male couples bickering but unable to part) and allegorize the knot by which master and slave are tied together. Lucky and Pozzo tweak the usual relationship, for Lucky seems happy to be a slave, which shocks Didi and Gogo. Lucky enjoys his servile abjection and is worried at the idea of being set free, which terrifies him: freedom is worse than slavery because one has to start making sense of one's life. Hamm and Clov repeat this play in *Endgame*: Hamm keeps telling Clov that he is free to go, knowing that he cannot free himself without killing him either literally or metaphorically.

Anders's thesis is that the irruption of the second couple provides meaning: history acquires dynamism. What Hegel and Marx defined as the engine of history, the mechanism of exploitation and alienation, is projected on the stage in a bitter farce that nevertheless reminds us that history has a collective meaning. Anders's powerful reading saves *Waiting for Godot* from nihilism. For Anders, Beckett goes back to the tradition of anarchist humor ushered in by Charlie Chaplin. Behind the apparent cynicism and derision of all the higher values, there is an ethos marked by human solidarity and a pervasive but saving humor. Ander's groundbreaking interpretation of *Godot* provides a blueprint for Adorno's reading; however, Adorno, unlike Anders, refuses to see humor or clowning as *Endgame*'s saving grace. He writes more dourly:

> Psychoanalysis explains the clown's humor as a regression to an extremely early ontogenic stage, and Beckett's drama of regression descends to that level. But the laughter it arouses ought to suffocate the ones who laugh.

This is what has become of humor now that it has become obsolete as an aesthetic medium and repulsive, without a canon for what should be laughed about, without a place of reconciliation from which one could laugh, and without anything harmless on the face of the earth that would allow itself to be laughed at. (Adorno 257)

Such strictures are loaded with presuppositions about laughter and call up an earlier discussion with Walter Benjamin about those who laugh at films in theaters:

The laughter of a cinema audience [. . .] is anything but salutary and revolutionary; it is full of the worst bourgeois sadism instead. [. . .] the idea that a reactionary individual can be transformed into a member of the avant-garde through an intimate acquaintance with the film of Chaplin strikes me as simple romanticization.[8]

Indeed, Anders, like his cousin, may have been guilty of such romanticism. This echo sends us to the question of sadism in Beckett's works, and to allusions to horror in the play. Adorno makes an interesting comparison between *Endgame* and the pathos deployed by expressionist plays or films. Adorno mentions sketchily a novella by Leonhard Frank, "Die Ursache," in which a young man returns home to make sense of his troubled past and catches up with Herr Mager, the teacher who bullied and humiliated him; when he sees Herr Mager torturing a young student in the same manner, he kills him. The passage quoted comes from the novel *Die Räuberbande* (1922) in which the same tyrannical Herr Mager is seen peeling an apple with unbearable slowness. But the hero who murders this despicable sadist is unable to explain the rationale of his impulsive action, and is condemned to death. For Adorno, who knew how much the theme of sadism pervades Beckett's works, Mager is "a figure of sadism" (Adorno 253) flirting with that of the victim.

Beckett's dark humor cannot be condoned by Adorno, even when he calls it "Jewish" as when he alludes to the famous story of the "world and the pair of trousers," in which a fastidious tailor praises his work as perfect once compared to the total mess the world is in. God cannot be invoked to shame him! Adorno calls this a "metaphysical Jewish joke" (Adorno 256). Later he compares the scene in which Clov uses an alarm clock to show he is alive with a gag in the Busch circus: August catches his best friend with his wife on the sofa, and being unable to throw away either the wife or the friend decides to get rid of the sofa! Funny as the joke is, Adorno's tone is dark: "The only thing that is still funny is the fact that humor itself evaporates along with the meaning of the punchline" (Adorno 258).

Adorno makes witty observation that in *Endgame*, all four characters have names that are "four letter words" (Adorno 266), that is, they are living obscenities. This corresponds to a trick he finds in Kafka as well, the literalization of a colloquial phrase—if the parents are to be thrown to the garbage, here they indeed survive in garbage bins (Adorno 266).

Finally, Adorno had duly noted that Beckett compared *Endgame* to a chess problem, the type of problem called an "endgame." Even if all is lost from the beginning, the game has to be played to the end all the same. But truly the issue is whether the end can really end or not, an issue underpinning Adorno's reading of *Endgame*. The play's meaning would not be provided by death as in classical tragedy but from the opposite, the "abortion of death." The pathos of the play derives from the sense that even after all is over, one has to go on. This corresponds to a post-Holocaust situation, when the mechanization of death in the camps has increased the unspeakable. The best denunciation of a postapocalyptic post-Holocaust situation, a predicament in which we are still caught, will be achieved by a dramatization of the non-death of the subject. Hamm's actions and speeches in *Endgame* do not betray a fear of death, for what he really fears is that "death could miscarry" (Adorno 269–70). Immediately after, Adorno adds, "—an echo of Kafka's motif in 'The Hunter Gracchus'" (Adorno 270), referring to his own "Note on Kafka."

In this analysis, Kafka's parable of Hunter Gracchus provided a key to the sense of blocked time and negativity deployed by Beckett. Kafka told the story of a hunter who had missed his own death by accident. Even though Gracchus has died, he is condemned to roam the earth, and turns into an immortal being in spite of himself. In Adorno's reading, the undead Gracchus is like the bourgeoisie that failed to die in a Marxian scheme, while adumbrating a more sinister meaning: it is the theme of being "between life and death" that the death camps of the Nazis enacted with a vengeance: "In the concentration camps, the boundary between life and death was eradicated. A middle ground was created, inhabited by living skeletons and putrefying bodies, victims unable to take their own lives, Satan's laughter at the hope of abolishing death."[9]

For Adorno, *Endgame* had less to do with the Cold War and the fear of a universal atomic annihilation than with Auschwitz, that is, with an event that was so traumatic that it cannot be named: "The violence of the unspeakable is mirrored in the fear of mentioning it. Beckett kept it nebulous. About what is incommensurable with experience as such one can only speak in euphemisms, the way one speaks in Germany of the murder of the Jews" (Adorno 245–6). The restraint of that muted reproach impressed Adorno all the more. "Beckett too could claim what Benjamin praised in Baudelaire, the ability to say the most extreme things with the utmost discretion; the consoling platitude that things could always be wore becomes a condemnation" (Adorno 266).

Adorno anticipates Giorgio Agamben when he talks of reducing all subjects to mere existence or to "bare life" (*vita nuda*): "(Beckett) extends the line taken by the liquidation of the subject to the point where it contracts into a 'here and now,' a 'whatchamacallit,' whose abstractness, the loss of all qualities, literally reduces ontological abstractness *ad absurdum*, the absurdity into which mere existence is transformed when it is absorbed into naked self-identity" (Adorno 246).

During their first conversation in Paris, Adorno expressed some incomprehension about the issue of negativity, and noted: "Very enigmatic remark about a kind of positivity contained in pure negativity. In view of such absolute negativity, one could be said to *quasi* live" (Tiedemann 24). This point condenses what was baffling for Adorno. Soon after, he meditated on the paradox and teased out its consequences, which appears in the notes taken in the summer of 1960 in which we see him pondering the Beckettian oxymoron of "Life does not live."

However, Adorno had also registered Beckett's passion for music and rhythm: "B. said that his plays were as much music as play, following a purely immanent logic of sequences, not of meaning" (Tiedemann 24). This was enhanced by Adorno's habit of dotting his copies of Beckett's works with marginal F (forte) or FFF (fortissimo). One can say that his essay is a musical fugue as well, with several themes intertwining, vanishing, and recurring modulated with variations and then taken up at another level.

From *Endgame* to *The Unnamable* and *Aesthetic Theory*

Beckett and Adorno met a second time in Frankfurt. This was in the spring of 1961, when Beckett had come for a celebration of his work. Adorno gave a lecture that condensed "Trying to understand *Endgame*." Adorno left a less congenial impression on Beckett then. Beckett, always a stickler for linguistic detail and precision, had explained to Adorno that the name "Hamm" contained no reference to Hamlet. However, in his lecture Adorno developed his thesis on the links between *Hamlet* and *Endgame*.[10] Adorno thus embodied for Beckett the typical German professor whose watertight architecture of concepts is impervious to facts. This led Beckett to give a series of ironical remarks in German when he was questioned about *Endgame* in 1967: "*Endgame* will be just play. Nothing less. Don't worry about enigmas and solutions. For these, we have well-equipped universities, churches, cafés du commerce and so on."[11] These questions and answers, added to the program of *Endgame* when produced in Berlin in 1967, can be seen as barbs addressed to Adorno as well.

A rapprochement came when they met again, this time in Berlin on September 23, 1967, after which Beckett could write, "Don't know why he likes me or why I like him" (Quoted in Beckett 96). In January 1968, Beckett and Adorno met cordially and for the last time in Paris. Adorno had come to give a lecture at the Collège de France. Beckett gave him the idea that his work amounted to a "desecration of silence" (in English) (Tiedemann 25), a phrase found in the pages of *Aesthetic Theory*:

> Whereas each artwork that succeeds transcends the nexus (of guilt), each must atone for this transcendence, and therefore its language seeks to withdraw into silence: An artwork is, as Beckett wrote, a *desecration of silence*. (Adorno 134)

Confessing to his incipient minimalism, Beckett confided to Adorno that everything that mattered depended less upon "man's maximum" than on "man's minimum."[12] Then Adorno left for Cologne, where he participated in a heated discussion on Beckett with Martin Esslin and others for a German radio network. In the discussion typically entitled "It would be criminal to think optimistically," Adorno reiterated the principle of negative dialectics: everything would hinge around "determined negation"—a phrase that was heard repeating at the end when the discussion got lost in a cacophony of voices. This was the negation he saw at work in Beckett's oeuvre.

Adorno and Beckett were not to meet again in person. On February 15, 1969, Beckett thanked Adorno who had suggested he should direct Godot in Hamburg and also complimented him on the imminent publication of *Aesthetic Theory*. Adorno confessed that he had been shocked at being called "reactionary" and prevented from teaching by his students in Frankfurt. Beckett answered him to reassure him on the issue of leftist politics prevalent among German students: "I have not yet been *conspué* so far as I know and that is not far, by the *Marcusejugend*. As you said to me once at the Îles Marquises, all is *malentendu*. Was ever such rightness joined to such foolishness?"[13] With *conspué*, ("publically heckled, pilloried"), Beckett accused the German leftists of being no more than a new *Hitlerjugend*. Marcuse had broken with Adorno at the time, and supported the more radical fractions, for whom Adorno was a liberal professor comfortably inserted in the bourgeois world who merely paid lip service to Marxism and the Revolution.

The shock of this heckling triggered a depression that contributed to the heart attack he died from in August 1969. When *Aesthetic Theory* was published posthumously, it was dedicated to Beckett. Adorno had planned another essay on Beckett. Among his papers were notes on Beckett's *Unnamable*. Quite rightly, Adorno had come to consider that novel as Beckett's literary masterpiece. These notes were accompanied by a rough draft of an essay on the novel. Adorno multiplies parallels with Bertold Brecht, Gotfried Benn, Kafka, Benjamin, Bloch, Wittgenstein, and Hegel. Gertrude Stein, James Joyce, and Descartes are mentioned. The discussion would have been highly philosophical, and launched a new motto: "The path of the novel: reduction of the reduced" (Tiedemann 38). Adorno still harps on the dialectics of negativity: "L'innommable is the negative subject-object" (Tiedemann 67). "With Beckett, positive categories as hope turn into absolutely negative ones. Here hope goes to the nothing" (Tiedemann 44). The last pages of the draft meditate on the nature of this nothing: "Is the nothing only nothing? This is the central issue in Beckett. Absolute rejection, because hope is only where there is nothing to keep. Plenitude of the nothing. This is the explanation of his remaining in the zero-point" (Tiedemann 73). This negativity has nothing to do with the "absurd," and Beckett should not be compared with Ionesco.

In *Aesthetic Theory* Adorno revisited his analysis of *Endgame*:

> Beckett's plays are absurd not because of the absence of any meaning, for then they would be simply irrelevant, but because they put meaning on trial; they unfold its history. His work is ruled as much by an obsession with positive nothingness as by the obsession with a meaninglessness that has developed historically and is thus in a sense merited, though this meritedness in no way allows any positive meaning to be reclaimed. (Adorno 153)

The dialectics of content and form are coupled with a Hegelian *Aufhebung* of negativity, as we see in the "draft introduction":

> In Beckett the negative metaphysical content affects the content along with the form. [. . .] A relation, not identity, operates between the negativity of the metaphysical content and the eclipsing of the aesthetic content. The metaphysical negation no longer permits an aesthetic form that would itself produce metaphysical affirmation; and yet this negation is nevertheless able to become aesthetic content and determine the form. (Adorno 347–8)

Form determines content while sublating negativity to another level in a Hegelian progression. Along with vaulting parody in the realm of ideas and slapstick in the realm of the theater, we have a fusion of a verbal dynamism and an ontological immobility thanks to which Beckett launches his tragicomedy. Beckett's exemplary position explains why he exerts a political impact even when he did not explicitly engage with politics. It was revealing that the right-wing junta of Greek colonels who had seized power banned his works: "Greece's new tyrants knew why they banned Beckett's plays in which there is not a single political word" (Adorno 234). Beckett exemplifies the spirit of resistance in art, an obstinate ethical perseverance facing barbarism, all the while to make explicit political statements. We see this in *Negative Dialectics*, revisiting an idea jotted down in Paris with Beckett:

> Beckett has given us the only fitting reaction to the situation left by concentration camps—a situation he never calls by name, as if it were

subject to an image ban. What is there, he says, is like a concentration camp. He spoke once of a lifelong death penalty, implying as only hope for the future that there will be nothing any more. This, too, he rejects. From the rift of inconsistency thus found it is the imagery of the Nothing as Something that emerges, and it will then stabilize his poetry. (Adorno 380–1)[14]

The particular negativity deployed by Beckett is not "nothing" for it retains historical, hence dialectical, properties: "Such nihilism implies the contrary of an identification with nothingness" (Adorno 372). Like Paul Celan but with different rhetorical strategies, Beckett provides an answer to Adorno's self-imposed quandary: how to write poetry after Auschwitz? Beckett's alleged "nihilism" ends up figuring as the opposite of nihilism: he is a "true nihilist" only when attacking the faded positivities of a post-Auschwitz restoration of values in which no one believes.

Aesthetic Theory generalizes to Beckett's novels what Adorno had perceived in *Endgame*: "they present the reduction of life to basic human relationships, that minimum of existence that subsists *in extremis*" (Adorno 30). Here we see the introduction of a protocol of reading in the concept of subtraction. Subtraction entails an anti-dialectical dialectics of a Nothing that reverts to a positive affirmation. In *Aesthetic Theory* Beckett finally allowed Adorno to achieve a posthumous reconciliation with Walter Benjamin:

> "*Il faut continuer*," the conclusion of Beckett's *The Unnamable*, condenses this antinomy to its essence: that externally art appears impossible while immanently it must be pursued. [. . .] The political significance, however, which the thesis of the end of art had thirty years ago, as for instance indirectly in Benjamin's theory of reproduction, is gone; incidentally, despite his desperate advocacy of mechanical reproduction, in conversation Benjamin refused to reject contemporary painting: Its tradition, he argued, must be preserved for times less somber than our own. (Adorno 320–1)

As Benjamin insisted in his *Arcades Project* against Adorno's unshakeable confidence in "progressive" versus "regressive" art, any revolutionary work will embody a rejection of the idea of progress—such a refusal would be allegorized by the lack of movement in Beckett's plays and novels:

> His narratives, which he sardonically calls novels, no more offer objective descriptions of social reality than—as the widespread misunderstanding supposes—they present the reduction of life to basic human relationships, that minimum of existence that subsists *in extremis*. These novels do however, touch on fundamental layers of

experience *hic et nunc*, which are brought together into paradoxical dynamic at a standstill. (Adorno 30)

Thanks to Beckett, Adorno finally understood that the negative could only turn into a positive if one posited a "dialectics at a standstill," the phrase by which Benjamin defined his method in the *Arcades Project*. Adorno praised the heroism of modernist artists who rejected a bourgeois mass culture dominated by Kitsch. Beckett occupies a place of honor in this pantheon, next to Schönberg and Kakfa: their works destroy a shallow capitalistic culture of commodification. Beckett stands out as a defiant bearer of negativity who debunks a world dominated by the ethical entropy of late capitalism, while identifying his characters with the trash of a debased culture. While dismantling the remnants of a classical culture that he parodies, he can give us reasons to believe in man's resilience in front of catastrophe. "Dialectics at a standstill" culminating in the music of thought reconcile Benjamin and Adorno via Beckett. Adorno understands that the act of thinking is similar to music for both, which does not entail an adherence to Schopenhauerian mysticism. If the music of thinking stresses form more than content, its brilliant forms open new holes for truth in our outmoded ideologies. Art will allow truth to shine in spite of its relentless reductio ad absurdum operating via ironical subtraction.

Notes

1. After Adorno had read passages from his "Attempt to Understand Endgame" on February 28, 1961, Beckett mentioned to Barbara Bray hearing "the homage with profundities from Adorno." Letter of 1 March 1961 to Barbara Bray, Beckett 401.
2. See Stefan Müller-Doohm 357.
3. Adorno, "Versuch, das Endspiel zu verstehen," in Adorno 214.
4. Benjamin to Adorno, May 7, 1940, in *Theodor W. Adorno and Walter Benjamin*, 1999, p. 333.
5. Walter Benjamin, "The Image of Proust," in Benjamin, 1968, p. 202.
6. Günther Anders, "Being without Time: On Beckett's Play *Waiting for Godot*," (1954), trans. Martin Esslin, revised by the author, in Esslin, 1965, pp. 140–51. The original "Sein ohne Zeit: Zu Becketts Stück 'En attendant Godot,'" to be found in Anders 213–31.
7. Anders's "Being without Time," in Esslin, 1965, p. 149. The German text is, "... *weil das Paar selbst eine Dechiffrierung ist*," emphasis in original, in Anders 228.
8. Adorno to Benjamin, March 18, 1936, in *Adorno and Benjamin*, 1999, p. 130.
9. Adorno, "Notes on Kafka," in Adorno 227. For the "The Hunter Gracchus," see Franz Kafka 226–30.

10 This was Siegfried Unseld's account reported by James Knowlson in Knowlson 428.
11 "*Endspiel* wird blosses Spiel sein. Nichts weniger. Von Rätseln and Lösungen also kein Gedanke. Es gibt für solches ernstes Zeug Universitäten, Kirchen, Cafés du Commerce usw." In Beckett 114.
12 See T. W. Adorno, "Notes on Beckett," *Journal of Beckett Studies*, 19. 2 (2010), p. 169.
13 Letter to Adorno of February 15, 1969, Beckett 151.
14 Adorno 371–2. I have modified Adorno, 380–1.

Works Cited

Adorno, Theodor. *Aesthetic Theory*. Trans. Robert Hullot-Kentor. Minneapolis, MN: University of Minnesota Press, 1997.

Adorno, Theodor. *Can One Live after Auschwitz? A Philosophical Reader*. Ed. Rolf Tiedemann. Stanford, CA: Stanford University Press, 2003.

Adorno Theodor. *Negative Dialectics*. Trans. E. B. Ashton. New York: Continuum, 1981.

Adorno, Theodor. *Negative Dialektik*. Frankfurt: Suhrkamp, 1970.

Adorno, Theodor. *Noten zur Literatur II*. Frankfurt: Suhrkamp, 1969, p. 214.

Adorno, Theodor. "Notes on Beckett." Trans. Dirk Van Hulle and Shane Weller. *Journal of Beckett Studies* 19, no. 2 (2010): 157–95.

Adorno, Theodor. *Notes to Literature*, vol. II. Trans. Shierry Weber Nicholsen. New York: Columbia University Press, 1991.

Adorno, Theodor and Walter Benjamin. *The Complete Correspondence, 1928–1940*. Trans. Nicholas Walker. Cambridge, MA: Harvard University Press, 1999.

Anders, Günther. *Die Antiquiertheit des Menschen I*. New ed. 2010. Münich and Frankfurt: Beck, Nördlingen, 1956.

Beckett, Samuel. *Disjecta: Miscellaneous Writings and a Dramatic Fragment*. London: Calder, 1983.

Beckett, Samuel. *Endgame*. New York: Grove Press, 1958.

Beckett, Samuel. *The Letters of Samuel Beckett*, vol. II. Ed. George Craig, Daniel Gunn, Martha Fehsenfeld and Lois Overbeck. Cambridge, UK: Cambridge University Press, 2011.

Beckett, Samuel. *The Letters of Samuel Beckett*, vol. III. Ed. George Craig, Daniel Gunn, Martha Fehsenfeld, and Lois Overbeck. Cambridge, UK: Cambridge University Press, 2014.

Beckett, Samuel. *The Letters of Samuel Beckett*, vol. IV. Ed. George Craig, Daniel Gunn, Martha Fehsenfeld, and Lois Overbeck. Cambridge, UK: Cambridge University Press, 2016.

Benjamin, Walter. *Illuminations*. Trans. Harry Zohn. New York: Schocken, 1968.

Esslin, Martin, ed. *Samuel Beckett: A Collection of Critical Essays*. Englewood Cliffs, NJ: Prentice-Hall, 1965.

Graver, Lawrence, and Federman, Raymond, eds. *Samuel Beckett; The Critical Heritage*. London: Routledge and Kegan Paul, 1979.

Kafka, Franz. *The Complete Stories*. New York: Schocken, 1983.

Knowlson, James. *Damned to Fame*. New York: Simon Schuster, 1996.
Müller-Doohm, Stefan. *Adorno, A Biography*. Trans. Rodney Livingstone. Cambridge, UK: Polity, 2005.
Rickert, Heinrich. *Unmittelbarkeit und Sinngebung*. Tübingen: Mohr, 1939.
Tiedemann, Rolf. "Eine Dokumentation zu Adornos Beckett-Lektüre." *Frankfurter Adorno Blätter III*. Münich: Text+Kritik, 1994.

8

Thinking through and beyond Modernism

Adorno and Contemporary Performance

Sabine Wilke

In a recent collection of essays on *Adorno and Performance* (2014), Will Daddario and Karoline Gritzner introduced the idea of performance as a central category in Adorno's philosophical project of thinking about modernist artistic practices in terms of social form and innovation. With this essay collection, Daddario and Gritzner offer the novel idea that Adorno thinks philosophically with various forms of expression, including performative artistic practices (see 1). They provide commentary on Beckett's performance score for *Act without Words I: A Mime for One Player* (1956), that is, a short play with one single male character, a mime, who is cast into a desert environment illuminated by a "dazzling light" (see Beckett 35). At the beginning of the play, the mime hears and reacts to a whistle and, later on, to various objects that present themselves to him:

> Desert. Dazzling light.
>
> The man is flung backwards on stage from right wing. He falls, gets up immediately, dusts himself, turns aside, reflects. Whistle from right wing. He reflects, goes out right. Immediately flung back on stage he falls, gets

up immediately, dusts himself, turns aside, reflects. Whistle from left wing. He reflects, goes out left. Immediately flung back on stage he falls, gets up immediately, dusts himself, turns aside, reflects. Whistle from left wing. He reflects, goes toward left wing, hesitates, thinks better of it, halts, turns aside, reflects. (Beckett 35)

The mime's endless attempts to pursue an object on stage present a multifaceted allegory that opens up numerous ways of thinking about Adorno in the context of performance:

Object always precedes subject. That which flings the man onstage commences the action of this piece. Man himself, once flung, slowly comes around to thinking, here phrased as reflection. Negative dialectical thinking takes its cue from this order of events. (Daddario/Gritzner 2)

This is an important step in framing the relationship between Adorno and performance: an idea that was already addressed in the preceding chapter by Jean-Michel Rabaté in the context of thinking about Beckett in terms of negative dialectics applied to theater. Despite Adorno's disparaging statements about contemporary popular culture and 1960s performance art in some of his later works, we can now see how some of the principles of Adorno's aesthetics of modernism can be productively applied to understanding contemporary performance styles as radical versions of that project in a contemporary context that is informed by environmental debates. Thinking through modernism begins with understanding the relationship between performance and aesthetic expression.

Not only the preponderance of objects but also the recovery of the individual experience and the critical negativity of the artwork that transports the message of freedom and entanglement are central to Adorno's aesthetics (see Sakoparnig 54). This critical negativity also applies to contemporary performances, especially when understood as environmental practices in terms of their sheer materiality, corporeality, and the copresence of human performer, objects, machines, nonhuman actors, and the audience. Contemporary performances emphasize the inescapably social character of the situation. In her contribution to Daddario and Gritzner's volume, Anja Nowak reminds us of the constitutive temporality of theater which is a central element in Adorno's aesthetics, revealing the essential fleetingness of performances and opening us up for "the instantaneousness of the artwork's appearance and the process of re-dynamization through reception" (144). Nowak draws on Erika Fischer-Lichte's idea articulated in *The Transformative Power of Performance: A New Aesthetics* (2008) that performances should be understood as art events, putting them on equal footing with art in terms of aesthetic value as well as social and cultural meaning. With the help of the concept of the transformative power or performance we can understand theater and performance as artistic expressions that seek to make a contribution to social thought and perennial concerns of justice (see Fischer-Lichte 15ff.). I read the bodily copresence of human and nonhuman performers in contemporary performance styles as phenomena that build on Adorno's reliance on modernist aesthetic practices but develop them further in a context that emphasizes the radical interconnectedness of life spheres and their environmental settings (for more theoretical background see Wilke, "Critical Theory and Ecology," 25ff.). This idea can be framed productively with the concept of the Anthropocene, that is, a term that refers to the newly pronounced geological age of the human which highlights human agency in changing the Earth's atmosphere and biological mechanisms, perhaps most prominently featured in discussions of climate change, energy, and species extinction (see Crutzen/Stoermer 12; Zalasiewicz et al. 2228ff.). Performance in the Anthropocene highlights this agency and the radical interconnectivity between life forms and material practices. Understood through the lens of Adorno's aesthetic theory, contemporary performances in the Anthropocene build on radical versions of modernist artistic practices to advance a conception of art as critical-creative and historical practice.

In this chapter on thinking through and beyond modernism, I discuss contemporary theater and performance styles as radicalized modernist practices. Many contemporary performance styles rely on Beckett in developing human-nonhuman relations on stage that leave neat conceptions of the humanist stage behind and instead focus on putting the human into his/her environmental context by emphasizing ways of co-construction and co-inhabiting the world. I focus on four select elements to discuss the concept of performance in the Anthropocene, that is, the importance of deceleration, the need for rethinking aesthetic semblance, reframing identity-logic in the context of geo-power, and, finally, highlighting the role of volatility and risk. I am interested in the concept of the Anthropocene not so much as a scientific but as a critical concept that helps facilitate possible models for rethinking the humans' place in the world (see Heise 6). In the Anthropocene, cultural expressions like theater and performance explore the radical interconnectedness between the sphere of the human and the nonhuman, that is, animals, plants, biological agents, but also objects, machines, and the technosphere (see Davies 7). They blur the boundaries between these spheres by focusing on the radical idea of how these spheres might work together—perhaps in a state of mutual thriving that philosopher Glen Mazis proposed as a new ethics that does justice to overlapping relations between different life forms (see 206). Anthropocene performances cast human beings into broader networks as human beings that live among and with other life forms, objects, and machines in an augmented sphere that is constantly changing and proliferating, recasting itself, and redefining our social, political, and cultural realities (see Campos 37ff.; Yusoff 12ff.; Galloway 15ff.). At the same time, they address issues of environmental and social justice at a variety of levels, referencing and thinking through Adorno's modernist project of social thought and critique. They also provide new impulses for understanding modernism as a form of thinking about society and culture that is still relevant today (see Wilke, "Enlightenment, Dialectic, and the Anthropocene," 83ff.).

The French sociologist Bruno Latour began writing his "Compositionist Manifesto" in order to find an alternative expression to Adorno's modernist critical theory. Rather than moving radically away from Adorno's project, however, I contend that Latour is offering a radicalized version of it. He sets out by confirming that "[c]ritique was meaningful only as long as it was accompanied by the sturdy yet juvenile belief in a real world beyond. Once deprived of this naïve belief in transcendence, critique is no longer able to produce this difference of potential that had literally given it stream" (Latour 475). If there is no world beyond, "ecology seals the end of nature" (Latour 476). For Latour, modernism reveals the belief in a world beyond whereas his alternative expressions are cultural assemblages to be slowly composed without any reference to a greater project. In other words, Latour articulates a theory of social and cultural construction that uses the theater as epistemological model for the creation of knowledge, thereby unleashing Fichter-Lichte's concept of the transformative power of theater. Whereas modern mise-en-scènes reveal a world beyond, contemporary performances bring together actors, performers, nonhuman performers, and spectators in a slow process of composition, interweaving, and compromise that involves discontinuous pieces, fragmented acts, and unbound technical and digital forces. In the following, I discuss four examples of Anthropocene performances that build on Adorno's modernist aesthetic project and offer insights into environmental entanglements and their sociocultural meaning.

Deceleration or the Preponderance of Objects

Building on Adorno's modernism expressed in the preponderance of the object and Beckett's emphasis on objects that surround the human actor who reacts to them on stage, the German playwright and director Heiner Goebbels radicalized this idea by proposing a stage that emphasizes things and objects where human performers are absent in "Stifters Dinge" (Stifter's Things) (2007).[1] "Stifter's Dinge" is a performative installation in which the experience of things is explored and where the spectators become the sovereigns of their own experiences. Adalbert Stifter was a nineteenth-century Austrian writer and painter (1805–68) whose work played a central role in shaping German-language prose styles. Stifter's poetic realism also influenced modern writers like Franz Kafka by focusing on a character's moral striving in a world that is more and more characterized by the excessive, the catastrophic, and the pathological. Stifter pioneered the language that we use to describe landscapes even today. In that context, he is known for his "aesthetics of the small" that he articulated in the preface of *Limestone, and Other Stories* (1853). In contrast to Immanuel Kant's conception of the sublime, Stifter states that phenomena such as lightning, wild storms, volcanic eruptions, and other atmospheric events that threaten human life are small compared to the power that makes milk bubble and rise in the pot of a poor woman. It is these occurrences that are commonly looked at as "small" that come into focus in his aesthetics, whereas the Kantian sublime is revealed as an effect of much larger causalities (see Stifter 12f.).

Stifter's aesthetics of the small led Sean Ireton to propose the concept of the gentle Anthropocene on the example of Stifter's prose—an idea that helps us understand "Stifters Dinge" as an environmental practice (see 195ff.).[2] The gentle Anthropocene evident in Stifter's nature scenes, however, nevertheless also hints at the destruction of nature by modern civilization. In "Stifters Dinge" this predicament is translated into a stage concept that emphasizes the need for deceleration as critical intervention into an Anthropocene world that is more and more characterized by an unbound technosphere that is proliferating at alarming speeds. Like Adorno's modernist artworks, "Stifters Dinge" offers what Carl Lavery calls a "performative critique of the temporal models that have not only produced global warming but are also increasingly unable to respond, in any effective way, to the temporal 'weirding' that it has given rise to" (305). Instead of resigning to the temporal regimes of a technosphere unbound, "Stifters Dinge" models new and different temporal repertoires to include multiple forms of human and more-than-human timescales.

Time is indeed a central concept of the Anthropocene, perhaps best captured in the metaphor of the "long durée" (see Saywer). In his commentary on "Stifters Dinge," Lavery is drawing on Barbara Adam's concept of "time ecology," that is, "a mode of thinking that stresses the necessity of expanding our temporal repertoire to include a multiplicity of competing human and 'more than human' time scales (geochronology, planetary time, the gestation period of animals, the times of migration, the cycles of seasons, etc.)" (305). Deceleration becomes a means of accelerating perception and creating complex time-scapes that avoid binary oppositions between slowness and fastness (see Lavory 308). In "Real Time in Oberplan: On Stifters Dinge—A Theatre of Deceleration" Goebbels explains that

> We are powerless against other things, strange things: this is where our sense of time no longer takes effect [. . .] you could call it, perhaps a little lofty, the time of the other. It is rather the unfamiliar time, the duration of which we cannot estimate, as it follows other rules and other powers: those of nature, gravity, mechanics, arts, or even the rules and powers of other cultures and traditions. (32)

To produce this effect on stage, Goebbels rids the stage of the human presence and instead emphasizes the presence of nonhuman elements: objects, lighting banks, and the performance space itself. In his review of the performance, Lavery describes the 2012 version of "Stifters Dinge" that he saw in London in the underground bunker of Ambika P3 on Marylebone Road:

> On entering the cavernous, industrialised space, the spectators are greeted by an intermittent and discordant sound scape composed of diegetic and non-diegetic sounds: the "hum" of the building, the mechanical noises of machines, the intermittent chords of an atonal piano and a scratchy, analogue field recording of an incantatory chant from Papua New Guinea. [. . .] After an indefinable period of time, two stagehands, dressed in black, emerge from the wings, mix a white substance into two large sieves, and proceed to sprinkle what looks like salt crystals into the rectangles. As the room ticks and reverberates, coming alive we might say, the sound of running water is heard, and the rectangles slowly fill up with liquid. The banks of LED lights framing the stage illuminate the salt that is now dissolving into the water. The space glows white, with patterns of straight lines crisscrossing the rectangles. (310)

As the performance proceeds, the spectators hear a recording with passages from one of Stifter's novellas, overlaid with parts of Bach's Italian concerto and a projected image of Jacob Van Ruisdael's painting *Swamp* (1660), layering text, audio, and image files in a complex web of synesthesia. Critical voices from cultural theory and diverse musical scores were added to the performance at a later point, mesmerizing an audience that was free to wander around and explore these complex theatrical environments on their own time.

The effect of this performance was to model a renewed emphasis on perception. With references to Beckett's preponderance of objects on stage and the notion of the critical negativity of the modern artwork that Adorno valued so highly, "Stifters Dinge" resulted in a new form of environmental aesthetic practice that disclosed multiple ways of being in time simultaneously. "Stifters Dinge" introduced a performance style and a theatrical language that thinks beyond modernism by radicalizing its core concern with time, encouraging sovereign spectatorship and the experience of complexities on a variety of levels, including different time-scapes and atmospheres. While we can characterize this performance as artistic practice that engages with time-scapes in the Anthropocene, understanding it through Beckett's and Adorno's modernism adds an entire level of meaning to our appreciation of contemporary performance styles: the critical negativity of the modernist artwork is radically extended to the level of the spectator who is experiencing deceleration as an intervention into being and time.

Geo-Logic or an Identity-Logic for the Capitalocene

Aside from the displacement of the human performer from stage, a renewed interest in objects, and the need for deceleration and an awareness of different time-scapes, contemporary performance styles are also building on Adorno's concept of ideology. Ideology critique focuses on the dialectical relationship between the individual and the socioeconomic system culminating in his concept of logocentrism and the culture industry, that is, concepts that he first developed together with Max Horkheimer in their California exile (see *Dialectic of Enlightenment,* 23ff.). Contemporary performances that address climate change, for example, explore the idea of the geo-logic that goes deeper and beyond modernist conceptions of identity-logic. Instead, they develop performance styles that stage the technosphere unbound by flooding the stage in a literal as well as metaphoric sense, perhaps most radically seen recently in Ulrich Greb's "Futur II" (Future Perfect) from 2013 and Thomas Köck's *paradies fluten* (Flooding Paradise) from 2017. Greb's performance and Köck's play articulate a project that addresses and makes visible the principle of slow violence that underlies climate change and its environmental effects thus visualizing the principles of Adorno's identity-logic in a radicalized sense as a geo-logic for fossil cultures (see Nixon 12ff.).

Greb's "Futur II" was first produced at the Schlosstheater Moers in Germany in 2013.[3] It featured a handful of actors sitting on stage, debating the reality of climate change in a moderated talk-show format borrowed from television while the stage was slowly being flooded. In the last scene, the stage was flooded not only with water but also with all kinds of material waste, uprooted objects, sneakers, pieces of clothing, and even two corpses. Greb's production presented climate change in form of a theatrical farce for which the material was taken from our discourses on climate change stitched together into a collage. This is contrary to Goebbel's human-less stage where the importance of things and the need for deceleration was emphasized. Performances that address climate change feature our addiction to energy and our failure to take note and embrace structural and behavioral change. Adorno's Marxist strand of a critique of capitalism is developed into a much more comprehensive critique of what Jason Moore and others have called the Capitalocene in a conversation about geohistory and the attempt to rethinking ecological crisis (15ff.). Performances of climate change stage this crisis with the help of modernist aesthetic strategies that include collage, humor, and farce, with water assuming a form of agency on stage questioning the ago-old humanist tradition of theater. Adorno's modernism becomes the radicalized core of the performance of geo-logic, building on aesthetic practices derived from the critique of identity-logic.

Thomas Köck's first part of his climate trilogy, *paradies fluten* (2017),[4] continues this analysis of the geo-logic on stage. The Austrian playwright asks what social and political conditions define a culture that is so addicted to energy that it is no longer capable of ridding itself from it? In Köck's play, historical forms of colonialism are linked to social and cultural practices that are supplying the raw materials for modern technologies. Specifically, the play focuses on the story of rubber and its transformation into a variety of modern materials with the help of vulcanization. Rubber is pervasive; it is found everywhere: in the tires of our airplanes, cars, trucks, busses, and, of course, our tanks and military machines. Rubber fueled European expansion; it was the source of the Western hegemony over the rest of the world. In Köck's play rubber becomes a theme as well as an aesthetic practice that translates its material qualities into a performance style that links the principle of energy abundance to material floods. Like Greb's performance, Köck's play also takes place in the future perfect where the catastrophe has already happened and the characters on stage are only able to react to it, thus finding a theatrical model for Fredrick Buell's trope for oil cultures as merger of catastrophe and exuberance (Buell 273). Two figures who live in climate capsules and seem to be the only "humans" left in this postapocalyptic future perfect time-scape frame the play with their cynical comments, yet, as opposed to the Greek chorus, they no longer have any influence over the fate of these humans or the rest of the world for that matter. The only communal act they are capable of committing in their capsules is lighting a cigarette. After that, the stage turns black.

Köck's play stages the poetic interweaving of catastrophe and exuberance by "flooding" the stage with materials, memories, objects, and many of the other things that were excluded from geo-power. The play upholds the centrality of Adorno's doctrine of remembering the subject, that is, his insistence on the central importance of the fragmented, the marginalized, and the nonidentical. Yet these memory floods can no longer be attached to a specific character. The classical humanist stage centered on the exemplary political individual and/or the idea of the political family becomes a tableau vivant for the staging of global neoliberal practices of exploitation. Through the lens of Adorno's modernism we are able to retain a critical understanding of the performance of climate change as radicalized artistic practice that is rooted in a critique of identity-logic that has been elevated to a critique of the geo-logic. Köck stages a geological critique of the historical forms of colonial exploitation that led to global neoliberal economic-political regimes. He shows us why and over what wars are fought in the twenty-first century (see Welzer 12ff.).

Augmented Reality or an Enhanced Truth Content

The increasing augmentation of the technosphere as a product of oil cultures is a central concern of contemporary performances. Understanding it as an artistic version of Adorno's idea of an enhanced truth content ties these performances back to his project of critical modernism. US-American performance artist Tamico Thiel envisioned "Gardens of the Anthropocene" by providing spectators an artistic model for exploring an augmented reality facilitated by oil and offering techniques to adapt to a constantly changing environment. "Gardens of the Anthropocene," an artistic installation that was made available to visitors of the Olympic Sculpture Park in Seattle, Washington, United States, from June 25 to September 30, 2016, "posits a science fiction future in which native aquatic and terrestrial plants have mutated to cope with the increasing unpredictable and erratic climate swings."[5] While the project relied in part on scientific research into the question of which plants might develop a tolerance to extreme environmental conditions, "the artwork takes artistic license to imagine a surreal, dystopian scenario in which plants are 'mutating' to breach natural boundaries: from photosynthesis of visible light to feeding off of mobile devices' electromagnetic radiation, from extracting nutrients from soil to feeding off of man-made structures, and to transgressing boundaries between underwater and dry land, between reactive flora and active fauna."[6] The staging of such an augmented reality in form of a dystopic science fiction future explored notions of adaptation and mutation to a different reality, artistically rethinking the conceptions of nativity and tolerance, photosynthesis, extraction, as well as boundaries between fauna and flora that have collapsed in the Anthropocene.

"Bullwhip Kelp Drones (*Nereocystis volans*) Feeding off of Elliot Avenue Street Signs" was a performative installation that envisioned underwater plants used by Native Americans for centuries for food and storage. These plants mutate into flying drones that move freely through the Olympic Sculpture Park and are able to feed off of man-made structures and detritus left over in the aftermath of a violent storm that uprooted these structures and destroyed many buildings. Through specially designed 3-D glasses, visitors were able to see these drones and how they were able to carry off these roadside fixtures and building parts in the vortex of their rotor blades. Several aspects of the concept of the Anthropocene are explored in this performance: a world of extreme weather conditions caused by anthropogenic climate change, the role of indigenous knowledge systems and epistemologies in this new world defined by extremes and insecurities, the significance of local ecosystems in relation to that paradigm, the principles of adaptation and mutation as possible strategies of survival in the Anthropocene, and the significance of flourishing life forms beyond the human. In fact, no humans were visible in "Garden of the Anthropocene," even though visitors were able to imagine them driving their cars and inhabiting their apartments in the vicinity of Elliot Avenue which is a major road connecting the downtown area with the waterfront and nearby neighborhoods. Through augmentation the truth content of these artworks was enhanced and a hybrid version of the sublime emerged in the bright colors of the digital image that was superimposed over nature and the environment with flying kelp drones, thus visualizing a radical version of Adorno's understanding of modernist art.

Another installation, "Radar Camas: Alexandrium Giganteous Spores," also featured Bullwhip kelp drones, although here the fleshy green leaves of the succulent plant had mutated into the blue camas, a poisonous plant, that was shown framing Alexander Calder's abstract statue of an "Eagle" (1971) in the background. This artistic engagement with an iconic modern artwork is central to my claim that this augmented reality explores the relationship between seventies conceptual art, its historical ties to corporate financial sponsors—the statue was commissioned by Forth Worth National Bank and was first placed outside of their corporate headquarters in Texas—and the financial regime of the Capitalocene. But perhaps the most striking installation in Thiel's "Garden of the Anthropocene" was "Antennate Farewell to Spring," an artwork that overlaid enhanced digital images of bullwhip kelp drones in the foreground with an expansive view of the landscape of the Puget Sound with Calder's "Eagle" in the distant background framed by the Olympic Mountains against a beautiful clear blue sky. In this image, Calder's statue was relegated into a background image. What were shown in the foreground were several steps of mutation and the eventual status of plants that have adapted to feed off of electromagnetic emissions from our mobile devices. No humans were present in these images. Instead, the effect of this augmented reality was a result of the blending of biology, landscape, geology, and art with man-made environments that inhabit this "Garden of the Anthropocene."

Finally, "Alexandrium Giganteous" showed how algae caused red toxic tides and how they will flourish in the warming waters of the Puget Sound. This was a strangely gigantic mutation: "no longer a single-celled microscopic algae, the mutated species has transformed into what could be termed *Alexandrium Giganteous* because of its size" (http:/tamicothiel.com /gota/m.html). This gigantic structure functioned as a parent pod that was able to emit large numbers of smaller child spores. With this image Thiel was engaging in the discussion of "toxic discourse" begun by ecocritic Lawrence Buell referring to the "forms, origins, uses, and critical implications of toxic rhetoric, conceiving it as an interlocked set of topoi whose force derives partly from the exigencies of an anxiously industrialized culture, partly from deeper-rooted Western attitudes" (639). Toxic discourse characterizes the language and aesthetic strategies that we use to express deeply rooted fears about environmental problems. Thiel's mutated gigantic algae in her "Garden of the Anthropocene" is so toxic that it provides a stage for the technosphere unbound, signaling the urgent need for rethinking the concepts of volatility and risk in an Anthropocene world. Through augmentation and digitally enhanced images these performative installations present a platform for reframing Adorno's modernist aesthetic into a globally reaching critique of the conditions that inform life and matter in the Anthropocene. A radicalized form of modernity emerges through augmentation based on critical reflection of these new paradigms. With the help of Adorno's modernist framework, we are able to retain a critical platform on which these performances speak to current sociocultural conditions and environmental change. Without that reference, these performance styles simply express anxieties of life in precarious times but no longer hark back to the project of critique.

Volatility and Risk

The project "1948 Unbound" at the House of World Cultures in Berlin (December 2017) introduced visitors to some of the most significant changes in the transformation of the technosphere after the Second World War: biology is turning to become a new platform for innovation, nature seems reprogrammable, and theories of genetic control and mastery over humans, animals, and agriculture abound.[7] The end of the Second World War and the beginning of the Cold War also coincided with the beginning of the new geological era of the Anthropocene, that is, the great acceleration of human impact on nature and the environment in the 1950s that Will Steffen and others have located in the scientific models that they use for charting the changing surface of the Earth and subsequently referred to as "The Great Acceleration" (see Steffen et al.). The explosion of the atom bombs in Japan was an important milestone in that trajectory, giving an entirely new meaning to the beginning phrases of Max Horkheimer and Theodor Adorno's *Dialectic of Enlightenment*: "Enlightenment, understood in the widest sense as the advance of thought, has always aimed at liberating human beings from fear and installing them as masters. Yet the wholly enlightened earth is radiant with triumphant calamity" (Horkheimer/Adorno 12). Perhaps *The Dialectic of Enlightenment* was the last and darkest articulation of an old-school (Holocene) theory of history. In light of such triumphant calamity, a new and critical understanding of the concepts of volatility and risk is at stake. Aside from the critique of rampant acceleration, man-made climate change, and a technosphere unbound, it is our era's nuclear threat that is explored critically in many contemporary performances.

Elfriede Jelinek's play "Kein Licht" (No Light) from 2013 is a musical theater of sorts (see the critical essays in Geilhorn/Weickgenannt).[8] Mindful of the 2011 Fukushima accident, the Austrian playwright and Nobel laureate provides us with a collage of idyllic scenes with pristine mountain streams, lush green vegetation, juxtaposed with scenes from oil-related catastrophes. These postapocalyptic hybrid nature scenes feature violent storms, a flooded stage, the lack of light, and radioactive waste that was left over from a former civilization. There is no life on stage left except for a dog that "sings" who has replaced the human as the measure of all things and is now the central character in the play. The Graz production featured video technology including zooms, fast cuts, and a pounding audio file, in order to question the principle of acceleration. But sound and action break apart and the instruments that are left on stage in the end turn silent. In that production, the instruments were played by human actors: they practiced language games, reorganized syllables, and translated the Fukushima iconology to a linguistic level, effectively radicalizing Beckett's preponderance of the object on stage. While the European concert and performance tradition is still referenced on stage, it no longer leads to new significations and musical meanings, just to new rhythms, seemingly underscoring Adorno's worst predictions about the hegemonic regimes of the culture industry and its iconic examples of popular music and swing-era jazz (see Adorno, *The Culture Industry*, 29ff). Reading the performance through the lens of Adorno's modernism enables us to understand the brightly lit female talking heads in the Graz production as expressions of the interweaving of exuberance and catastrophe that ecocritic Fredrick Buell attributes to the poetics of oil cultures (see 274ff.). While the play validates Beckett's idea of the preponderance of the object on stage, none of these performances, however, shed "light" on the condition of what it means to see and/or not to see. If there is "no light" the performers have to produce their own light and shine like stars. Adorno's metaphor and key concept for the meaning of art, that is, the constellation (of stars) as the central image in critical modern philosophy, becomes an aesthetic reference point for theater and performance in the nuclear age (see Cook 23ff.).

In sum, like theater productions that address climate change in an Anthropocene world, performances that engage questions of energy, radiation, and nuclear threat also deal with the problem of the invisibility of the phenomena, their effect of slow violence as described by Rob Nixon, and the meaning of so-called hyperobjects, that is, entities of such vast temporal and spatial dimension that can no longer be understood with the help of our traditional concepts of what constitutes a thing and an object in time and space (see Nixon 17ff. and Morton 12ff.). Volatility and risk assume entirely new meanings in the nuclear age as volatility becomes a new measurement for risk scenarios that embrace the idea of contingency. German sociologist Ulrich Beck's ideas of a "world risk society" is still framed as a self-reflexive development into and out of the calamity of a radiating Earth (see Beck 175). But with the help of and beyond Adorno's modernism, we can now understand these contemporary performance styles as artistic practices that engage with culture in the Anthropocene aesthetically and critically by modeling the need for deceleration while upholding the preponderance of objects, finding artistic expression for a geo-logic critique of the Capitalocene, developing new forms of an artwork's truth content in an enhanced and augmented environment, and staging volatility and risk in the nuclear age as a constellation that might propel us into a new and more diverse complexity of Anthropocene futures. These Anthropocene performance styles build on Adorno's insights into the meaning of modernist artistic practices while, at the same time, radicalizing their forms of expression and refining their theatrical strategies for coping with a new Anthropocene world beyond the compartmentalized forms of modern philosophy. Anthropocene performances highlight the condition of human and nonhuman entanglement while, at the same time, intervening in the culture of consumerism and global capitalism by modeling theatrical scenarios for experiencing and understanding a future complexity that is beyond the confines of Adorno's modernism. Understanding modernism becomes a project for thinking through contemporary performance styles and their relevance for a conception of art that is built on its role as social practice. Critique as an aesthetic project is alive and well if we allow it to expand into realms hitherto unexplored.

Notes

1 A 52-minute-long video documentation of the project by Mark Perroud from 2008 is available on YouTube; see www.youtube.com/watch?v1VV-mcuf-P8; last accessed December 4, 2017.
2 For video clips of the performance see Heiner Goebbels: "Stifters Dinge," (Ruhrtriennale Duisburg 2013, 31:02):https://www.youtube.com/watch?v=zazAuUhQrSkhttps://vimeo.com/134605443 (11:07).
3 See http://www.schlosstheater-moers.de/?produktion=futur-ii and https://www.youtube.com/watch?v=Vn8-p7NU4Ak.
4 See https://www.muenchner-volkstheater.de/spielplan/repertoire/paradies-fluten.
5 See link http:/tamicothiel.com/gota/m.html.
6 See link http:/tamicothiel.com/gota/m.html.
7 See the program brochure at: http://hkw.de/mediathek/hkw/_default/assets/000/061/712/61712_download_1948-unbound-programmzeitung-pdf_bkc6n.pdf.
8 See https://www.youtube.com/watch?v=OyhYPw2i07o (trailer of coproduction by Drama Graz and Theater FAIMME, KosmosTheater, Vienna, and the Musikfestival Bern in cooperation with the Hochschule der Künste Bern, 2013. 1:13).

Works Cited

Adorno, Theodor W. *Aesthetic Theory*. Trans. and Ed. Robert Hullot-Kentor. Minneapolis, MN: University of Minnesota Press, 1977.
Adorno, Theodor W. *The Culture Industry: Selected Essays on Mass Culture*. Intro. J. M. Bernstein. London: Routledge, 1991.
Beck, Ulrich. *World at Risk*. Trans. Ciaran Cronin. Cambridge, UK: Polity, 2009.
Beckett, Samuel. *Collected Shorter Plays of Samuel Beckett*. New York: Grove, 1984.
Buell, Fredrick. "A Short History of Oil Cultures: Or, the Marriage of Catastrophe and Exuberance." *Journal of American Studies* 46, no. 2 (2012): 273-93.
Buell, Lawrence. "Toxic Discourse." *Critical Inquiry* 24, no. 3 (1998): 639-5.
Campos, Luis. *Radium and the Secret of Life*. Chicago: University of Chicago Press, 2015.
Cook, Deborah, ed. *Theodor Adorno: Key Concepts*. London: Acumen, 2008.
Crutzen, Paul, and Eugene Stoermer. "The Geology of Mankind." *IGBP Newsletter* 41 (2000): 1-12.
Daddario, Will, and Karoline Gritzner. "Introduction to *Adorno and Performance*." In *Adorno and Performance*. Ed. Will Daddario and Karoline Gritzner. New York: Palgrave, 2014, pp. 1-12.
Davies, Jeremy. *The Birth of the Anthropocene*. Oakland: University of California Press, 2016.
Fischer-Lichte, Erika. *The Transformative Power of Performance: A New Aesthetics*. New York: Routledge, 2008.
Galloway, Alexander R. *Gaming: Essays on Algorithmic Culture*. Minneapolis: University of Minnesota Press, 2006.
Geilhorn, Barabara, and Kristina Iwata-Weickgenannt, eds. *Fukushima and the Arts: Negotiating Nuclear Disaster*. New York: Routledge, 2017.
Goebbels, Heiner. *Aesthetics of Absence: Texts on Theatre*. Trans. David Roesner and Christina M. Lagao. London: Routledge, 2015.
Heise, Ursula K. *Imagining Extinction: The Cultural Meanings of Endangered Species*. Chicago: University of Chicago Press, 2017.
Horkheimer, Max, and Theodor Adorno. *Dialectic of Enlightenment*. Trans. Edmund Jephcott. Stanford: Stanford University Press, 2002.
Ireton, Sean. "Adalbert Stifter and the Gentle Anthropocene." In *Readings in the Anthropocene: The Environmental Humanities, German Studies and Beyond*. Ed. Sabine Wilke and Japhet Johnstone. Rochester: Bloomsbury, 2017, pp. 195-219.
Jelinek, Elfriede. "Kein Licht." http://www.elfriedejelinek.com.
Kirkkopelto, Esa. "Species-Beings, Human Animals, and New Neighbors." *Performance Research* 22, no. 2 (2017): 87-96.
Köck, Thomas. *paradies fluten/paradies hungern/paradies spielen*. Frankfurt: Suhrkamp, 2017.
Latour, Bruno. "An Attempt at a 'Compositionist Manifesto.'" *New Literary History* 41 (2010): 471-90.
Lavery, Carl. "Theatre and Time Ecology: Deceleration in Stifters Dinge and L'Effet de Serge." *Green Letters* 20, no. 3 (2016): 304-23. DOI: 10.1080/14688417.2016.1191997.

Mazis, Glen A. *Humans Animals Machines: Blurring Boundaries*. Albany, NY: SUNY Press, 2008.
Moore, Jason. *Capitalism in the Web of Life: Ecology and the Accumulation of Capital*. London: Verso, 2015.
Morton, Timothy. *Hyperobjects: Philosophy and Ecology after the End of the World*. Minneapolis: University of Minnesota Press, 2013.
Nixon, Rob. *Slow Violence and the Environmentalism of the Poor*. Cambridge, MA: Harvard University Press, 2011.
Nowak, Anja. "On the Theatricality of Art." In *Adorno and Performance*. Ed. Will Daddario and Karoline Gritzner. New York: Palgrave, 2014, pp. 143–54.
Sakoparnig, Andrea. "Performativization and the Rescue of Aesthetic Semblance." In *Adorno and Performance*. Ed. Will Daddario and Karoline Gritzner. New York: Palgrave, 2014, pp. 53–66.
Sawyer, Stephen W. "Time after Time: Narratives of the *Long Durée* in the Anthropocene." *Transatlantica* 1 (2015). Online: https://transatlantica.revues.org/7344.
Steffen, Will, Wendy Broadgate, and Lisa Deutsch. "The Trajectory of the Anthropocene: The Great Acceleration." *The Anthropocene Review* 2, no. 1 (2015): http://journals.sagepub.com/doi/abs/10.1177/2053019614564785?journalCode=anra.
Stifer, Adalbert. *Limestone, and Other Stories*. Trans. David Duke. New York: Hartcourt, Brace & World, 1968.
Welzer, Harald. *Climate Wars: What People Will Be Killed for in the Twenty-First Century*. London: Polity Press, 2012.
Wilke, Sabine. "Critical Theory and Ecology: The Shape of Performance in the Anthropocene." *Telos* 183 (2018): 25–46.
Wilke, Sabine. "Enlightenment, Dialectic, and the Anthropocene: Bruised Nature and the Residues of Freedom." *Telos* 177 (2016): 83–106.
Yusoff, Kathryn. "Epochal Aesthetics: Affectual Infrastructures of the Anthropocene." *E-flux* (2017). http://qmro.qmul.ac.uk/xmlui/handle/123456789/28686.
Zalasiewicz, Jan, Mark Williams, Will Steffen, and Paul Crutzen. "The New World of the Anthropocene." *Environmental Science & Technology* 44 (2010): 2228–31.

9

Rereading Adorno's Reading of Eichendorff in the Context of 1957

Christian P. Weber

Disruption, Fragmentation, Friction

Professor Theodor Adorno's piece "Zu Eichendorffs Gedächtnis" [. . .] will hardly deepen our understanding of the poet: shot through with needless and aggressive polemics, arbitrary in some of its claims, presumptuous in tone, it feigns a philosophical profundity which, at a closer look, is not much more than verbal and stylistic opaqueness, and buries some truly interesting insights under a modernist critical jargon, which, in Germany even more than here, is the hallmark and blight of the avant-guard [sic].

(SEIDLIN, "1957," 187)

With this verdict, Oskar Seidlin, one of the leading scholars of German literature in the United States at the time, concluded his survey of many remarkable scholarly contributions about Joseph von Eichendorff that appeared in the year 1957, on the 100th anniversary of the German romantic poet's death. It is the only negative statement after much praise for all those, including the author himself, who helped to rectify "the all too pat conception of Eichendorff as the carefree and unproblematic 'letzte Ritter der Romantik' [*last knight of Romanticism*]" (Seidlin, "1957," 187). For Seidlin, apparently, Adorno's piece must have gone too far in this effort and touched a sensitive spot in the self-understanding of scholarly literary criticism. Today, however, Adorno's essay on Eichendorff is considered "perhaps the single most important work on this poet" (Plass 62). To assess Adorno's modernism and originality as a literary critic, it may be a worthwhile task to reread his essay in the backlight of other major contributions (first and foremost Seidlin's) that commemorated the Eichendorff year. Through this juxtaposition we will gain a better understanding of the "break in the continuity of historical consciousness" (ME 55/69),[1] which Adorno performed by breaking away from the false consciousness of a traditionalism that he detected in many of his Germanist colleagues. Instead, he inscribed himself explicitly into the modernist genealogy of "great avant-garde artists like Schönberg" who "knew that they were fulfilling the secret purpose of the tradition they were shattering [*zerbrachen*]," because only those who "break" [*durchbrechen*] and "try [their] strength against it" gain a positive and productive attitude to tradition. According to Adorno, "it is up to advanced consciousness to correct the relationship to the past, not by glossing over the breach [*Bruch*] but by wresting what is contemporary away from what is transient in the past and granting no tradition authority" (ME 56/70).

Sixty years after its first appearance, we may entertain a similar attitude when assessing the lasting value of Adorno's "Eichendorff" essay, which, together with its complementing "Speech on Lyric and Society," articulates a striking theory of poetic language that may actually be less modernist than commonly thought, but remains thought-provoking, nonetheless. My hermeneutic method of rereading Adorno's essay and speech both along and against the lines of his Germanist contemporaries will crack open the protection shield of the modernist jargon under which Adorno concealed that his indebtedness to a Germanist tradition was deeper than he wanted to acknowledge. Seidlin detected that correctly, I think, but the reverse holds true as well: Seidlin and his fellow Germanists were, as we shall see, more inspired by Adorno's essay than one would expect after this scathing review. My analysis of the constellation of essays that appeared or were written during the commemorative year of 1957 reveals a highly productive and still very impressive intellectual engagement with the celebrated poet, an engagement stimulated by frictions but also, as a positive effect of these frictions' repercussions, by mutual inspiration.

What may have sparked the interest of the critical philosopher in one of the most conservative romantic poets has baffled many commenters. It certainly cannot be simply explained by referring to the odd historical analogy that Eichendorff lamented the decline and fall of the aristocratic culture of his Silesian home during the French Revolution and in the aftermath of the Napoleonic Wars, while Adorno bemoaned the failure of a highly cultivated German bourgeoisie during and after the two world wars.

Apart from this coincidence, Adorno is guided by a much more fundamental interest in a very pressing topic of his time that he addresses explicitly in the "Eichendorff" essay early on:

> [a]t a time when no artistic experience is accepted unquestionably any more, when, as children, no textbook authority can appropriate beauty for us any more—the beauty we understand precisely because we do not yet understand it—every act of contemplating beauty demands that we know why the object of our contemplation is called beautiful. A naiveté that would exempt itself from this demand is self-righteous and false; the substance of the work of art, which is itself spirit, does not need to be afraid of the mind that seeks to comprehend it; rather, it seeks out such a mind. (ME 57/71)

Beauty, Adorno claims here, has become problematic in a culture ruined by the war and the naive attitude of many vis-à-vis the products of the culture industry. Adorno's task is to present exemplary objects of beauty that he salvages from the ruined past and to facilitate an understanding of their beauty without any traditionalist aesthetic preconceptions, by plainly appealing to the spirit of those whose minds are still open to experience beauty as it appears. He selected the example of Eichendorff's poems because they are written in a rather simple language that is particularly inviting to enter its world of poetic beauty; hence, the essay can be read as an investigation of how specifically the language of lyric poetry can produce such beauty. To accomplish this, Adorno must let poetry speak for itself. By disrupting the traditionalist context of interpretation, he aims to reestablish direct communication between the artistic/poetic and the hermeneutic/aesthetic spirit. Accordingly, Adorno disentangles Eichendorff's poetry both from its mostly academic history of reception—this explains the almost complete lack of engagement with literary criticism in his essay that must have upset Seidlin—and from the romantic discourse by emphasizing that Eichendorff himself severed bonds with his fellow poets and appeared to have intentionally misunderstood the philosophy of German idealism, whereas "he had insightful and respectful things to say about Kant himself" (ME 72/86). By hinting at the poet's positive relationship to Kant,[2] Adorno indicates that these two, the critical philosopher and the practicing poet, together contributed significantly to an understanding of aesthetic and poetic beauty in ways that Adorno's "Eichendorff" essay replicates and that my own contribution aims to retrace.

Under these circumstances, Adorno's "modernist critical jargon" is certainly not, as Seidlin alleged, an empty pose but a necessary method to regain direct access to the lyrical subject matter. If it was meant to be an affront, it was one first and foremost against the common hermeneutical method of the time, that is, the close reading propagated by the school of New Criticism and practiced by the Germanists that will be featured in this article. Richard Alewyn's much-celebrated essay on Eichendorff's construction of poetic landscape as an "experienced space" ("erlebter Raum"; "Landschaft Eichendorffs," 38), for example, derives its insights from the minute analysis of just a single sentence from one of the poet's lesser-known novellas. Similarly, Seidlin's impressive interpretation of the poem "Sehnsucht" offers a minute, richly imaginative line-by-line analysis over seventeen pages ("Eichendorffs Sehnsucht"); in contrast, Adorno spends not even two pages for his discussion of the same poem, which by far is the most space he granted any of Eichendorff's texts. His essay addresses, if I have not miscounted, altogether twenty-five different texts by the poet, often citing only single lines of poems without providing their titles (moreover, he references at least twenty other poets, philosophers, and composers). He does so in accordance with the principle of fragmentary form that he outlined in the programmatic opening essay of *Notes on Literature*, of which the first volume (of four) also features the piece on Eichendorff:

> [The essay] has to be constructed as though it could always break off at any point. It thinks in fragments, just as reality is fragmentary, and finds its unity in and through its breaks and not by glossing them over. An unequivocal logical order deceives us about the antagonistic nature of what that order is imposed upon. Discontinuity is essential to the essay; its subject matter is always a conflict brought to a standstill. (EF 16/24–5)

The dialectic between fragments and (an imaginary) whole does not just concern the essay's form but constitutes an essential tension for any artwork and its reception as is reflected by the hermeneutic circle, in which the reader's attention continuously shifts back and forth from the perception of discrete parts to attempts of comprehending their ultimately incomprehensible unity and identity. Humans, as mortal beings with limited life span and world experience, are always only transient and fragmentary figures within the greater totalities of society, nature, and history. Adorno embraces the existential limitations of the human condition instead of searching for an all-encompassing ontology like Heidegger. The essay pays tribute to this reality by maintaining a flexible form open to thought experiment and linguistic playfulness. It congeals into what Adorno thought inspired Walter Benjamin's "dialectical image," in which the dialectic comes to a standstill while its movement in history continues (see Tiedemann 132–6).

Similarly, the poem, in its attempt to capture the transience of a moment or instance, is marked by both the extrinsic tensions of the poet's individual subjectivity in conflict with the objectivity of society on the one side and intrinsic tensions between the poetic spirit and the linguistic material on the other. According to Adorno, "lyric poetry has a moment of discontinuity [*Moment des Bruches*] in it" (LPS 40/53) and expresses "the cleft [*Riß*] between what human beings are meant to be and what the order of the world has made of them" (ME 57/71). While the norms and rules muted and concealed the many social tensions and societal rifts, the seamlessness and harmony with which "pure subjectivity" appears in lyric form—"all the more so, the more pure [sic] it claims to be"—bears witness "to the suffering in an existence alien to the subject and to love for it as well" (LPS 41/53) by presenting their opposite. *Qua* the individualistic placement and relatively free association of words, each poem generates an alternative reality to the linguistic conventionality and ideological complicity that defines each society at a certain moment of its history; the poem's "social substance is precisely what is spontaneous in it, what does not simply follow from the existing conditions at the time" (LPS 43/55, see also Kaufmann).

Constructing Allegorical Flashes of Illumination and Symbolic Landscapes of Beauty

The will to disrupt and fragment thus coincides with a will to experiment in the construction of new intellectual and poetic experiences that Adorno finds not only in the modernist avant-garde but already in the poet of late romanticism: "Eichendorff was probably the first to discover the expressive power in fragments [*Bruchstücken*] of the *lingua mortua*" (ME 66/81). Again, it is the programmatic "Essay as Form" in its philosophical self-reflection that provides a foundation for also understanding poetic form and the question of what precisely makes Eichendorff's poetry "spontaneous" and "expressive" in a modernist sense. Lyric poetry in general rejects, just like the essay, the definition of concepts (EF 12/19); one could even say that the lyric, in contrast to the still discursively operating essay, does away with concepts altogether and operates, instead, only with words and associations. Then the task becomes to find a nonconceptual "manner of expression" that defies definition without salvaging precision. If, indeed, an alternative, more intuitive model can be found, it is of utopian promise by circumventing the understanding while still maintaining the possibility of communication and communality, by establishing an ideal of communication that could be performed without the threat of conceptual misunderstanding and an ideal of community that functions beyond the imposition of linguistic normativity and ideological constraints as they have manifested in language itself.

Concerning the essay, Adorno names Benjamin the "unsurpassed master" of a "more than [. . .] definitional procedure" that

> presses for the reciprocal interaction of its concepts in the process of intellectual experience [*geistiger Erfahrung*]. In such experience, concepts do not form a continuum of operations. Thought does not progress in a

single direction; instead, the moments are interwoven as in a carpet. The fruitfulness of the thoughts depends on the density of the texture. The thinker does not actually think but rather makes himself into an arena for intellectual experience, without unraveling it. (EF 12–13/20–1)

The essay has to cause the totality to be illuminated [*die Totalität aufleuchten lassen*] in a partial feature . . . without asserting the presence of the totality. (EF 16/24–5)

Adorno clearly follows this example by reconfiguring fragments from Eichendorff's poems, accompanied by rather sparse commentary, into the tension-filled whole of his essay. Indeed, he emulates here the poet's own method. Eichendorff's verses still fascinate so much, Adorno writes, because they achieve "the most extraordinary effects with stock images that must have been threadbare even in his day. The castle that forms the object of Eichendorff's longing is spoken of only as the castle; the obligatory stock of moonlight, hunting horns, nightingales, and mandolins is provided, but without doing much harm to Eichendorff's poetry" (ME 66/81). His poems basically are collages—as modernist aesthetics would call them—made from always the same "things, which have become reified," but which are brought back to life by endowing them "with the power to signify, to point beyond themselves. This momentary lightning flash from a thing-world that is still quivering with life internally [*Augenblick des Aufblitzens einer gleichsam noch in sich erzitternden Dingwelt*] may explain to some extent the unfading quality of the process of fading in Eichendorff" (ME 67/81-2). On a grander scheme, Adorno notes, the same effect has been accomplished by Schumann's "Liederkreis opus 39," which rearranged Eichendorff's poems "through a process of construction" into a whole that "emerges from the complex of miniature-like elements" (ME 73/87–8). Adorno's review of the song cycle puts great emphasis on the order of arrangement and the echo effects it generates among the individual poems and songs. The process of de-conceptualization that has been set in motion with the production of each individual poem increases by its transposition into music and reaches its greatest resonance with the creation of the cycle. Instead of just measuring the "Eichendorff" essay philologically as a failed contribution to a deeper understanding of the poet's work (as Seidlin does), it is important to notice that Adorno used the poems (as well as his insight in the method of their poetic production) also as material for his reconstruction of yet another collage originating from a very similar spirit of melancholy to that which characterized Eichendorff's late romanticism.

Not by coincidence does Adorno relate the Catholic Silesian aristocrat Eichendorff to the era of the Baroque (ME 67/81) and refer to Benjamin's famous study on *The Origin of German Tragic Drama* as a theoretical model for his essayistic concept of allegorical collage (see Jameson 49–58; Weber Nicholsen 103–10; Plass 60–6). Adorno thereby inscribes himself into a genealogy of modernity as mourning the disenchantment of the world and the loss of a specific culture: while the Baroque poets lamented the breakdown of the Catholic worldview and order after the Reformation and the Thirty Years' War and many late romantics lamented the collapse of aristocracy as a consequence of the French Revolution and the Napoleonic secularization of Central Europe, Benjamin and Adorno mourned the decline of the *Bildungsbürgertum* (cultivated upper middle-class), to which they undoubtedly belonged, after the First World War. For Adorno this negative experience was further enhanced by the horrors of the Holocaust which canceled out the idea of humanism and with it any hope for social betterment in the future. This experience explains the general negativity—the transience, nostalgia, anti-subjectivist tendency, and even self-extinction—that Adorno detects in Eichendorff's poetry and in its aspiration "to attain the darkness of language" (ME 67/81).

"Darkness of language" means, as I will elaborate in the next section, nonconceptual language, that is, words without objective and subjective meaning that have resorted to a purely intuitive level on which "allegorical moments" (ME 68/82) can occur in the flash of "contact with one another" (ME70/84). In other words, the poet produces an aesthetic condition where "defunct words [*abgeschiedene Worte*]" (ME 73/87), that is, concepts that have been deprived of their schematic input and semantic historicity and therefore lost their ability to signify, light up another meaning derived from the associations that these ruins of signification generate in the specific constellation of their placement. But this intuitive meaning cannot be captured again by any other language than poetry; it only occurs spontaneously when the aesthetic moment lifts the constraints of conventional language with all its historical and ideological baggage to offer a glimpse of autochthonic nature before it was linguistically codified and commercially reified into what Lukács termed "second nature" (see Plass 59–60). "In Eichendorff," Adorno writes, "what was nonsensuous and abstract became a metaphor [*Gleichnis*] for something formless: an archaic heritage, something earlier than form and at the same time a late transcendence, something unconditioned, beyond form [*das Unbedingte über die Gestalt hinaus*]" (ME 63/77). As a result of referencing the void, "[n]one of Eichendorff's images is only what it is, and yet none can be reduced to a single concept: this lack of resolution of allegorical moments [*dies Schwebende allegorischer Momente*] is his poetic medium" (ME 68/82). Yet, at the same time, these moments promise, through the revelation of archaic formlessness, the possibility of an entirely new creation, one that is not imposing a form by a law from above, but one that is constituted by a self-generating and self-organizing interplay of the fragments and remnants left behind from the previous order of things.

Adorno's association of Eichendorff with this modernist-inflected notion of allegorical temporality distinguishes his approach most significantly from those of his Germanist colleagues who aimed to unravel the symbolism of his poetic landscapes. Oskar Seidlin's article on "Eichendorff's Symbolic Landscape" from 1957 serves as an excellent example for this distinction. He regards the nature and landscape in Eichendorff's work as "a system of symbols, . . . a cryptogram which has to be deciphered" as a "visible theology" (646–7). For Seidlin, Eichendorff's landscape is symbolic and not allegorical in the Adornian sense because in it, all things and beings are integrated in a transcendental context that maintains the unity between sign and meaning. Hence, this landscape's "iconography will again and again reveal the existential condition of man" (649). Insofar this frail human condition agrees with the Catholic belief system, Seidlin can still identify Eichendorff's poetic landscapes as symbolical. However, Seidlin nonetheless detects an absence and lack in them (due to the withdrawal of God from the world because of vanishing belief), that also aligns him closely with Adorno's allegorical reading. For he also acknowledges that the many representations of ruins and enchanted gardens in Eichendorff's work show traces of temporality, so that his poetic landscape is "not revelation, not the manifestation of the eternal spirit, but it is creature, and as such finite," symbolizing "lived time which is being kept slumbering or imprisoned by nature" (657). These enchanted landscapes and their visitors exist in "a state of life arrested within its own magic circle, and incapable of breaking through its own shell" (659). Seidlin even associates this state with Dürer's famous print "Melencolia," which served Benjamin as an important artistic model for his reconceptualization of allegory. The consequence that Seidlin draws from this association sounds very much like a blueprint of modernist aesthetic: "What this landscape needs to return to life is a shock, a sudden act of awakening, a quick tearing away of the heavy shroud. [. . .] Here we may find the answer to the question why Eichendorff so persistently prefers one specific mode of daybreak. It is literally a break stressing the suddenness, the almost explosive quality, the momentous act of awakening" (659). Yet, again, instead of a new beginning with the potential for creating an entirely different world order with an unknown outcome, Seidlin sees in Eichendorff the history of nature and culture embedded in a "history of salvation," as merely episodic manifestations of a "religious tension between distance from God and closeness to grace" (658). Whereas Adorno perceives Eichendorff's "uncontained Romanticism" at the threshold of modernity as a "genuinely anti-conservative . . . renunciation of the aristocratic, a renunciation even of the dominion of one's own ego over one's psyche" in so far as subjectivity suspends itself in a poetry that "confidently lets itself be borne along by the st[r]eam of language" (ME 64/78), Seidlin beholds quite the opposite: the human condition is unconditionally connected with the divine and nature "by the concept of analogy" within "a system of vast and subtle correspondences, a multiple design of perspectives all of which point to the ultimate question: What is the meaning and destiny of life as God created it?" (660).

By means of this comparison we are now in a better position to characterize Adorno's modernism. In Seidlin's reception, Eichendorff's poetry integrates all its fragmented, disjointed, and ruined images and motifs in a theological context that interconnects everything by assuming a symbolic copresence of everything based on the fundamental identity of all things created, even though the Creator may seem absent from the world. For Adorno, absolute certainty does not exist or no longer exists—neither in the divine nor in the human. If there is an absolute for him at all, it resides in the autochthonic, formless nature of an archaic past, to which there is no other access than in those rare allegorical glimpses of illumination when it abruptly (re)appears under the condition that all layers of subjectivity and semantics are stripped away. Alternatively, the absolute may be found negatively in the unsublatable differentiation between the signs and things and the arbitrariness of meaning production in the flow of language. Pure language's torrents of permanent contingency dissolve the cognitive foundations of subjectivity and carry away what is left of it into an incalculable future of potential (re)construction.

For Adorno, Eichendorff's work exemplifies, like no one else's except perhaps Baudelaire's, the possibility of a poetic regeneration of language itself. Adorno could have found support for his argument in Richard Alewyn's celebrated contribution to the Eichendorff year, which ventured in a similar direction by reconstructing meticulously how the poet has constructed a symbolic landscape not by resorting to an ontological system of analogies among all beings à la Seidlin but, instead, by creating an entirely different, poetic nature purely emerging from the grammatical relations and poetic associations of a set of recurring linguistic patterns and semantically discharged words that are formulaically arranged in the poem and rearranged with every new poem. Alewyn shows at the example of one sentence from Eichendorff's story "Viel Lärm um Nichts" how from the distinguished elevated viewpoint of a mostly anonymous observer (the narrator as stand-in for the reader), an "experienced space" unfolds that has its own depth, width, and height. Neither the observer nor the entities that act in the described landscape—in the given example "der herrlichste Sommermorgen" ("the most magnificent summer morning"), "alle Vögel" ("all birds"), and "die Morgenglocken" ("the morning bells")—are specified or identified; moreover, all other nouns are subordinated as objects to mainly verbs of motion, which are reinforced by coupling them with uncommon prepositions of direction: "*ging* an allen Fenstern des Palastes *vorüber*" ("went on by all windows of the palace"), "*klangen* über den Garten *herauf*" ("sounded upward from across the garden"). These motions are carried out by predominantly immaterial substances, such as light and sound, "traversing the landscape on rays [and waves] that are all directed toward one point, the here, to which corresponds another point in the distance at the fringe of this landscape. Between the here and a distant there unfolds communication . . . , and between these two poles, the landscape expands in all three dimensions of the 'experienced space,' which is specified—with the help of prepositions and plural forms—by some scattered points within this landscape that emit or relay signals" ("Landschaft Eichendorffs," 42). The result is a physically dematerialized, de-historicized, and de-subjectivized, yet, poetically charged and spiritualized landscape. I find it very probable that Adorno had Alewyn's article, which appeared in the spring of 1957, in mind, when he conceived his own speech on "The Memory of Eichendorff" that was first presented to a German radio audience a couple of months later in the same year. Whether Adorno knew of it or not, Alewyn's analysis has clearly demonstrated that, in Eichendorff's poetry, a subject can give itself over to language and construct in and with it an alternative poetic space for the experience of a more harmonious world.

But this poetically created "second nature" (which, to distinguish it from Lukács's use of the term, would be better called "third nature") still retains its allegorical origin per Adorno. The beauty that Eichendorff's poems create is momentary, a transient effect; conversely, their beauty relies on and emerges from the allegorical constellation of linguistic and poetic elements that embody transience. They are, as Adorno aptly labels them, "allegories of longing" (ME 73/87), because they enact and preserve the "mourning for the lost moment [*Trauer um den verlorenen Augenblick*]": a loss that is felt intermittently whenever the poetic force of the lyric and the ensuing aesthetic experience break through the world of our quotidian routines. To give this beauty more permanence, Eichendorff put out an enormous number of repetitive poems that are essentially variations of the same theme and method of allegorical constellation. Altogether, they form the super-constellation of an allegorical space of reverberation; the resounding beauty of this space becomes evident in the history of Eichendorff reception, but especially in its creative adaptations like Schumann's song cycle.

The Sources of Eichendorff's "Rauschen"

Recapitulating what we have reconstructed so far from Adorno's modernist reading of Eichendorff's poetry, it appears as if his essay presents a dialectical process of lyric subjectivity: we noticed how the subject alienated itself from society, broke off from the continuity of (false) historical consciousness, and shattered the world, the ideologically infected language, and along this trajectory its own subjectivity into pieces; we then noticed how it momentarily regained glimpses of consciousness through the flashing up of autochthonic nature from an archaic past, and these flashes of illumination confronted the subject with the idea of a non-reified world and utopian potentiality; finally, we saw how the subject was swept away by the torrents and sucked into the darkness of language. Yet, as shown, Eichendorff's poetry embodies for Adorno a model of recovery and regeneration through rebuilding an alternative world of beauty out of shattered experiences and "defunct words." The following course of inquiry will examine more closely the poetic modus operandi that reanimates the ruined language to beautiful effects with the capacity to resurrect the human as an aesthetic subject.[3] For this purpose, we need to consider the role of aesthetics in this reconstruction process and look beyond the limits of the "Eichendorff" essay.

If Adorno has pursued a theory of language, it is one expressed through the filter of poetic language. Hence, it is important to distinguish these two modes of language: whereas communicative language operates conceptually and discursively with the purpose of facilitating and serving understanding, poetic language relates to communicative language as do concepts relate to the phenomenal world of things and societal relations. Since Kant we know that the "things in themselves" remain out of reach for the human cognitive apparatus. One of Eichendorff's most famous poems seems to acknowledge and yet, at the same time, protest against this condition: "Schläft ein Lied in allen Dingen, / Die da träumen fort und fort, / Und die Welt hebt an zu singen, / Triffst du nur das Zauberwort." ("A song sleeps in all things / that are dreaming on and on, / and the world begins to sing / if you only hit the magic word.") For Eichendorff, "dreaming" is the fundamental state of the natural world that cannot be accessed by conventional language but only through poetical divination. (The poem's title is "Wünschelrute" / "Divining/Wishing Rod.") Accordingly, he defined "poetry" in his treatise "Zur Geschichte der poetischen Literatur Deutschands" ("Toward a History of German Poetic Literature") as a work of art "that renders tangible the hieroglyphic inscription, quasi the song without words, . . . through which the hidden beauty of each particular region wishes to communicate with us" (821). Adorno, however, recognizes in "Wünschelrute" a different, modernist spin: "The word for which these lines . . . yearn is no less than language itself. What decides whether the world sings is whether the poet manages to hit the mark, to attain the darkness of language, as if that were something already existing in itself. This is the anti-subjectivism of Eichendorff the Romantic (ME 67/81)." A bit later, citing from Theodor Meyer's book *Das Stilgesetz der Poesie* (*The Stylistic Law of Poetry*), he adds,

> "Language as the representational means [*Darstellungsmittel*] of poetry," as something autonomous, is [Eichendorff's] divining rod. The subject's self-extinction is in the service of language. [. . .] The subject turns itself into *Rauschen*, the rushing, rustling, murmuring sound of nature: into language, living on only in the process of dying away, like language. The act in which the human being becomes language, the flesh becomes word, incorporates the expression of nature into language and transfigures the movement of language so that it becomes life again. (ME 68–9/83)

Language means here not the communicative language of understanding (cp. Tiedemann 128–9) but *poetic* language, that is, a language distant from meaning (ME 69/83) no longer in the service of representation. Instead, it is forming its own "autonomous" system in which, as with Saussure, the relation between the signified (image) and signifier (word) of the sign (concept) is completely arbitrary. Liberated from the duty of representation and uncoupled from the concepts, images and words are no longer static but in a constant flow out of which poetic language can produce its own kind of meaning and even truth by making new contingent associations. As such, poetic language operates as a "means of presentation" (which is a more adequate translation of "Darstellungsmittel"), that is, it presents the virtual reality of a parallel existing universe without direct connection to the reality of things (their thingness), but much more in sync with the general flow of things than the language of understanding in its effort to arrest this flow by the damming means of concepts and their "stereotypical" symbolism (ME 70/84). By restoring the fluidity of language, poetry truly deserves the name "second nature." It resembles nature in a manner that Benjamin attempted to capture in the essay "On the Mimetic Faculty" by the notion of "nonsensuous similarity" (336).

We have therefore two parallel systems of arbitrariness: the things "dreaming" in themselves (Eichendorff with Kant) and the "streaming" of poetic language (Adorno with Saussure) that both create their own specific *Rauschen* and share this noise in common. In order to establish a relation between these two parallel dynamisms a third dynamism needs to be introduced that mediates between the flows of language and things, not by assuming a transcending position outside of it—this would repeat the "failure" of conceptual language—but by immanently floating with the general flow of words and things. This mediating force is "imagining," the imaginative power of the human mind to form poetical associations based on analogical similarity, which combines, to stress once more Adorno's indebtedness to Benjamin, the "sensuous similarity" of "natural correspondences" with the "nonsensuous similarity" of language. To do so, Adorno asserts, the subject needs to "giv[e] itself up to *Rauschen*," that is, adapt to the fluid imaginary potentiality of a poetic language that is as dynamic, flexible, and transient in a similar manner as the constantly changing phenomena of "dreaming" things. (Cp. Plass 57–58, who reads Adorno's association of "[t]he act in which the human being becomes language" with "the flesh becom[ing] word" as a "parodistic inversion of the *Gospel According to John*.") Weaving both planes together in imaginary associations—the fleeting images of the perceived phenomenal world of things on the one side and the floating sounds and de-conceptualized words of language on the other—the productive imagination composes them into a poetic text, a creation per se, that is intrinsically brimming with the tensions that exist within and between all three dynamisms (of things, language, and imagination). In these poetic presentations, "things, which have grown cold, are brought back to themselves by the similarity of their names to themselves, and the movement of language [*Zug der Sprache*] awakens that resemblance" (ME 69/84). In short, poetry revitalizes the ossified and commodified world of things, reveals the mimetic potential stored in language, and restores the faculty of imaginative play from which humans have been alienated in the historical process of industrialization.

Two aspects still require further explanation: First, we need to describe in greater detail the relation between the imaginative subject and language; that is, we must explain the transition from the conceptual language of pseudo-objective understanding to an imaginative poetic language *in* which subjectivity—the subject in unison with language—speaks (and not *through* which the subject expresses itself). Second, we must describe how the imaginative language does relate to the world of things. In short, it is still unclear how precisely the imagination operates in the poetic mode of associating. Concerning the first aspect, we find an important passage in the speech "On Lyric Poetry and Society" that is the closest that Adorno has reached in conceiving a theory of language:

> [L]anguage is itself something double. Through its configurations it assimilates itself completely into subjective impulses; one would almost think it had produced them. But, at the same time, language remains the medium of concepts, remains that which establishes an inescapable relationship to the universal and to society. Hence the highest lyric works are those in which the subject, with no remaining trace of mere matter, sounds forth in language until language itself acquires a voice. [. . .] The moment of unself-consciousness [*Selbstvergessenheit*] in which the subject submerges itself in language is not a sacrifice of the subject to being. It is a moment not of violence, nor of violence against the subject, but reconciliation: language itself speaks only when it speaks not as something alien to the subject but the subject's own voice. (LPS 43/56)

Subject and language merge when the subject submits itself to the "descending flow of language" instead of aiming for "the power to control it" (ME 70/84) and when, in return, language is loosening up on its ambition of conceptual understanding and making itself malleable again by "washing words away from their circumscribed meanings and causing them to light up when they come in contact with one another" (ME 70/84). It is an operation reminiscent of Kant's conceptualization of the aesthetic experience of beauty in terms of a reflective judgment in the mode of a "free play" between the schematizing imagination and the law-giving understanding. Kant's explanation of aesthetic beauty is compatible with Adorno's conception of poetic language in that it stipulates the failure and negation of conceptual understanding as a precondition for the liberation of the productive (poetic) imagination that drives the free play of the aesthetic experience.[4] In this mode, the subject's "allegorical intention" can discover new potentiality for expressing itself and the world of things in metaphorical language and rediscover its originary creativity by experimenting with alternative configurations of constructing meaning.

Concerning the second aspect, Adorno has not much to say in these essays, especially since it is not his intention to conceive of poetry as a positive medium of representation, but rather as one of negation: "the lyric reveals itself to be most deeply grounded in society when it does not chime in with society, when, instead, the subject whose expression is successful reaches an accord with language itself, with the inherent tendency of language" (LPS 43/56). "In the lyric poem," he continues, "the subject, through its identification with language, negates both its opposition to society as something merely monadological and its mere functioning within a wholly socialized society [*vergesellschaftete Gesellschaft*]" (LPS 44/57). However, things look a bit different regarding nature. If nature should function as a critical positive counterimage to society in poetry, as Eichendorff intends it in his poems, then it must express also truth about the dynamic state of natural things. Here is not the place to venture into specifics, but I will say in general that Adorno's praise of Goethe's lyric poetry, shining through both the "Eichendorff" essay and the speech "On Lyric Poetry and Society," stresses the capacity especially of young Goethe to restore nature from alienation "through animation [*Beseelung*], through immersion into the 'I' itself," and "through humanization [*Vermenschlichung*]" (LPS 41/53), whereas the mature Goethe's essentially poetic, morphological conception of an ever-changing nature has found Eichendorff's praise (ME 69/84).

Given that I have treated the delicate and esoteric subject matter of Adorno's theory of poetic language rather abstractly so far, I would like to add some concreteness to the argument by letting poetry speak for itself. Adorno himself points to a beautiful line from Eichendorff's poem "Zwielicht" ("Twilight") that helps to elucidate the complex of lyrical associations:

> The line "Wolken ziehn wie schwere Träume" ["clouds move like heavy dreams"] procures for the poem the specific kind of meaning contained in the German word *Wolken*, as distinguished for example from the French *nuage*: in this line it is the word *Wolken* and what accompanies it, and not merely the images the words signify, that move past like heavy dreams. (ME 65/80)

Adorno suggests, in the words of his reader Ulrich Plass, "that Eichendorff's line does not merely signify or represent clouds; rather, it is the word *Wolken* itself that moves like a heavy dream" (63). But I think that Adorno implies more than what Plass says. The constellation here is a variation on a theme in Benjamin's seminal essay "On the Mimetic Faculty": "If words meaning the same thing in different languages are arrayed about that thing as their center, we have to enquire how they all—while often possessing not the slightest similarity to one another—are similar to what they signify at their center" (335). In Adorno's example, however, the aim is not to establish the hidden similarity between words of different languages meaning the same thing but to uncover the "specific kind of meaning" that distinguishes them and that a word can take on only in the context of its particular language. What Adorno wishes to explore is, in fact, poetic meaning, meaning that is associative. One must play along with the associations evoked by the line to experience their full poetic potential and magic. First, the word *Wolken* forms an assonance with the word *Worte* (words), suggesting that the words themselves are moving with the same heaviness as the clouds. (Curiously, Benjamin reports in his memories of *A Berlin Childhood around 1900* that he "learned to disguise [him]self in words, which were actually clouds" [qtd. in Weber Nicholsen 143].) Second, the comparison of the *Wolken* with *Träume* (dreams) recalls the essential quality of "all things," of thingness itself, from the previous poem: "Schläft ein Lied in allen Dingen, die da träumen fort und fort." Applying, conversely, to this line the line from "Zwielicht" as its intertext, the dreaming *fort und fort* ("on and on") has no longer just a temporal dimension (as the translation suggests) but also gains a spatial dimension in the sense of "further and further" away. Consequently, the full poetic meaning expressed here is that the dreams of things are moving away and dissolving like clouds in the sky, but more generally also that clouds (nature), words (language), and dreams (the human imagination) share an intrinsic dynamism and chime in a similar, harmonious tone when their cords are struck with the same gentle touch. This resounding meaning turns each line ambiguous (i.e., conceptually indeterminate) and mysterious, and from it emerges the beauty so characteristic for Eichendorff's *lyric* poetry.

Another fascinating example that Adorno uses for his theory of poetic language appears in Eichendorff's "Sehnsucht" ("Longing")—a poem he considers "as immortal as any ever written" (ME 71/85). It is the only text that his essay renders in full length and honors with an interpretation of some substantiality. Adorno notices and imagines an entire "associational field" of phonetic, semantic, intra-, and intertextual references, for example, when he compares the representation of a mountainous landscape in the second stanza with one in Goethe's poem "Kennst du das Land": "how far from Goethe's powerful and spellbinding 'The rock plunges and over it the torrent' is the pianissimo of Eichendorff's 'where the woods rustle [*rauschen*] so softly,' the paradox of a light rustling still perceptible virtually only in an inner acoustic space, into which the heroic landscape dissolves, sacrificing the sharpness of the images to their dissolution in open infinity" (ME 71–2/86). The demarcation between subject and object and between language and the sound of nature dissolves in the indistinct sounds of rustling. In another context, Adorno stresses that "[Eichendorff's] language in its distance from meaning . . . imitates *Rauschen* and solitary nature. It thereby expresses an estrangement which no thought, only pure sound can bridge" (ME 69/84). *Rauschen* thus represents the sound of nature, language, and the subject colliding at the threshold of their contact points; it is the sound that emerges when the three dynamisms dissolve by fusing into each other in a free play of associations. Eventually, the poem as such fades away (*verrauschen*) and performs the eponymous longing through the collapse of its beginning (the lyric "I" stands alone at the window in a magnificent summer night and listens to the song of two young journeymen passing by, which incites in the subject a great longing to join them) with its ending (the poem closes with the song's evocative image of "palaces in the moonlight, / where the maidens listen [*lauschen*] at the window / when the sound of the lutes [*Lauten*] awakens / and the fountains murmur [*rauschen*] sleepily / in the magnificent summer night"). Adorno regards this circular structure as the transformation of "an erotic desire" into "that supreme idea of happiness in which fulfillment reveals itself to be longing, the eternal contemplation of the godhead" (ME 72/86).

Most surprisingly, especially when considering the quotation from the beginning of my article, Adorno found an unexpected ally in his reading of the poem in none other than Oskar Seidlin, whose masterful interpretation of "Sehnsucht" came out at around the same time as Adorno's speech "In Memory of Eichendorff." Their similarity is striking, indeed. It almost seems as if Seidlin listened to Adorno; but, in fact, it is more likely that Adorno read Seidlin, since the speech aired a month after the article's publication in October. Anyway, Seidlin's interpretation states many crucial points that matter to Adorno: First, there is the notion of poetic "delimitation" ("Entgrenzung"), which for Seidlin amounts not just to the dissolution of world and subject but culminates in a "magical transformation," in which the original state is "sublated" ("aufgehoben") in the threefold meaning of the word: "preserved, annulled, and raised to another level" ("Eichendorffs Sehnsucht" 524). Second, Seidlin also praises the artistry of the poem's circular structure. Third and most importantly, he agrees with Adorno on the significance of sound as the only medium that guarantees cohesion (cf. ME 69/84, as quoted earlier). For Seidlin as well, "everything is held together by sound," and "at the end, the poem flows into 'pure' sound ['*reiner' Klang*], in a sound [*Tönen*] that does no longer signify anything, that no longer means anything: music of the instruments and sound of nature" (525). He finds the pure, non-referential sound not just in the sleepy "murmur" ("Rauschen") of the fountains but first and foremost in the awakening sound of the "lutes" ("Lauten"), which in the German word not only refers to the instrument but references the "sound of tonality" ("Klang der Klanglichkeit") as such. "In this primordial ground [*Urgrund*] flows the poem, as it had sprung up from the ground of sound [referring to the sound of the post horn at the poem's beginning, addition mine]. Ascending from the ground to return into it: this appears to be the poem's innermost rhythm" (526). This is also Adorno's notion of transience that affects, for Seidlin, all figures of the poem by drawing them into the vortex of dematerialization so that, in the end, nothing remains of this magnificent summer night but the pure sound of the *Lauten*, the *Rauschen* of the fountains, and the shining glimmer of the stars.

Concluding Correspondences

What, we may finally ask, remains of the magnificent Eichendorff year of 1957? In my recapitulation of the main contributors to this year of commemoration, we have seen a concerted effort to elevate a poet previously decried as conservative, even reactionary by reassessing him as an innovate, even proto-modernist author. Adorno associates Eichendorff's poetry explicitly with the founding text of modernist poetry, Baudelaire's "Fleurs du mal," stating that Eichendorff's "uncontained Romanticism leads [insensibly] to the threshold of modernity" (ME 64/78). Alewyn and Seidlin do not stand back, though. Both establish links to Baudelaire's poem "Correspondances" from the "Fleurs du mal" (see Seidlin, "Symbolic Landscape," 661 and Alewyn, "Wort," 17). This is hardly a coincidence. Instead, we have traced back the many correspondences between Adorno, Alewyn, and Seidlin that have elevated not just our understanding of Eichendorff but also of poetic language as such and of the power of resistance embedded in its aesthetic beauty.

A résumé of these multiple correspondences and of Adorno's unique contribution to 1957 has been aptly articulated by another of the leading Germanists of this time, Wilhelm Emrich, in an article that, as already the title indicates, pays homage to Adorno's speech "On Lyric Poetry and Society":

> Forest, heimat, moonshine, rambling, the good old time turn into images and signs of a poetic process of lyrical enchantment in which nothing signifies anymore itself, in which everything refers to something else that can be no longer articulated in accordance to the common forms of intuition and cognition. This Other not only withdraws itself from all limiting propositions, it also assumes a critical stance against the concrete lifeforms themselves, which have emerged under the command [*Herrschaft*] of this limiting, virtually palpable type of thinking during the nineteenth and twentieth centuries. Poetry becomes the antagonist of an increasingly reifying world. [. . .] The audaciousness of [Eichendorff's] poetry does not only consist in elevating itself as a mysteriously luring, even puzzling enchantment above the philistine-bourgeoise society,

but also in revealing that the enlightened civil world itself has lost an understanding of itself and become itself a riddle as if it had fallen under an evil spell. (Emrich 55–6)

Around this time, it has become an avant-gardist endeavor to exorcize the evil spell of the capitalist-industrial society with the counterspell of critical thinking. But one should not forget that the foundations were laid by the generation of postwar literary scholars who, like Adorno, looked for a positive counterimage to their reality in ruin and being ruined once more by a consumer culture and a mass audience at the verge of losing the sense of/ for beauty. They found it in the poetic constructivism of the reputed arch-romanticist Eichendorff, who has made an extraordinary comeback in the shape of an avant-garde modernist. It remains now for a new generation to rediscover this legacy or find beauty elsewhere.

Notes

1   I cite from Adorno's *Notes to Literature / Noten zur Literatur* by using an acronym for the individual essay title (EF: "The Essay as Form," LPS: "On Lyric Poetry and Society," and ME: "In Memory of Eichendorff") followed by a page number referring to the English edition and a second page number referring to the German edition.

2   This reference appears even more significant given that Eichendorff's assessment of Kant is, in fact, far less positive than suggested by Adorno; at least I cannot find any statements in Eichendorff's oeuvre that would justify the term "insightful."

3   Adorno's theory of subjectivity is inspired by and reflects the historical situation of the postwar era. I would like to specify my use of metaphors in this context. Certainly, Adorno does not envision regeneration in terms of a cyclical, organic temporality, as a return to a previous stage, but rather in the more constructive sense of reorganization and transformation that reaches a new plane of consciousness without the possibility of a return or relapse. The goal (although Adorno never defines one as such) would be the creation of a subjectivity that retains the self-image of its previous failure and false consciousness as a warning negative counterimage by building consciously onto the ruins and from the fragmented material of the past. Ideally, the subject would thereby immunize itself against the recurrence of false consciousness in this process—although Adorno was, of course, too realistic to not be pessimistic about this prospect. Nonetheless, Adorno's aesthetic theory holds on to the promise or at least the possibility that beauty can rise again from the ashes of the past.

4   For the argument that Kant's notion of individual aesthetic experience, grounded in subjective freedom, should have formed the basis for Adorno's aesthetic theory to counter its tendency "toward dogmatic self-validation" for certain preferred objects of art, see Bubner 167–70.

Works Cited

Adorno, Theodor W. *Noten zur Literatur*. Ed. Rolf Tiedemann. Frankfurt am Main: Suhrkamp, 1974.
Adorno, Theodor W. *Notes to Literature*, vol. 1. Ed. Rolf Tiedemann. Trans. Shierry Weber Nicholsen. New York: Columbia University Press, 1991.
Adorno, Theodor W. "In Memory of Eichendorff" [ME], pp. 55–79.
Adorno, Theodor W. "On Lyric Poetry and Society" [LPS], pp. 37–54.
Adorno, Theodor W. "The Essay as Form" [EF], pp. 3–23.
Alewyn, Richard. "Eine Landschaft Eichendorffs." In *Eichendorff heute. Stimmen der Forschung mit einer Biographie*. Ed. Paul Stöcklein. Darmstadt: Wissenschaftliche Buchgesellschaft, 1966, pp. 19–43. (Originally published in *Euphorion*, vol. 51, 1957, pp. 42–60).
Alewyn, Richard. "Ein Wort über Eichendorff." In *Eichendorff heute. Stimmen der Forschung mit einer Biographie*. Ed. Paul Stöcklein, Darmstadt: Wissenschaftliche Buchgesellschaft, 1966, pp. 7–18. (Originally published in *Neue deutsche Hefte*, vol. 43, February 1958, pp. 977–85).
Benjamin, Walter. "On the Mimetic Faculty." In *Reflections*. Ed. Peter Demetz. Trans. Edmund Jephcott. New York: Harcourt Brace Jovanovich, 1978, pp. 333–6.
Bubner, Rüdiger. "Concerning the Central Idea of Adorno's Philosophy." In *The Semblance of Subjectivity: Essays in Adorno's Aesthetic Theory*. Ed. Tom Huhn and Lambert Zuidervaart. Cambridge, MA and London, UK: MIT Press, 1997, pp. 147–75.
Eichendorff, Joseph von. "Zur Geschichte der poetischen Literatur Deutschlands." In *Geschichte der Poesie. Schriften zur Literatugeschichte*. Ed. Hartwig Schultz. Frankfurt am Main: Deutscher Klassiker Verlag, 1990, pp. 805–1074.
Emrich, Wilhelm. "Dichtung und Gesellschaft bei Eichendorff." In *Eichendorff heute. Stimmen der Forschung mit einer Biographie*. Ed. Paul Stöcklein. Darmstadt: Wissenschaftliche Buchgesellschaft, 1966, pp. 55–65. (Originally published in *Aurora*, vol. 18, 1958, pp. 11–17).
Jameson, Fredric. *Late Marxism: Adorno, or, the Persistence of the Dialectic*. London and New York: Verso, 1996.
Kaufmann, Robert. "Adorno's Social Lyric, and Literary Criticism Today: Poetics, Aesthetics, Modernity." In *The Cambridge Companion to Adorno*. Ed. Tom Huhn. Cambridge: Cambridge University Press, 2004, pp. 354–75.
Plass, Ulrich. *Language and History in Theodor W. Adorno's Notes to Literature*. New York and London: Routledge, 2007.
Seidlin, Oskar. "1957: The Eichendorff Year." *The German Quarterly* 31, no. 3 (1958): 183–7.
Seidlin, Oskar. "Eichendorffs Sehnsucht." *The Journal of English and German Philology* 56, no. 4 (1957): 511–27.
Seidlin, Oskar. "Eichendorff's Symbolic Landscape." *PMLA* 72, no. 4 (1957): 645–61.
Tiedemann, Rolf. "Concept, Image, Name: On Adorno's Utopia of Knowledge." In *The Semblance of Subjectivity: Essays in Adorno's Aesthetic Theory*. Ed. Tom Huhn and Lambert Zuidervaart. Cambridge, MA and London, UK: MIT Press, 1997, pp. 123–45.
Weber Nicholsen, Shierry. *Exact Imagination, Late Work: On Adorno's Aesthetics*. Cambridge, MA and London, UK: MIT Press, 1999.

10

Adorno and the Ethics of Camp

Heidi Schlipphacke

For only what does not fit into this world is true. (59)[1]

In his posthumously published *Aesthetic Theory* (1970, composed between 1956 and 1969), Theodor Adorno locates suffering as the expression of "authentic art." The experience of engaging with art reveals, for Adorno, the sedimented expression of suffering that animates the artwork in the "unbefriedete" (Adorno 386 ["not at peace" 260]) society of the post-Holocaust West. Even when positing a future liberated society, Adorno reminds us that art in this society would continue to carry the aesthetic and ethical burden of revealing the barbarism of history: "Regression threatens unremittingly, and freedom—surely freedom from the principle of possession—cannot be possessed. But then what would art be, as the writing of history, if it shook off the memory of accumulated suffering" (261). These are the last words of the last section (on "Society") of the main portion of the *Aesthetic Theory*, as edited by Gretel Adorno and Rolf Tiedemann. They remind us of the unbreakable bond in Adorno's aesthetic theory between aesthetics and ethics, between the artwork itself, autonomous yet always already embedded within the socioeconomic structures of production, and the barbarism of history. The expression of suffering, of the pain of those who have been "repressed" and "dominated" (336)[2] is, Adorno reminds us again and again, the single authentic expression the modernist artwork can utter in a post-Holocaust age.

Adorno links the expression of suffering in the artwork to mimesis, conceived as a dialectical process that occurs both within the artwork itself and between the subject who experiences the work of art and the artwork. The artwork unfolds the dialectical process of history via the "sedimentation," as Adorno calls it, that takes place in the work of art; the artwork reveals, in a moment like a "firework" or a "dialectical image" (23; Adorno cites Benjamin here), the socioeconomic processes that produce suffering. Indeed, if the artwork does not stand in dialectical relation to the social, then it is, for Adorno, "kitsch." "Kitsch" art is the product of the culture industry and hence stands in a non-dialectical relationship to the processes of production and consumption. Rather than revealing the processes of domination and suppression that turn the wheels of the culture industry, kitsch represses the truth behind the culture industry's mask and conceals the suffering that expresses the truth of art after Auschwitz.

In this essay, I will explore the limits of this understanding of kitsch through a discussion of kitsch's queer cousin Camp. For Adorno, kitsch is understood to be a false catharsis: "Kitsch parodies catharsis" (239). Camp can be viewed as a mode of art that self-consciously celebrates the inevitable irreconcilability between the subject and the artwork, between the representation and that which it represents, via a kitsch-like excess. Camp reveals in a particularly flamboyant manner the gap at the heart of Adorno's understanding of mimesis. Does Camp, then, engage affect in a manner that is "false"? On the contrary, I contend that Camp, as a specifically queer mode of aesthetics, produces affective responses that are anything but "false"; rather, the affect of Camp, as epitomized in drag but represented in a variety of objects and performances, is one of pain, of the suffering produced through the failure of the drag performance. Camp reminds us of the pain of marginality, the falseness of approximation, and, in this sense, the truth that there is no perfect mimesis. Adorno's utopian notion of mimesis as the disappearance of the subject within the work of art and within the other, the mimesis that is the residue of a premodern relationship to the Other, always retains in the modern age a residue of incommensurability. What might be called the inevitable "failure" of the Camp work of art is, in essence, its plain representation of the truth of mimesis. Always already aware of its own failure, Camp art mimetically produces the queer pain of marginalization, thus itself remaining other. Along these lines, I suggest that Camp art presents us with a (queer) example of non-"high," non-dialectical art that nevertheless expresses the suffering of the "repressed" and "dominated." Adorno's own understanding of mimesis, I propose, opens a door to this interpretation, paving a path for correspondences between Adorno's aesthetics and a queer mode of aesthetics.[3]

Queer interventions into Adorno's works, in particular *Aesthetic Theory*, are few and far between. Adorno's name does not appear in the bibliographies and indexes for some of the seminal works of queer theory of the past few decades. Pioneers Judith Butler and Eve Kosofsky Sedgwick tend not to cite him or engage with his work in their field-changing analyses of sexuality and queer thought, and more recent theorists like Jack

Halberstam, Heather Love, or Sara Ahmed likewise offer queer critiques of Western thought that generally shy away from Adorno.[4] There are, in fact, two major queer theorists who do make some use of Adorno's thought: Lee Edelman and José Muñoz. In his *No Future: Queer Theory and the Death Drive*, Edelman cites Adorno's *Negative Dialectics* once in the context of the queer rejection of "the good"—a mode of negation that opens a path for, as Edelman writes, something "better" (Edelman 5). Adorno is here a marker of negation. Muñoz similarly cites Adorno in his *Cruising Utopia: The Then and There of Queer Futurity* (2009) as a figure of negative dialectics. Muñoz, however, turns Edelman's negation of the future into a negation of the "here and now" (Muñoz 99). Muñoz focuses on the dialogue between Adorno and Ernst Bloch on "the utopian function of art" (37) in which they define utopia as a critique of the present. Muñoz cites Adorno here: "Adorno: Yes, at any rate, utopia is essentially in the determined negation, in the determined negation of that which merely is, and by concretizing itself as something false, it always points, at the same time to what should be" (Muñoz 37). Interestingly, both Edelman and Muñoz pick up on Adorno's trope of negation, overlooking, as do other queer theorists, Adorno's concept of mimesis or his critique of interiority in the *Aesthetic Theory*—concepts that, to my mind, could be made fruitful for a queer project.[5]

It is Amy Villarejo who in her recent monograph on queer television, *Ethereal Queer: Television, Historicity, Desire*, takes up Adorno's aesthetic and social critique of television as a way of mobilizing Adorno for queer purposes. Villarejo focuses on Adorno's 1954 essay "How to Look at Television," in which he makes a plea for facing social injustice head-on, despite the fact that seeing these things makes, as he puts it, "life more difficult for us than it already is" (cited in Villarejo 65). As Villarejo shows, Adorno offers some unusual ways of thinking about identification via looking and typology (including the type of the "homosexual"), and she concludes her close reading of his essay with a turn to Adorno's ethics of "intellectual resistance" as "negative utopia: the belief that vigilant thought can bring us closer to justice without the necessary accompanying idea of a material utopia" (Villarejo 65). Here, Villarejo emphasizes that she sees Adorno's writings "as inviting and worthy of much further scrutiny by queer readers in response to my initial forays" (65). I take up that invitation here with a focus on the moments in the *Aesthetic Theory* that reveal slippages between kitsch and Camp and that open up the affect of suffering to an aesthetic experience that is not explicitly dialectical.

There are many reasons for the lack of synergies between queer thought and Adorno, and the limits of dialectical thought are surely a central factor. Queer theory is predicated upon the notion of performance, of multiplicity over a binary. A queer perspective would offer a peripheral, askance, or askew perspective. This is not a dialectical worldview. Process is not at the center of queer theory. But this does not mean that queer identity imagines itself to be identical to the social environment in which it exists. Queer identity does not stand cleanly in a dialectical relationship to the social, but it likewise cannot be simply equated with the culture industry. Queer art, then, likewise occupies a position between identity and nonidentity, neither embracing the culture industry as kitsch presumably does nor resisting the status quo in an oppositional manner. If the dialectic in some sense always depends upon a binary, then this is surely the crux of much of queer theory's resistance to Adorno's theories of culture.[6]

On the other hand, it is clear that, as Villarejo points out, Adorno shares an ethical agenda with queer theorists, and that agenda is revealed again and again in the *Aesthetic Theory*—a work that has not had any pride of place within queer theoretical works. Whereas the *Dialectic of the Enlightenment* might succeed too well in its dialectical polemics, Adorno's *Aesthetic Theory* highlights Adorno's ethics of pain and frequently offers insights into an aesthetic experience that seems to exceed or elide the dialectic. These insights speak, at times, the language of the queer. One of the many such moments occurs when Adorno refers to the structure of the "messianic," as an order "just like the habitual order but changed in the slightest degree" (138) ("der in allem sei wie der gewohnte und nur um ein Winzig anders") (208). This formulation is reminiscent of the "traces of something better" (114) that Horkheimer and Adorno link to the circus performer in the *Dialectic of the Enlightenment*. But here the language mirrors precisely a queer (*quer*) perspective: messianic truth is in this instance in every way a replica of the status quo, but just the tiniest bit (*ein Winzig*) different. The German word *quer* emphasizes the oblique, non-oppositional nature of queer orientation, and this is exactly what Adorno describes here. A similar formulation occurs in the section on "Semblance and Expression" in the *Aesthetic Theory*: Adorno posits that even in art that is generally perceived as being harmonious "das Desperate" survives (167) ("something desperate and mutually contradictory") (109). Even the formulation ("something desperate") recalls the Camp excess of a queer aesthetic.

Adorno's critique of interiority and various formulations of the concept of mimesis likewise open the door to queer interventions in his *Aesthetic Theory*. As Judith Butler pointed out in her early queer work, the ideology of interiority is linked to a "construction of coherence" that conceals differences that do not map along a clear sex/gender binary (138). As Moe Meyers puts it in his introduction to *The Politics and Poetics of Camp*, "queer" indicates "an ontological challenge that displaces bourgeois notions of the Self as unique, abiding, and continuous while substituting instead a concept of the Self as performative, improvisational, discontinuous, and processually constituted by repetitive and stylized acts" (2–3). Queerness is a critique of the "depth model of identity"[7] created by the bourgeoisie, an interior identity that is, as Foucault points out in *Discipline and Punish*, marked on the body by a dominant culture (Butler 135). What do queer theorists make, then, of Adorno's passionate distaste for interiority as expressed in the *Aesthetic Theory*? Adorno attacks the process of interiorization that, for Kant, reflects the subject's protest against an outside force of domination but that, in the twentieth century, becomes the internalization of an anthropological type (177). Here Adorno cites Benjamin's disdain of interiority: "Benjamin once said that in his opinion inwardness could go fly a kite" (116).[8] Later in the *Aesthetic Theory* Adorno criticizes the concept of artistic duration, pointing rather to the quality of ephemerality that is at the heart of "authentic" artworks. In this context, interiority ("Innerlichkeit"), imagined by the bourgeois as an opposing image to ephemerality, is a concept that "has been compromised politically as well as aesthetically by its incapacity for exteriorization and a stubborn limitation to individual quiddity" (178). Here Adorno shares with the lover of Camp a resistance to the ideology of interiority as well as an affinity for the ephemeral.

Adorno's mimesis is likewise a concept that has the potential to open up a queer discourse. As Shierry Weber Nicholson elegantly shows in her analysis of mimesis and form in the *Aesthetic Theory*, Adorno produces what she calls "interlaced constellations" (88) in his work; perhaps we might think of them as "dialectical images" that produce a variety of intertwined but always slightly changing concepts. She presents eighteen quotes on mimesis from the *Aesthetic Theory* (there are, of course, more), illustrating the constellational quality of the work's presentation of its central ideas—a quality that invites the reader to likewise approach a conception of the ideas in the work through the construction of a constellation. Based on the eighteen quotes, Weber Nicholson can draw out recurring ideas that are linked to mimesis in *Aesthetic Theory*, such as "assimilation of the self to the other" (Weber Nicholson 62); a migration of behavior from an "archaic context" (62), and, among other things, both a relationship between the subject and the artwork and one between the artwork and its own objectivity. As Weber Nicholson puts it, Adorno "is interested in the work as well as in the subject's mimetic activity" (62). Weber Nicholson elucidates, based on the many loosely related passages she has cited, some of the central qualities of Adorno's notion of mimesis in order to reflect on the process of reading Adorno's work. In order to undertake the hermeneutic work of coming to an understanding of Adorno's terminology in the *Aesthetic Theory*, one would do well to follow Weber Nicholson's example: collecting quotations that engage particular concepts, noticing correspondences between these quotations, and distilling some shared qualities that emerge from the constellation of ideas presented, all the while retaining a sensibility for difference. As Weber Nicholson points out, each notion in the *Aesthetic Theory* emerges like a "flame" and resembles the other related iterations about this notion but is not identical to it. Weber Nicholson calls these iterations "opaque similarities" (68)—a term that highlights a queer sensibility in the structure and style of Adorno's work.

As Weber Nicholson underscores, we have at least two sets of relationships in Adorno's mimesis: the relationship between the subject and the artwork and the one between the artwork and its expression (also linked to its objectivity). A queer-inflected combing of passages in the *Aesthetic Theory* would look for points where the binary is not fixed, where subject and object are neither identical nor purely oppositional. Indeed, the *Aesthetic Theory* presents frequent iterations of the subject and object relationship in which dominance is not the primary mode at play. Whereas a mimetic negation of the subject's autonomy through partial assimilation to an other was possible in a premodern world, this relationship of mimesis is only possible in a post-Enlightenment era through the medium of the artwork. The "[m]imetic comportment—an attitude toward reality distinct from the fixated antithesis of subject and object—is seized in art—the organ of mimesis since the mimetic taboo—by semblance and, as the complement to the autonomy of form, becomes its bearer" (110).

For Adorno, mimesis holds the potential to destabilize binaries, but only via the modernist work of art, and this is one of the many reasons why Adorno's *Aesthetic Theory* holds great promise for queer theory. The potential of mimesis is its link to a premodern "magical" relationality between humans and an other (i.e., animals), and this potential is preserved, Adorno writes again and again, through an incommensurable residue that cannot ever be fully integrated into the culture industry. "Ridiculousness is the residue of the mimetic in art, the price of its self-enclosure" (119). Adorno posits in the *Aesthetic Theory* a space for truth (in the modernist artwork) in a post-Auschwitz world. In this sense, the *Aesthetic Theory* offers a response to the questions posed by the *Dialectic of the Enlightenment*: Where is there a space outside the universal "delusive context" (171) ["Verblendungszusammenhang" (Horkheimer and Adorno, *Dialektik*, 216)] that characterizes the post–Second World War West? How does one access a space and time of reflection within this world? It is the *Aesthetic Theory* that offers in its constellational form possible answers to these questions, and the artwork is at the crux of these answers. These answers are likewise linked to a mode of relationality that resists both identity and sameness, one that is dialectical but that always retains a non-dialectical residue, one that consistently produces incongruencies, and one whose central affective force is based on the truth of suffering of the oppressed: "Artistic expression comports itself mimetically, just as the expression of living creatures is that of pain" (110). Indeed, dissonance, "the seal of everything modern" (15), transfigures the sensuous into pain, and pain, according to Adorno, is "an aesthetic archetype of ambivalence" (15). How, we might ask, but in the expression of pain and in the enduring presence of ambivalence does the queer work of art speak?

As Adorno points out in the *Aesthetic Theory*, the "intolerance of ambiguity" (115) is precisely a sign of the "authoritarian personality," a personality typology he tried to systematize and analyze in the *Authoritarian Personality* project. It is precisely those who cannot tolerate ambiguity who respond to the fascist message and who are liable to become anti-Semites. In truth, suffering is ambivalent, and difference produces ambivalence; indeed, the queer cry of frustration is often a response to the "intolerance of ambiguity" reflected in mainstream cultures and laws.

How, then, do we square Adorno's empathy for the marginalized with his seeming homophobia, and even his equivalence between totalitarianism and homosexuality expressed in some of his writings? Most famously, in his critique of masculinity in the piece called "Tough Baby" in *Minima Moralia*, Adorno writes, "Totalitarianism and homosexuality belong together" (46).[9] Here he is surely integrating Freudian thought into his cultural analysis. But how are we to understand this statement that effects a reversal of the linkage between totalitarianism and the "intolerance of ambiguity"?[10] It is highly likely that, along with a resistance to the entrenched binary of dialectical thinking, statements like these have soured queer theorists on Adorno's more usable concepts. In *Queer Social Philosophy* Randall Halle offers a critical reading of Adorno's engagement with the trope of homosexuality that is based on the psychological model of latency that Adorno uses frequently in his social theories. Halle highlights the link between anti-Semitism and repressed or hidden homosexuality that Adorno and Horkheimer already posit in the *Dialectic of the Enlightenment*. As they understand it, aggressive (anti-Semitic) acts are driven by the repression of a forbidden act: "the forbidden action which is converted into aggression is generally homosexual in nature" (cited in Halle 138). As Halle puts it, "The psychoanalytic map they employed took them to the source of this abnormal prohibition: 'the homosexual character'" (Halle 138). Halle traces Adorno's use of the homosexual trope throughout a number of his works, focusing, in particular, on Adorno's critique of the latent homosexual in the "Tough Baby" piece in *Minima Moralia*. In "Tough Baby," Adorno critiques contemporary masculinity, linking the "he-men" of film to repressed homosexuality:

> He-men are thus, in their own constitution, what film plots usually present them to be, masochists. At the root of their sadism is a lie, and only as liars do they truly become sadists, agents of repression. This lie, however, is nothing other than repressed homosexuality presenting itself as the only approved form of heterosexuality. (*Minima Moralia*, 45–56)

Both Halle (140) and Michael Warner (22) point to Adorno's progressive role in the postwar social reform period in Germany (he even supported arguments for the decriminalization of homosexuality and abortion in "Sexual Taboos and Law Today" from 1963). Nevertheless, Halle convincingly lays out the troubling link Adorno makes in multiple works between a perceived crisis of masculinity that helped produce Nazism and a repressed or latent (or sometimes overt) homosexuality. Indeed, as Halle shows, Adorno was not alone in drawing the connection between homosexuality and totalitarianism; many of his social theory contemporaries (Wilhelm Reich and Erich Fromm, for example) did the same in their writings. Debunking the latent homosexuality theory that he detects in the works of all three thinkers, Halle asks, "How can a new mode of social psychology approach fascism? The problem of fascism is not a failure of heterosexuality. Heterosexuality acts as a chief normalizing mechanism of fascism. Heterosexuality is part of the problem, not part of the solution" (165).[11]

How do we bring together the multiple Adornos (the social reformer; the social theorist who locates homosexuality, always linked to effeminacy, at the root of sadism; the anti-totalitarian thinker who pinpoints the "intolerance of ambiguity" as a key quality of fascist thought) in order to take stock of the elements of his thought that might be productive for queer theory's purposes? In my view, his *Aesthetic Theory* more than any of his other works offers grounds for kinship between queer theory and Adorno. Indeed, if we are to redeem Adorno for queer studies, then we would do well to consider the correspondences between queer aesthetics and Adorno's aesthetic theory.

The path to these correspondences leads through the distinction between kitsch and "authentic" art and the slippage between kitsch and Camp (itself a queer mode of aesthetics). And Camp aesthetics, I will argue, closes the loop between the presumed dichotomy between kitsch and high modernist art, sharing precisely in the nonidentical identity that opens up access to the sedimentation of suffering in Adorno's authentic artwork. For the expression and experience of affect in and through the artwork ultimately locates this experience as a moment of redeemed truth.

In defining kitsch, Adorno gravitates to the question of affect in order to underscore its collusion with the culture industry: "Kitsch parodies catharsis" (239). Whereas Greek tragedy's catharsis had been a purification and simultaneous sublimation of emotions (238), kitsch takes this process of "repression" of the emotions further: "Although kitsch escapes, implike, from even a historical definition, one of its most tenacious characteristics is the prevarication of feelings, fictional feelings in which no one is actually participating, and thus the neutralization of these feelings" (239). In this sense, kitsch—for example, a painting of the Matterhorn or, for Adorno, any representation of nature—both produces false emotions and neutralizes/represses them. The process of catharsis is carried out but with emotions that have no connection to truth in a post-Holocaust world. Of course, the term "Kitsch" is littered throughout Adorno's writings, but it is the connection to affect and truth that is essential for Adorno. As "sensual satisfaction" (276), kitsch produces numbingly affirmative feelings that repress the truth.

In *The Five Faces of Modernity* Matei Calinescu borrows from Adorno's understanding of kitsch as false catharsis, writing that kitsch is not only guilty in aesthetic but also in moral terms. For Calinescu, an element of

> evil can be identified in the fundamental characteristic of kitsch, that of lying. [. . .] The temptation to believe the aesthetic lies of kitsch is a sign of either undeveloped or largely atrophied critical sense. Mental passivity and spiritual laziness characterize the amazingly undemanding lover of kitsch. Theologically, then, Richard Egenter may be right when he identifies kitsch as the sin of 'sloth.' (259–60)

This is a dramatic formulation, but it is essentially not at odds with Adorno's understanding of kitsch as producing a false sense of well-being that forecloses those true emotions linked to suffering that would reveal an ethical truth.

Adorno's understanding of kitsch in the *Aesthetic Theory* emerges from a series of metonymic slippages, from catharis to the culture industry to kitsch to the category of "the vulgar" and, by association, to queerness. All concepts are contained in one paragraph of *Aesthetic Theory* that presents Adorno's understanding of bad art in a series of associative connections. Indeed, just before the attempt to define kitsch (as false catharsis), Adorno calls the "sensational" Oscar Wilde, Gabriele D'Annunzio, and Maurice Maeterlink "preludes to the culture industry" (239). A discussion of the category of the "vulgar" follows, connecting the queer and Camp Wilde to the culture industry and kitsch.[12] The notion of the vulgar is linked to "every salable feeling" (239): "Art is vulgar when it degrades people by canceling its distance from an already degraded humanity; it confirms what the world has made of them rather than that its gesture revolts against it. Insofar as they embody the identification of people with their own debasement, the grinning cultural commodities are vulgar" (314–15). Vulgarity stands in a metonymic relationship to the culture industry, engendering a lack of distance and, hence, blindness to the truth.

A nationalist and queer-phobic sensibility hovers around Adorno's notion of kitsch. Adorno points out that the French have no term for "kitsch" and have produced writers like Colette, who irritates Adorno: "The most significant objection to French art, which nourished the whole of modernism, is that the French have no word for kitsch, precisely that which is a source of pride in Germany," Adorno writes in the *Parilipomena* of *Aesthetic Theory* (314). Perhaps there is a very subtle irony in the phrase "a source of pride in Germany," but in his rejection of kitsch and kitsch-associated artists, Adorno resists naming German names. The names of Maeterlinck, D'Annunzio, and Wilde are joined in this section by Colette—the famously bisexual French woman of letters. Adorno's complains about "the pseudo-individualization of novels à la Colette" (314) in his section on kitsch and the vulgar, linking one of the very few women artists mentioned in *Aesthetic Theory*, all of whom were writers of novels,[13] to a form of kitsch that tries to mask its kitschness (lowbrow masquerading as middlebrow, as Adorno suggests). What do we do with the coding of these writers (two of which were famously queer) with kitsch?

As frustrating as Adorno's seemingly queer-phobic vague associations between queerness and kitsch/culture industry/vulgarity might be, he is also aware of the toxic nature of categorical rejection. In his critique of modernist "Sachlichkeit" (New Objectivity) in *Aesthetic Theory*, Adorno calls out the barbarism of the "allergy to kitsch" (61) that infuses the ideology of "Sachlichkeit":

> Thought through to the bitter end, *Sachlichkeit* itself regresses to a preartistic barbarism. Even the highly cultivated aesthetic allergy to kitsch, ornament, the superfluous, and everything reminiscent of luxury has an aspect of barbarism, an aspect—according to Freud—of the destructive discontent with culture. (61)

Aesthetic barbarism is the rejection of historical truth, and the allergy to kitsch itself might reveal an oversimplification and a marginalization, that is, an untruth. Likewise, in the draft introduction to *Aesthetic Theory*, an introduction presumably composed before the other parts, Adorno discusses the "obsolete category of taste" (342) as a part of his critique of Kant's aesthetic theory. "Significant contemporary art" that engages its "power of reflection" is the product of an aesthetics that is "obliged to renounce the concept of taste, in which the claim of art to truth is in danger of coming to a miserable end" (342). Truth (linked to a notion of objectivity)[14] trumps taste. So where does this leave the vulgar, the distasteful kitsch products about which Adorno complains?

The realm of the vulgar and distasteful takes us easily to the aesthetics of Camp. During the post–Second World War period when Adorno was working on *Aesthetic Theory*, any understanding of Camp would link it to the homosexual. In Susan Sontag's 1964 "Notes on Camp," she writes that Camp is an aesthetic realm controlled and curated by the modern dandy and "aristocrat" of taste and the "homosexual" (63–4). Moe Meyer traces the origins of Camp to Oscar Wilde's dandyism, Wilde's study of the French Delsarte method of gesture for acting and his famous indecency trial ("Under the Sign of Wilde," 105). As Meyer shows, the word "Camp" first appeared in a dictionary of Victorian slang in 1909 and was defined as "Actions and gestures of exaggerated emphasis. Probably from the French. Used chiefly by persons of exceptional want of character" ("Under the Sign of Wilde," 75). Meyer's interest is in linking once and for all the postures and aesthetics of Camp to queer culture.[15] Indeed, it is difficult to give a genealogy and etymology of the term without returning again and again to queerness. Christopher Isherwood's 1954 novel *The World in the Evening* is often cited as a seminal moment in literary history in which the term "Camp" appears in the text and is clearly linked to the emerging homosexuality of the protagonist. As Meyer shows, prior to the emergence of pop art in the 1960s the term "Camp" would have been immediately linked to queerness. Meyer argues convincingly that pop art appropriated the queer aesthetics of Camp, rebranding it as a mere celebration of consumer culture, but that Camp can nonetheless never detach itself fully from queer culture. "Camp is solely a queer (and/or sometimes gay and lesbian) discourse; and Camp embodies a specifically queer cultural critique" ("Introduction," 1).

All of the seminal essays on Camp (Sontag, Booth, Meyer) must contend (if they do not all agree) with the queerness at the heart of Camp aesthetics, and, conversely, no theory of queer aesthetics can separate itself completely from the concept of Camp. The term is linked to notions of exaggeration, bad taste, extreme aestheticization, excess and lack,[16] the recuperation of what is old and dead,[17] and affective detachment, among other things. In "Notes on Camp" Sontag emphasizes not only Camp's exaggeration and potentially bad taste, but also highlights the way in which Camp is intrinsic to the artwork: it is "not only in the eye of the beholder" (54). This means that Camp is an aesthetic, not just a posture. Though Sontag points out that Camp is directly linked to homosexual taste,[18] she likewise insists that we cannot locate the quality of Camp solely in its reception. Another central claim that Sontag makes is that Camp's affect can be "serious,"[19] but that Camp fosters moral agnosticism[20]—an assertion that has provoked some vigorous critique.[21]

Adorno never uses the term Camp in his *Aesthetic Theory*, though he mentions the original Camp dandy Wilde in loose connection to kitsch and vulgarity. The slippage between kitsch, the vulgar, and homosexuality in Adorno is apparent at numerous points. Indeed, kitsch and Camp might occupy some shared ground, and Adorno would certainly have been familiar with the ways in which homosexuality and effeminacy are linked to Camp/kitsch style in the 1950s and 1960s. He likely would have seen no reason to delineate one term from the other.

To the extent that Camp aesthetics are linked from their inception to queerness and queer aesthetics to Camp, we are invited again to consider the potential correspondences between Adorno's reflections on "authentic" art's ability to reveal truth as suffering and Camp/queer art's capacity to do the same. A recent issue of *Modernism/Modernity* (2016) focused on "Camp Modernism," exploring the aesthetics and affect of Camp and its organic connection to modernism. Camp grew out of modernist movements and, according to the editors of the issue, Camp and modernist aesthetics mirror each other in multiple ways, most strikingly in the fact that both modes of aesthetics are "over the top," as the editors write (Bryant and Mao 2). Hence, Camp is here not the bastard child of modernist art that destroys its inheritance and empties it of value; rather, Camp is modernism's queer cousin, living in tandem with, but in the shadow of, its more famous kin.

But let us not forget that Adorno's aesthetics are deeply concerned with the interests of the oppressed: "For art allies itself with repressed and dominated nature in the progressively rationalized and integrated society" (336). Adorno repeats this social/aesthetic function of modernist art at interludes in *Aesthetic Theory*: "This is the locus of the idea of art as the idea of the restoration of nature that has been repressed and drawn into the dynamic of history" (131). The suffering that the authentic work of art should express is that of the oppressed of history. Camp's inseverable link to queerness is predicated upon the same affective truth. Numerous theorists of Camp remind us of the link between Camp aesthetics and the suffering of the minority, revealing that which is not deemed valuable by the dominant culture (Ross, Booth).[22] As Christopher Nealon writes, Camp aesthetics produce the "polemical affection for what is obsolete, misguided or trivial" (581), a symptom, as he puts it, of the "damage" of late capitalism, an attempt to recuperate and repair the discarded and devalued materials of culture (583).

Allan Pero's "Fugue on Camp," published in the "Camp Modernism" *Modernism/Modernity* issue, underscores the relationship between Camp and the melancholy linked to "damaged life": "Camp has an aesthetic, rather than forensic, relation to the anatomy of melancholy" (29). Pero likewise makes direct reference to Adorno's "high art": "Camp's loyalty to aestheticism, like Adorno's to so-called 'high art,' is grounded in the art object's beleaguered nonidentity" (29). Camp functions, for Pero, as Adorno's "high art" does, as "a glittering bulwark against the twin forces of philistinism and utility" (32). And "Camp," Pero writes, "is not kitsch. In Lacanian terms, camp is the Real of kitsch" (31). Camp is, then, the experience of the artwork that precedes culture and sublimation, mirroring Adorno's articulation of aesthetic perception and knowledge: as Adorno writes, aesthetic experience "reaches back far behind aesthetic sublimation, where it is indivisible from lived perception" (345).

If Camp is the Real of kitsch and resides, as does Adorno's aesthetic perception, *behind and before* sublimation, then how is it linked affectively to the "underinvolvement" and "detachment" produced by Camp posited by theorists like Sontag?[23] If we think with Adorno, then "underinvolvement" does not, in fact, follow from "detachment." Whereas kitsch, for Adorno, allows no distance between the subject and the artwork, creating identity between the subject and the culture industry, authentic art should produce distance. Adorno gives as an example the polemicism of Mozart that is "central in the power ['Gewalt'] by which the music sets itself at a distance that mutely condemns the impoverishment and falsity of that from which it distances itself. In Mozart form acquires the power of that distancing as determinate negation; the reconciliation that it realizes is painfully sweet because reality to date has refused it" (177). Distance produces the reflection that is key to both the experience and objective reality of the artwork and that can allow the truth of suffering to be revealed. Camp similarly produces an experience of distance that, as Jack Babuscio beautifully put it already in 1978, engenders profound empathy for the suffering of the marginalized. Babuscio reminds us that the aesthetic mode of Camp, predicated on exaggeration, artifice, and incongruencies, mimics structurally the passing and performance that are part and parcel of every queer's daily life (124–5). Identification with the "failing diva" is, as Babuscio points out, an affective and cognitive experience of one's own oppression (126), producing a moment of empathy "with the typical gay experiences, even when this takes the form of finding beauty in the seemingly bizarre and outrageous, or discovering the worthiness of a thing or person that is supposedly without value" (127–8). Detachment is key to the emotional impact: exaggeration and excess engender both reflection and emotional access.

The empathy resulting from the experience of Camp is a product of failure. The performances of the aging diva and the drag queen must fail; Camp reveals the truth that "wholeness" is unattainable, mirroring the inevitable gap between the queer subject and an unattainable idealized identity. Adorno privileges the aesthetics of dissonance; scars and ugliness function as "a cipher of resistance" (my translation).[24] The new work of art, Adorno writes, must fail in order to critique the false ideology of capitalist success: "Modern art, with its vulnerability, blemishes, and fallibility, is the critique of traditional works, which in so many ways are stronger and more successful: It is the critique of success" (160). In contrast to classicism's cold and harmonious mode of distancing, "new," authentic art, for Adorno, reveals its scars and stains: "Scars of damage and disruption are the modern's seal of authenticity" (23). Aren't these scars precisely the ones that are revealed in the drag performance, in the aging diva's mournful song, and even in the seemingly smooth pop art silk screens of an artist like Andy Warhol? His silk screens of celebrities—take, for instance, the silk screens of Jackie Kennedy or of Marilyn Monroe (rivals, of course)—are a case in point. Reproduced as negatives, silk-screened and multiplied, the beauty of these two cultural icons is ironically revealed to be more vulnerable and less perfect with each reproduction. There is no original, no natural beauty, and Warhol's use of imperfectly colored silk reproductions of photographic negatives renders Monroe and Kennedy overly made-up drag queens, ironically revealing the true labor underneath their performances of iconic femininity. Warhol's reproductive process does not produce the sameness of the culture industry but rather reveals the incommensurability that is truth.

Juliane Rebentisch eloquently links the Camp aesthetics of the cult filmmaker Jack Smith to the melancholic representation of the transience of nature. She connects this aesthetic mode to Adorno's notion of "critical melancholy"—a "melancholic perception that recognizes the transience in all historical phenomena is characterized as the epitome of criticality" (241). Rebentisch quotes Adorno from his 1964–5 lectures, *History and Freedom*: "This is a melancholy that has become active, not a melancholy that makes do, that remains stuck fast in an unhappy consciousness, not at home with itself, but a consciousness that exteriorizes itself as a critique of existing phenomena. Such a melancholy is probably the pre-eminent critical, philosophical stance" (Rebentisch 241). Smith's works are imbued with the aesthetics of the ephemeral, and, as Rebentisch writes, for critical theory "the utopian perspective only emerges via an insight into the perishability, deficiency, and fallibility of mere being" (241).

"In the end," Adorno writes in *Aesthetic Theory*, "the artwork's unfolding is one with its ruin."[25] Aesthetic time cannot be equated with empirical time: "[. . .] actually, aesthetic time is to a degree indifferent to empirical time, which it neutralizes" (107). The temporality of the artwork is both slower and faster than empirical time—both the "flash" of the dialectical image and a slow unfolding. In both cases, the scars are made visible, the experience of ephemerality, of suffering, is revealed where empirical reality would mask these truths. Is there any great work of Camp/queer aesthetics that aims for anything less?

I turn in closing to one of my favorite works of Camp, R. W. Fassbinder's film *The Bitter Tears of Petra von Kant* (1972) that appeared in Germany three years after Adorno's death. This beautiful, ugly, scarred work about impossible queer love plays out in front of Poussin's masterpiece of baroque art, *Midas and Dionysis* (1629–30),[26] a life-size reproduction of which covers the wall of the eponymous character's home. Petra von Kant (Margit Carstensen) is a fashion designer and, simultaneously, Immanuel Kant's distorted (queer) mirror image. Petra conducts a love affair riddled with unequal power dynamics with the young, beautiful, and brutal Karin (Hanna Schygulla) that takes place in front of both the Poussin painting and Petra's assistant Marlene (Irm Hermann), whom Petra sadistically neglects. The aesthetics of excess and exaggeration (the absurdly stylized costuming and mise-en-scène, the "over-the-top" melodramatic narrative, and the unnatural posturing) culminates in Petra's epic humiliation in the penultimate scene after Karin has left her. Vamped up in a ball gown and wig fit for a drag queen, lying on the floor by the phone drinking vodka to excess in front of the already overcoded Poussin painting, Petra's abjection and the excess and artifice of the scene produce simultaneously emotional distance/repulsion and empathy. The cruelty of this scene is underscored by the utopian hopes that had been expressed earlier in the film. In a discussion with her friend Sidonie, Petra had expressed the anti-utopic sentiments that "here things rarely change. In Germany things are as they are. One can't do anything about it." But Petra's express promise to Karin had been that they would enjoy a relationship of equals, that things "shall now be completely different." Of course, the Camp work of art never once indicates that utopia will be possible; rather, the negation of this possibility is always already evident in each moment. Camp, in fact, doesn't lie. What Camp brings to the table is an image of suffering that is not assuaged by pleasure but rather sutured to it. Might this be the critical melancholy that could reconcile reflection and affect? Adorno's conception of the critical and affective potential of art helps unlock the queer aesthetics at the core of Fassbinder's film in a manner that revives all the more urgently the enduring relevance of Adorno's *Aesthetic Theory*.

Notes

1. Adorno, Theodor W., *Aesthetic Theory*. All English translations from Adorno's *Ästhetische Theorie* will be from this work, unless otherwise indicated. "Wahr ist nur, was in dieser Welt nicht passt" (Adorno, Theodor W., *Ästhetische Theorie*, 93).
2. "For art allies itself with repressed and dominated nature in progressively rationalized and integrated society" (336).
3. Indeed, we might ask here whether "mimesis" is a fully dialectical concept in Adorno's work.
4. Heather Love refers briefly to the *Dialectic of the Enlightenment* in *Feeling Backward*, 9–10.
5. Fred Moten makes ample use of Adorno's *Aesthetic Theory* in *Black and Blur* (one of the *Consent Not to Be a Single Being* volumes), a black/queer meditation on music.
6. This is, of course, not a wholesale resistance, but it is striking to see how rarely Adorno's works are cited in the seminal texts of queer theory. Walter Benjamin, by contrast, is a Frankfurt School thinker whose works are frequently used for queer projects.
7. See Moe Meyer's queer critique of this model in introduction, 3.
8. "Benjamin sagte einmal: die Innerlichkeit kann mir zum Puckel herunterrutschen" (177).
9. ("Totalität und Homosexualität gehören zusammen"): Adorno, *Minima Moralia: Reflexionen aus dem beschädigten Leben*, 52.
10. Villarejo interestingly points to Adorno's sympathetic representation of the 'homosexual type.' See in particular pp. 55–65.
11. "All homosexuals know, or at least intuit, that heterosexuality is the determinate of fascism" (Halle 159).
12. In "Under the Sign of Wilde: An Archeology of Posing," Moe Meyer argues elegantly that Oscar Wilde is the father of Camp.
13. Adorno mentions Weimar novelist Vicki Baum, Wilhelminian romance novelist Hedwig Courts-Mahler, and the Swedish writer Selma Lagerlöf, who won the Nobel Prize in literature in 1909. For more on Adorno's uses and limitations

for feminist purposes, see Heidi Schlipphacke, "A Hidden Agenda." For a related essay that focuses more closely on the *Aesthetic Theory*, see Sabine Wilke and Heidi Schlipphacke, "Construction of a Gendered Subject."
14 "It is to Kant's credit that he recognized the aporia of aesthetic objectivity and the judgment of taste" (343).
15 Mark Booth denies this link: "Troglodytes sometimes confuse camp with homosexual" (70). See also Andrew Ross, who marginalizes "gay camp" vis-à-vis pop art (323).
16 See Meyer, who presents a queer etymology of Camp, "Under the Sign," 76.
17 Andrew Ross calls Camp the "re-creation of surplus value from forgotten forms of labor" (320).
18 Sontag's somewhat homophobic point is that homosexuals pretend to be aristocrats and try to marginalize others by being the arbiters of taste themselves.
19 After claiming in previous notes that Camp is not serious, Sontag writes the following: "There is seriousness in Camp (seriousness in the degree of the artist's involvement) and, often, pathos" (62).
20 "Homosexuals have pinned their integration into society on promoting the aesthetic sense. Camp is a solvent of morality. It neutralizes moral indignation, sponsors playfulness" (64).
21 See, for example, Juliane Rebentisch's critical engagement with "Notes on Camp" in "Camp Materialism," 237–8.
22 Mark Booth writes with some contempt for the narrative of the queer origins of Camp (which he is eager to dispel): "*To be camp is to present oneself as being committed to the marginal with a commitment greater than the marginal merits*" (69).
23 "44. Camp proposes a comic vision of the world. But not a bitter or polemical comedy. If tragedy is an experience of hyperinvolvement, comedy is an experience of underinvolvement, of detachment" (63).
24 Hullot-Kentor translates this as "a cipher of the opposition" (93). "Chiffre des Widerstands" (144).
25 "Am Ende ist ihre Entfaltung eins mit ihrem Verfall" (266). I use Eva Geulen's translation here as cited in her essay "Endgames," 156. In the essay, Geulen intriguingly argues that Adorno's style moves him away from the dialectic.
26 See Lynne Kirby, "Fassbinder's Debt to Poussin," in which she offers a detailed analysis of the role of Poussin's painting in Fassbinder's film.

Works Cited

Adorno, Theodor W. *Aesthetic Theory*. Trans. Robert Hullot-Kentor. Minneapolis, MN: University of Minnesota Press, 1997.
Adorno, Theodor W. *Ästhetische Theorie*. Suhrkamp: Suhrkamp verlag, 1970.

Adorno, Theodor W. *Minima Moralia: Reflections from Damaged Life.* Trans. E.F.N. Jephcott. New York: Verso, 1978.
Adorno, Theodor W. *Minima Moralia: Reflexionen aus dem beschädigten Leben.* Suhrkamp: Suhrkamp Verlag, 1987.
Babuscio, Jack. "The Cinema of Camp (*aka* Camp and the Gay Sensibility)." In *Camp: Queer Aesthetics and the Performing Subject: A Reader.* Ed. Fabio Cleto. Ann Arbor, MI: University of Michigan Press, 1999, pp. 117–36.
Booth, Mark. "*Campe-Toi*! On the Origins and Definitions of Camp." In *Camp: Queer Aesthetics and the Performing Subject: A Reader.* Ed. Fabio Cleto. Ann Arbor, MI: University of Michigan Press, 1999, pp. 66–80.
Bryant, Marsha and Douglas Mao. "Camp Modernism." In *Introduction. Modernism/Modernity,* 23, no. 1 (January 2016): 1–4.
Butler, Judith. *Gender Trouble: Feminism and the Subversion of Identity.* New York and London: Routledge, 1990.
Calinescu, Matei. *Five Faces of Modernity: Modernism, Avant-Garde, Decadence, Kitsch, Postmodernism.* Durham, NC: Duke University Press, 1987.
Edelman, Lee. *No Future: Queer Theory and the Death Drive.* Durham, NC: Duke University Press, 2004.
Geulen, Eva. "Endgames: Reconstructing Adorno's 'End of Art.'" *New German Critique* 81 (Autumn 2000): 153–68.
Halle, Randall. *Queer Social Theory: Critical Theory from Kant to Adorno.* Urbana, Champagn, IL: University of Illinois Press, 2004.
Horkheimer, Max, and Theodor Adorno. *Dialectic of the Enlightenment: Philosophical Fragments.* Ed. Gunzelin Schmid Noerr. Trans. Edmund Jephcott. Stanford, CA: Stanford University Press, 2002.
Horkheimer, Max, and Theodor Adorno. *Dialektik der Aufklärung: Philosophische Fragmente.* Frankfurt am MainFischer, 1993.
Kirby, Lynne. "Fassbinder's Debt to Poussin." *Camera Obscura: A Journal of Feminism, Culture and Media Studies* 13-14 (1985): 5–27.
Love, Heather. *Feeling Backward: Loss and the Politics of Queer History.* Cambridge, MA: Harvard University Press, 2007.
Meyer, Moe. "Reclaiming the Discourse of Camp." In *Introduction. The Politics of Poetics of Camp.* Ed. Moe Meyer. New York and London: Routledge, 1994, pp. 1–22.
Meyer, Moe. "Under the Sign of Wilde: An Archeology of Posing." In *The Politics of Poetics of Camp.* Ed. Moe Meyer. New York and London: Routledge, 1994, pp. 75–110.
Moten, Fred. *Black and Blur.* Druham, NC: Duke University Press, 2017.
Muñoz, José Esteban. *Cruising Utopia: The Then and There of Queer Futurity.* New York: New York University Press, 2009.
Nealon, Christopher. "Camp Messianism, or, the Hopes of Poetry in Late-Late Capitalism." *American Literature* 76, no. 3 (September 2004): 579–601.
Nicholson, Shierry Weber. "*Aesthetic Theory*'s Mimesis of Walter Benjamin." In *The Semblance of Subjectivity: Essays in Adorno's Aesthetic Theory.* Ed. Tom Huhn and Lambert Zuidervaart. Cambridge, MA: MIT Press, 1997, pp. 55–93.
Pero, Allan. "A Fugue on Camp." *Modernism/Modernity* 23, no. 1 (January 2016): 28–36.

Rebentisch, Juliane. "Camp Materialism." *Criticism* 56, no. 2 (Spring 2014): 235–48.
Ross, Andrew. "Uses of Camp." In *Camp: Queer Aesthetics and the Performing Subject: A Reader*. Ed. Fabio Cleto. Ann Arbor, MI: University of Michigan Press, 1999, pp. 308–30.
Schlipphacke, Heidi. "A Hidden Agenda: Gender in Selected Writings by Theodor Adorno and Max Horkheimer." *Orbis Litterarum* 56, no. 4 (2001): 294–314.
Sontag, Susan. "Notes on 'Camp.'" In *Camp: Queer Aesthetics and the Performing Subject, A Reader*. Ed. Fabio Cleto. Ann Arbor, MI: University of Michigan Press, 1999, pp. 53–66.
Villarejo, Amy. *Ethereal Queer: Television, Historicity, Desire*. Durham, NC and London: Duke University Press, 2014.
Warner, Michael. *The Trouble with Normal: Sex, Politics and the Ethics of Queer Life*. Cambridge, MA: Harvard University Press, 1999.
Wilke, Sabine, and Heidi Schlipphacke. "Construction of a Gendered Subject: A Feminist Reading of Adorno's *Aesthetic Theory*." In *The Semblance of Subjectivity: Essays in Adorno's Aesthetic Theory*. Ed. Tom Huhn and Lambert Zuidervaart. Cambridge, MA: MIT Press, 1997, pp. 287–308.

PART THREE

Adorno's Constellations

11

Art and Animals in Adorno

Camilla Flodin

Introduction

While establishing a dividing line between art and nature can be regarded as constitutive for aesthetics, relating the natural world to man-made artworks has been of equal importance for theories of art. Some kind of mimetic relation is often emphasized; through human means, art imitates, if not nature per se, then at least what the beauty of nature seems to imply: the meaningful unification of sensuous multiplicity. For Adorno as well, the relationship between art and nature, and between artistic beauty and natural beauty, is crucial. In *Aesthetic Theory* Adorno claims that "reflection on natural beauty is irrevocably requisite to the theory of art" in order to do justice "to what is located beyond aesthetic immanence and yet is nevertheless its premise" (62). There is no theory of art, then, without a reflection on what is beyond the seemingly self-enclosed sphere of art. This "beyond" is a prerequisite that has to be acknowledged, in order for aesthetic theory not to succumb to the domination of nature which directs the rest of human practice. The "beyond," properly acknowledged, thus also holds the utopian promise of a nature liberated from domination.

For one of Adorno's most important philosophical interlocutors, Hegel, natural beauty is insignificant compared to artistic beauty, and aesthetics is for Hegel defined as the philosophy of art (Hegel, *Aesthetics*, 1–2). Adorno's effort to rehabilitate natural beauty's importance for aesthetics is aimed at the idealistic belief in the supremacy of reason and reason's detachment from nature. This is a trait that Adorno argues is already present in Kant's *Critique of the Power of Judgment*. Despite the importance of natural beauty in the third *Critique*, reason ultimately triumphs over nature in the feeling of the sublime, which is caused by the human subject's experience of his own determination over nature (Kant, *Critique of the Power of Judgment*, 145). While Kant separates between the experience of natural beauty and the experience of the sublime, for Adorno they are intimately related. Both experiences hinge on the promise of "that which surpasses all human immanence" (Adorno, *Aesthetic Theory*, 73). That is to say, these experiences point to the possibility of transcending the existing order of things.[1] For Adorno, genuine freedom is not achieved by exalting human being above nature and conceiving dignity as a mark of exclusion from the natural and animal world, authorizing mastery over the rest of nature. That is why Adorno claims, "If the case of natural beauty were pending, dignity would be found culpable for having raised the human animal above the animal" (*Aesthetic Theory*, 62). Reflecting on the problem of especially Kant's concept of dignity, Adorno writes in his unfinished book on Beethoven,

> Ethical dignity in Kant is a demarcation of differences. It is directed against animals. Implicitly it excludes man from the rest of creation [*Schöpfung*] so that its humanity threatens incessantly to revert to the inhuman. It leaves no room for compassion [*Mitleid*]. Nothing is more abhorrent to the Kantian than a reminder of man's likeness to animals [*Tierähnlichkeit*]. This taboo is always at work when the idealist berates the materialist. . . . To revile man as an animal—that is genuine idealism. To deny the possibility of salvation for animals absolutely and at any price is the inviolable boundary of its metaphysics. (Adorno, *Beethoven*, 80 [translation altered]; *Beethoven: Philosophie der Musik*, 123–4)

For Adorno, the possibility of salvation for animals hangs on human being's ability to remember and acknowledge her likeness to them, and recognizing her inclusion in the rest of the natural world. As I have indicated earlier, and will elaborate further in the chapter, art and aesthetic experience play a crucial role for this work of remembrance.

The Song of the Blackbird

In the section "Natural Beauty" in *Aesthetic Theory*, Adorno reflects on the beauty of bird song, and argues that "[t]he song of birds is found beautiful by everyone; no feeling person in whom something of the European tradition survives fails to be moved by the song of a blackbird after a rain shower. Yet something frightening lurks in the song of birds precisely because it is not a song but obeys the spell [*Bann*] in which it is enmeshed" (*Aesthetic Theory*, 66 [translation altered]; *Ästhetische Theorie*, 105).[2] It is easy enough on a careless reading to assume from this passage that Adorno sees the world of birds as the eternal repetition of the same, that blackbirds and other birds are forever entrapped in nature, their song merely originating in instinct, while the song and music of humans marks a distance from the natural world. But as Lydia Goehr rightly points out, the frightening aspect lies "not so much in the song itself as in the spell within which the song has historically become enmeshed," that is to say the spell of domination of nature, which turns nature into myth ("For the Birds / Against the Birds," 104). The spell that we are all under, blackbirds and the rest of us, is thus not the spell of so-called first nature, but of human being's own creation; in other words, it is the spell of second nature.

Nature-dominating society has petrified into precisely what it wanted to escape by reducing nature to the backdrop of human affairs, calling it to the foreground chiefly when it can be used as an area of projection for socially conditioned inhumanities we wish to preserve (*qua* "natural" they are regarded as impossible to change). There is no nature that is not under this spell, which also implies that there is no direct access to the beauty of nature: "Natural beauty is the trace of the nonidentical in things under the spell of universal identity. As long as this spell prevails, the nonidentical has no positive existence" (Adorno, *Aesthetic Theory*, 73). There is truth content in the experience of natural beauty, namely in the resistance against domination that the trace of the nonidentical indicates, or to put it differently, in the promise of that which is beyond domination. That is why Adorno thinks that the sound of a blackbird after a rain shower has not completely lost its appeal to the European sensibility. But the assurance it gives us to think that there still is beauty in the natural world, that it has not been damaged by domination, conceals the suffering that is the prerequisite for this experience. For this reason, Adorno insists that natural beauty must be mediated through art: "Only what had escaped nature as fate would help nature to its restitution" (*Aesthetic Theory*, 67). In other words, only an artwork that does not pretend to be nature, or to have access to the beauty of nature, is able to do nature justice as something beyond its current reduction to myth or fate. Such artworks hold on to what natural beauty promises: that which is beyond domination.

Man-made art is thus both a distancing and an approaching of nature. (Increasingly in modernity, it is an approaching through distancing, as we will see.) Art can point beyond the entrapment in a society that has turned into petrified second nature and beyond society's false conception of nature as a thing to be mastered. It does not achieve this, however, through imitation *qua* copying of, for example, beautiful birdsong: "nature, as something beautiful, cannot be copied" (Adorno, *Aesthetic Theory*, 67). This is so because natural beauty is already an image: it is something which appears as more than what merely is, and "by objectifying what appears" art would eradicate it (67). Authentic artworks have to allow natural beauty to appear as a moment (*Moment*) of the artwork itself. This can only come about if the artwork does not itself give the false appearance of an already attained reconciliation by appealing directly to a nature beyond distortion.

Suffering Nature and Human Being's Likeness to Animals

In the end of the section on natural beauty, Adorno writes, "With human means art wants to realize the language of what is not human" (*Aesthetic Theory*, 78). And he argues that this is achieved in "Webern's most authentic works" (78). Already in the early essay "On the Social Situation of Music" (1932), Adorno claims that Anton Webern's compositions aim "for the liberation of a type of natural language of music, of pure sound" without appealing to some sort of "natural *material*, to tonality and to the 'natural' overtone relations" (emphasis in original, 402–3). Adorno regards the atonal music of the Second Viennese School, with its questioning of tonality—the critique, that is, of the hierarchical way of organizing musical compositions around a tonal center—as the foremost example of the increasingly self-reflective character of music in modernity. What Webern's music wants is "[t]o produce the image of nature within historical dialectics" and the "enigma" that Webern's music proposes is the antithesis to "all positive nature-romanticism" ("On the Social Situation of Music," 403 [translation altered]; "Zur gesellschaftlichen Lage der Musik," 742).

In *Aesthetic Theory* as well, Webern's music exemplifies the nonhuman language that art attempts to realize. "[T]he pure tone" in Webern "reverses dialectically into a natural sound" and demonstrates art's effort "to imitate an expression that would not be interpolated human intention" (78). This effort should thus not degenerate into a romanticism of the kind that believes itself to have immediate access to a nature in itself, outside of the dialectic of natural history. There is no such nature: "One cannot make unmutilated nature speak, for this unmutilated nature, a pure nature—that is to say, a nature that has not gone through the mediation processes of society—does not exist. . . . It is the task of art to give a voice to mutilated nature, meaning nature in the respective form in which it exists through its historical mediations at a particular stage in history" (Adorno, *Aesthetics*, 77). It is the suffering nature that music living up to its name expresses, that is to say, nature as deformed by human being's denial of her dependence on nature and by a social practice stemming from this denial— a denial which has led to the metaphysical position of regarding nature as void of meaning, a mere object of mastery. Paradoxical as it may seem—that is why Adorno writes of Webern's music as offering us an enigma—art that seems to be furthest from nature, like Webern's music, is capable of giving voice to it.

In an early radio talk on Webern, also from 1932 (and published later on), Adorno refers to Webern's Trakl song cycle, Op. 14 (consisting of six pieces based on poems by Georg Trakl), and specifically to the last song "Gesang einer gefangenen Amsel" (Song of a captive blackbird):[3]

> This is the deep and fruitful contradiction in Webern: the highest art of compositional technique, the most alert critical consciousness, the most conscious discipline of form, only serves to rid music of all given rules, of all bonds that are intentionally posited by spirit, of all architecture and symmetry, until it really sounds like the song of a captive blackbird. In him nature does not let itself become spiritualized—in the end of its journey spirit reveals itself as creaturely [*kreatürlich*], as nature. But only at the end of the journey and not through a recourse to what is past. (Adorno, "Anton von Webern," 207)

In Webern's music, as in authentic art in general, technique and mastery of the material does not serve nature-dominating spirit; instead, it strips spirit of the delusion of supremacy and utter independence, and makes spirit aware of itself as something created, creaturely. When the captive blackbird is given voice, the possibility of the end of confinement and suffering is also heard. That is why Adorno claims that giving voice to suffering nature (which always includes both human and nonhuman nature, as they are not ultimately completely separable) also involves the element of joy.[4] Allowing spirit to recognize itself in the song of a captive blackbird is one way of becoming aware of human being's likeness to animals.

Ridiculousness and Mimetic Behavior

In *Aesthetic Theory*, Adorno connects the awareness of human being's likeness to animals with art's ridiculousness (*Albernheit*), which he sees as an essential part of art's critique of the dominant order outside art, claiming that ridiculousness is "part of a condemnation of empirical rationality; it accuses the rationality of social praxis of having become an end in itself and as such the irrational and mad reversal of means into ends" (119). The increasing domination of nature and the accompanying exemption of reason from the natural world, according to Adorno, have not led to a genuinely rational social praxis but instead resulted in a society where rationality is reduced to nature-dominating rationality, which no longer works for the sake of actual progress but operates as an end in itself.

It is not that Adorno regards art as the irrational counter to nature-dominating rationality; art is not exempt from the process of rationalization. However, art is able to preserve mimetic comportment, according to Adorno. In his lectures on aesthetics, he characterizes mimetic comportment, or behavior, as "direct imitation [*Nachahmung*] in general" (*Aesthetics,* 41). In previous magical practice, human beings sought to influence nature directly through imitation: Adorno gives the example of how the magic priest's imitation of the sound of rain was supposed to evoke rain (41). Mimesis and domination of nature are thus bound up with each other from the start. But this kind of imitation is qualitatively different from dominating and classificatory rationality. First, in mimetic comportment the affinity between subject and object, between humankind and nature, is preserved. Second, the imitated object is acknowledged in its particularity and attention is given to its sensuous qualities, and the object is thus not treated as a generic representative or an exemplar. With increasing rationalization (on the level of both theory and social praxis) the attention toward the particular and its unique qualities diminishes; the logic of nature-dominating rationality instead follows the law of quantification, exchangeability, and subsumption. "Art," however, "is a mimetic behaviour that is captured, preserved in an age of rationality" (41). Being part of the process of rationalization, art has left behind the magical belief in directly influencing nature through imitation. However, art preserves the idea of affinity between humankind and nature (in epistemological language: between subject and object), and it holds on to the importance of sensuous uniqueness. According to Adorno, art thus implies "the restoration of nature in a certain sense, because it is part of the prehistory of art itself—the idea of art itself, if you will—that that which would otherwise perish because of rationale, law, order, logic, classificatory thought, because of all these categories, finds its voice and receives its due after all" (41).

In his lectures on aesthetics, Adorno associates mimetic behavior to the "childlike" (41) and, as we saw earlier, argues that it was prominent in the early stages of human civilization, and that art preserves certain important aspects of it. In *Aesthetic Theory*, he in a similar manner claims that "[r]idiculousness is the residue of the mimetic in art" and connects it to intentionlessness, arguing that "the ridiculous elements [*Momente*] in artworks are most akin to their intentionless levels and therefore, in great works, also closest to their secret" (119). Through the ridiculous elements and the remembrance of human being's likeness to animals that these elements allow for, art can remind us of the necessary softening of "the stony heart of infinity" which Adorno and Horkheimer write about in the fragment "Man and Beast" in *Dialectic of Enlightenment*. At the beginning of the fragment, it seems as if the writers are of the opinion that the other animals are once and for all at the mercy of nature (qua mere drive toward self-preservation) since they lack reason. But then it dawns on the reader that this image of the other animals actually says more about human beings of today than about the other animals, because Adorno and Horkheimer write, "the animal's lack of reason holds it eternally captive in its form, unless man, who is one with it through his past, can find the redeeming formula and through it soften the stony heart of infinity at the end of time" (*Dialectic of Enlightenment*, 206). It is human being who, by acknowledging her origin, and the origin of reason (spirit), in the animal world, can transform the view of the other animals as merely imprisoned in coercive nature.

An acknowledgment of human being's likeness to animals is also necessary for the liberation from the grips of petrified second nature, as we saw in Adorno's discussion of Webern's music. Adorno also links human being's likeness to animals to the clownishness of art—a version of its ridiculousness—which likewise serves as a reminder of the shared past of human being and animals:

> In its clownishness, art consolingly recollects prehistory in the primordial world of animals. Apes in the zoo together perform what resembles clown routines. The collusion of children with clowns is a collusion with art, which adults drive out of them just as they drive out their collusion with animals. Human beings have not succeeded in so thoroughly repressing their likeness to animals that they are unable in an instant to recapture it and be flooded with joy; the language of little children and animals seems to be the same. In the similarity of clowns to animals the likeness of humans to apes flashes up; the constellation animal/fool/clown is a fundamental layer of art. (*Aesthetic Theory*, 119)

The human likeness to animals is for Adorno both a critical and a utopian concept. Human behavior in nature-dominating society is spellbound, and to be able to break out of the spell human beings need to recognize themselves in the image of imprisoned animals behaving in a repetitive manner. But in the sudden reminder of their own repressed likeness to animals that human beings experience in their encounter with art's ridiculous aspects, the possibility of a reconciliation of human being and animal is also glimpsed. The reminder is therefore a source of joy: it testifies to the possibility of a transformed relationship between human beings and the other animals. Authentic art reminds us of the common past in a manner that does not indicate the past as something we should return to, but rather as a memory that can point toward the possibility of a transformed relationship between human beings and other animals in the future. Adorno connects art's remembrance with the longing for "the reality of what is not" and to Plato's idea of *anamnesis*: "Ever since Plato's doctrine of anamnesis the not-yet-existing has been dreamed of in remembrance, which alone concretizes utopia without betraying it to existence" (*Aesthetic Theory*, 132).

As we saw in relation to Webern's music, there are no shortcuts to the self-reflection of spirit as creaturely, animal-like, and natural. The problem with Stravinsky's music, which Adorno pits against Webern's in "On the Social Situation of Music," is precisely that it attempts to circumvent the demanding process of reflection by using previous musical forms as though they were untouched by sociohistorical mediation. Adorno argues that Stravinsky's compositions strive to correct human being's domination of nature (which has led to a hierarchical society from which the individual subject feels alienated) "through regression to older, totally pre-bourgeois musical forms, within which an effort is made to affirm an original natural state of music" ("On the Social Situation of Music," 403). For example, Stravinsky and his successors use "rhythms originating in the dance" as if they were "elevated above historical change and accessible to every age" (403). Stravinsky's neoclassical works in particular are regarded by Adorno as aiming to overcome the alienation that the domination of nature has entailed by going back to a presumed more original natural state. These works thus fail to give voice to nature in its sociohistorical state, as mutilated.[5]

Adorno contrasts Webern's works against Stravinsky's failure to express subjugated nature. Webern's music avoids the naively romantic illusion of the pure natural material, pure nature. Instead of, in the manner of Stravinsky, returning to musical forms from a time when the domination of nature was less intense and society appeared as less antagonistic, Webern develops the inner dynamic of the material. As Adorno points out in *Aesthetic Theory*, "material is not natural material even if it appears so to artists; rather, it is thoroughly historical" (148). Adorno agrees with the "almost universally accepted terminology in all the arts," namely, "material is what is formed" (147). However, material should not be conflated with content (*Inhalt*). He explains this by using music as an example: the content of music is "what occurs—partial events, motifs, themes, and their elaboration: changing situations"; thus content is "essential" to musical time, and vice versa: "content is everything that transpires in time" (147–8). "Material," however, "is what artists work with: It is the sum of all that is available to them, including words, colors, sounds, associations of every sort and every technique ever developed," which implies that "forms too can become material" (148). Musical material is not, then, an unchangeable resource for the composer to use according to personal taste; rather, it is something that develops historically and makes demands on the composer. Every new composition is an effort to respond to the needs of the historically conditioned musical material. A certain chord, for example, does not have a given meaning but gains its significance through the place it occupies in the constellation that the musical composition constitutes.[6] It is by focusing on the inner logic of the development of musical material that music can point beyond nature-dominating society. This logic is music's own, but it is simultaneously marked by the logic that operates outside music: the logic of the domination of nature. The increased domination of nature has involved an even more oppressed nature together with an increasingly tight-knit society (with an even stricter division of labor and a deepened antagonism between the individual subject and society), and this is something that will be expressed if the composer follows the logic of the musical material, according to Adorno. By concentrating on its own unique logic, music is able to reveal itself as second nature, that is, as construction. Only by being as subjectively mediated as possible and by not giving the illusion of having immediate access to nature in itself is music able to give voice to nature as it is in its sociohistorical mediation: broken, deformed, subjugated, and suffering on account of this subjugation. It is through this expression of suffering, Adorno claims, that the possibility of the end of suffering is kept alive, and therefore the expression of suffering always also contains "the happiness of giving nature its voice" (*Aesthetics,* 40).

Adorno's Reinterpretation of Stravinsky

Adorno's conception of the development of musical material and his focus on the Austro-German tradition of modern music has been criticized for being too narrow. Albrecht Wellmer argues that Adorno ignored the "line of development in modern music which links Debussy with Stravinsky, Messiaen, and Ligeti" ("Adorno, Modernity, and the Sublime," 179). Wellmer argues for a widening of Adorno's aesthetic theory and claims that such a widening needs to be accompanied by a simultaneous distancing from the latter's claim about a possible reconciliation between humanity and nature (180). However, Wellmer neglects to explore how Adorno in his late writings was much more open toward other directions in music than the one represented by the Second Viennese School.[7] In *Philosophy of New Music* from 1949, Schoenberg and Stravinsky are indeed opposed in polemical fashion: here, Schoenberg's music exemplifies the most advanced state of musical material, while Stravinsky's music is described as a kind of regression, which, as we saw earlier, was also the case in "On the Social Situation of Music." In both these examples it seems as if Adorno's concept of musical material is only able to account for *one* possible direction for authentic music. But in *Philosophy of New Music,* Adorno also suggests the possibility that the concept of musical material is too narrow to be able to include a composer like Stravinsky: "The concept of a musical material inhering in the work itself, fundamental to the Schoenberg school, has no strict application in Stravinsky" (135). Already here, Adorno thus implicitly admits that there can be other standards for music than the concept of the advancement of musical material. And in the late essay "Stravinsky: A Dialectical Portrait" (1962), he attempts to give a more nuanced interpretation of Stravinsky, arguing that "[a]fter the Second World War" the latter's music "entered into an entirely transformed constellation" (145 [translation altered]; "Strawinsky," 382). This allows Adorno to discover genuinely progressive traits in Stravinsky's music. As we will see here, Adorno furthermore detects these traits in passages that enable an awareness of human being's likeness to animals, that is to say, in precisely those passages where the hope of reconciliation survives.

The development of art music after the Second World War, and in particular the rise of serial music, sheds new light on Stravinsky's oeuvre, according to Adorno. In the essay, he argues that Stravinsky may actually be closer to serial music than Schoenberg, "from whom it more visibly derives" ("Stravinsky," 146).[8] Indeed, Adorno remained ambivalent toward serial music and its pseudoscientific attempt to achieve objectivity through complete control of the material—at the same time as it drives twelve-tone music's control of the material to its extreme, it also appears as a musical dead end to him[9]—but the revaluation of Stravinsky in the light of the later development in music still shows an openness toward the possibility that other kinds of music than the one composed by the Second Viennese School can reveal the truth about unreconciled society. Even if Adorno in his late essay on Stravinsky claims that *Philosophy of New Music* has been misunderstood, he also develops the argument that Stravinsky's music at least occasionally is able to point beyond unreconciled society, something which was denied in the previous work. There are thus tendencies in Stravinsky's music that point in another direction than the archaizing traits that attempt to return to previous stages in order to solve current problems. Late Adorno finds truth content in some passages of Stravinsky's works—and, notably, above all in such passages where he detects the animal/fool/clown layer of art. The late essay on Stravinsky closes with the following observation, which is worth quoting at length:

> In the moments in Stravinsky's music when feeble-minded or idiotic characters make themselves heard, for example in the imagery of the clown that has recurred again and again ever since *Petrushka* [1911], the reified consciousness, of which he was the exemplary composer, dramatizes itself without turning itself into something else or acquiring another identity by false pretences, and yet it becomes something greater than itself. He is indebted for this to that form of comedy in which mere nature [*bloße Natur*] helplessly, speechlessly, opens its eyes. It alone allows his music to suspend for a moment its identification with the objects of fear, without depicting false meaning in a rosy light. Repetition is a characteristic of what has been reduced to the animal plane. By entrusting itself to it music transforms the extreme remoteness from nature into its own animal nature. Its spirit becomes animal [*Kreatur*]. The passages in Stravinsky in which this transformation occurs successfully are indelible. ("Stravinsky," 174–5 [translation altered]; "Strawinsky," 408–9)

Adorno thus claims that in certain passages of Stravinsky's works the animal/fool/clown layer is evident, and that this enables the music to point beyond the current reification and domination of nature, without falsely claiming an immediate access to this "beyond" as an already realized meaning. Through the returning theme of the clown, the music occasionally manages to overcome the distance to nature and offers a momentary glimpse beyond mythic entrapment.

Even though Adorno in his book on Mahler is still careful to distinguish between the brokenness characterizing Mahler's music and the archaizing trait in Stravinsky's (*Mahler*, 39), he nonetheless, in the Stravinsky essay, finds that also in the latter's music there are passages which reveal the potential for transformation and which break through reified human consciousness, in a way that is actually reminiscent of what Mahler, according to Adorno, achieves in the Third Symphony. Adorno argues that, in the third movement of Mahler's Third Symphony, the music identifies with the presumed closed world of animals. Simultaneously, through the careful inclusion of a simple folk musical-like tune which is never fully integrated but constitutes a rupture in the symphony, the music discloses this conception of animals—and the hierarchical division between high and low as such, whether in music or regarding living beings—as artificial and determined by a nature-dominating society (*Mahler*, 8–9). Mahler's symphony reveals that, because of the domination and denial of nature, it is in fact the world of humans that is closed, while the symphony simultaneously succeeds in pointing toward the possibility of an altered relationship between humans and animals that would lead out of this closed world.[10] Through incorporating the constructed image of the closed and static world of the animal, music is able to break reified human consciousness stuck in compulsory behavior because of its denial of its likeness to animals (and thus also able to halt the regress into the false image of the animal as a mere reflex being). Even though it does not happen to the same extent as in Mahler, Stravinsky's music still contains instants when nonlinguistic nature can become eloquent in its subjugated condition—where it is reduced to "mere nature"—instead of being misrepresented as archaic and "pure," or as already reconciled with humanity.[11]

Conclusion

Reading Adorno's aesthetics through the prism of the art–nature relationship allows for both connecting it to the history of aesthetics, where this relationship has a long tradition, and emphasizing his original contribution: the conception that authentic artworks are capable of giving voice to the subjugated natural and animal world. Art remembers what is repressed for the sake of progress, and is able to reveal that the notion of animals as trapped in nature says more about the current human condition, than about animals themselves. This is also the reason for Adorno's insistence on "the possibility of salvation for animals": if the dominant conception of freedom as demarcating human beings from animals by exalting the former and denigrating the latter could be transcended by taking the cue from what art reveals as genuine freedom, namely the self-recognition of humanity as creaturely and part of nature, then salvation is indeed still conceivable, for both human and other-than-human animals.

Notes

1. I discuss Adorno's critique of Kant's and Hegel's aesthetics in relation to natural beauty and the sublime further in "Of Mice and Men," see especially 143–9.
2. For some reason, Hullot-Kentor translates Adorno's "Amsel" (*Turdus merula*), that is, common blackbird, as "robin," but Adorno here specifically discusses the survival of tradition in a *European* individual, and the blackbird, both the actual bird and its representation, is more typically European than the robin; there *is* of course the European robin (*Erithacus rubecula*; "Rotkehlchen" in German), which, in its turn, should be distinguished from the American robin (*Turdus migratorius*), see "Robin." *Britannica Academic*, Encyclopædia Britannica, May 28, 2008. academic-eb-com.ezproxy.its.uu.se/levels/collegiate/article/robin/63907. Accessed January 21, 2019.
3. The poem originally appears in Trakl's collection *Sebastian im Traum* from 1915.
4. See, for example, Adorno, *Aesthetics,* 40.
5. As Paddison also notes in *Adorno's Aesthetics of Music,* 268, Adorno in this early essay is moderately approving of some of Stravinsky's works, chiefly *L'Histoire du soldat* (1918), see Adorno, "On the Social Situation of Music," 406.
6. For an elaborated account of Adorno's conception of musical material, see Paddison, *Adorno's Aesthetics of Music,* especially chapters 4–7.
7. In Flodin, "Adorno and Schelling on the Art–Nature Relation," 193, I briefly discuss the possibility of Ligeti's *Atmosphères* (1961) as an example of what Adorno termed *musique informelle*, and how this kind of music accomplishes an open, informal unity resembling the way early Schelling describes natural construction.
8. In later works, Stravinsky was himself influenced by serial music.
9. See, for example, Theodor W. Adorno, "The Aging of the New Music," especially 194.
10. I discuss Adorno's interpretation of Mahler's Third Symphony further in Flodin, "The Wor(l)d of the Animal."
11. Paddison also notes Adorno's changed attitude toward Stravinsky's works and the feasible link to Mahler's music in general, see *Adorno's Aesthetics of Music,* 268–70.

Works Cited

Adorno, Theodor W. *Aesthetics 1958/59*. Ed. Eberhard Ortland. Trans. Wieland Hoban. Cambridge, UK: Polity Press, 2018.
Adorno, Theodor W. *Aesthetic Theory*. Ed. Gretel Adorno and Rolf Tiedemann. Trans. Robert Hullot-Kentor. New York: Continuum, 2002.
Adorno, Theodor W. "Anton von Webern." In *Gesammelte Schriften* vol. 17. Ed. Rolf Tiedemann. Frankfurt am Main: Suhrkamp, 2003, pp. 204-9.
Adorno, Theodor W. *Ästhetische Theorie*, vol. 7 of *Gesammelte Schriften*. Ed. Rolf Tiedemann and Gretel Adorno. Frankfurt am Main: Suhrkamp, 2003.
Adorno, Theodor W. *Beethoven: Philosophie der Musik*, vol. I: 1 of *Nachgelassene Schriften*. Ed. Rolf Tiedemann. Frankfurt am Main: Suhrkamp, 1993.
Adorno, Theodor W. *Beethoven: The Philosophy of Music*. Ed. Rolf Tiedemann. Trans. Edmund Jephcott. Cambridge, UK: Polity Press, 1998.
Adorno, Theodor W. *Mahler: A Musical Physiognomy*. Trans. Edmund Jephcott. Chicago, IL and London: The University of Chicago Press, 1996.
Adorno, Theodor W. "On the Social Situation of Music." In *Essays on Music*. Ed. Richard Leppert. Berkeley, CA: University of California Press, 2002, pp. 391-436.
Adorno, Theodor W. *Philosophy of New Music*. Ed. and Trans. Robert Hullot-Kentor. Minneapolis, MN and London: University of Minnesota Press, 2006.
Adorno, Theodor W. "Stravinsky: A Dialectical Portrait." In *Quasi una Fantasia: Essays on Modern Music*. Trans. Rodney Livingstone. New York, NY and London: Verso, 1992, pp. 145-75.
Adorno, Theodor W. "Strawinsky: Ein dialektisches Bild." In *Gesammelte Schriften*, vol. 16. Ed. Rolf Tiedemann. Frankfurt am Main: Suhrkamp, 2003, pp. 382-409.
Adorno, Theodor W. "The Aging of the New Music." In *Essays on Music*. Ed. Richard Leppert. Berkeley, CA: University of California Press, 2002, pp. 181-202.
Adorno, Theodor W. "Zur gesellschaftlichen Lage der Musik." In *Gesammelte Schriften* vol. 18. Ed. Rolf Tiedemann. Frankfurt am Main: Suhrkamp, 2003, pp. 729-77.
Flodin, Camilla. "Adorno and Schelling on the Art–Nature Relation." *British Journal for the History of Philosophy* 26, no. 1 (2018): 176-96.
Flodin, Camilla. "Of Mice and Men: Adorno on Art and the Suffering of Animals." *Estetika: The Central European Journal of Aesthetics*, no. 2 (2011): 139-56.
Flodin, Camilla. "The Wor(l)d of the Animal: Adorno on Art's Expression of Suffering." *Journal of Aesthetics & Culture* 3 (2011). DOI:10.3402/jac.v3i0.7987.
Goehr, Lydia. "For the Birds / Against the Birds: Modernist Narratives on the End of Art." In *Elective Affinities: Musical Essays on the History of Aesthetic Theory*. New York: Columbia University Press, 2008, pp. 79-107.
Hegel, G. W. F. *Aesthetics: Lectures on Fine Art*. Vol. 1. Trans. T. M. Knox. Oxford, UK: Clarendon Press, 1975.
Horkheimer, Max, and Theodor W. Adorno. *Dialectic of Enlightenment: Philosophical Fragments*. Ed. Gunzelin Schmid Noerr. Trans. Edmund Jephcott. Stanford, CA: Stanford University Press, 2002.
Kant, Immanuel. *Critique of the Power of Judgment*. Ed. Paul Guyer. Trans. Paul Guyer and Eric Matthews. Cambridge, UK: Cambridge University Press, 2000.

Paddison, Max. *Adorno's Aesthetics of Music*. Cambridge, UK: Cambridge University Press, 1993.
"Robin." *Britannica Academic*, Encyclopædia Britannica, 28 May 2008. academic-eb-com.ezproxy.its.uu.se/levels/collegiate/article/robin/63907. Accessed 21 January 2019.
Wellmer, Albrecht. "Adorno, Modernity, and the Sublime." In *Endgames: The Irreconcilable Nature of Modernity. Essays and Lectures*. Trans. David Midgley. Cambridge, MA: The MIT Press, 1998, pp. 155–81.

12

The Art of Dehumanization

Adorno's Animals

Natalie Lozinski-Veach

It is a moment of utter absurdity: a mere few pages from the end of Franz Kafka's *Metamorphosis*, Gregor Samsa, enthralled by sister's violin play, considers his animality for the very first time: "Was he an animal, that music so moved him" (39)?[1] The question appears deeply ironic, for Gregor's transformation into a vague, but distinctly insectile, shape has dominated the narrative from its famous opening sentence on. Since then, his human characteristics have fallen away one after another: he has lost his ability to speak and developed strange appetites; his sight, this most human of all senses, has increasingly deteriorated, even as his newly discovered joy in crawling on the walls and the ceiling has provided him with new perspectives. And yet, Gregor's question remains essentially unanswerable even now, prompting a particular combination of amusement and horror that spills beyond the page, unsettling all ontological certainties. For where does the distinction between human and animal fall if neither Gregor nor we ourselves can determine his humanity with confidence?

Such uneasy fascination with the arbitrary limits of the human traverses much of Kafka's work, prompting Theodor W. Adorno's observation that "instead of reflection on the human," Kafka's works provide "the trial run of a model of dehumanization" (Adorno 254). In the context of Adorno's oeuvre, this remark is high praise. Throughout his own writings, the philosopher remains suspicious of any unthinking attribution of intrinsic value to the concept of the human, since critical theory reveals our understanding of humanity to be as historically contingent as all other aspects of life under late capitalism. What appear to be transcendent truths about human nature are in fact culturally constructed ideas that emerge from as well as maintain society in its current, reified state. Within this structure, what is perceived to be true humanity in fact promotes its opposite, an "ideology of inhumanity," that relies on exclusion and violence to sustain itself (*Aesthetic Theory*, 15).[2]

Yet if the concept of the human serves as a tool of oppression, its corrosion contains redemptive potential. A "trial run" of ontological destabilization, modernist art contains such disruptive force. In the encounter with the artwork, the hierarchical relationship between subject and object that dominates our quotidian perceptions momentarily collapses, unsettling the notion of human exceptionalism by confronting instrumental reason with its other. It is no mere stylistic idiosyncrasy that in *Aesthetic Theory*, the artwork's resistance to identity thinking takes shape in animal figures. What Adorno refers to as "the salutary recollection of the similarity between man and animal" in Kafka is, in fact, a seminal component of any authentic aesthetic experience (Adorno 269). In the face of the nonidentity of the artwork, this memory overwhelms us, revealing the fragile nature of human self-comprehension. The artwork, split against itself, is both a human conception and its renunciation; a product of human creativity, it transgresses subjective intentions through its own expression (*AT* 63). Precisely as manifestations of human distinction, then, modern artworks also have the capacity to topple such anthropocentric assumptions. Gregor's question, in all its ambiguity, reverberates through Adorno's aesthetics, where art establishes the possibility of humanity only in its negation. What remains is the disquieting awareness of human animality, negatively delineated in the dissonances of modernist art.

Clever Animals

In all of its absurdity, Gregor's question is of its time: in the early twentieth century, the notion of the human had become incongruous with its former self, nonidentical in a way that simultaneously bore rich potential and the seeds of the catastrophe to come. If the once so secure binary between human and animal had begun to disintegrate with the popularization of Charles Darwin's theory of evolution, Friedrich Nietzsche's nonanthropocentric philosophy and Sigmund Freud's ideas of the unconscious brought it to the brink of collapse.[3] The Darwinian model of evolution not only destabilized the absolute difference between humans and other animals, it also challenged progressive conceptions of history. For if evolutionary adaptations were, as Darwin's work convincingly argued, non-teleological and arbitrarily determined by environmental factors, the human could neither be the pinnacle of creation nor its final conclusion.[4] A new narrative haunted modernity instead, aptly captured in Nietzsche's fable of the "clever animals," whose invention of knowledge comprises "the most arrogant and mendacious moment in the 'history of the world,'" and which is nothing but a flicker against the vast expanse of nonhuman nature (Nietzsche 141). In Nietzsche's account, even human reason, our most fundamental claim to distinction from other beings, is a mere evolutionary oddity. Independent of his physical form, then, the ostensive answer to Gregor's question in its historical context would have to be a resounding "Yes!", for in 1915 when *The Metamorphosis* was published, there was little doubt that humans were, in fact, animals. Yet even as the paradigm of a common ancestry between humans and other animals transformed what used to be a difference in kind into one in degree, human exceptionalism adapted and survived.[5] Humans might be animals, the counterargument went, but they were superior ones, rendering the difference between a man and an insect so great as to be insurmountable.

Maintaining the guise of scientific progress, this claim permitted a sociocultural return to the comforts of the long-held distinction between the human and all other species—a paradigm that Adorno and Horkheimer summarize in the fragment "Man and Animal": "The idea of the human in European history expresses itself in contradistinction to the animal. With its lack of reason, they prove human dignity" (*Dialectic,* 203).[6] Arising out of the distinction between reason and its other, the idea of the human is a persistent mirage, a metaphysical addendum to the biological corporeality of Homo sapiens. The concept's origins are marked by a knot of slippages, for the idea that *is* the human is both a consequence of the distinction from the animal and its precondition, while the idea *of* the human multiplies yet again, splitting like a cell to denote rational thought as well as the conceptualization of the human being that such thought produces.[7] Despite the self-perpetuation of this idea, which "expresses itself" like a dominant genetic trait, the human is not its passive victim, for in the second sentence of the fragment, a grammatical subject appears: "With its lack of reason, they prove human dignity." At once clearly the agent of the sentence and impossibly vague, "they" does not have a preceding referent. It enters the sentence as if through spontaneous generation—a stubborn vestige of the pre-Darwinian theory of life that Adorno and Horkheimer reject a few pages earlier.[8] The human species is not, as they write, a "freak event in natural history, an incidental and abnormal formation produced by hypertrophy of the cerebral organ," but constitutes instead "a regular epoch of the earth's history" (*DE* 184). Yet the sudden appearance of the pronoun as a grammatical subject implies a different story in regard to the *idea* of the human, as if the concept could break the laws of evolution in a manner impossible for the biological being.

This suggestion is, in fact, not without merit, as the sudden appearance of the pronoun in the text mirrors that of reason in Adorno and Horkheimer's account of human history. At the root of the simultaneous entanglement and discrepancy between Homo sapiens and the concept of the human, it is *ratio* that emerges as a mutation in and of natural history. Based in the materiality of the body, human intelligence, along with its inventions of "machines, chemicals, and organizational powers," first develops as a successful evolutionary adaptation for the sake of survival, essentially no different than the teeth of a carnivore, even if far more destructive. In this regard, reason is natural. At the same time, this particular "instrument of adaptation" also appears to be essentially *un*natural, since it preserves human existence only by means of the domination of nature. If other forms of life are subjugated to the arbitrary ebb and flow of the natural world, reason has seemingly liberated humans from this oppression, but only at the cost of imposing its own yoke. As rational animals, we may have escaped the immediate compulsions of the natural world, conquered sickness and even delayed death, yet these achievements are indissolubly intertwined with a repression of not only external but also internal nature:

> The domination of the [animal] self, on which the [intelligible] self is based, is inevitably the destruction of the subject in whose service it is undertaken because the substance that is dominated, repressed, and dissolved by self-preservation is nothing other than that very life by which the efforts of self-preservation are exclusively defined; that very life that is to be preserved.[9]

This idea is one of the core arguments of the *Dialectic of Enlightenment*, and it remains central throughout Adorno's oeuvre. In *Negative Dialectics*, Adorno continues to describe this tension in evolutionary terms:

> The primacy of subjectivity is a spiritualized continuation of Darwin's struggle for existence. The suppression of nature for human ends is a mere natural relationship, which is why the supremacy of nature-controlling reason and its principle is a delusion. (179)[10]

In its domination over nature, reason, itself a part of nature, "unreconciled and self-estranged," inevitably also mars itself (*DE* 31).

The very constitution of the idea of the human as rational and autonomous depends on the "domination of the [animal] self, on which the [intelligible] self is based (*Die Herrschaft des Menschen über sich selbst, die sein Selbst begründet*)"[11] (ND 294). In Adorno and Horkheimer's original, the distinction between these two selves is expressed in the subtle contrast between a pronoun and a noun. J. M. Bernstein's parenthetical differentiation between the two kinds of self in his adjusted translation earlier sacrifices this subtleness with good reason. His brackets allow an often-neglected truth to surface: with the appearance of rational thought, the human does not cease to be an animal in order to become something else entirely; instead, human animality is subjugated, or, as Adorno repeatedly writes in relation to nature more generally, "mutilated."

The notion of mutilation tends to appear in Adorno's writing as a figurative term, but its implementation is anything but gratuitous. When Adorno writes of the "pain of the subject, that in what became of them, in their reality, all humans are mutilated," he refers to intangible forms of violence such as the psychological suppression of instincts by the ego and the all-pervasive compulsions of living in a sociocultural totality (*ND* 297).[12] Such forms of oppression cannot, however, be separated from their material consequences, just as rational thought cannot be severed from the organic matter that gives rise to it. The dominance of reason over nature that leads to a division between subject and object also entails the conceptual oppression of the latter. Always more than can be expressed in words, objects are necessarily diminished when they are transposed into thought, which identifies them with their concepts as if these were fully sufficient. In substituting an abstract notion for the ungraspable multiplicity of an object, identity thinking insists on their equivalence, subsuming the world into categories that turn things into resources and people into means (*ND* 12). A seminal non-concept in Adorno's thinking, the nonidentical, escapes and resists such conceptualization, and thereby indicates the limits of systematic thought. Reason's response is to repress what it cannot grasp—a gesture that imbues all rational thinking with an inevitable element of violence. Adorno sees the suppression of the nonidentical as inseparable from the domination of nature on which administered society depends, where it manifests as psychological and physical violence toward the external world, both human and nonhuman. These forms of suffering are neither virtual nor self-contained; they are corporeal, even in their psychological incarnation, experienced in the flesh and imposed upon bodies.

Although the Enlightenment model of the human may be nothing but a concept, the actions necessary to maintain it are quite real. While Adorno and Horkheimer note "that few other ideas are so fundamental to Western anthropology" as the disparity between human and animal, this notion might not be all-encompassing because it contains some fundamental truth but because it needs to be continuously reiterated in order to be maintained. In *Dialectic*, such reverberation takes on a religious cast, as the antithesis is "recited (*herbeten*)" like a prayer that accompanies human history from its earliest beginnings to modernity. In *Minima Moralia*, meanwhile, its reiteration materializes in a more violent manner. In the section "People are Looking at You," Adorno writes,

> The possibility of pogroms is decided in the moment when the gaze of a fatally-wounded animal falls on a human being. The defiance with which he repels this gaze—"after all, it's only an animal"—reappears irresistibly in cruelties done to human beings, the perpetrators having again and

again to reassure themselves that it is "only an animal," because they could never fully believe this even of animals. (*Minima Moralia*, trans. E.F.N. Jephcott 105)[13]

The entanglements suggested by Adorno's thought-image run deep. What distinguishes this fragment from the common idea that a lack of compassion toward animals leads to violence against fellow humans is its insight into the stimulus behind this transference. Here, cruelty toward human others is not the perversion of a warranted attempt to maintain a preexisting hierarchical difference from other animals, but instead an effort to establish such superiority in the first place. The constitution of the idea of the human depends on a notion of bare animality as its opposite, which is justifiably repressed as an instance of the domination of nature that makes civilized society possible. The logic of such repression, however, is once more haunted by an aporia: bare animality is not an essential truth, but must be continuously established through violence in order to be propagated. Colonialism, pogroms, wars—the barbaric practices that are repeatedly enacted in the name of civilization, and therefore humanity, even humaneness, have their origin here, in reason's manic attempt to hold on to its supremacy by rejecting its similarity to nature.

Yet Adorno's thought-image makes visible how precarious such a binary is. The title of the passage, "People (*Menschen*) Are Looking at You," suggests an ontological certainty that cannot be maintained, as the text slowly strips away the equivalence between the idea of the human and its biological incarnation. Noting how racism undercuts empathy through a perceived multiplication of differences between humans, the thought-image suggests that perhaps "the social schematization of perception in antisemites is developed in such a way [*so geartet*] that they do not see Jews as human beings at all."[14] Adorno's expression *so geartet* is seminal, for it undermines the very humanity to which antisemites lay claim by denying it to Jews. The adjective *geartet* is etymologically related to *die Art*, meaning "species," and indicates a natural constitution. The line between first and second nature withers to a point here, as sensory perception, warped by social mutation, obscures the humanity of the other. Adorno's language indicates that this mutation, antisemitism, has become so ingrained that it takes on the semblance of a hereditary trait. If the concept of humanity is aligned with rational control over one's choices, the antisemites in Adorno's thought-image are themselves not human, since their socially conditioned hate against Jews is as compulsive as any animal instinct. The denial of the humanity of others, meant to establish one's own, calls the very notion of humanity into question. In its ideological incarnation, the human is an aberrance whose taxonomy is not only entirely severed from other species but also split against itself:

In repressive society, the concept of the human is itself a parody of divine likeness. The mechanism of "pathic projection" determines that those in power perceive as human only their own reflected image, instead of reflecting back the human as precisely what is different.

That such a narrow conception of humanity would even be possible in the first place reveals for Adorno that the *idea* of the human—an enlightened, rational individual, that is diametrically opposed to the animal—is by no means the same as Homo sapiens. Instead, this idea is a fabrication that serves as a double-edged tool of oppression, always cutting both ways: its external propagation culminates in murder, the final attempt to confirm the inhumanity of the other through absolute reification, while at the same time establishing the inhumanity of the human beyond any doubt (*MM* 105).

Inhuman Reflections

The aphorism's bleak assessment of human nature, however, leaves behind a small shard of hope. Instead of the current self-identical image of the human, Adorno indicates the possibility of "reflecting back the human as precisely what is different (*das Menschliche gerade als das Verschiedene zurückzuspiegeln*)." This alternative enters the thought-image in a phrase whose calm common sense belies the complexity of the issue, as if it were merely a question of replacing one mechanism with another. Yet precisely the simplicity of the sentence makes visible the intricacies that this reflection would entail. Despite the grammatical correspondence between *das Menschliche* and *das Verschiedene*, such a reflection would also have to be a distortion. The mirror line between the two terms is the word *gerade*, accurately translated as "precisely," but also meaning "straight." In the process of such a strange reflection, however, this line would not straighten but warp; in order to return *das Menschliche* as *das Verschiedene*, the line would have to become the locus of a refraction. This multiplication would align only through fragmentation, returning not one image but an infinite number of them. As reflections, all these images would have *some* resemblance to the original; at the same time, they would be radically different. Their affinity with the original might lie merely in the process of reflection, in the recognition of a kinship with the other. Yet Adorno's mirror imagery implies that such a similarity would have to run deeper, for something can only be reflected if it is already *there*. In other words, the reflection of such difference would depend on the recognition of an innate alterity within the human. But if the human is an idea that emerges precisely through the suppression of such otherness, this reflection would be inherently impossible. Perhaps this is why Adorno does not actually use the noun human (*der Mensch*) at this point, but turns instead to the less definite term *das Menschliche*. In replacing the former with the latter, Adorno's text breaks open the reflective possibilities at play by shifting away from all of the rigid connotations that construct the traditional idea of the human. In *Mensch-lich*, the suffix itself implies a similarity, something *like* the human, imbued with its qualities, but also inherently unlike itself. *Das Menschliche* does not abide by the sociocultural conventions that rely on binary thought structures, including the one that separates the human from everything that is animal. Its amorphous shape resists any predetermined definition, promising radical openness that might well be able to reflect the difference called for if the human is to leave behind its oppressive conceptual carapace.

Adorno's conception of human being is marked by just such radical indeterminacy. For him, it is impossible to determine what the human is now or might become eventually. What we take to be humanity does, in fact, not exist, at least not yet. This openness, however, is not simply a positive quality of human distinction, a comforting sign of a sanguine futurity. In its current form, the human is obscured by sociocultural structures and repressed by its own reason, which render it as indefinable and as inhuman as the true form of Kafka's Gregor after his metamorphosis (*ND* 124). Neither is it guaranteed that this condition will eventually transform into something better. Over the course of his oeuvre, Adorno suggests a series of disquieting possibilities to indicate the potential for further human degeneration, including the purposefully bizarre notion of a "human super-amphibian" (*DE* 185). Strange as it may be, the horror in this image lies not in the—distinctly modernist, even Lovecraftian—grotesque aesthetic of such a being but in the destructive potential of its technological advancement. Yet precisely this uniquely human industrial evolutionary component also makes highly questionable that such a development would ever take place, for Adorno and Horkheimer were well aware of the human animal's devastating potential when they first released *Dialectic* in 1944, five years into the Second World War. Instead, further evolution is likely to be foreclosed by a cataclysm of human origin that does not require any additional developmental metamorphoses, but can occur solely by means of technological innovations. The eventual result of such ruinous progress would be a catastrophic *tabula rasa*, as the human species destroys either merely itself or all life on Earth. While Adorno and Horkheimer's *Dialectic of Enlightenment* thrives on hyperbole, this apocalyptic scenario seems to be less a stylistic exaggeration than an indication of the one aspect of human being that can be determined with relative certainty: whatever the human may be, it has not yet reached its destructive potential. As Adorno notes, "inhumanity has a great future" (228).

Yet if reason is the compulsive force behind such progressive degeneration, it also contains the potential to disrupt this development. In its "pure form," that is, as a self-reflexive thought that would also radically call its own conditions of possibility into question at every juncture, reason would be aware of the nonidentity that both inhabits and surrounds it. Such a form of thinking would no longer be entirely rational, at least not within the parameters of our current hierarchical relationship to the world. This form of thought would break away from its instinctive domination of nature, and therefore also give up its antagonistic struggle for survival. Instead, it would recognize itself as an alienated part of nature, making possible—but by no means guaranteeing—a new, reconciled relationship between subject and object, in which their mutual constitution would not depend on hierarchical repression.[15] In order to take up a fundamentally noninstrumental relationship to the world, this thinking would have to recognize the preponderance of nature that takes shape in our inevitable reliance on the material world.

Considered through the distorting perspective of the current conditions of human existence, such thinking would be infected with more than a trace of madness: it would threaten the "predominance of the species" (*DE* 185). Yet what would such a loss entail? *Would* it even be a loss? Adorno and Horkheimer's wording suggests that, instead, a shift might take place, for the kind of thinking that would unsettle the unquestioned dominance of the subject over the object by repudiating its own systematic structures would no longer have any need for such categories as "species." Taxonomies that reify the living would have to make way for encounters with individuals, always attuned to the most minute particularities of the other. In relation to other animals, the notion of species is a tool of epistemic mastery that eradicates singularity and ossifies nonhuman lives into an undifferentiated background against which human history plays out; in relation to the human, the framework of species projects the illusion of evolutionary supremacy through denial. In this manner, the term "species" serves a double function. On the one hand, it integrates the human into this self-created taxonomy in order to claim a position as the apex of animal life. On the other hand, however, the term contains its own transgression: having established human exceptionality, it also situates the human beyond its own classificatory reach. The unexpected result of the emergence of a self-critical reason that subverts the "predominance of the species," then, would be finally to prove humanity's exceptionality by breaking once and for all with the violent impulses that mark both natural existence and human reason in its current form. If and in how far a reconciled humanity would still be recognizably human, however, has to remain an open question; in such a state, after all, humanity would reflect back "the human as precisely what is different," shattering accepted norms.

Adorno's mirror metaphor is doubly relevant in this regard, as it combines the necessity for an alternative cognitive approach with an aesthetic aspect that would be integral to such non-systematic thinking. The broken reflections in the thought-image that adjust social perception by diffracting it find their philosophical counterpart in Adorno's notion of a "second reflection"—reason's self-critical turn toward its own limits in and through art. According to Adorno, when we contemplate an artwork, our conceptual tools never quite suffice to permeate its enigma. In the aesthetic experience, the artwork's nonidentity makes itself felt in its defiance of systematic comprehension. While for Adorno all objects contain nonidentical elements that elude reason's grasp, artworks, which are always more than their tangible components, are special in that they pose a challenge to conceptual subsumption and so make us aware, even if only briefly, of the limitations of rational thought. This is true especially when it seems that we are at the cusp of truly understanding a piece of art: "If a work unlocks itself completely, its question-form is reached and forces reflection; then the work withdraws, only to ambush those who feel certain about the object for a second time with the What is it" (*AT* 121).[16] Adorno's words imbue the aesthetic experience with an objective force that invests the artwork with the agency to invert the subject's control. As if making a choice, the artwork opens itself up, only to reveal a dark nucleus that triggers reflection like a nerve impulse triggers pain. Resistance is futile: just as we feel that we know the artwork, that we can grasp it, its impermeability assails us once more. In this instance, second reflection takes place, as thinking turns to the concepts by means of which it tries to understand the artwork in order to trace their shortcomings (*AT* 314; *ÄT* 465).

Second reflection, then, offers a momentary disruption of the hegemony of identity thinking, as it serves as a reminder of the ways in which such thought persistently misses its mark (*AT* 67; *ÄT* 105). Its aim is not to get at the immediate truth of the artwork, which is, after all, mere semblance; in a corrupted world, not even the artwork with its claim to autonomy is beyond mediation. Rather, second reflection is a thinking attuned to the many discrepancies that separate its concepts from the objects that they try to approach. A reflection of and on reflection, this form of aesthetic cognition harbors the possibility of the utopian diffraction necessary to shatter the self-identical image of the human reliant on its opposition to animality—it is the condition of possibility to reflect back "the human as precisely what is different." After all, the concept of the human is not exempt from the taxonomies that structure society; it, too, is both limiting and limited. Once prompted by the artwork's resistance to systematic understanding, the critical force of second reflection ricochets uncontrollably, shattering any number of conceptual formations. Most of all, this explosive energy turns back on the thinking subject itself, whose epistemic dominance over the world collapses along with the hierarchies on which it depends.

Animal Expressions

Without such reflection, human beings have fallen short of their potential, proving true Nietzsche's dark fable by devolving into "the cleverest animals, which subjugate the rest of the universe when they happen not to be tearing themselves apart" (*DE* 211). Modernist art, however, harbors the promise to suspend this deterioration by, however briefly, rupturing human self-certainty. Adorno insist that the truth content of art is inseparably conjoined with the notion of a "changed humanity," but he might as well omit the adjective, for, as he also writes, humanity does not yet exist. We are, instead, a species, "which is not human as long as it [. . .] is fused with domination," that is, driven by the urge to instrumentalize and exploit the world and the beings around us (*AT* 241). In order to remain true to what humanity might eventually become, art has to resist what it currently is: "[Art's] humanity [*Humanität*] is incompatible with any ideology of service to humankind. It is loyal to humans [*den Menschen*] only through inhumanity [*Inhumanität*] against it" (*AT* 197; *ÄT* 293). In keeping with his commitment to a constellatory, non-systematic philosophy, Adorno does not apply the words *Humanität* and *Menschlichkeit* with any conceptual consistency throughout his oeuvre (Basnett 210). Rather, the meaning of these terms must be devised anew each time they appear, always with careful attention to the slightest nuances. In this specific case, such attentiveness reveals the marked difference between humans and humanity (*Humanität*). The latter's etymological link to the Latin *humanitas* aligns it with the kind of Enlightenment humanism that has an ideological dark side in Adorno's work. If humanity, as we currently understand it, is, as Adorno contends, actually an ideology of inhumanity hidden behind a thin veneer of sociocultural conventions, art presents us the distorted mirror image of this condition: here, the possibility of true humanity flashes up in the negation of traditional humanism through an aesthetic *in*humanity. Loyalty to human beings as breathing, embodied creatures depends on a disavowal of the kind of exclusionary conceptual humanity that is purged of any trace of living animality.

Yet how does such inhumanity find its expression in art, and what shape would it take in modernism? One thing, after all, is beyond doubt: what art *cannot* do is simply to represent humanity or nature in a unified state of reconciliation. From the vantage point of the world as it is, any definite vision of utopia would be an untrue projection. Adorno's "prohibition of graven images" is equally applicable to art as it is to society, for any form that reconciliation might take within wrong life would have to be corrupted (*AT* 241). Its positive depiction would either confirm the status quo or betray the true, inconceivable potential of freedom by suggesting an alternative that would inexorably fall short. Instead, art's utopian vision takes shape negatively, not as representation but as interference. Authentic art pretends to be more than the oppressive conditions of the world permit; at the same time, it exposes its own claim to be pure artifice and so remains true to its utopian promise. Modern art's self-reflexive tendencies have the power to pierce the mollified state in which we exist, perforating its own spell along with our unthinking acceptance of the world as it is. Rather than return an image of a better world, then, art diffracts our vision—as Adorno famously writes, the splinter in one's eye can be the best magnifying glass (*MM* 80). Artworks are just such splinters; they make visible the distortion of our self-perception.

In regard to the idea of the human, this distortion emerges especially in the kinship between artworks and animals. Throughout *Aesthetic Theory*, animals appear in unexpected constellations with key elements of Adorno's philosophy of art, including the notion of artistic expression (*Ausdruck*):

> The expression of artworks is the nonsubjective in the subject, less its expression than its impression; there is nothing so expressive as the eyes of animals—great apes (*Menschenaffen*)—which seem (*scheinen*) objectively to mourn that they are not human. (*AT* 113; *ÄT* 172)[17]

Unlike fabular beasts, Adorno's animals, thoroughly modern, do not have a clarifying function. Their meaning is not too complex to be devised; rather, their very complexity rejects meaning. Adorno's attention to the nonidentical becomes particularly evident in relation to his animals, who always exceed any signification that the text would impose on them.[18] While the eyes of the great apes may *seem* to lament their inhumanity, this suggestion is semblance—*Schein*—and, like the artworks it purports to describe, reveals itself as such. In a world in which reason dominates nature, nothing that seems objective can truly be so, since experience is necessarily warped as long as the subject denies its dependence on the object. Under such circumstances, the very notion of objectivity is necessarily a result of subjective compulsion. At the same time, however, the great apes' lament is not so easily brushed aside, either, for in a coercive society in which animals are objects to be controlled and repressed, their pain and its expression *are* quite real. The specificity of our interpretation is an imposition. The idea that the apes are mourning their inhumanity is more likely to be a projection arising from guilt and the nagging awareness, however repressed, that our own claims to humanity are equally uncertain.[19]

Instead of offering a clarification, then, the appearance of the animals seems to constitute an unexpected aside—a digression that interferes in Adorno's meditation on the artwork at least as much as it contributes to it. Yet this intractable quality is precisely the point: after all, the text claims that animals and artworks coincide in their capacity for expression. A nonverbal, intransitive language, aesthetic expression speaks only through disruption. *That* artworks have an expressive quality is beyond question, but what exactly this expression might mean and how it is constituted eludes theoretical comprehension. Expression, writes Adorno, is "qualitatively contrary to the concept per se"; in other words, it comprises part of what makes the artwork resistant to identity thinking (*AT* 111). Thus, linked to nonidentity, expression is both a lament of the status quo and its defiance.

In the moment in which we acknowledge the expression of an artwork, the possibility of a nonbinary relation between subject and object makes itself felt, albeit in a form that—at least for now—remains beyond realization.

Adorno's attribution of expression to animals suggests that they have a similar disruptive potential. Once more it is the nonhuman gaze that contains the possibility of destabilizing the dichotomies on which identity thinking depends.[20] Adorno's specific choice of great apes is salient here, for, especially in German, these animals are our mirror images. *Menschenaffen*, human apes, they are living reminders of our shared evolutionary roots, which are reflected in the imitative quality of their very names: split into two and with the addition of an umlaut, *Menschenaffen* transforms into *Menschen äffen*, humans imitate. Adorno's text, too, indulges in such broken reflections: "the subject" encounters "the nonsubjective" as "expression" and "impression" come face to face, emphasizing the reflection across species lines between humans and apes as one of many. These reflections, however, are no simple imitations; rather, they are instances of mimetic affinity.

Adorno's notion of mimesis has little to do with the term's traditional understanding as artistic replication, although it does have its origins in premodern attempts to appease or comprehend nature through ritual mimicry. Mimetic comportment, a deeply empathetic bodily impulse, is based on an awareness of kinship with the object. In its utopian form, the mimetic relation between subject and object would be unmarked by predetermined thought structures; it would be an expression of radical openness toward alterity. In the administered world, such a relation to the other has been displaced by identity thinking, but its traces survive in art. Rather than being an imitation of something else, aesthetic mimesis attempts to restore a reconciled state, in which "kinship prevailed between subject and object, rather than the antithetical separation of the two elements we find today" (*Aesthetics*, 42). In this way, art is the mimesis of a nature that has never existed, one that is no longer entangled in a web of violence and domination (*AT* 131). While artworks themselves are not exempt from the hegemony of reason, their mimetic vestige suggests an alternative to identity thinking (*AT* 54). Yet another form of reflection, aesthetic mimesis is an affective relation to the object that does not attempt to force it into preexisting schemata and so holds the as of yet undetermined promise of a form of thought that would do justice to the nonidentical.

Expression facilitates "art's mimetic consummation" by interfering with the absorption of the artwork into the heteronomous structures of the culture industry (*AT* 112). In its expression, art resists imposed meaning, so that its independent objectivity can make itself known. While this objectivity has to be mediated by subjective experience, the artwork's expressive quality shapes this encounter in such a way that it does not transform into a subsumption; instead, aesthetic experience permits the reified subject a brief manifestation of its own mimetic impulses (*AT* 111). Through expression, subject and object encounter each other in a mutually constitutive reflection, which does not, however, return the image of a harmonious whole. Rather, aesthetic expression "is the nonsubjective in the subject, less its expression (*Ausdruck*) than its impression (*Abdruck*)"—it is a negative manifestation of the other of subjectivity, an objectivity which does not and cannot find its voice apart from the artwork (*AT* 112; *ÄT* 172). Adorno's term *Abdruck* denotes the kind of imprint left behind by something that is no longer there— an absence that insists on the actuality of a former presence while also mourning its loss. Despite the fact that for an instant, aesthetic expression comes close to a glimpse of a mimetic relationship between subject and object, it is always also a mark of the impossibility of such a noncoercive affinity in the administered world. In its expression, the artwork grieves not only repression of the object, but also the reification of the subject, which cannot be thought apart (*AT* 117).

Although aesthetic expression does not actually articulate anything, it does manage to give voice to something, even if only negatively. In its impossible allusion to a reconciled world, art contributes to "the movement of a humanness, which is not yet" (*AT* 117).[21] While the expression of artworks alone is not capable of changing the world, its mimetic manifestation resonates, contributing to a "movement" toward something that cannot exist within the confines of reason's hegemony. This something is not humanity, but "a humanness," *ein Menschliches*, akin to that which would, in a reconciled world, be reflected back as what is different. Adorno's phrase in *Aesthetic Theory* is even more open-ended than that in *Minima Moralia*, since here, the indirect article *ein* replaces the specificity of the earlier *das*. While we may not have moved any closer to a reflection *of* difference with the transformation of "the human" (*das Menschliche*) into "a humanness" (*ein Menschliches*), the slight disparity between these two expresses a reflection *on* difference that keeps open the possibility of change within the indeterminacy of the human itself. That Adorno refers to the eyes of animals in both passages is no coincidence, for if the ideological notion of the human is founded on its imaginary distinction from the animal, the mimetic impulse is its antidote, and nowhere can the dual meaning of such reflection make itself felt as distinctly as in the recognition that another consciousness is looking at us. The acknowledgment of a nonhuman gaze complicates the simplicity of a binary difference; when gazes meet, the awareness that two beings look at and *see* each other challenges the attribution of subjectivity to only one of them. Meeting the gaze of an animal, we see ourselves reflected, in all senses of the word.

In Adorno, the artwork, too, has this capacity to look: "Expression is the gaze of artworks" (*AT* 112). Like that of the animal, the expression of this aesthetic gaze unsettles our secure hold on our humanity. Expression is a form of disruption, or, more specifically, dissonance (*AT* 110). A mark of modern artworks, dissonance expresses the suffering of repressed nature and so fulfills what is, according to Adorno, the primary task of all art (*AT* 15).[22] In its moments of dissonance, modern art reveals itself as pure artifice, fragmenting its own harmonious illusions along with those that constitute the social totality. Thus, art rejects the world as it is and so negatively imitates one that does not yet, and may never, exist (*AT* 131). In this manner, the dissonant elements in art are instances of remembrance of the domination of nature on which human culture and society are founded (*Aesthetics*, 39).

In this moment of dissonance, the expressive capacities of the artwork and the animal meet to remind us of the untenability of our humanity in its current form. If expression is dissonance, its reverberations disrupt the calm surface of a reflection that allows us to see only our own image as human. Aesthetic expression, like the gaze of the great apes, bears a memento of the "prehistory of the subject"—a term that Adorno elsewhere connects to our "prehistory in the primordial world of animals" (*AT* 119). This memory makes itself felt in a "tremor" in the artwork, which recollects the emergence of reason and with it the all-encompassing domination of nature. The expression of the artwork, with its vestige of mimetic comportment, however, can only educe this past because this prehistory survives in the subject itself (*AT* 113). In this regard, Adorno connects the artwork's expressive capacity to his notion of "shudder" (*Schauer*)—a sudden and overwhelming remembrance of a prehistoric fear of nature that arises from the aesthetic experience's capacity momentarily to demolish the hierarchy between subject and object. This shudder is terrifying in its reiteration of an existence threatened by a treacherous nature, but it is also a reminder of the possibility of a mimetic relation between subject and object (*AT* 80).[23] Mediated through the artwork, the shudder becomes a physical impression of dissonance, a future-oriented memory that breaks through the reification of the subject for the briefest moment (*AT* 356).

In the aesthetic experience, this memory makes itself felt as a wave of dissolution of the subject and her humanity; it is "a memento of the liquidation of the I, which, shaken, perceives its own limitedness and finitude" (*AT* 245). The shudder (here *Erschütterung*) perforates the seeming coherence of the human subject: "this shock is the moment in which recipients forget themselves and disappear into the work [. . .] the possibility of truth, embodied in the aesthetic image, becomes tangible" (*AT* 244; *ÄT* 363). This "possibility of truth" that overwhelms us is that of a noncoercive relation to nature, and as such, a rupture of the idea of the human and its violent underpinnings. In rendering both *Erschütterung* and *Schauer* as "shudder," the English translation of *Aesthetic Theory* emphasizes an important connection between these two components of the aesthetic experience: the encounter with the artwork has the capacity to destabilize the dominant idea of the human in the now by contrasting it with its past and future reflections, however blurred these may be.

The "salutary recollection of the similarity between man and animal" that Adorno locates in Kafka comprises a seminal element of this aesthetic capacity, but it is only one aspect of modernist art's ability to project the possibility of a humaneness that does not yet exist by fracturing the cohesion of the existing concept of the human.[24] The constellatory relation of animals and artworks in Adorno points us into the direction of such a disturbance, but as notions such as aesthetic expression and the shudder make clear, artworks need not actually contain animals to destabilize the idea of the human, just as nature need not appear in an artwork for it to express its suffering. As Walter Benjamin notes about Kafka's animals, they "are not the goal, to be sure, but one cannot do without them" (132). A similar point could also be made about Adorno's animals; reminders of a shared past, they hold the fragile promise of a different future (*DE* 205f). If Kafka's works present us with "the trial run of a model of dehumanization," Adorno's aesthetics reveals that all modernist art has such a capacity: in their dissonant challenge to the conventional notion of the human, artworks perform determinate negation. In this way, modernist artworks subvert the concept of "degenerate art (*entartete Kunst*)" attributed to them by the National Socialists. *Entartet*, so closely related to the term *geartet* used by Adorno to describe the social mutation of antisemitism, contains the same stem, *die Art*, the species. If the National Socialist concept was meant to imply that these artworks deviate from the standard of an accepted normalcy, displaying troublesome and unhealthy aberrations, one could think of modernist art and its expressive capacities as a form of *entartende Kunst*—degenerating art: an art of dehumanization that perturbs ontological certainties in favor of mimetic affinities. Blind mirrors, such artworks unsettle the order of taxonomic systems along with our humanity, and so illuminate the possibility of reflections that return not identity but difference.

Notes

1 Susan Bernofsky translates the German *Tier* as "beast"; I have rendered it as "animal" to better fit my argument. In what follows, modified translations will be marked as tm.

2 Hereafter cited as *AT*. Tm: "Ideologie der Unmenschlichkeit." *Ästhetische Theorie* 30, cited as *ÄT*. For a detailed account of the nuances of Adorno's negative notion of the human and its political implications, see Basnett.

3 Despite the centrality of this disintegration of the human-animal binary in modernism, there are surprisingly few studies that explore the topic in depth, particularly in the German context. One notable exception is Margot Norris, whose *Beasts of the Modern Imagination: Darwin, Nietzsche, Kafka, Ernst, & Lawrence* traces the influence of these developments on modernist literature and thought. She develops a theory of her subjects as "biocentric" thinkers,

who write "with their animality speaking" (1). In a more recent article, Kári Driscoll explores a shift in the depictions of animals in German literature around 1900, when animals ceased to hold merely symbolic value and began to be invested with significance on their own terms. Finally, while Carrie Rohman's *Stalking the Subject* is primarily concerned with the question of the animal in the British tradition, it contains detailed readings of Darwin and Freud in the greater contexts of modernism.

4 See also Norris 223.
5 One of the most horrific consequences of human exceptionalism in the context of pseudo-evolutionary thought was indubitably social Darwinism along with its fascist and racist permutations. See Rohman, especially 29–62; on the relation between Nazism and biocentrism, see Norris 23–4.
6 Hereafter cited as *DE*. Tm, Horkheimer and Adorno, *Dialektik* 262. Cited as *DEG*.
7 In this regard, Adorno and Horkheimer's self-generating difference between human and animal displays an affinity with Jacques Derrida's notions of *différance* or trace. Derrida discusses the interconnections between animals and these structures in *The Animal That Therefore I Am*. See also Kari Weil, "Difference," 112–24.
8 See also Cook 65.
9 This translation is cited from J. M. Bernstein's *Disenchantment and Ethics*, 200.
10 Cited as *ND*.
11 German original: *Negative Dialektik* 289, hereafter cited as *NDG*.
12 Tm, *NDG* 292.
13 Hereafter *MM*. German original 118.
14 Tm.
15 For a thoughtful exploration of the notion of reconciliation in relation to nature, see Düttmann.
16 Tm, *ÄT* 184.
17 Tm: Hullot-Kentor translates "great apes" as "especially apes."
18 Christina Gerhardt reads this affinity between Adorno's animals and the nonidentical as the one consistent aspect of their signification across his work (160).
19 Robert Savage comes to a similar conclusion about the reflective properties of the apes' eyes (110).
20 For Adorno, acknowledging the animal gaze is both a moral and a philosophical imperative. He even cites it as the central task of philosophy, which "is actually there to redeem what lies in the gaze of an animal" (Horkheimer 58). Here, too, there is an affinity with Derrida, for whom the penetrating gaze of an animal constitutes the condition of possibility for thinking (29).
21 Tm, *ÄT* 179.

22 Camilla Flodin offers a meticulous account of the relation between the dissonances of art and its expression of nature's suffering.
23 For more on the shudder, see Bernstein, *The Fate of Art* and Ball, "Shudder."
24 Basnett explores an alternative way in which art can challenge accepted notions of humanity by focusing on how art can denaturalize "those aspects of humanity that are understood as being naturally part of a person" (221).

Works Cited

Adorno, Theodor W. *Aesthetics. 1958/59*. Ed. Eberhard Ortland. Trans. Wieland Hoban. Medford, MA: Polity Press, 2018.

Adorno, Theodor W. *Aesthetic Theory*. Trans. Robert Hullot-Kentor. Minneapolis, MN: University of Minnesota Press, 1997.

Adorno, Theodor W. *Ästhetische Theorie*. Ed. Rolf Tiedemann and Gretel Adorno. Frankfurt am Main: Suhrkamp, 1973.

Adorno, Theodor W. "Aufzeichnungen zu Kafka." In *Kulturkritik und Gesellschaft I. Prismen. Ohne Leitbild*. Ed. Rolf Tiedemann, Gretel Adorno, Susan Buck-Morss und Klaus Schultz. Frankfurt am Main: Suhrkamp, 1977, pp. 254–83.

Adorno, Theodor W. *Minima Moralia. Reflections from Damaged Life*. Trans. E. F. N. Jephcott. New York: Verso, 2005.

Adorno, Theodor W. *Minima Moralia. Reflexionen aus dem beschädigten Leben*. Ed. Rolf Tiedemann. Frankfurt am Main: Suhrkamp, 1980.

Adorno, Theodor W. *Negative Dialectics*. Trans. E. B. Ashton. New York: Routledge, 2004.

Adorno, Theodor W. *Negative Dialektik. Jargon der Eigentlichkeit*. Ed. Rolf Tiedemann. Frankfurt am Main: Suhrkamp, 1973.

Adorno, Theodor W. "Notes on Kafka." In *Prisms*. Trans. Sam and Shierry Weber. London: Spearman, 1967, pp. 243–70.

Adorno, Theodor W. and Arnold Gehlen. "Ist die Soziologie eine Wissenschaft vom Menschen? Ein Streitgespräch." In *Adornos Philosophie in Grundbegriffen*. Friedemann Genz. Frankfurt am Main: Suhrkamp, 1974.

Ball, Karyn. "Shudder." *German Aesthetics. Fundamental Concepts from Baumgarten to Adorno*. Ed. J. D. Mininger and Jason Michael Peck. New York: Bloomsbury Academic, 2016, pp. 227–35.

Basnett, Caleb J. "Without Banisters: Adorno Against Humanity." *Contemporary Political Theory* 16, no. 2 (2017): 207–27. http:// doi:10.1057/cpt.2016.24.

Benjamin, Walter. *Illuminations. Essays and Reflections*. Ed. Hannah Arendt. Trans. Harry Zohn. New York: Schocken Books, 1968.

Bernstein, J. M. *Disenchantment and Ethics*. Cambridge: Cambridge University Press, 2001.

Bernstein, J. M. *The Fate of Art: Aesthetic Alienation from Kant to Derrida and Adorno*. The Pennsylvania State University Press, 1992.

Cook, Deborah. *Adorno on Nature*. Durham: Acumen Publishing Limited, 2011.

Derrida, Jacques. *The Animal That Therefore I Am*. Trans. David Wills. Fordham University Press, 2008.

Driscoll, Kári. "The Sticky Temptation of Poetry." *Journal of Literary Theory* 9, no. 2 (2015): 212-29. DOI 10.1515/jlt-2015-0011.
Düttmann, Alexander García. "Can There Be Reconciliation with Nature?". *MLN* 133, no. 3 (2018): 709-19. http://10.1353/mln.2018.0047.
Flodin, Camilla. "The Wor(l)d of the Animal. Adorno on Art's Expression of Suffering." *Journal of Aesthetics and Culture* 3 (2011). http:// DOI: 10.3402/jac.v3i0.7987.
Gerhardt, Christina. "The Ethics of Animals in Adorno and Kafka." *New German Critique* 33, no. 97 (2006): 159-78.
Horkheimer, Max. *Nachträge, Verzeichnisse und Register*. Frankfurt am Main: Fischer, 1996.
Horkheimer, Max and Theodor W. Adorno. *Dialectic of Enlightenment. Philosophical Fragments*. Ed. Gunzelin Schmid Noerr. Trans. Edmund Jephcott. Stanford: Stanford University Press, 2002.
Horkheimer, Max and Theodor W. Adorno. *Dialektik der Aufklärung. Philosophische Fragmente*. Frankfurt am Main: Fischer, 2011.
Kafka, Franz. *The Metamorphosis*. Ed. Mark M. Anderson. Trans. Susan Bernofsky. New York: W.W. Norton & Company, 2016.
Nietzsche, Friedrich. "On Truth and Lying in a Non-Moral Sense." In *The Birth of Tragedy and Other Writings*. Ed. Raymond Geuss and Ronald Speirs. Trans. Ronald Speirs. Cambridge: Cambridge University Press, 1999, pp. 139-53.
Norris, Margot. *Beasts of the Modern Imagination: Darwin, Nietzsche, Kafka, Ernst, & Lawrence*. Baltimore, MD: Johns Hopkins University Press, 1985.
Rohman, Carrie. *Stalking the Subject*. New York: Columbia University Press, 2009.
Savage, Robert. "Adorno's Family and Other Animals." *Thesis Eleven* 78, no. 1 (2004): 102-12.
Weil, Kari. "Difference." In *Critical Terms for Animal Studies*, Ed. Lori Gruen. Chicago: Chicago University Press, 2019, pp. 112-24.

13

Social Labor and the Work of Art, According to Adorno

Ulrich Plass

Art's Mode of Production

According to Adorno's most well-known argument about the relation between art and society, works of art negate the social order to which they belong by virtue of their autonomy: artworks and artistic processes of production follow their singular "inner consistency" (*Stimmigkeit*) (AT 9) and are therefore exempt from the socioeconomic rationalities of self-preservation, utility, and profit-making that tend to determine people's lives. Although this argument about art's autonomy is derived from the idealist aesthetics of thinkers such as Kant and Schiller, Adorno's aesthetics probe it from a materialist point of view. Here is a passage from the beginning of *Aesthetic Theory*'s section "Society" that states the dialectic of art and society cogently: "Art, however, is social not only because of its mode of production [*Modus ihrer Hervorbringung*], in which the dialectic of the forces and relations of production is concentrated, nor because of the social derivation of its thematic material. Rather, art becomes social by its opposition to society, and it moves into this position only as autonomous art" (GS 7: 335; AT 225; trans. modified).

Because much critical attention has been dedicated to Adorno's thoughts on art's autonomy as constituted by its determinate negation of heteronomous social conditions,[1] I want to explore instead the first claim of Adorno's sentence, which, although it has received less critical attention, also pertains to how art relates to society: *art is social because of its mode of production*; which is to say: because of the specific kinds of artistic *labor*

(*Arbeit*) that crystallize into the work of art.[2] My discussion is not meant as a refutation of the autonomy thesis; both aspects of Adorno's claim about art's social character are dialectically related and hence inseparable.[3] In shifting the accent from art's opposition to society to its partaking in and affinity with social forms, I seek to gain a better understanding of the role Marx's critique of political economy, arguably the most central richest source of Adorno's social theory, plays in Adorno's aesthetics. Put differently, the purpose of this contribution is to underscore that Adorno's insistence on autonomy as resistance to social unfreedom is not only a critique of the politics of artistic commitment he attributes to two of his most important interlocutors, Bertolt Brecht and Georg Lukács, and a pitting of modernist against realist aesthetics,[4] but also an attempt to account for the historically evolving meaning and function of art against the backdrop of capitalist labor processes characterized by fragmentation, separation, and alienation. Throughout *Aesthetic Theory*, Adorno theorizes the work of art in relation to capitalist social forms of labor, conjoining the term "labor" with critical Marxian attributes such as "useful," "unfree," or "productive." Adorno's frequent references to Marx's analysis and critique of the labor process as "unfree" point to the paradoxical utopian horizon of Adorno's aesthetics: The ultimate end of art is to become superfluous in a society in which unfree labor has been abolished.

Modernism, then, is the cultural expression of a state in which art remains necessary because unfree labor has not been abolished. The necessity of art is dictated by the relations of production, vis-à-vis which art is powerless: To want to abolish art without abolishing labor would be, according to Adorno, misguided "practicism" (GS 7: 473; AT 419) rather than genuinely transformative praxis. Adorno's radical aesthetic modernism remains wedded to the idea of abolishing the very social and economic conditions from which modernist art emerges. Therefore, it is crucial for an understanding of Adorno as a theoretician of art and society, I claim, to move the focus of analysis from *modernism* as the framework of Adorno's aesthetics[5] to the *capitalist mode of production* as providing the historical conditions for art's *Modus der Hervorbringung*.

"Relation" or "Affinity": Adorno's Equivocation

Adorno's repeated statements according to which works of art are products of social rather than merely private labor will strike most readers as intuitively correct; after all, the conditions under which artworks are produced are not fundamentally different from the conditions under which other products are made: Even the most private of artistic productions, the writing of a poem or the drawing of a picture, occur under conditions brought about by the long history of socially divided labor that enables the artist to benefit from past know-how and labor, objectified in the artist's materials, tools, and machinery (such as the now indispensable personal computer). Capitalist modernity, the social form that makes possible the emergence of the autonomous creative artist (as distinct from the artisan and handicraftsman) as a distinct socioeconomic type, takes shape only under conditions of a *socially universalized* division of labor, brought about, as Marx shows in *Capital*, by a bloody history of primitive accumulation that separated workers from their means of production and compelled them to enter the labor market and their new workplace of the factory as expropriated and thus "free" sellers of their labor-power. To express the same fact structurally, there can be no capitalist system of commodity production without a social division of labor that relegates private labor—that is, labor for the satisfaction of one's own needs—to the margins of society.

To appreciate the significance of art's autonomy, it is crucial to state that as labor becomes socialized, a system of mutual dependency develops. Human needs can only be satisfied by the work of others, and hence all needs are mediated by the market, where commodities are exchanged. In Hegel's words, "Need and labor, elevated to the level of generality, form [. . .] a tremendous system of commonality and mutual dependence [. . .]" (Hegel, *Jenaer Systementwürfe*, 231). As Marx argues, this commonality is mediated through the commodity form (or value-form)—"social labor" does not appear directly in society, *as* labor, but only in the objectified form of commodities exchanged on the market. Commodities do not only contain the concrete labor-power of the person who produced them but also embody the inherited social labor on which the individual producer drew during the process of production, such as skills and knowledge learned from others and tools and machinery developed and made by others. Therefore, Marx states, "To produce a commodity, a certain amount of labour must be bestowed upon it, or worked up in it. And I say not only *Labour*, but *Social Labour*." And he goes on to explain what he means by "social labor":

> A man who produces an article for his own immediate use, to consume it himself, creates a *product*, but not a *commodity*. As a self-sustaining producer, he has nothing to do with society. But to produce a *commodity*, a man must not only produce an article satisfying some *social* want, but his labour itself must form part and parcel of the total sum of labour, expended by society. It must be subordinate to the *Division of Labour within Society*. It is nothing without the other divisions of labour, and, on its part, is required to *integrate* them. (Marx, "Value, Price and Profit," 406)

Without a specialized and technologically enhanced division of labor, a system of capital accumulation for its own sake could not have come into being; by the same token, autonomous art would not have evolved, either, because it is precisely in response to the increase in labor productivity, the growth of wealth in the form of accumulated capital, and the rise of the bourgeois class that new social needs for leisure and play developed. As Peter Bürger puts it,

> The evolution of art as a distinct subsystem that began with l'art pour l'art and was carried to its conclusion in Aestheticism must be seen in connection with the tendency toward the division of labor underway in bourgeois society. The fully evolved, distinct subsystem "art" is simultaneously one whose individual products tend to no longer take on any social function. (Bürger 32)

Unlike Bürger, Adorno does not unequivocally endorse the idea according to which art's social function consists precisely in its lack of function and purpose. On occasion, Adorno does replicate this thesis, perhaps most powerfully when he toys with the idea that "artworks are in fact absolute commodities" because they have abandoned the ideological illusion of serving a social good and instead admit, truthfully, that they exist only "for those who hold power," that is, for the capitalists overseeing the production and distribution of commodities (AT 236). In this chapter, however, I am interested in how Adorno theorizes artistic work as a productive force subject to the same historical tendencies as commodity-producing industrial labor. Arguing sociohistorically, Adorno does not exempt art and artistic production from the evolution of nonartistic productive forces.

> The productive forces, in the last analysis, are human forces and as such are identical too, in all areas. The subjects on whose faculties the material form of production always depends are historically concrete, formed in their turn by the total society of their time; they are not absolutely other subjects than the makers of works of art. [. . .] However much the groups may be estranged by the division of labor, all individuals working in each phase are socially joined, no matter what they are working on. Their work, even the artist's most individual one in his own consciousness, is always "social labor" [Adorno's scare quotes]; the determining subject is far more of a total social subject [*Gesamtsubjekt*] than privileged brain workers in their individualistic delusion and arrogance would like. (Adorno, *Sociology of Music*, 201–2/GS 14: 403; translation modified)

This passage is taken from the chapter "mediations" in Adorno's *Sociology of Music*. As the concept of "mediation" implies, Adorno's insistence on the *general* identity of human productive forces is countenanced by his seemingly contradictory insistence that musical production is not to be equated with material production: "[The latter] is constitutively different from an aesthetic formation [*Gebilde*]," because art cannot be reduced to a thing; artistic production, Adorno notes, is primarily nonmaterial production. Without the hierarchical separation of mental and manual labor, art would not have come into existence in the first place. Adorno's adamant use of the Marxian terms "production" and "productive forces" in relation to artistic making indicates an equivocation that one can observe from his earliest to his latest aesthetic writings. For instance, in *Aesthetic Theory*'s section "Mediation of Art and Society," Adorno vacillates between describing works of art as products of social labor and describing artistic productive forces as being "related to" and having an "affinity" with social production (AT 236).

A similar equivocation marks one of Adorno's first attempts to theorize the commodity-character of artworks. In his 1938 essay "On the Fetishism in Music and the Regression of Listening," Adorno claims that "all contemporary musical life is dominated by the commodity form" (*Culture Industry*, 37) and underscores, "The application of the category of the commodity is not an analogy. Indeed, the exchange of 'cultural goods,' however mediated, terminates in material things: opera and concert tickets, piano reductions of popular hits, gramophone records, radios and, fully so in America, the objects to whose praise the musical performances contribute" ("Über den Fetischcharakter," 330; my translation). Without much ado, Adorno's point here is "vulgarly" materialist: beneath the veneer of cultural values, there lurks the profit motive. Far from being autonomous, artworks serve the economic functions of advertising, of creating new needs and hence of satisfying new forms of consumption, such as the solitary reception of music in one's living room rather than in a public setting.

In a long letter to Adorno and Horkheimer, the literary critic and social theorist Hans Mayer faulted Adorno's essay for offering merely suggestive analogies rather than genuinely striking dialectical mediations between economic and aesthetic categories. In their response to Mayer's criticism, Adorno and Horkheimer conceded the "immeasurable difficulties" of such mediations and suggested that most "mediating concepts of the bourgeois sciences" (Adorno/Mayer, "Dokumentation einer Kontroverse," 404) could be unmasked as ideological by grounding them, as Marx did, in the process of production itself. Still, Mayer's criticism had a lasting effect: in the 1956 republication of his essay, Adorno omitted the passage in which he had preemptively dismissed the anticipated reproach of offering mere analogies between economic and aesthetic categories. Nonetheless, rather than retreating from Marxian concepts, Adorno's postwar work indicates that he hoped to find material categories that would allow the sort of persuasive mediation between aesthetic and social form that Mayer found missing in his fetishism essay.

Productive Labor and the Culture Industry

In a 1963 lecture on Marx's materialism, Adorno discusses two meanings of the concept of productive labor that inform his understanding of artistic labor. Adorno first cites Marx's quintessentially Hegelian concept of labor as a *transformative* activity: "The [labor] process is extinguished in the object. [. . .] Labour has become bound up in its object: labour has been objectified [. . .]. The worker has spun, and the product is a spinning" (Marx, *Capital*, 287; cited in PT 270). In this first sense of the concept, labor is productive when human labor-power, aided by instruments, affects a change in the materials and objects provided by nature. "The product of [this] process is a use-value, a piece of natural material adapted to human needs by means of a change in its form" (*Capital*, 287). Although artistic labor is frequently unintentional labor and hence most akin to "the free play of [a human being's] own physical and mental powers" (*Capital*, 284), Adorno nonetheless claims a historical evolution of art from use-value to exchange-value. Yet this development is not an absolute "historical law" but rather a tendency, a never fully completed shift from art as use-value to art as exchange-value. This "transvaluation" occurs in tandem with the unfolding of the "occult ability" of value to become "self-valorizing value," operating as an "automatic subject" that shapes the social form of modernity (*Capital*, 255). As Adorno underscores in his lecture on Marx, "productive labor" under capitalism no longer means the production of useful objects; rather "in bourgeois society, only labor that creates capital and possesses exchange-value is considered productive" (PT 275). Adorno illustrates the capitalist distinction between productive and unproductive labor by citing Marx's famous depiction of how Milton wrote *Paradise Lost*: "Milton produced *Paradise Lost* as a silkworm produces silk, as the activation of *his* own nature" (*Capital*, 1044; cited in PT 275–6).

Marx's example shows that from the point of view of capital accumulation, the productivity of labor bears no relation to the concrete object labor produces: "[L]abour with the same content can be either productive or unproductive. For instance, Milton, who wrote *Paradise Lost*, was an unproductive worker" (1044; cited in PT 275). Adorno follows Marx in underscoring that, in capitalism, the "essence" or value of artistic productivity is not to be found in the labor itself but rather in how totally the process of production has been subsumed under exigencies demanded by the value-form (see PT 274): "[Milton] later sold his product for £5 and thus became a merchant. But the literary proletarian of Leipzig who produces books, such as compendia on political economy, at the behest of his publisher is pretty nearly a *productive worker* since his production is taken over by capital and only occurs in order to increase it" (1044; cited in PT 275–6). This distinction is crucial for contextualizing Adorno's claim that artistic labor is social labor: In Milton's case, the artist product becomes a commodity only in the sphere of circulation. The poet's artistic labor remains private and unwaged and, as the silkworm metaphor suggests, almost instinctively natural; and so Milton's creative work process remains non-alienated. In the case of a writer employed to produce articles or books under conditions heteronomously imposed upon them, artistic production assumes *from the start* the alienated form of waged commodity production, requiring an industrialized work process in which all labor can yield a steady output of surplus-value. Marx refers to the first as "formal subsumption" and to the latter as "real subsumption" (645), and he illustrates this distinction as follows: "A singer who sings like a bird is an unproductive worker. If she sells her song for money, she is to that extent a wage-labourer or merchant. But if the same singer is engaged by an entrepreneur who makes her sing to make money, then she becomes a productive worker, since she produces capital directly" (1044; cited in PT 275).[6]

In his collaboration with Max Horkheimer, Adorno coined the term "culture industry" to describe precisely this tendency toward a real subsumption of artistic production under capital. Rather than a fixed and static form of cultural production, the term "culture industry" indicates a historical transformation of artistic labor's process and scale, over the course of which the imperative to accumulate capital acquires an increasingly "direct control over the labour process" (*Capital,* 645). The industrial mode of artistic production changes the entire social mode in which art is produced. Arguably, the real subsumption of labor under capital not only eradicates obsolete individualistic methods of artistic production but also paves the way for new forms of socialized labor to emerge that are not necessarily always hierarchically organized—a possibility that Adorno concedes in *Aesthetic Theory*: "Collective modes of production by small groups are already conceivable, and in some media even requisite" (259).[7] In this vein, Benjamin and Brecht saw in the production and reception of film, a large-scale mode of artistic production that requires an industrial division of labor, the possibility of rehearsing new forms of social labor: more collective and more horizontal than the established bourgeois arts. Although Adorno rejected this view as too optimistic because it did not sufficiently take into account the monopolistic relations of production embodied in the Hollywood studio system, he nonetheless emphasized, in his collaboration with Hanns Eisler, the possibility of a transformed, collective mode of artistic labor.[8] In a similar vein, modernist art on par with the highest level of the technical division of labor entails, in contrast to the "silkworm-like" unconscious labor of the private poet, conscious planning, and it does so precisely where it is seemingly at its most spontaneous and free, that is, when it experiments: "The . . . idea of the experimental . . . transfers from science to art the conscious control over materials" (*AT* 37).

Art's Self-Reification

In conceptualizing works of art as products of social labor, Adorno draws on Marx's summing up the gist of Hegel's *Phenomenology of Spirit*:

> The importance of Hegel's *Phenomenology* . . . lies in the fact that Hegel conceives the self-creation of man [*Selbsterzeugung des Menschen*] as a process, objectification as loss of object [*Vergegenständlichung als Entgegenständlichung*], as alienation and as supercession of this alienation; that he therefore grasps the nature of *labour* and conceives objective man—true, because real man—as the product of his *own labour*. (*Early Writings*, 385–6, emphasis in original)

Marx credits Hegel for conceptualizing the dual character of human labor as, on the one hand, the alienation or objectification of human labor-power, and, on the other hand, self-creation through this very process of alienation. But he criticizes that Hegel's notion of labor is limited to "abstract mental labour" (386). Similarly, in his essay "Aspects of Hegel's Philosophy," Adorno insists that Hegel's formulation of "the labor of the concept" means that to read Hegel correctly entails "translating Hegel's concept of spirit into social labor" (*Three Studies*, 18). In *Aesthetic Theory*, Adorno likewise "translates" the concept of the artwork into a product of social labor. Adorno's debt to Hegel's dialectics is doubly reflected in his aesthetics: At the particular level of experiencing an artwork, Adorno insists that all aesthetic experience terminates in judgment and concept (AT 245)—and thus aesthetic experience, however enigmatic, is structurally analogous to the journey of spirit coming fully to know itself as outlined in Hegel's phenomenology. At the level of universality, art is itself a historical phenomenon, and Adorno follows Hegel quite faithfully in noting art's becoming increasingly conceptual and reflective: "Philosophy and art converge in their truth content: The progressive self-unfolding truth of the artwork is none other than the truth of the philosophical concept" (AT 130). Nonetheless, rather than restating Hegel's progressive evolution of art as "the self-unfolding Idea of beauty" (*Aesthetics*, 97), Adorno insists on there being an unintelligible aesthetic remainder that no labor of the concept can ever transform into thought: "Artworks that unfold to contemplation and thought without any remainder are not artworks" (AT 121).

For Adorno, it is precisely this nonconceptual remnant in works of art rather than the synthesis of experience and knowledge that attests to the truth-value of art. This truth-value is contradictory, and its contradictory character cannot be fully grasped as an immanent aesthetic matter, simply because for Adorno artworks can only be artworks by virtue of being somehow other than the "regular" objects that make up human reality.

But because they are also products of social labor, works of art lead a precarious existence: they are at risk of becoming commodities like all others, and Adorno notes that they survive only by doing to themselves what society is already doing to them—"Art keeps itself alive" when it "reifies itself" (AT 226). Throughout AT, Adorno pursues a double strategy of keeping art alive: On the one hand, he pursues an almost "realist" or reflective aesthetics that reads artworks as incorporating, in their form, the very social contradictions at the core of the capitalist mode of production. As he puts it in his *Philosophy of New Music*, "The works themselves are successful to the extent that they shape the contradiction and in this shaping allow the contradiction to reappear in the marks of their own imperfection" (24). On the other hand, Adorno insists that this structural doubling of social contradictions in artworks does not affirm but rather negates and critiques them—to the point where artworks run the risk of ceasing to be works of art at all: "the force of the contradiction defies the forming process and destroys the works" (24). Dialectically, it is this fracturing of artistic form that accounts for the success of art as critique. Put differently, the "labor" performed by works of art is both the alienated labor of social reproduction of the status quo, the bad universal, and the (second-order) labor of "pure means": the more artworks replicate an (inherently irrational) capitalist logic of "production for the sake of production" (*Capital*, 742) and the more they labor for the sake of laboring, the closer they move, paradoxically, to articulating freedom from the abstract domination of the law of value—I will return to this thesis in my conclusion.

Artistic Labor: Concrete *and* Abstract

Despite the deceptively static appearance of Adorno's syntax, his aesthetic theory conceives of the dual character of art as contradictory movement, pulling, as it were, in two directions simultaneously. As products of social labor, artworks are like other social objects—in Adorno's depiction, their growing identity with society looks like reconciliation, but is actually compulsion (*Three Studies,* 20). As autonomous products without a clearly defined social use, however, works of art lag behind the technological and economic progress of society. What art is becomes uncertain, and therefore Adorno begins *Aesthetic Theory* by observing "that nothing concerning art is self-evident anymore," and states "For absolute freedom in art, always limited to a particular, comes into contradiction with the perennial unfreedom of the whole" (AT 1). Adorno's reference to "unfreedom of the whole" is not a reference to any particular political order and its specific limitations on individual freedoms. Rather, Adorno is drawing on Hegel's concept of alienated labor, according to which "the world as a whole [is] the product of labor" (*Three Studies*, 45):

> As the unity of human subjects who reproduce the life of the species through their labor, things come into being within society objectively, independent of reflection, without regard to the specific qualities of those who labor or the products of labor. The principle of the equivalence of social labor makes society in its modern bourgeois sense both something abstract and the most real thing of all, just what Hegel says of the emphatic notion of the concept. (*Three Studies*, 20)

In his lectures on *The Philosophy of Spirit* (1805–6), Hegel argued that as the instruments, uses, and aims of labor become more varied, more specialized, and more sophisticated, not only labor but social reality as a whole becomes more alienated and more abstract:

> [The individual] labors for the needs of many, and so does everyone. Each satisfies the needs of many and the satisfaction of one's own many particular needs is the labor of many others. Since his labor is abstract in this way, he behaves as an abstract I [. . .] not as an all-encompassing Spirit, rich in content, ruling a broad range and being master of it; but rather, having no concrete labor, his power consists in analyzing, in abstracting, dissecting the concrete world into its many abstract aspects. (*Hegel and the Human Spirit*, 121)

In depicting the emergence of modernity as a progressive, totalizing process of abstracting from the concrete and particular, Hegel is not advancing an idealist claim but rather anticipates Marx's critique of the capitalist mode of production as bringing forth a social reality, the constitutive parts of which are related to one another abstractly, through the market and thus through the "appearance-form" of abstract labor: exchange-value. Bearing in mind the materialist dimension of Hegel's dialectics, when Adorno "translates" Hegel's *Phenomenology of Spirit* into sociological terms, he actually only retranslates the *Phenomenology* into an earlier stage of Hegel's thought. Crucially, in moving back and forth between the more concrete economic and the more abstract speculative dimension of Hegel's dialectic, Adorno finds a model for the dialectical motion of his aesthetic theory: Because the tension between artworks as social facts and as autonomous *Gebilde* (built forms or shapes) is not static and not absolute but mediated socially, labor is not only the power that makes and shapes artworks but is also the mediating social force that keeps works of art alive in their very contradictoriness. In other words, artistic labor is both concrete—it creates particular works of art—and abstract: it automatically subsumes the particulars it creates under a preexisting social category that renders them identifiable and experientiable as works of art. This can be expressed in a somewhat abbreviated fashion: abstract artistic labor both alienates artworks from their concrete being by producing them as "artworks" and renders them socially real as *artworks* precisely by virtue of this abstraction.

Neither Declinist nor Elitist

It is important to underscore that two prevalent and usually directly interrelated popular views of Adorno's aesthetics often voiced in conversations and Q&As after lectures miss the mark: Adorno is neither interested in a declinist critique that merely bemoans the commercialization and commodification of artworks nor interested in an elitist veneration of "high art" as exempted from universal commodification. Rather, the insightfulness of Adorno's aesthetics lies, on the one hand, in his *externally* historicizing method of reflecting on art's transformation in an increasingly abstract social reality and, on the other hand, in the close attention he pays to the *inner* historical dynamics of artistic genres, types, and individual artworks. Because history is both internal and external to works of art, and because their internal and external historicity are often at odds with one another, artworks are unstable entities. Their reality is not exhausted by their phenomenal "thingness"; rather, once they enter the sphere of circulation and reception (or, consumption) they gain value, not just subjectively, for the recipient who appreciates them, but also objectively, in being like other works of art.

Against the backdrop of an advanced division of labor, Adorno's insistence on works of art being products of social labor points to a historical trajectory tending toward the end of art: this end of art, however, is not to be viewed as the fulfillment of the task nineteenth-century Idealist philosophy assigned to it: to reconcile spirit and matter, freedom and nature, internal and external reality. Rather, the end of art should be construed as the always present real possibility of concrete artistic labor and hence artistic use-value becoming dissolved by the intangible universal product of abstract labor: the value-form. If concrete artistic labor were to become secondary in relation to exchange-value producing abstract labor, art would be "falsely" reconciled with bourgeois society's demand for productive labor. In Adorno's aesthetic thought, the existence of the culture industry is a constant reminder that potentially every work of art made today can be standardized and replicated as a commodity like any other: works of art can become mere social facts devoid of autonomy.

Marx's theoretical stipulation that the amount of socially necessary labor-time embodied in a commodity determines its value is a useful foil for highlighting the *ideal-typical* contrast between commodity production and artistic production: In the case of individualistic, nonindustrial art, exchange-value emerges only after the fact, as the price a work of art realizes when it is sold. The retroactive commodification of art gained by appraisal and purchase (not infrequently as investment object) is a familiar phenomenon. However, Adorno's insistence on artworks being products of social labor is focused primarily on *how* art is being made, implying that even works that are not produced under the direct dictates of commodity production ("real subsumption") nonetheless are affected by it—in Adorno's Hegelian-Marxian language: Even works that are not commodities are socially mediated by the commodity form, and hence the fetishism of commodities—the appearance of a social relation as a relation between things—also affects the appearance and reception of works of art, as Adorno shows in his fetishism essay and his monograph on Wagner. Adorno's recourse to the notion of fetishism as well as to Lukács's almost identical concept of reification is crucial, for it allows him to gloss over the fact that, of course, the value of most works of art cannot be determined according to the amount of labor-time embodied in them and, instead, to focus on the distorting, ideological effects of commodity fetishism.

Modernism: Fetishism and Industrialization

In Adorno's aesthetic writings from the late 1930s, commodity fetishism is presented as a sort of Debordian spectacle avant la lettre. For instance, Adorno depicts Wagner's music drama as a *total* phantasmagoric spectacle designed to obscure the *specific* kinds of artistic labor that went into it: "Works of art owe their existence to the division of labour in society, the separation of physical and mental labour" (*In Search of Wagner*, 72). Instead of owning up to their quasi-industrial and inherently hierarchical mode of production, Wagner's works create a veil of false naturalness that articulates the dangerous ideological distinction between "good" concrete and "bad" abstract labor. The anti-Semitic strain in Wagner's modernism serves as a kind of dark mirror for Adorno's AT, especially in passages that read as if they were conceived of as antidotes to Wagner's aesthetic ideology. Here is one such passage:

> The substantive element of artistic modernism draws its power from the fact that the most advanced procedures of material production and organization are not limited to the sphere in which they originate. In a manner scarcely analyzed yet by sociology, [the most advanced procedures] radiate out into areas of life far removed from them, deep into the zones of subjective experience, which does not notice this and guards the sanctity of its reserves. Art is modern when, by its mode of experience and as the expression of the crisis of experience, it absorbs what industrialization has developed under the given relations of production. (AT 34)

Art's "absorption" of industrialization[9] does not primarily appear in its themes or in its contents: art that directly represents industrial production was never dominant, not even during the period of the Industrial Revolution. Instead, the modernity of art is measured by the degree to which it does away with techniques and procedures that have been rendered superfluous by the progress of production methods (laborsaving devices, logistics, automation, etc.): "Modern art is equally determined socially by the conflict with the conditions of production and inner-aesthetically by the exclusion of exhausted and obsolete procedures" (AT 34). Again, what makes art modern is not its progressive content but rather its being produced and shaped as rationally and unsentimentally as if it were an industrial product: "[T]he material concept of the modern implies conscious control over its means. Even here material production and artistic production converge" (AT 34–5). Adorno thinks that the various challenges posed by dealing with techniques, procedures, and material subsumed under the category of aesthetic form provide a historically precise index of "the socially most advanced level of the productive forces" (35). He imagines the historical dynamic of art's ongoing practices of modernization and internal "industrialization" as a dramatically contentious, antagonistic process of correction, critique, and negation: "each artwork is the mortal enemy of the other" (35). This seems to reflect the historical tendency of free competition becoming centralized and monopolistic: just as capitalism self-antagonistically strives toward the elimination of the market,[10] art strives toward its own elimination. Indeed, the analogy can be extended: The very existence of art is an index of social antagonisms.

For Adorno, as for other thinkers in the Frankfurt School such as Horkheimer and Marcuse, a reconciled society is one in which the "law of value" no longer applies universally. In Orthodox Marxist terms, they view the forces of production as being advanced enough to abolish most forms of alienated labor. It is only the "fetters" of the capitalist relations of production that prevent a postcapitalist society from becoming reality. For Adorno, the productive forces that bring forth advanced art express a dawning consciousness of the possibility of abolishing value-producing abstract labor.

"This Is What It's Like Out There"

Comparing the work of art to a monad (AT 35), Adorno suggests that art articulates inwardly, in its own formalized representations, types, and plots, the bourgeois rationality that dominates "outside" the sphere of art:

> The reprise, peculiarly long-lived in the history of music, embodies to an equal degree affirmation and—as the repetition of what is essentially unrepeatable—limitation. Intrigue and development are not only

subjective activity, temporal development for itself. They also represent unleashed, blind, and self-consuming life in the works. Against it, artworks are no longer a bulwark. Every intrigue, literally and figuratively, says: This is how things are, this is what it's like out there. In the portrayal of this "Comment c'est" the unwitting artwork is permeated by its other, its own essence, the movement toward objectivation, and is motivated by that heterogeneous other. (AT 223)

Adorno detects the ubiquitousness of the *problem* of social labor in, on the one hand, standardized aesthetic formats such as the reprise in the sonata: "To the extent to which a drama—itself a sonatalike product of the bourgeois era—is in musical terms 'worked,' that is, dissected into the smallest motifs and objectivated in their dynamic synthesis, to this extent, and right into the most sublime moments, the echo of commodity production can be heard" (AT 223). On the other hand, what can be heard "objectively" in the work of art is not only the echo of commodity production but also, in the age of the potential abolition of compulsive labor, its irrationality. When works of art state implicitly "so it is," they not only confirm the way things are. They also lend a formalized expression to the uncanny, semiconscious experience shared by most workers in advanced capitalist societies: that the work they perform with ever fewer reprieves is personally pointless and, potentially, even superfluous.[11] Because aesthetic conventions such as dramatic intrigue and sonata development assume, once they are integrated into the work, the fetishistic character of objective necessity, they reveal, Adorno argues, the coercive character of social labor and, in doing so, implicitly gesture toward the "potential superfluousness" of "social labor." Adorno adds, "This superfluousness is truly the point at which art coincides with the real world's business" (AT 223). Works of art can be experienced as critiques of potentially superfluous abstract social labor only at the point where "commodity production not only migrates into artworks in the form of heterogenous life but indeed also as their own law" (223). Works that become "unwitting *tableaux économiques*" (223) avoid, by virtue of their conscious *formal* commitment to artifice and construction, Wagner's regressive solution of providing to the passive observer temporary relief from the toil of labor barely concealed by the phantasmagoria of the performance (*In Search of Wagner*, 72).

Toward Collective Labor

As cited earlier, Adorno describes the process of art's becoming integrated into the "administered world" of bourgeois rationality as one of "migration." Rather than repelling commodity production, modern artworks internalize the instrumental rationality of industrial production processes. In this "migration" of the logic of commodity production into the construction of the work of art, Adorno locates the "origin of modern humor": On the surface, bourgeois society's economic organization is a means to an end. Industrial labor processes are assumed to be designed to guarantee the supply of sufficient consumer goods for human life to reproduce itself, reduce suffering, and eliminate scarcity. Capitalist industry is a means to an end. However, as Adorno underscores, the immanent historical dynamic of capitalist production is toward an irrational logic of production for its own sake:[12]

> [Industry] subordinates all ends until it itself becomes an end in itself and truly absurd. This is recapitulated in art in that the intrigues, plots, and developments, as well as the depravity and crime of detective novels, absorb all interest. By contrast, the conclusions to which they lead sink to the level of the stereotypical. Thus real industry, which by its own definition is only a for-something, contradicts its own definition and becomes silly in itself and ridiculous for the artist. (AT 223)

Adorno here depicts art as comically distorted mirror image of economic rationality. In referring to modern artworks as economic tables, he alludes, on the one hand, to the purposeful function of these representations as being designed to render economic processes evident and transparent and thus rationally governable (Foucault 285). On the other hand, his reference to *tableaux économiques* is tongue-in-cheek, because works of art are economic tables only insofar as they reveal the irrationality of economic rationality. Here, Adorno the aesthetic theorist seeks to appropriate for himself the artistic humor that knows more about bourgeois economy than the latter knows about itself. Yet art does so not because it is some sort of higher knowledge, but precisely because artworks are social labor—brought to the level of ironic consciousness through aesthetic form. With regard to Beckett, Adorno notes, "Consciousness recognizes the limitedness of limitless self-sufficient progress as an illusion of the absolute subject, and social labor aesthetically mocks bourgeois pathos once the superfluity of real labor came into reach" (AT 225). In this and similar passages, Adorno does not separate artistic from social labor and, by implication, does not pit artistic autonomy against social heteronomy. Rather, he theorizes art as a medium of social labor in which the latter is temporarily relieved of the ideological burden of self-justification as a rational means toward an end and is, thereby, brought to a consciousness of itself. Much is at stake in this claim: Because Adorno understands artistic work not in psychological terms as "creativity" or "innovation," but rather as a productive force in which individual labor is necessarily mediated by the social labor of a potential "collective subject" (*Gesamtsubjekt*) "watching over the artist's shoulder" (AT 231), he views art as providing a model[13] for social productive forces liberated from the irrational requirements of the capitalist relations of production—artistic labor could indicate how social labor can be realized as concrete, collective labor rather than abstract labor.

Notes

1. For introductory purposes, see O'Conner 173–184 and Wilson 45–53.
2. The index of the *Adorno-Handbuch* (edited by Richard Klein, Johann Kreuzer, and Stefan Müller-Doohm, Metzler, 2011) lists forty-four passages on "aesthetic autonomy" but does not contain the term "Arbeit" (work/labor). For notable exceptions to this relative neglect of reflecting on social and artistic labor in Adorno's aesthetics, see Roberts, *Intangibilities of Form* and *Revolutionary Time and the Avant-Garde* and Robinson 163–99.
3. One of the most illuminating exemplifications of this dialectic can be found in Roberts' interpretation of Duchamp's readymades in *Intangibilities of Form*.
4. See Jameson's afterword in *Aesthetics and Politics*.
5. For one of the most compelling interpretations of Adorno in terms of artistic modernism, see Bernstein.
6. For a lucid summary of Marx's distinction between productive and unproductive labor, see Braverman chapter 18. For recent discussions on formal and real subsumption in relation to the work of art, see Beech chapter 8, Bernes/Spaulding, Brown introduction, and La Berge introduction.
7. Marx himself and also Lukács make similar observations: "a utopian configuration (socialism) [. . .] already exists in the capitalist mode of production" (Best 23).
8. Adorno/Eisler, *Composing for the Films*, 15–16.
9. Despite the rise of the postindustrial artwork discussed in Bernes, most work processes today retain an industrial rationality.
10. Inspired by Friedrich Pollock's concept of state capitalism, this was an important claim in "classical" Frankfurt School Critical Theory.
11. See, for instance, Graeber and Weeks.
12. For a canonical critique of this inner logic of capitalism see Postone.
13. I thank Matthias Rothe for insisting on this point and for his criticisms of other aspects of my essay.

Works Cited

Adorno, Theodor W. *Aesthetic Theory*. Minneapolis, MN: University of Minnesota Press, 1997. Cited as AT.

Adorno, Theodor W. *Gesammelte Schriften*, 20 vols. Ed. Rolf Tiedemann. Frankfurt am Main: Suhrkamp, 1997. Cited as GS.

Adorno, Theodor W. *Hegel: Three Studies*. Cambridge, MA: MIT Press, 1994.
Adorno, Theodor W. *In Search of Wagner*. Brooklyn, NY: Verso, 2005.
Adorno, Theodor W. *Introduction to the Sociology of Music*. New York: Seabury, 1976.
Adorno, Theodor W. *Philosophische Terminologie*, vol. 2. Berlin: Suhrkamp, 1974. Cited as PT.
Adorno, Theodor W. *Philosophy of New Music*. Minneapolis: University of Minnesota Press, 2006.
Adorno, Theodor W. *The Culture Industry: Selected Essays on Mass Culture*. Ed. J. M. Bernstein. New York and London: Routledge, 1991.
Adorno, Theodor W. "Über den Fetischcharakter in der Musik und die Regression des Hörens." *Zeitschrift für Sozialforschung* 7 (1938): 321–56.
Adorno, Theodor W., and Hanns Eisler. *Composing for the Films*. New York: Continuum, 2007.
Adorno, Theodor W., and Hans Mayer. "Dokumentation einer Kontroverse." *Mit den Ohren denken: Adornos Philosophie der Music*. Ed. Richard Klein and Claus-Steffen Mahnkopf. Berlin: Suhrkamp, 1998, pp. 369–442.
Adorno, Theodor W. and Walter Benjamin, Ernst Bloch, Bertolt Brecht, and Georg Lukács. *Aesthetics and Politics*. Brooklyn, NY: Verso, 2007.
Beech, Dave. *Art and Value: Art's Economic Exceptionalism in Classical, Neoclassical and Marxist Economics*. Chicago, IL: Haymarket Books, 2015.
Bernes, Jasper. *The Work of Art in the Age of Deindustrialization*. Stanford, CA: Stanford University Press, 2017.
Bernes, Jasper, and Daniel Spaulding. "Truly Extraordinary." *Radical Philosophy* 195 (January/February 2016): 51–4.
Bernstein, J. M. *Against Voluptuous Bodies: Late Modernism and the Meaning of Painting*. Stanford, CA: Stanford University Press, 2006.
Best, Beverly. *Marx and the Dynamic of the Capital Formation: An Aesthetic of Political Economy*. New York: Palgrave Macmillan, 2010.
Braverman, Harry. *Labor and Monopoly Capital: The Degradation of Work in the Twentieth Century*. New York: Monthly Review Press, 1974.
Brown, Nicholas. *Autonomy: The Social Ontology of Art under Capitalism*. Durham, NC: Duke University Press, 2019.
Bürger, Peter. *Theory of the Avantgarde*. Minneapolis, MN: University of Minnesota Press, 1984.
Foucault, Michel. *The Birth of Biopolitics*. New York: Palgrave MacMillan, 2008.
Graeber, David. *Bullshit Jobs: A Theory*. New York: Simon & Schuster, 2018.
Hegel, Georg Wilhelm Friedrich. *Hegel and the Human Spirit: A Translation of the Jena Lectures on the Philosophy of Spirit (1805-6)*. Detroit, MI: Wayne State University Press, 1983.
Hegel, Georg Wilhelm Friedrich. *Introductory Lectures on Aesthetics*. New York: Penguin, 2004.
Hegel, Georg Wilhelm Friedrich. *Jenaer Systementwürfe I: Das System der spekulativen Philosophie*. Ed. Klaus Düsing and Heinz Kimmerle. Hamburg: Felix Meiner, 1986.
La Berge, Leigh Claire. *Wages Against Artwork: Decommodified Labor and the Claims of Socially Engaged Art*. Durham, NC: Duke University Press, 2019.

Marx, Karl. *Capital: A Critique of Political Economy*, vol. 1. New York: Vintage Books, 1977.
Marx, Karl. *Das Kapital: Ökonomisches Manuskript 1863–65, Marx-Engels Gesamtausgabe*, section II, vol. 4.1. Ed. Internationale Marx-Engels Stiftung. http://telota.bbaw.de/mega/. Access date January 10, 2019.
Marx, Karl. *Early Writings*. New York: Penguin, 1992.
Marx, Karl. "Value, Price and Profit." *Collected Works of Marx and Engels*, London: Lawrence and Wishart (1985), 20: 101–49.
O'Connor, Brian. *Adorno*. New York: Routledge, 2013.
Postone, Moishe. *Time, Labor, and Social Domination: A Reinterpretation of Marx's Critical Theory*. Cambridge, UK: Cambridge University Press, 1996.
Roberts, John. *The Intangibilities of Form: Skill and Deskilling in Art After the Readymade*. Brooklyn, NY: Verso, 2007.
Roberts, John. *Revolutionary Time and the Avant-Garde*. Brooklyn, NY: Verso, 2015.
Robinson, Joshua. *Adorno's Poetics of Form*. Albany, NY: SUNY Press, 2018.
Weeks, Kathy. *The Problem with Work: Feminism, Marxism, Antiwork Politics, and Postwork Imaginaries*. Durham, NC: Duke University Press, 2011.
Wilson, Ross. *Theodor Adorno*. New York and London: Routledge, 2007.

14

Conspiracy against Theory

Superagents, Conspirators, and the Educational Legacies of Positivism

Kenneth J. Saltman

The Alienation of Fact, Educational Reform, and Conspiracy Theory

A number of professional and academic fields have increasingly embraced a positivist rationality. Within this rationality, data is said to drive inquiry and displays of numerically quantifiable progress stand in place of efficacy. Managers, police officers, teachers, and administrators are supposed to be "data-driven." Numerous academic fields in the social sciences and humanities have eschewed theory and interpretation in favor of radical empiricism and certain strains of what is called materialism. This trend owes in part to the expansion of instrumental, vocational, and commercial justifications for the remaking of fields. A few glaring examples in higher education include the ontological turns in philosophy and anthropology, the replacement of mass communication studies with telecom, the advent of the "digital humanities" as the humanities are being defunded and dismantled, and the gutting of social justice standards and educational theory from teacher and leadership preparation programs.

The neoliberalization of institutions promotes radical empiricism as part of an application of "scientific management" industrial efficiency models. Ever-greater efficiencies of production can only be achieved through ever-greater controls over workers and knowledge. Numerical quantification lends itself to this cult of industrial control as commercial or exchange logic infiltrates every last social space. Yet, all of this rationalization does not promote greater efficiencies, and it comes with tremendous social costs. For example, the knowledge disciplines such as philosophy, history, literature, art criticism, and social and cultural theory that are central to societal self-reflection are being radically reduced. At the same time, policy has become increasingly unmoored from rational or evidence-based justification. Some glaring examples of this include the United States' executive branch's refusal to accept the scientific consensus on climate change, the more than 8,459 documented lies that Donald Trump has told in office as of February 2019 (Factchecker), the intentional federal defunding of scientific research, and research showing that money buys policy changes but that citizens, movements, and evidence-based demands from the public have little to no policy impacts (Gilens & Page). In education, there is no evidence to support such neoliberal privatization schemes as vouchers, chartering, and "portfolio districts," yet these initiatives have been promoted and implemented nonetheless. Trump's secretary of education Betsy DeVos spent her career promoting unsupported voucher schemes, profiting from brain treatment centers that are unsupported by scientific evidence, and justified arming teachers on the basis that children are endangered by grizzly bears—a claim unsupported as well by evidence or any bearing on reality. Her signature achievement as secretary of education has been to roll back regulations on the for-profit college industry that were in place to stop epidemic fraud (including the fraud practiced by Trump University). On the one hand, everything must be data-driven and, on the other, information, evidence, argument, and particularly theory have little place in policy. From the 1940s onward, Theodor Adorno noted and criticized these trends in the growth of positivism in social and cultural spaces. Though the forms of positivism have changed with growing uses of technology and reductions in the traditional institutional avenues for the exercise of democratic participation, Adorno's warnings about the stakes are still relevant.

In what follows, I first discuss the recent expansion of positivism. I then consider the radical transformations to knowledge in education through three phases of the different capitalist uses of positivism in education. I then discuss positivism in and outside of education as a force propelling and complementing the dangerous rise of conspiracy theory. Comprehending the legacy of positivism aids in understanding the distinct forms that conspiracy theories now take. The commonly given reasons for the recent expansion of conspiracy theory include the proliferation of information on the internet—news provision coming from unedited social media sources such as Facebook, social insecurity, precarity, and inequality—that is, social conditions that render people powerless such that conspiracy theory provides feelings of power and control. I suggest here that what also makes conspiracy theory particularly alluring at present involves the transformation of how knowledge and information are taught and have been taught about in both K-12 and higher education. The educational conditions for conspiracy theory have been largely absent from the public and academic discourse on expanding conspiracy theory. In addition, I want to emphasize that conspiracy theory is a form of social theory, albeit bad social theory, that has to be taught and learned in place of better social theories that comprehend experience in terms of broader social forces, systems, and structures. As Adorno argued, such better social theory provides individuals with the capacity to interpret and collectively act on public problems—conditions necessary for the development of a democratic society. I conclude by arguing, with Adorno, that valuing theory in education and challenging positivism are crucial aspects of a struggle against not just rampant conspiracy theory but the broader phenomenon of rising authoritarianism.

Positivism

Truth, in the ideology of positivism, appears as a collection of facts. Facts, in this view, appear as objects without history that appear to become meaningful on their own, without theoretical assumptions or interpretations. Facts appear at once ungrounded and at the same time all powerful. Fact decreasingly depends upon reasoned argument or evidence. Fact increasingly depends upon assertion and hence the social authority of the speaker. Positivism is an ideology about truth claims that delinks from facts the conditions of their making and interpretation. The ideology of positivism is built into daily life and institutions, such as the guise of disinterested objectivity in journalism that obscures the social positions and ideologies of journalists while effacing the values, assumptions, and ideologies that inform reporting; CompStat that quantifies police work and transforms policing into boosting the numbers rather than community engagement; standardized testing in schools that falsely claims as universal and neutral the partial, class, and culturally based truth claims that appear on tests and treats the numbers of test outcomes as learning. As the ideology of positivism alienates facts, facts appear, on the one hand, to come from nowhere and, on the other hand, to be almighty and determining of social outcomes, the required focus of managers and workers.

Adorno's criticism of positivism was integral to his broader philosophy. Adorno develops his philosophy of negative dialectics as a theory of mediation between the subject and the social. Negative dialectics is a philosophy of difference presupposing "the divergence of concept and thing, subject and object, and their unreconciled state" (*LND* 6). Negative dialectics notes the disruption built into any representation in the same way that modernism, for example, distorts reality, suggesting the limitations of representation and the potentials of other social orderings that are already contained inside the present moment. That is, negative dialectics understands facts as antagonistic to their historical moment and, as such, always in the process of reconstitution in response to historical challenges. Contrary to negative dialectics, positivism is an ideology that presumes truth to be in correspondence to its representation, a pure reflection of reality, and facts that are allegedly collected by a knowing subject. Adorno explains "that the concept of the fact, of data, that is canonical for empiricist philosophies and which is based on sense experience, that is, on sense data, has no validity for intellectual experience, which is the experience of something already intellectual and is an intellectually mediated experience" (*LND* 89). Unlike positivism, for Adorno intellectual experience is not based in brute facts but sets facts in their context and meaning. In contrast to positivism, Adorno's negative dialectics recognizes that concepts are not selfsame but rather are constituted by antagonism and require interpretation by subjects. Essential social antagonisms structure concepts. The subject who does the work of interpretation is an aspect of social objectivity and as such is also structured by social antagonisms. Another related dimension of Adorno's criticism of positivism can be traced to Nietzsche's (*TI* 43) criticism of positivity as a cult of rationality that effaces difference and darkness. Adorno's rejection of positivity dismisses the logic of identity, and the tendency of thought in the rationalized society to capture alterity and make it more of the same. The rejection of positivity eschews affirmation of the world as it is, a world structured through domination and mastery of nature. Positivity for Adorno mistakenly affirms the rationality of the irrational society, wrongly suggesting transcendent meaning when the only meaning in the present historical conjuncture is the mastery of nature (*LND* 19). Negative dialectics makes philosophy about what Adorno calls the essential—human suffering, social structures, and systems. In contrast, positivism through scientism (the misapplication of scientific method) makes truth the accumulation of decontextualized facts.

The possibility of the good society demands thinking people who can make experience and facts objects of critical analysis. Such social philosophy holds promise for the development of a reflective society capable of collective self-governance and commitments to justice and equality. Education structured through positivism is culpable of producing miseducated subjects who learn that only that which can be numerically quantified as knowledge, that experience and truth claims do not require interpretation, and that knowledge and learning are not political. Adorno's critique of positivism has had a long-standing influence on educational scholarship. It has provided crucial criticism of the ways positivism has concealed the politics of knowledge and deterred critical forms of teaching and learning. As well, critical pedagogy has been and continues to promise to enact Adorno's critical theory as an educational practice concerned with examining how claims to truth relate to social authority, how experience and the subject are social products, and how acts of interpretation can form the basis of agency and acts of social intervention. At the same time, critical pedagogy embraces the negative dimension of Adorno's dialectics that rejects Hegelian positivity—to have knowledge be resolved, secured, and guaranteed through harmony, totality, and universality.

Adorno, drawing on the sociologist Georg Simmel, suggests that the allure of positivism derives from the false promise of certainty and solidity of numbers in a world of exchange in which everything is made abstract by being rendered into its exchange-value (*ItS*). Adorno also comprehends the logic of positivism and this promise of control as an expression of the tendency of enlightenment rationality toward conquest—the mastery and domination of nature and the inclination to eradicate difference (*History and Freedom*, 43). We might add to Adorno that positivism and the allure of the seeming solidity and certainty of numbers is a response as well to ubiquitous screens and the expansion of what Hubert Dreyfus called "disembodied telepresence" that replaces bodies with digital images, erodes one's sense of corporeal agency, and shears away social context for social exchange (Dreyfus 59).

Schooling produces and promotes particular conceptions of knowledge. As well, it is a site of cultural struggle. Positivism as an ideology that delinks knowledge from its conditions of production falls on a side of cultural struggle that is hostile to theory, interpretation, judgment, and comprehension of how truth claims relate to social authority, material and symbolic interests, and social antagonisms. Positivism instead most often aligns with dogma and increasingly with market fundamentalism dressed as progress and irrationalism posing as reason.

Three Phases of the Capitalist Use of Positivism in Education

Three modern phases of educational positivist rationality have been interwoven with the capitalist uses of schooling: the industrial scientific management phase, the postindustrial neoliberal privatization/accountability phase, and the new data/body privatization phase.

Throughout most of the twentieth century, schooling was based on industrial efficiency models. Scientific management developed by Frederick Taylor sought to break down the tasks of teachers and students, to routinize them, and to measure them for ever-greater control and efficiency. Taylorism was imported into public schooling in the early twentieth century, and it expanded greatly during the postwar industrial era. Critical education scholars describe how the time and space of school was largely organized for social and cultural reproduction: teaching skills and know-how in forms ideologically compatible with prescribed economic roles for different classes of students. Schooling in the Fordist era created the exploitable workforce by investing long term in knowledge, skills, and dispositions compatible with the making of workers whose time and labor-power could be shortchanged for owner profit. Most significantly, schools taught working-class children obedience to the authority of the boss—the assumption that knowledge is grounded by authority rather than argument. Professional class students learned different skills and ideologically bounded dispositions of dialogue, debate, and dissent that would aid them in taking leadership roles in the public and private sectors.

Positivist rationality played a central role in concealing the hidden curriculum of Fordist schooling—that is, the ways that a capitalist basis for education was obscured by tropes of merit and talent through seemingly disinterested, universally valuable, and allegedly objective mechanisms such as testing and grades. Positivist ideology obscured and concealed the values, assumptions, and interests of those claiming official knowledge in the form of the curriculum. Testing and grades, for example, naturalized and depoliticized the unequal distribution of life chances by making the production of inequality appear to be the result of neutral disinterested mechanisms. Positivism also played a key role in shutting down a recognition by teachers and students of the cultural politics of knowledge and curriculum by misrepresenting truth claims as outside of contestation, conflict, and interpretation. Liberal and conservative critics of standardized testing typically at most sought to root out test bias, affirming the guise of disinterested objectivity rather than recognizing the inherently political nature of the curriculum and making such antagonism the basis for linking learning to material and symbolic contests. As such, positivism was instrumental in deterring progressive and critical traditions of education that connect learning and knowledge to the experiences of students, the social world, and that highlight relationships between truth claims and authority.

From the late 1980s to the present, the neoliberal restructuring of public education paired with the standards and accountability movement utilized positivist ideology in a revised fashion. Neoliberal education represents another form of social and cultural reproduction in the postindustrial era. With working-class industrial jobs becoming increasingly offshored and a growing segment of the population rendered marginal to the economy, schools, particularly in working-class and poor communities, moved away from reproducing the labor force through time and labor-intensive preparation for work. Increasingly, profits could be made for capitalists through short-term strategies of commodifying students and schools. Like for-profit prisons, bodies in seats became the new means of profiting through contracting. Profit-taking schemes include privatizing public schools with giant educational management companies winning contracts to cut overhead and inflate profits; union-busting to drive down teacher pay and drive up management income; contracting, massifying, and homogenizing corporate curriculum products; and replacing teacher labor with technology products. By the 1990s the ideology of corporate culture became open and dominant rendering the hidden curriculum overt. That is, a capitalist basis for schooling itself became dominant. In the post-Fordist era, positivism was paired with heavy and frequent standardized testing and standardized curriculum as a multibillion dollar business itself (McGraw-Hill, Pearson, Houghton Mifflin, ETS, and Kaplan). Neoliberals used test scores as evidence of school "failure" and public sector failure to justify turning schools into businesses in the form of charters, private voucher schools, and a bevy of corporate reform schemes.

Post-Fordist schooling continued to be characterized by disciplinary power, learned self-regulation, but also by what Deleuze characterized as "societies of control." Often the imperatives for control follow a class-based pattern in the post-Fordist era. Working-class and poor students have been subject to ever-greater repression and direct control as their use for capital involves students themselves being commodified objects in an increasingly commercialized educational system that merges with for-profit communications and media sectors. Professional class students, on the other hand, continue to be disciplined entrepreneurial subjects of learned self-regulation who aim to self-manage the body, the brain, and affect. They learn that they need to manage their own bodies for competitive advantage with nootropic drugs such as amphetamines, anxiety-control drugs, and antidepressants—all to win on positivist testing regimens that ultimately can be exchanged for economic opportunity. Technologies of direct physical control include not just the modeling of schools on the prison and military but massive overdiagnosis and prescription of ADHD amphetamine attention drugs and antianxiety drugs, behaviorist grit pedagogies, and increasing employment of biometric pedagogical apparatus.

Positivist testing and declarations of educational failure grounded in test outcomes are used to justify these corporeal controls. The exponential increase in ADHD prescriptions for children coincided with the advent of high stakes standardized tests as teachers and parents began drugging kids to game the tests and increase the chance of ongoing school funding or to drug the kids out of distracting other test takers. Grit pedagogy, a neoliberal form of character education, employs behaviorist strategies of conditioned response to teach in ways that avoid reflection and dialogue. Biometric pedagogies use real-time webcams to measure the faces of students and translate bodily stature into claims about student attention, interest, and, allegedly, learning. Biometric pedagogy alleges to measure and translate body movement into student learning and teacher performance. The pharma and media technologies make learning into a material impact on a body, evacuating mediation, thinking, critical consciousness, and knowledge production through dialogic exchange. Similarly, learning analytics, Pay for Success, and grit pedagogies all merge corporeal control with surveillance and measurement of bodies. Scripted lessons, a kind of quasi-religious practice of indoctrinating dogma, have continued to expand for teachers. They are now widespread, imposed under the guise of accountability and standards with the profits flowing to the large publishing companies. What is significant is that dialogue between teachers and students, the relationship between student subjectivity and social context, and consciousness play no part in this concept of learning. Learning is what is done to a body. Data gleaned from surveillance of bodies appears to seamlessly translate to control and measurement of both student learning and teaching as a scripted performance.

We are now entering a new phase of the uses of positivism for capitalism through education that builds on the neoliberal/accountability phase and its fever for direct corporeal control. Corporeal control through direct coercion and surveillance connects with the making of youth into commodified data and investment securities. Though this phenomenon of making youth into investment securities joining with corporal security began close to twenty years ago, it is now developing through data science and learning analytics, social media, and impact investing schemes.

A few key reforms are converging that typify the data/body privatization phase: Pay for Success, Adaptive Learning Technologies, and Social Emotional Learning. Pay for Success or Social Impact Bonds, which are promoted in the federal Every Student Succeeds Act (the latest iteration of the Elementary and Secondary Education Act), bring together banks and philanthropic foundations with governments in order to privatize public services. This is justified on the basis that measurement provides accountability and the public will not have to pay if the metrics do not show success. Schooling, juvenile justice recidivism reduction, and childcare are some of the services targeted for Pay for Success. Banks such as Goldman Sachs largely finance an already-established public service in order to limit the risk of not getting paid. The service is measured, and if the program "succeeds" then the bank can double its initial investment at the public's expense. Banks aim to influence the selection of programs and the terms of evaluation. This public skimming scheme is sold under the guise of innovation, cost savings, and accountability. The privatization of the service is made into an investment bond that can be securitized by an investment bank. Increasingly the surveillance of clients is done through data technology. In Pay for Success positivism, privatization, surveillance, and corporeal control merge as quantitative measurement becomes the justification for the value of a public project.

Another scheme of the data/body privatization phase, Adaptive Learning Technology, promoted as a part of the Personalized Learning movement, has been referred to as the "Netflixing of education." In this scheme teachers are imagined as facilitators and curriculum software on screens stands in place of the teacher. Students choose lessons based on interest and test performance. Adaptive Learning Technology is a kind of new techno-tracking in which a case of the student is built over time out of data collected by the student's use of the software. The numbers then falsely appear as a neutral, disinterested, and objective record of the student and her performance. Adaptive Learning Technology builds standardized testing into lessons, deepening and expanding on the legacy of excessive testing and teaching to the test. Teaching and test preparation merge. Proponents of these schemes commonly claim that such technologies are "personalized" because students can move at different speeds.[1] However, under the guise of personal student choice, the subjective experiences and the particular context are utterly disregarded as is the relationship between knowledge, experience, and the social world. As such Adaptive Learning Technology represents a deepening and expansion of the positivism that has defined the era of test-based accountability. What is also new about Adaptive Learning Technology and Pay for Success is that the capture and commodification of student data are becoming the basis for corporate profit. Adaptive Learning Technology projects such as the Chan Zuckerberg Initiative's Summit is being widely implemented in schools without a fee, but Summit/CZI, which is financially interwoven with Facebook and other for-profit education companies, is able to take student data and use it for other educational projects. CZI's other educational projects include pay for fee services as well as advertising driven platforms with profit models like Facebook's. These trends are converging. Pay for Success profiteers are moving to use Adaptive Learning Technologies to measure and justify further Pay for Success projects.

The data/body privatization phase includes Social Emotional Learning schemes, such as "grit pedagogy," that are promoted through the Every Student Succeeds Act. These projects aim to make individual subjects resilient, able to withstand the disinvestment in schools and communities and withstand poverty and other ill effects of such disinvestment. Grit, for example, is a kind of neoliberal character education in the age of austerity that has been popularized in privatized charter schools. Like biometric pedagogy, it aims to replace learning through dialogue and student questioning and thinking with automatic response to rapid fire scripted teacher lessons. Grit emphasizes physical control and measurement of that control as a means of learning. Learning in this view does not involve dissent, dialogue, questioning, and curiosity but learned dispositions for obedience to authority. There is an industry in selling grit pedagogy, and grit has been promoted through privatization of schools.

The data/body privatization phase allows media corporations to hijack decisions about pedagogy and curriculum from teachers and communities, representing a hollowing out of the nation-state's sovereignty over one of the last large-scale public institutions. Positivism allows the values and ideologies of the corporations to be concealed under the guise of disinterested objectivity and neutrality, numerical quantification, the ideology of technological innovation, and an alibi of accountability.

Conspiracy Theory

Conspiracy theories are everywhere: Vaxxers, Chemtrails, Climate Change Hoax, Birtherism, Qanon, Pizzagate, Deep State, 9/11, Holocaust Denial, Immigrant Replacement, Incel, War against Islam, and Creeping Shariah. Their adherents are making headlines with mass shootings and determining elections with the support of reactionary populist politicians. According to a Cambridge University six-year international empirical study, "conspiracy theories are, nowadays, mainstream rather than marginal beliefs" (CRASSH News). New and long-standing scholarship on conspiracy theory offers insights into the resurgence of white supremacy, anti-Semitism, xenophobia, and authoritarian politics and identifications.

Donald Trump typifies the extent to which conspiracy theory is now mainstream. Trump launched his political career on the birther conspiracy and ran on anti-immigrant racial and religious replacement conspiracy— Latin Americans and Muslims are replacing white Christians from the nation; women are replacing men. Trump propelled previously fringe conspiracy theorists such as Alex Jones into the mainstream and has propounded conspiracy theories of which he is the principal victim: a deep state witch hunt of his presidency, mainstream news conspiring to lie to the public with "fake news."

According to Richard J. Evans, director of the Conspiracy and Democracy project at Cambridge University,

> A *conspiracy theory* is an attempt to explain an event, or a series of events, or a phenomenon of some sort, as the outcome of a secret plot aiming to deprive the people illegally of money, liberty, power, or knowledge. . . . Conspiracy theories are a form of alternative knowledge that regards knowledge produced by experts on events as unreliable; conspiracy theories posit an "establishment" that produces "official" knowledge, often with the ulterior motive of covering up the "real truth" about something. (Evans)

Conspiracy theorists find in conspiracies easy answers, certain knowledge in uncertain times, and feelings of agency. Conspiracies provide easy answers because they come ready-made and require neither evidence, nor the work of research, nor a broader interpretive theory that can explain patterns of social phenomena. Conspiracies appear to provide certain knowledge because they place explanation in the persons of discreet actors. They provide the conspiracy theorist with feelings (albeit false feelings) of agency by offering an explanation for inexplicable and uncertain conditions. Conspiracy theories appeal to those who experience powerlessness, and evidence suggests that, in turn, exposure to conspiracy theory (such as a viewing of the Oliver Stone film *JFK*) results in reported increases in political cynicism and feelings of diminished political agency (Koerth-Baker; Swami & Coles 561).

Conspiracy theory flourishes in contexts of inequality and political misrecognition. Evans claims, "More unequal countries with a lower quality of democracy tend to display higher levels of belief in the world cabal." As economic inequality and social precarity have radically increased in the new gilded age and political power has become concentrated, and as ecological precarity looms, conspiracy theory finds widespread use.

Conspiracy theories tend to be less attractive to those with higher levels of education (Drochon). As well, skepticism toward science, academics, journalists, and expert knowledge is growing. This is in part by design. Trump, Orban in Hungary, Duterte in the Philippines, Bolsonaro in Brazil, Erdogan in Turkey, and other right-wing populists who trade in conspiracy theory, actively seek to erode, destroy, or co-opt knowledge-making institutions including independent media, schools, and universities. By disseminating an abundance of lies, they undermine confidence in the possibility of using knowledge and education to act on and shape the social world. Epistemologically, conspiracy theory works much like Donald Trump's yellow hair and speech: ersatz, outlandish, clownish, and dubious on the surface. The real function of persistent bullshit is to undermine confidence in the capacity of individuals to obtain knowledge and act on that knowledge and to discredit knowledge-making institutions. As Jason Stanley points out, this is a standard move of fascists dictators to make the strongman's assertions the only ones that can be accepted as truth. Truth then is grounded in the body of the strongman (Stanley 71).

What do the latest uses of positivist ideology have to do with the expansion of conspiracy theory? Each of the phases of schooling that I have outlined has contributed to the development of an approach to knowledge that has created the conditions for conspiracy theory to flourish. Positivist standardized testing promoted the equating of knowledge with authority. In the neoliberal and data/body phases, positivism is also used to justify an approach to knowledge characterized by dogma and faith, particularly in markets. In place of dialogue, argument, and evidence, positivism erases the conditions of production for truth claims as well as disappearing the actual people who make the tests and curriculum and the relationship between their social locations and their claims to truth. As Adorno pointed out, positivism locates the concept in the subject rather than in the dialectical relationship between the subject and society (*ItS* 32). Positivism appeals to people because it seems to offer certainty and foundations for truth through the apparent concreteness of numbers. The neoliberal and data/body phases of positivism increasingly locate truth in the bodies of students and teachers. Yet, the latest uses of positivism render these subjects ever more ephemeral and fleeting as subjects become data and abstract investment securities.

Conspiracy theory appears to overcome positivism's erasure of the social origins of facts by locating truth in the essentialized bodies of agents. Karl Popper who is credited with first naming conspiracy theory described the religious character of it. Conspirators have a mystical omnipotent agency. In contrast to the superagents of conspiracy theory, regular people have no agency at all. Conspiracy theories locate inflated agency, total agency in two figures, god and the devils: gods take form as salvational "superagents" such as strongmen who embody truth through aggressive assertion; conspiratorial "secret agents" (Muslims, Jews, blacks, women, and deep state puppet masters, according to such conspiracy theorists) corporeally ground the truth and threat of the precarious social order. Strongmen aim to make themselves the embodiment of security, promising to protect the people who they allege are threatened by vilified others, the conspiratorial "secret agents" who themselves are positioned as having total agency and an existential threats to the order. Trump put it succinctly: "Only I can protect you." The conspiracy theory of replacement suggests that Muslims, Jews, and Latin American immigrant are conspiring to replace white Christians from the nation-state.

The replacement alleged is a physical displacement. The beleaguered masses in this narrative are defined by their racial essence—the fear expressed is one of "white genocide." The conspiratorial secret agents are also defined by their racial essence grounded in the body—marchers in Charlottsville chanted "Jews will not replace us," Trump advocates a Muslim ban, and the "caravans" of central American refugees are deemed a threat. The Squirrel Hill Pittsburgh synagogue shooting of 2018 clearly expressed the logic: Jews were conspiring to help Muslim refugees enter the nation and the response was a sudden violent superman act of physical annihilation of the secret agents of the replacement threat. Similarly, the involuntary celibacy conspiracy theory, which expresses male fears of being replaced by women, locates the threat to men in the bodies of women who are framed as "harpies"—seducing destroyers—and danger takes form in the material fabric of their pernicious yoga pants. The Incel boys do not lobby congress to outlaw yoga pants or develop educational projects to end women's suffrage. Instead, they idealize and emulate their supermen Incel heroes who murder women in mass shootings. The men's alienation, misery, and feelings of rejection are comprehended as an effect of the women's bodies. Deep state conspirators who are invisible bodies seem always to target the bodies of their victims: 9/11 conspiracy, Vaxxers, and chemtrails. The mystified social origins of facts are located in the alleged physical effects.

Conspiracy theory sees the social as largely static and consensually formed with the exception of the changes accomplished by superagents and the changes threatened by secret agents. As such, conspiracy theory largely fails to recognize the multiple contests of classes and cultural groups and their symbolic and material interests, instead focusing on the perceived and typically misrepresented interests of a small number of historically vilified groups. Conspiracy theory typically inverts power relations when it comes to these vilified groups, ascribing to them exceptional power and agency. Conspiracy theory displaces social theory capable of providing a full picture of the workings of the social order by displacing structure with mystified agency.

Conspiracy theory, by grounding truth in the body, offers explanatory power in which material essence stands in for theory, evidence, and argument. Both positivism and conspiracy theory invert essence. As Adorno pointed out, the essential, the principle of exchange, is precisely what seems evacuated in the view of the social proposed by positivism. Yet, both positivism and conspiracy theory erase the essential, not just exchange but the relationship between the subject and the social. Positivism replaces the essential with numbers. Conspiracy theory replaces the essential with bodies who have mystified and inflated agency.

The antidote to conspiracy theory is not merely more facts or better facts. Rather, the antidote to conspiracy theory is the ruthless interrogation of the social assumptions, values, interests, and ideologies undergirding claims to truth. As Adorno said, facts are always social facts. Conspiracy theory deprives people of agency because it undermines the capacity of knowledge for social agency. It locates social agency and social change in the essentialized "facts" of groups of people rather than recognizing the material and symbolic power struggles among groups and classes. Conspiracy theory is against theory itself. Theory is a crucial tool to make experience, knowledge, and the social world into objects of critical analysis. The educational task to dismantle conspiracy theory involves a project of evacuating positivism from educational practices and institutions and replacing it with a culture of education that makes central the politics of culture and knowledge.

Both liberal and conservative educational thinking have come emphatically to embrace the ideology of positivism and frame projects for educational equality in terms of positivism. Perhaps nothing could be more pernicious than the language of the "achievement gap" that suggests that the aim for educational justice is to have nonwhite and poor students scoring the same as rich white children on standardized tests. Such a concept affirms the knowledge and culture of dominant class and racial groups as a universal norm to which all other groups ought to aspire. Moreover, the concept conceals the question of who made these standardized tests, what their class and cultural positions are, and what material and symbolic interests and contests inform the embrace of particular claims to truth. The antidote to rising authoritarianism is the embrace of cultures of democracy everywhere. Cultures of democracy in educational institutions flourish when educative practices foster the development of critical consciousness and modes of interpretation that can form the basis for social intervention and agency. Educational practices can foster critical consciousness by using theory to make experience an object of critical reflection, to contextualize experience and claims to truth in terms of broader structures and systems, social forces, and antagonisms.

Note

1 I detail how Adaptive Learning Technology is promoted as "personalized learning" in the chapter on the Chan Zuckerberg Initiative of Kenneth J. Saltman *The Swindle of Innovative Educational Finance*, Minneapolis: University of Minnesota Press 2018.

Works Cited

Adorno, Theodor. *History and Freedom: Lectures 1964–1965*. English Reprinted First Edition. Ed. Rolf Tiedmann. Trans. Rodney Livingstone. Malden, MA: Polity, 2008.
Adorno, Theodor. *Introduction to Sociology*. English First Edition. Ed. Christoph Gödde. Trans. Edmund Jephcott. Stanford, CA: Stanford University Press, 2000.
Adorno, Theodor. *Lectures on Negative Dialectics*. English First Edition. Ed. Rolf Tiedemann. Trans. Rodney Livingstone. Malden, MA: Polity, 2008.
CRASSH News. "Brexit and Trump Voters More Likely to Believe in Conspiracy Theories, Survey Shows." Centre for Research in the Arts, Social Sciences and Humanities. University of Cambridge. http://www.crassh.cam.ac.uk/blog/post/brexit-and-trump-voters-more-likely-to-believe-in-conspiracy-theories-surve.
Dreyfus, Hubert. *On the Internet*. New York: Routledge, 2010.
Drochon, Hugo. "Britains Are Swallowing Conspiracy Theory: Here's How to Stop the Rot." *The Guardian*, November 28, 2018. Available at http://www.conspiracyanddemocracy.org/blog/conspiracy-theories-and-antisemitism/. Accessed May 15, 2019.
Evans, Richard J. *Presentation to the All-Party Parliamentary Group against Antisemitism, Palace of Westminster, 19 June 2018*. Posted in Conspiracy Theories on June 22, 2018 by Conspiracy Democracy. http://www.conspiracyanddemocracy.org/blog/conspiracy-theories-and-antisemitism/. Accessed May 15, 2019.
Factchecker. "In 745 Days, President Trump Has Made 8459 False or Misleading Claims." *The Washington Post*, February 3, 2019.

Gilens, Martin, and Benjamin I. Page. "Testing Theories of American Politics: Elites, Interest Groups and Average Citizens." *Perspectives on Politics* 12, no. 3 (2014): 564–81.

Koerth-Baker, Maggie. "Why Rational People Buy into Conspiracy Theories." *The New York Times Magazine*, May 21, 2013.

Nietzsche, Friedrich. *Twilight of the Idols/ The Anti-Christ*. Trans. R. J. Hollingdale. New York: Penguin, 1990.

Saltman, Kenneth J. *The Swindle of Innovative Educational Finance*. Minneapolis, MN: University of Minnesota Press, 2018.

Stanley, Jason. *How Fascism Works: The Politics of Us and Them*. New York: Random House, 2018.

Swami, Viren and Rebecca Coles. "The Truth Is Out There." *The Psychologist* 23, no. 7 (July 2010). www.thepsychologist.org.uk. Accessed 15 May 2019.

Taylor, Frederick. *The Principles of Scientific Management*. New York: Harper and Brothers, 1915.

15

Aspects of Adorno's Critical Theory of Culture

Stefan Müller-Doohm and Trans. Daniel Steuer

Adorno often points out that there are no commonalities between critical theory and the kind of cultural criticism one finds in Oswald Spengler or Ortega y Gasset.[1] He develops this claim in his article "Cultural Criticism and Society" ("Kulturkritik und Gesellschaft"; GS 10.1, 11–30), first published in 1951, which presents his understanding of cultural analysis.[2] Right at the outset, he clarifies that not only intellectual culture and the values embedded in its ideational material but also contemporary pessimistic criticisms of civilization and the cultural phenomena of modernity are an integral part of a society "in which all being is merely there *for* something else" ("Cultural Criticism and Society," 20; GS 10.1, 12). In capitalistically organized societies, everything, without exception, is a commodity; everything, without exception, is there to be exchanged. This also applies to the individual, who has to sell herself as a "personality," while familiarity with aesthetic qualities is a hindrance rather than a help: "who still knows what a poem is, will hardly find a well-paid position as a copywriter" (GS 8, 101f.). It applies to language, which, as a medium of communication, has become a means for "advertising" thoughts as commodities that must prevail on the market of communication (*Dialectic of Enlightenment*, xiv [transl. amended]; GS 3, 12). And it applies to education and the arts: as half education and merely decorative arts, they ultimately amount to forms of regression.

This fundamentally critical attitude toward the function of culture within an integrated society includes cultural criticism within its scope: there is a "complicity" between the critic of culture and his or her object domain, and this makes cultural critique an element within what Adorno calls the culture industry. "By making culture his object, he objectifies it once more. Its very meaning, however, is the suspension of objectification" ("Cultural Criticism and Society," 22; GS 10.1, 15).

Cultural criticism ignores the genesis of culture within the functional context of society, viewing it instead as an independent sphere. Culture originates from the division between manual and intellectual labor. This division is the "original sin" of bourgeois culture and the *thema probandum* of critical theory. This is what gives its analysis of culture its depth. It does not adopt a backward-looking perspective that is critical of civilization and simply laments the decline of bourgeois values brought about by the commercialization of culture; rather, it concentrates on the separation of culture from the living process of society, its reification, the "fetishization of the intellectual sphere." Part of the ambition of Adorno's interpretation of culture is to combine a transcendent approach with the immanent approach he prefers. "Immanent criticism of intellectual and artistic phenomena [geistiger Gebilde] seeks to grasp, through the analysis of their form and meaning, the contradiction between their objective idea and that pretension [of correspondence with reality]. It names what the consistency or inconsistency of the work itself expresses of the structure of the existent [Verfassung des Daseins]" ("Cultural Criticism and Society," 31f.; GS 10.1, 26f.).

Adorno's critical theory of culture culminates in the conclusion that the "triumph of culture" is at the same time its failure (*Negative Dialectics*, 366; GS 6, 359), that in the course of bourgeois history it has ceased to be a bourgeois emancipatory achievement and has come to exist only as a façade: "culture is still permitted to drive about in a type of gypsy wagon; the gypsy wagons, however, roll about secretly in a monstrous hall, a fact which they do not themselves notice. This might well explain to no small degree the loss of inner tension which is to be observed today at various points even in progressive cultural productions—to say nothing of the less progressive efforts. Whatever raises from within itself a claim to being autonomous, critical and antithetical—while at the same time never being able to assert this claim with total legitimacy—must necessarily come to naught; this is particularly true when its impulses are integrated into something heteronomous to them, which has been worked out previously from above, that is to say, when it is granted the space in which to draw breath immediately by that power against which it rebels" ("Culture and Administration," 118; GS 8, 133).[3]

From the perspective of the philosophy of history, Adorno sharpens this critique even further by juxtaposing Kant's expectation that freedom will be realized in the transcendental subject and Hegel's expectation that reason will realize itself in the world spirit, with the historical fact of the general failure of culture—a failure "demonstrated irrefutably" by Auschwitz. Adorno asks whether the idea of humanity can be rescued at all in the face of the reality of the death camps. He postulates that "all thoughts and actions" have to be arranged "so that Auschwitz will not repeat itself, so that nothing similar will happen" (*Negative Dialectics*, 356f.; GS 6, 358).

But Adorno would not be a dialectical thinker if his critique of cultural criticism were not also characterized by an attempt to rescue culture and salvage its promise of happiness. This is the promise of a space for the individual power of expression, for the peculiar and unique, as opposed to the machinery of business, the administered world, and the generality of society as a bad totality. Adorno is convinced that the complete disintegration of culture amounts to the condition of barbarism. "[T]oday, . . . the threat is a false destruction of culture, a vehicle of barbarism," he writes in *Aesthetic Theory*, a posthumous work to which we shall have occasion to return (*Aesthetic Theory*, 320; GS 7, 474). It follows that poetry is required even after Auschwitz, for poems register "the historical hours as they strike" (GS 11, 60; trans. D.S.). At the same time, we require more than just lyrics. As long as subjects are condemned to live the false life in a society that is ossified into a systemic objectivity, the negativity of the historical process needs to be made transparent, and this requires extremely exaggerated means of representation, both in social theory—which makes use of the intransigence of concepts—and in the arts, using the means of artistic representation. For the "[p]erennial suffering" throughout history has a "right to expression" (*Negative Dialectics*, 362; GS6, 355). Art must seize the opportunity—which still exists even under "civilized barbarism" (*Dialectic of Enlightenment*, xix; GS 3, 17)—to document the catastrophe that is the failure of culture by unfolding art's own contradiction. In the eyes of Adorno, Samuel Beckett stands out as having done this in the most uncompromising fashion in the areas of drama and prose.

Adorno develops his notion of critique as determinate negation as a means to the same end. Negation characterizes his conception of dialectics, which has "as its stage the tension between the insight into the complete impossibility of presenting a good life, and, concomitantly, the awareness of how it could be" (*Philosophische Terminologie*, vol. 1, 133).

Critique as Dialectical Thought Process

> To identify culture solely with lies is more fateful than ever, now that the former is really becoming totally absorbed by the latter, and eagerly invites such identification in order to compromise every opposing thought. (*Minima Moralia*, 44; GS 4, 49)

Adorno takes various things as the objects of his practice of critique, seeking to decipher the "internal texture of the thing" (GS 20.2, 765). He opposes this kind of immanent critique to instrumental forms of thought, which proceed deductively and by subsuming their objects under external categories. For Adorno, critique is a process of making visible what is possible, of making room for new perspectives through the determinate negation of what is posited and not questioned, whether this is a fact, an assertion, or a way of acting. While the truth content of critical thought is clear from the evidence it makes use of, the process of interpretation produces insights that are not at all "absolutely correct, irrefutable, watertight" (*Minima Moralia*, 71; GS 4, 79). For Adorno, if an insight is an exact statement that refers to a factually given reality, then it is really a tautology. The criterion for the truth of critique can therefore be neither the correspondence of propositions with the facticity of the given (as in correspondence theories of truth) nor something contained in the logical or systematic cohesion between propositions (as in coherence theories of truth). Critique uses the means of intentional exaggeration, which seeks to go beyond the pure representation of the given. The interpretative decipherment of social or cultural artifacts does not aim to produce an agreement between interpretation and what is interpreted, because in that case the interpretation would cease to be an interpretation; it would be a simple act of reproduction.

Adorno's interpretations of social and cultural phenomena uncover the concrete moments that determine them, moments that are mediated by society. "Being mediated," here, "is not a positive statement about being, but an instruction for knowers: not to be content with such positivity—in fact, this is the request to practice dialectics in concrete terms" (GS 5, 32; my translation, D. S.).

Adorno does not think that the way people and matters factually present themselves within society are the ways they necessarily have to be. Because social conditions and cultural achievements have been formed historically, they also contain the potential for change. Adorno therefore defines critique as "the power to resist . . . everything that is merely posited, that justifies itself with its existence" ("Critique," 281f.; GS 10.2, 785). However, because of the power of how things are, the space of freedom, as the space for what is different, does not lie in open view. Making it visible requires the capacity critique possesses to dismantle things. Critique produces new, alternative interpretations and opens up spaces in which the "distant and different" (*Negative Dialectics*, 192; GS 6, 192) can be thought. For Adorno, dialectic is "the consistent sense of non-identity" (*Negative Dialectics*, 5; GS 6, 17). In other words, "dialectics amounts to thinking so that the thought form will no longer turn its objects into immutable ones, into objects that remain the same. Experience shows that they do not remain the same" (*Negative Dialectics*, 154; GS 6, 157).

As part of his version of dialectics—an always incomplete and at the same time negative dialectics—Adorno puts forward the maxim that "the value of a thought is measured by its distance from the continuity of the familiar. It is objectively devalued as this distance is reduced; the more it approximates to the pre-existing standard, the further its antithetical function is diminished, and only in this . . . are the claims of thought founded" (*Minima Moralia*, 80; GS 6, 90).

For Adorno, dialectics is more than just a kind of oppositional thinking (thesis, antithesis) that is balanced out through a middle term (synthesis). Rather, between the oppositional moments exists an inner mediation without a middle ground, a mediation of the oppositions within themselves. This mediation consists in the fact "that the two opposed moments do not mutually point at each other, but that the analysis of each of them in itself points toward a sense implied in it, as its opposite, that is, actually, . . . the principle of dialectics in contrast to a purely external dualistic or disjunctive, distinguishing thinking" (*Philosophical Terminology*, 466).

In his reflections on "damaged life," Adorno tries to demonstrate that this form of dialectical thinking is associated with a specific linguistic mode of expression. The most striking feature of the fragments that make up *Minima Moralia*, first published in 1951, is their linguistic form, the way they lend the concepts of philosophy and social theory a literary or aesthetic quality and yet heed the rules of discursive logic. Thus, allegory and imploring linguistic gestures stand alongside strict conceptual explications. In particular, the "element of exaggeration, of over-shooting the object, of self-detachment from the weight of the factual" (*Minima Moralia*, 126; GS 4, 144) goes beyond the use of a language as merely a means of descriptive representation.[4] The artistry of Adorno's formulations shows how critical knowledge, as a kind of contrapuntal thinking, can be realized at the level of linguistic expression. The aphoristic miniatures of *Minima Moralia* create a tense field of paradox: "Only by the recognition of distance in our neighbour [Anerkennung von Ferne im Nächsten] is strangeness alleviated: accepted into consciousness" (*Minima Moralia*, 182; GS 4, 207). The contradictory form of presentation is precisely what gives rise to insight. By entering into oppositional configurations, individual perspectives point to the one-sidedness of their opposites. By illuminating the extremes of the matter in hand, Adorno creates a provocative excess of meaning which, in turn, leads the reader as well as the writer to further reflection.

With his *Negative Dialectics* (1966), Adorno provides an account of this kind of reflection: "The cognitive utopia [Utopie der Erkenntnis] would be to use concepts to unseal the nonconceptual with concepts, without making it their equal" (*Negative Dialectics*, 10; GS 6, 21). For Adorno, the most important condition that must be fulfilled if this cognitive goal [Erkenntnisziel], which he calls utopian, is to be realized is *unrestrained experience*: it requires that the subject "without anxiety, [. . .] entrusts itself to its own experience" ("On Subject and Object," 254; GS 10.2, 752). What is encountered in experience prior to any regimentation must, in a first step, be given over to *interpretation* by way of *conceptual reflection*. Such reflection "attempts to make this experience, or the wanting-to-say-it . . ., binding" (*Philosophical Terminology*, 108). For Adorno, to make something binding means—and this is the second step—entering into the process of *theoretical formation*, which moves toward the unity of the concept and its object. Just as interpretation distrusts the "deceit of appearance, . . . so the more smoothly the façade of society presents itself, the more profoundly does theory mistrust it. Theory seeks to give a name to what secretly holds the machinery together" ("Sociology and Empirical Research," 68; GS 8, 196).

This type of theory aims to produce "binding statements [Verbindlichkeit] without a system" (*Negative Dialectics*, 29; GS 6, 39). Adorno sees this ideal realized in what he calls thinking in constellations, or thinking in models: "A model covers the specific, and more than the specific, without letting it evaporate in its more general super-concept" (*Negative Dialectics*, 29; GS 6, 39). According to Adorno, the truth of a theory does not consist solely in "propositions or judgments or thoughts conforming to simply given states of affairs; rather, of primary importance is the expressive moment." That is, what is important is to express what "one becomes aware of about the world," while bearing in mind the possibility of a good life, one that provides an account of the false life, of the absurdity of the course the world is taking (*Philosophical Terminology*, 106f.).

The Culture Industry

The marks of disintegration are modernity"s seal of authenticity.

(*Aesthetic Theory*, 23; TRANSLATION AMENDED)

Adorno's theory of the culture industry can be taken as a "thought model" that he employs within the context of his cultural analyses. He developed this theory during his years in emigration, and it first appeared as a chapter with the subtitle "Enlightenment as Mass Deception" in *Dialectics of Enlightenment* (94–136; GS 3, 141–91), the book he coauthored with Max Horkheimer. In this text, Adorno substitutes the common term "mass culture" with the term "culture industry," "in order to exclude from the outset the interpretation . . . that it is a matter of something like a culture that arises spontaneously from the masses themselves, the contemporary form of popular art. . . . In all its branches, products which are tailored for consumption by masses . . . are manufactured more or less according to plan" ("Culture Industry Reconsidered," 98; GS 10.1, 337). Deploying the term "culture industry" is a way of critically pointing out that the aesthetic forms of expression in the areas of music, the visual arts, literature, and so on are mass produced as commodities. Their use-value consists in the distraction and amusement of consumers of culture. The gratification provided by cultural commodities in their mass consumption is the cause of "[t]he pernicious love of the common people for the harm done to them" (*Dialectic of Enlightenment*, 106; GS 3, 155). This idea finds its "classical" formulation early on in the essay on the culture industry in *Dialectic of Enlightenment*: "In reality, a cycle of manipulation and retroactive need is unifying the system ever more tightly" (*Dialectic of Enlightenment*, 95; GS 3, 142).

The term "culture industry" not only denotes the industrial production of the commodities, organized and administered from above, but also serves to overcome the flattening-out of the aesthetic sphere and to transcend a perspective centered on particular media: "culture industry" signifies the comprehensive network that provides culture in contemporary society. This includes the individual cultural sectors, the cultural goods that are made by the producers of culture and the associated distribution systems, the market for culture, and the consumption of culture. The culture industry includes media of mass communication, such as newspapers, journals, radio, records, film, and television, as well as institutions for the promotion of culture, such as theaters, festivals, the publishing industry, advertising, various sports, and other elements pertaining to the world of hobbies and entertainment. These institutions make up the system of the culture industry, and they are of enormous importance for social integration because they are responsible for the production of what is seen as reality and for the provision of meaning. In Adorno's view, the main function of the culture industry is to produce agreement with the way the world is organized. "The concepts of order which it hammers into human beings are always those of the status quo.... [T]he categorical imperative of the culture industry ... proclaims: you shall conform, without instruction as to what; conform to that which exists anyway. . . . The power of the industry's ideology is such that conformity has replaced consciousness" ("Culture Industry Reconsidered," 104; GS 10.1, 343). Adorno is convinced that the culture industry is incapable of producing culture of its own accord; it cannot be creative because it limits itself to "fus[ing] the old and familiar into a new quality" ("Culture Industry Reconsidered," 98; GS 10.1, 337).

The system of the culture industry—which today, in the wake of digitalization, has taken on a global dimension—is characterized by an ongoing process of staging and restaging culture in the form of mass entertainment and general information. These staging practices find a particular expression in the "star" system: "The more dehumanized" the operations of the culture industry become, "the more diligently and successfully the culture industry propagates supposedly great personalities and operates with heart-throbs" ("Culture Industry Reconsidered," 101; GS 10.1, 340). A large part of Adorno's critical attention is directed at this social phenomenon of personalization and emotionalization. The general tendency toward personalization in the media serves the purpose of making complex and hard to understand conditions within society and politics seemingly transparent by pretending that these are all down to the positive or negative influences of "great men." The culture industry's fixation on prominent individuals supports this false belief.

The overall effect of the culture industry on society runs counter to Enlightenment. It prevents the formation of "autonomous, independent individuals who judge and decide consciously for themselves. These, however, would be the precondition for a democratic society" ("Culture Industry Reconsidered," 106; GS 10.1, 345) because, according to Adorno, "[p]ublicness and democracy are thoroughly tied up with one another. Only under the guarantee of the democratic right to the free expression of opinions can publicness develop; only if the things on which citizens have to vote are public is democracy thinkable" ("Opinion Research and Publicness," 121; transl. amended; GS 8, 533).[5] Democracy puts autonomy and self-determination into practice by means of the processes of opinion and will formation, and for Adorno this provides the standard for his critique of culture and the media. When recapitulating his analysis of the culture industry in 1963 (GS 10.1, 337–45 ["Résumé über Kulturindustrie"; "Culture Industry Reconsidered"]; GS 10.2, 499–517 ["Jene zwanziger Jahre"; Prolog zum Fernsehen; "Those Twenties," "Prologue to Television"]), he not only focuses on the problem of how to organize the mass media so that they can act as mediators of public processes of opinion and will formation[6] but also asks whether the consumers of media can see through the staging practices of the culture industry. He reaches the conclusion that they want to be deceived, while being fully aware of the deception. According to Adorno, they are very well capable of distinguishing between media staging and their real interests in ordinary life.

In order to explain this, Adorno develops the theorem of the "split consciousness" ("Free Time," 196). On the one hand, the culture industry offers up the so-called Erlebniswerte (experiential value) of cultural commodities for almost compulsive consumption—the "displeasure in pleasure" belongs in this context ("On the Fetish Character in Music and the Regression in Listening," 33; GS 14, 19). On the other hand, the social position of individuals in the context of their real lives prevents them from taking the interpretative patterns of the culture industry at face value. Adorno assumes that "[t]he real interests of individuals are still strong enough to resist, within certain limits, total inclusion. That would concur with the social prediction that a society whose fundamental contradictions persist undiminished cannot be totally integrated even in consciousness" ("Free Time," 196f.; transl. mod.; GS 10.2, 655). To the other important question, namely how the audience as a sum of mature and responsible individuals can be motivated to want what is better and right, he responds as follows: "It would need to be brought to this point through itself, and at the same time against itself" (GS 20.1, 346; my translation, D. S.).

The Moment of Resistance in Aesthetics

The central point around which the philosophical reflections of *Aesthetic Theory* turn is the question of the possibility of an autonomous work of art today.[7] Adorno takes his cue from the categories of the aesthetic theories of Kant and Hegel, the epistemological substance of which he tries to make relevant for the present by confronting it with avant-garde modernist art.

Adorno concentrates exclusively on the aesthetics of the works themselves and for the most part leaves aside the question of the reception of the artwork. This orientation is in line with his postulate of the "primacy of the object" ("On Subject and Object," 249; GS 10.2, 746) over the subject, which he elaborates in *Aesthetic Theory* in the form of the primacy of the work of art. Compared to the work of art, the recipient—as well as the artist as subject—is of secondary importance. The primacy of the object not only expresses Adorno's plea for an *immanent analysis of artworks* but also points to the "character of art as the unconscious writing of history, as anamnesis of the vanquished, of the repressed, and perhaps of what is possible" (*Aesthetic Theory*, 259; GS 7, 384). While art is tied to empirical reality, Adorno, paradoxically, also takes it to be the plenipotentiary of the utopian moment—a moment which, like the riddle character of art, can never find a positive expression.

For Adorno—composer of free atonality, theoretician of the New Music, subtle interpreter of modern literature—theoretical engagement with aesthetics is a central pillar of philosophical work. Amid times of a seemingly revolutionary transformation of the art world, he was interested in rescuing it from decline; he was interested, as he put it, in the "rescue of semblance." The "emphatic right of art, the legitimation of its truth, depends on this rescue" (*Aesthetic Theory*, 107; transl. modified; GS 7, 164),[8] because only the great work of art is free of deceit. As he argues across many passages of *Aesthetic Theory*, these rescuing attempts fail when art, whose purpose is neither to console nor to produce emotional rapture, adapts itself (in the worst case to the taste and needs of the recipients) and thus engages with the sphere of communication.[9] Genuine art, by contrast, is the shadow cast ahead by what is not yet, and it provides us with a glimpse of what may be objectively possible under conditions of freedom. "Artworks have no truth without determinate negation" (*Aesthetic Theory*, 129; GS 7, 195), and in this consists their practically irreconcilable character. Although all art is a *fait social*, that is, part of the historical process, it is only valid inasmuch as it is a flat rejection of antagonistic society. "Art keeps itself alive only through its social force of resistance; . . . Its contribution to society is not communication with it but . . . resistance . . . Lest it risk its self-sublation, radical modernity preserves art's immanence by admitting society only in an obscured form, as in the dreams with which artworks have always been compared" (226; transl. modified; GS 7, 335f.).

For Adorno, art which leaves social reality undisturbed is merely decorative. Only those works of art that adopt an antithetical stance toward society contain any truth. This moment of truth, however, turns into its opposite if artworks pretend that complete success—"reconciliation" (*Aesthetic Theory*, 55; GS 7, 87)—is possible in existing society. Art cannot by itself dissolve the conditions which drive the world toward catastrophe. The "promise of happiness" that lies in the utopian moments of art is an "ever broken promise" (*Aesthetic Theory*, 136; GS 7, 205). This also applies to the most radical forms of artistic expression, such as Samuel Beckett's anti-dramatic plays. Such works are not free of deception: although they demand the abolition of the false, antagonistic, obviously absurd condition of reality, they are not themselves capable of bringing about this abolition. "Artworks draw credit from a praxis that has yet to begin and no one knows whether anything backs their letters of credit" (*Aesthetic Theory*, 83; GS 7, 129).

To the extent that art contains the power to resist, it shares with philosophy the impulse to rescue the nonidentical. Despite its utopian epistemological aim to "by way of the concept . . . transcend the concept" (*Negative Dialectics*, 15; GS 6, 27), philosophy operates through the medium of conceptuality, but art—as the sphere of the expressive—is the manifestation of the nonconceptual because it does not use discursive but in particular mimetic means. Adorno considers the arts as home to a specific form of reason that neither appropriates its objects for instrumental purposes nor attempts to dissect and analyze them by applying discursive epistemological procedures (cf. *Aesthetic Theory*, 54ff., 119ff. and 262f.; GS 7, 86ff., 185ff. and p. 391). Rather, art is characterized by empathy and mimesis, a distinct form of experience (*Aesthetic Theory*, 54f.; GS 7, 86f.). When discussing this aesthetic form of experience in his *Aesthetic Theory*, Adorno often refers to the concept of mimesis, mimetic capacity, or mimetic impulse.[10]

In a successful work of art, mimesis and the rational do not confront each other as incompatible opposites; rather, art is the result of the tension between those two poles. "Art is mimetic comportment that for the purpose of its objectivation disposes over the most advanced rationality" (*Aesthetic Theory*, 289; GS 7, 429). The rational moment consists in a complete mastery of the material and its design and in an application of the laws of aesthetic construction and form.

The mimetic impulses, by contrast, manifest themselves in the artistic process of creation. The mimetic moment in art should not be understood as pure imitation of a given matter; rather, mimesis gives expression to that which escapes objectifying representation. "The survival of mimesis, the nonconceptual affinity of the subjectively produced with its unposited other, defines art as a form of knowledge and to that extent as 'rational.' For that to which the mimetic comportment responds is the telos of knowledge, which art simultaneously blocks with its own categories. Art completes knowledge with what is excluded from knowledge" (*Aesthetic Theory*, 54; GS 7, 86f.). Art, however, should not be limited to its epistemological dimension. Adorno uses the concept of mimesis precisely in order to emphasize the expressive moment in art. That moment can hardly be imagined other than "as the expression of suffering—joy has proven inimical to expression, perhaps because it has yet to exist" (*Aesthetic Theory*, 110; GS 7, 169). For this reason, authentic contemporary art is dark [finster]; "its primary colour is black" (*Aesthetic Theory*, 39; GS 7, 65). In another key passage of *Aesthetic Theory*, Adorno states that in a world that is out of joint, all that is utopian in art is "draped in black"; yet, by virtue of its dissonances, art remains a "recollection of the possible in opposition to the actual . . . something like the imaginary reparation of the catastrophe of world history" (*Aesthetic Theory*, 135; transl. modified; GS 7, 204). When it expresses what is not yet—in music, literature, painting, and so on—art bears this aspect of reparation.

In this context, Adorno draws on Kant's category of natural beauty. However, as the "trace of the nonidentical in things," natural beauty is, according to Adorno, altogether "dispersed and uncertain" (*Aesthetic Theory*, 73; GS 7, 124). It should not be confused with pure nature, nor should it be confused with nature that has been shaped by the human hand. Rather, natural beauty is a cipher for what nature *could be*: "What is beautiful in nature is what appears to be more than what is literally there. . . . As true as the fact that every object in nature can be considered beautiful is the judgment that the landscape of Tuscany is more beautiful than the surroundings of Gelsenkirchen" (*Aesthetic Theory*, 70f. and p. 72; GS 7 111f.). The task of art is to serve as a reminder of this potentiality: "What nature strives for in vain, artworks fulfill: They open their eyes" (*Aesthetic Theory*, 66; GS 7, 104).

Aesthetic Theory represents a very complicated—and successful—balancing act: Adorno demonstrates the contradictory unity of the artwork, its construction out of a critical and an anticipatory aspect. Just as art can preserve its authenticity only by negating the catastrophic course the world is taking, so it must also simultaneously be the "plenipotentiary of a better praxis" (*Aesthetic Theory*, 12 and pp. 83f.; GS 7, 26 and p. 130). To the extent that the negation of the status quo is articulated in the artwork, it can change reality for the better: it can level charges against the world. For Adorno, this is the signature of modernity: the break with the principle of representation, with the concrete, with anything already known. In the avant-garde, one confronts the "entanglement" [Verfransung] (*Aesthetic Theory*, 182; my translation., D. S.; GS 7, 271)[11] of artistic genres that accompanies the disintegration of traditional norms.[12] What Adorno has in mind is the dissolution of the traditional borders between artistic genres, their confluence, a tendency that manifests itself in the fact that music-like structures can be found in paintings or in literary, and in particular lyrical, texts. With its claim that "the individual arts aspire to their concrete generalizations" ("Art and the Arts," 373; GS 10.1, 438), Adorno's reflections on aesthetic theory suggest a new concept of the avant-garde and a revision of concepts of art based on specific genres.[13]

Adorno, who did not live to see the publication of the book and its reception, understood *Aesthetic Theory* as exemplifying his epistemological model of thinking in constellations. This late work fully realizes one of the central tenets of negative dialectics: philosophy is not merely the application of categories; it must be self-composing, because "[t]he crux is what happens in it, not a thesis or a position—the texture, not the deductive or inductive course of one-track minds" (*Negative Dialectics*, 33; GS 6, 44).

Notes

1 Theodor Wiesengrund-Adorno (1903–69) was one of the most important philosophers, sociologists, and musicologists of the twentieth century. Following his dissertation on Edmund Husserl in 1924, he completed his Habilitation on *Die Konstruktion des Ästhetischen bei Kierkegaard* in 1931 (English: *Kierkegaard: Construction of the Aesthetic*, 1989) and became a Privatdozent (associate lecturer) at Frankfurt University. At the same time, he worked for the *Zeitschrift für Sozialforschung*, published by the Institute for Social Research, which was directed by Max Horkheimer. As a left-wing intellectual and so-called half-Jew, he experienced the repressive measures of the Nazi regime, and in 1934 emigrated to England, where he worked on a second dissertation at Merton College, Oxford. That work was only published in 1956 as *Metakritik der Erkenntnistheorie* (GS 5) (English: *Against Epistemology: a Metacritique*, 1982). In 1938, he accepted an invitation from Max Horkheimer and went to the United States, where he became a collaborator at the Institute for Social Research and director of music at the Princeton Radio Research Project. That project, under the leadership of Paul Lazarsfeld and financed by the Rockefeller Foundation, investigated the social function of radio. Horkheimer and Adorno subsequently moved from New York to Pacific Palisades, Los Angeles, where, from the early 1940s onward, they worked together on a fundamental critique of reason, published in 1947 under the title *Dialektik der Aufklärung* by Querido in Amsterdam (English: *Dialectic of Enlightenment*, 2002). Four years after the end of the war, Adorno returned to Germany and to the university of his hometown, Frankfurt am Main, for the winter term 1949. There, he published important works and taught philosophy and sociology until his untimely death in 1969. He also served as the director of the Institute for Social Research, which reopened in 1953. For the connections between Adorno's life history and his intellectual development against the background of the times, I refer the reader to my detailed biography (Müller-Doohm).

2 Culture is an object of sociological knowledge that was of particular concern to Adorno. His investigations cover somewhat unusual topics, such as popular

songs, jazz, horoscopes, or sexual taboos, and also areas that are well-established topics for sociology, for instance, mass media, leisure behaviour, the ideal of a "personality," or the transformation of education.

3 (Transl. note: The paragraph break introduced in the English translation has been removed.)

4 "All thinking is exaggeration, in so far as every thought that is one at all goes beyond its confirmation by the given facts" ("Opinion, Delusion, Society," 6; GS 10.2, 577; cf. also Müller-Doohm).

5 With Habermas, the perspective of an ideology critique of popular culture's function as a social glue that holds together the antagonistic social totality is no longer in the foreground. Rather, from the perspective of the theory of democracy, Habermas identifies the manifest danger to the public sphere from certain power structures. This focus on the phenomenon of the power of media indicates that Habermas is not at all interested in the media's role as a conveyor of meaning. Rather, he limits himself to an analysis of the spheres of communication whose shared interface is the politically functioning public sphere. Further, he investigates the institutional makeup of the mass media and describes their political function within the tense relation between "is" (the power of the media) and "ought" (the free flow of communication).

6 During his years in exile in America (1938–49), Adorno was involved in numerous empirical research projects. The best known of these, apart from the *Radio Research Project*, led by the Austrian emigrant Paul Lazarsfeld in New York, is the *Authoritarian Personality*. Adorno thus had practical knowledge in these areas of media research and research into prejudice (cf. Claussen 31, who rightly remarks: "Without the American experience, Critical Theory could not have been formulated." Cf. also Ziege 2009, 136ff.). Adorno's experience of Anglo-American culture not only led him to promote democratic forms of life but also taught him "no longer to regard as natural the conditions that had developed historically, like those in Europe: 'not to take things for granted.' ... In America I was liberated from a naïve belief in culture, and acquired this ability to see culture from the outside" ("Scientific Experiences of a European Scholar in America," 239; GS 10.2, 734).

7 Cf. Müller-Jentsch (2019; Kunstsoziologie, 351–80); Sonderegger.

8 Transl. note: The English translation renders "Rettung" sometimes as "redemption" [as in this case], sometimes as "rescue" [as, for instance, on p. 131: "The question of the truth of something made is indeed none other than the question of semblance and the rescue of semblance as the semblance of the true."]. Given the central importance of the "rescuing urge" [Begierde des Rettens] in Adorno's interpretation of Kant, "rescue" appears preferable.

9 The "sphere of communication," in this context, refers to processes of consumption, to the audience and its needs, and not to processes to do with reaching understanding.

10 Neither in *Dialectic of Enlightenment* nor in *Aesthetic Theory* does Adorno provide a theory of mimesis. On the concept of mimesis, see Früchtl; Scholze, 13ff. Jürgen Ritsert holds that the oppositional conceptualities of mimesis and

rationality form a main thread running through Adorno's *Aesthetic Theory*. In *Dialectic of Enlightenment*, the two fundamental categories, he says, are myth and enlightenment, and in *Negative Dialectics* identity and nonidentity. According to Ritsert, mimesis consists in "the praxis of the subject to surrender to the idiosyncratic sense and the particular details of the material, to seek the nearness of the individual object, so to speak." Further, mimesis "can be understood [as] perceptive sensibility [aesthesis], and thus as the subject's perceptiveness for a wealth of inexhaustible individual impressions." Ritsert concludes that Adorno linked mimetic experience to "thinking in configurations" along the lines expounded in *Negative Dialectics*. Ritsert 1996, 29ff.; cf. also Menke.

11 Transl. note: The English translation renders "Diese differieren ebensowohl spezifisch, wie sie sich verfransen" as "These [i.e., the artistic genres] differ as much specifically as they diverge from one another," instead of "become entangled with one another," thus missing the opposition between differing and being entangled.

12 Cf. Adorno, "Art and the Arts," 368ff.; GS 10.1, pp. 432ff.; Adorno, "On Some Relationships between Music and Painting," pp. 66ff.; GS 16, pp. 628ff.; see also Eichel.

13 On this thematic complex, see Wellmer, *Wahrheit*; Wellmer, *Zur Dialektik von Moderne und Postmoderne*.

Works Cited

A. English translations of texts by Adorno

Adorno, Theodor W. "Art and the Arts." In *Can One Live after Auschwitz? A Philosophical Reader*. Trans. Rodney Livingstone. Stanford: Stanford University Press, 2003, pp. 368–87.

Adorno, Theodor W. "Culture Industry Reconsidered." In *The Culture Industry: Selected Essays on Mass Culture*. Trans. Anson G. Rabinbach. London: Routledge, 1991, pp. 98–106.

Adorno, Theodor W. "Free Time." In *The Culture Industry: Selected Essays on Mass Culture*. Trans. Gordon Finlayson and Nicholas Walker. London: Routledge, 1991, pp. 187–97.

Adorno, Theodor W. Gesammelte Schriften 3. *Dialektik der Aufklärung*. Frankfurt am Main: Suhrkamp, 1997.

Adorno, Theodor W. Gesammelte Schriften 4. *Minima Moralia. Reflexionen aus dem beschädigten Leben*. Frankfurt am Main: Suhrkamp, 1997.

Adorno, Theodor W. Gesammelte Schriften 5. *Zur Metakritik der Erkenntnistheorie*, Frankfurt am Main: Suhrkamp, 1997.

Adorno, Theodor W. Gesammelte Schriften 6. *Negative Dialektik*. Frankfurt am Main: Suhrkamp, 1997.

Adorno, Theodor W. Gesammelte Schriften 7. *Ästhetische Theorie*. Frankfurt am Main: Suhrkamp. 1997.

Adorno, Theodor W. Gesammelte Schriften 8. *Soziologische* Schriften I. Frankfurt am Main: Suhrkamp, 1997.
Adorno, Theodor W. Gesammelte Schriften 10.1. *Kulturkritik und Gesellschaft* I. Frankfurt am Main: Suhrkamp, 1997.
Adorno, Theodor W. Gesammelte Schriften 10.2. *Kulturkritik und Gesellschaft II.* Frankfurt am Main: Suhrkamp, 1997.
Adorno, Theodor W. Gesammelte Schriften 11. *Noten zur Literatur.* Frankfurt am Main: Suhrkamp, 1997
Adorno, Theodor W. Gesammelte Schriften 14. *Dissonanzenten/Einleitung in die Musiksoziologie.* Frankfurt am Main: Suhrkamp, 1997
Adorno, Theodor W. Gesammelte Schriften 20.1. *Vermischte Schriften I.* Frankfurt am Main: Suhrkamp, 1997.
Adorno, Theodor W. Gesammelte Schriften 20.2. *Vermischte Schriften I.* Frankfurt am Main: Suhrkamp, 1997.
Adorno, Theodor W. *Philosophische Terminologie.* Nachgelassene Schriften. herausgegeben von Henri Lonitz. Berlin: Suhrkam, 2016.
Adorno, Theodor W. "On Subject and Object." In *Critical Models: Interventions and Catchwords.* Trans. Henry Pickford. Stanford: Stanford University Press, 1998, pp. 245-58.
Adorno, Theodor W. "On the Fetish Character in Music and the Regression in Listening." In *The Culture Industry: Selected Essays on Mass Culture.* Trans. Anson G. Rabinbach. London: Routledge, 1991, pp. 29-60.
Adorno, Theodor W. "Prologue to Television." In *Critical Models: Interventions and Catchwords.* Trans. Henry Pickford. Stanford: Stanford University Press. 1998, pp. 49-58.
Adorno, Theodor W. "Sociology and Empirical Research." In *The Positivist Dispute in German Sociology.* Trans. Glyn Adey and David Frisby. London: Heinemann, 1976, pp. 68-86.
Adorno, Theodor W. "Scientific Experiences of a European Scholar in America." In *Critical Models: Interventions and Catchwords.* Trans. Henry Pickford. Stanford: Stanford University Press, 1998, pp. 215-44.
Adorno, Theodor W. "Those Twenties." In *Critical Models: Interventions and Catchwords.* Trans. Henry Pickford. Stanford: Stanford University Press, 1998, pp. 41-8.

B. General

Claussen, Detlev 199. "Die amerikanische Erfahrung kritischer Theoretiker." In *Hannoversche Schriften I: Keine Kritische Theorie ohne Amerika,* S. 27-45. Ed. ders./Oskar Negt/Michael Wertz. Frankfurt am Main: Verlag Neue Kritik.
Eichel, Christine. *Vom Ermatten der Avantgarde zur Vernetzung der Künste.* Frankfurt am Main: Suhrkamp, 1993.
Früchtl, Josef. *Mimesis. Konstellation eines Zentralbegriffs bei Adorno.* Würzburg: Königshausen & Neumann, 1986.
Horkheimer, Max and Theodor W. Adorno. *Dialectic of Enlightenment: Philosophical Fragments.* Trans. Edmund Jephcott. Stanford: Stanford University Press, 2002.

Horkheimer, Max and Theodor W. Adorno. *Dialektik der Aufklärung.* Philosophische Fragmente. Amsterdam: Querido, 1947.
Menke, Christoph. *Die Souveränität der Kunst.* Frankfurt am Main: Suhrkam, 1991.
Müller-Doohm, Stefan. *Theodor W. Adorno. Eine Biographie.* Frankfurt am Main: Suhrkamp, 2003.
Müller-Doohm, Stefan. *Theodor W. Adorno: A Biography.* Trans. Rodney Livingstone. Cambridge: Polity, 2005.
Müller-Doohm, Stefan. *Sagen, "was einem aufgeht. Sprache bei Adorno – Adornos Sprache."* In *Wozu Adorno? Beiträge zur Kritik und zum Fortbestand einer Schlüsseltheorie des 20. Jahrhunderts.* Ed. Kohler, Georg/Stefan Müller-Doohm, Göttingen: Velbrück, 2008, pp.28-50.
Müller-Jentsch, Walter. *Die Kunst in der Gesellschaft.* 2nd ed. Wiesbaden: Springer, 2012.
Müller-Jentsch, Walter. Theodor W. Adorno (1903-1969). "Kunstsoziologie zwischen Negativität und Versöhnung." In *Klassiker der Soziologie der Künste. Prominente und bedeutende Ansätze.* Ed. Steuerwald, Christian. Wiesbaden: Springer, 2017, pp. 351-80.
Ritsert, Jürgen. *Ästhetische Theorie als Gesellschaftskritik.* Umrisse der Dialektik in Adornos Spätwerk. Frankfurt am Main: Suhrkamp, 1996.
Scholze, Britta. *Kunst als Kritik. Adornos Weg aus der Dialektik.* Würzburg: Königshausen&Neuman, 2000.
Sonderegger, Ruth. *Ästhetische Theorie.* In Adorno Handbuch. Leben, Werk, Wirkung, Ed. Richard Klein, Johann Kreuzer, Stefan Müller-Doohm. Stuttgart: Metzler, 2011, pp. 414-27.
Wellmer, Alfred. *Wahrheit, Schein, Versöhnung.* Adornos ästhetische Rettung der Modernität. In Adorno-Konfernz 1983. Ed. Ludwig von Friedeburg, Jürgen Habermas. Frankfurt am Main: Suhrkamp, 1983, pp. 138-76.
Wellmer, Alfred. *Zur Dialektik von Moderne und Postmoderne. Vernunftkritik nach Adorno.* Frankfurt am Main: Suhrkamp, 1985.
Ziege, Eva-Maria. *Antisemitismus und Gesellschaftstheorie. Die Frankfurter Schule im amerikanischen Exil.* Frankfurt am Main: Suhrkamp, 2009.

NOTES ON CONTRIBUTORS

Stefanie Baumann is currently a contracted researcher at CineLab/ IFILNOVA (New University of Lisbon, Portugal). She obtained her PhD in philosophy in 2013, with a doctoral thesis on Walid Raad's artistic project *The Atlas Group*. She taught philosophy, aesthetics, and contemporary art theory at University of Paris VIII (Paris, 2007–10), Ashkal Alwan (Beirut, 2013), ALBA—the Lebanese Academy of Fine Arts/University of Balamand (Beirut, 2012–15), and the Maumaus Study Program (Lisbon, since 2016). She also worked with the artist Esther Shalev-Gerz as personal assistant from 2005 to 2010, and collaborated with video artists Marie Voignier and Mounira Al Solh.

Jeffrey R. Di Leo is Professor of English and Philosophy at the University of Houston-Victoria, United States. He is the editor and publisher of *American Book Review*, and the founder and editor of *symplokē*. His recent books include *Corporate Humanities in Higher Education: Moving Beyond the Neoliberal Academy* (2013), *Criticism after Critique: Aesthetics, Literature, and the Political* (2014), *Dead Theory: Death, Derrida, and the Afterlife of Theory* (2016), *Higher Education under Late Capitalism: Identity, Conduct and the Neoliberal Condition* (2017), *American Literature as World Literature* (2017), *Bloomsbury Handbook of Literary and Cultural Theory* (2018), *The End of American Literature: Essays from the Late Age of Print* (2019), *Biotheory: Life and Death under Capitalism* (2020, with P. Hitchcock), *What's Wrong with Antitheory* (2020), and *Vinyl Theory* (2020).

Camilla Flodin holds a PhD in Aesthetics from Uppsala University and is currently Lecturer and Research Fellow in Comparative Literature at Södertörn University, Stockholm, Sweden. She has published in, for example, *Adorno Studies* and *British Journal for the History of Philosophy*. She is co-editor of *Beyond Autonomy in Eighteenth-Century British and German Aesthetics* (Routledge, 2020) and a contributor to the *Oxford Handbook of Adorno* (forthcoming).

Robin Truth Goodman is Professor of English at Florida State University, United States. Her prior publications include *The Bloomsbury Handbook of 21st-Century Feminist Theory* (edited collection; 2019); *Gender for the Warfare State: Literature of Women in Combat* (2017); *Literature and the Development of Feminist Theory* (edited collection; 2016); *Gender Work: Feminism After Neoliberalism* (2013); *Feminist Theory in Pursuit of the Public: Women and the "Re-privatization" of Labor* (2010); *Policing Narratives and the State of Terror* (2009); *World, Class, Women: Global Literature, Education, and Feminism* (2004); *Strange Love: Or, How We Learn to Stop Worrying and Love the Market* (cowritten with Kenneth J. Saltman; 2002); and *Infertilities: Exploring Fictions of Barren Bodies* (2001).

Birgit Antonia Hofstätter is a lecturer at the Department of German at Stockholm University, Sweden. She was awarded a PhD in 2017, with a thesis entitled "The Fabric of Critique: 'Lending Voice to Suffering' in the Work of T.W. Adorno." Her research focuses on early critical theory, in particular on the relationship between aesthetics and critique. Recent articles appeared in *Adorno Studies* and *Zeitschrift für kritische Theorie*. Together with Daniel Steuer, she is the co-editor of a forthcoming collection of essays on *Adorno's Rhinoceros: Art, Nature, Critique*.

Natalie Lozinski-Veach is an assistant professor of German in the School of International Letters and Cultures at Arizona State University, United States. Her work focuses on the intersection between critical aesthetic theory and the environmental humanities, especially animal studies, in twentieth- and twenty-first-century German and Polish literature. She has published on Paul Celan, Walter Benjamin, and the Polish modernist writer and artist Bruno Schulz; her forthcoming work includes an article on the notion of poetic involution in Celan and Adorno. Her current book project is a study of creaturely expression in literature after the Shoah.

Stefan Müller-Doohm studied in Frankfurt under Theodor W. Adorno and Max Horkheimer and is now Professor Emeritus of Sociology and Director of the Forschungsstelle Intellektuellensoziologie (Research Centre on the Sociology of Intellectuals) at the University of Oldenburg. Among his more recent publications are: *Adorno: A Biography* (2005) and *Habermas. A Biography* (2016).

Max Paddison is Professor Emeritus of music aesthetics at the University of Durham, United Kingdom. He studied music theory, piano, and composition at the Royal Manchester College of Music, musicology at the University of Exeter, where he also did his doctorate. He was a DAAD scholarship holder at the Goethe University Frankfurt am Main, where he worked on Adorno's music aesthetics and music sociology. His work focuses on critical theory, philosophy, and contemporary music. Publications include *Adorno's*

Aesthetics of Music (1993); *Adorno, Modernism and Mass Culture* (1996); *Musique Contemporaine: Perspectives Théoriques et Philosophiques* (ed. jointly with Irène Deliège, 2001); "Die vermittelete Unmittelbarkeit der Musik: Zum Vermittlungsbegriff in der Adornoschen Musikästhetik" (in *Musikalischer Sinn*, eds. Becker & Vogel, 2007); and *The Philosophy of Rhythm: Aesthetics, Music, Poetics* (ed. jointly with Andy Hamilton and Peter Cheyne, 2019).

Ulrich Plass is Professor of Letters and German Studies at Wesleyan University, United States. He has published monographs on Kafka and on Adorno's literary criticism, articles on aphoristic ethics (Nietzsche, Adorno), alienation and literary form (Brecht), neoliberalism and the novel (Bolaño), and postmodern realisms (Kracht, Sebald). He is finishing a book on the genealogy of the Frankfurt School's concept of the culture industry. His forthcoming work includes articles on realism debates and on economics and aesthetics in Marx, Lukács, and Sohn-Rethel.

Larson Powell is Professor of German and Film Studies at the University of Missouri—Kansas City, United States. He has published *The Technological Unconscious in Modern German Literature* (2008); *The Differentiation of Modernism* (2013), and two edited volumes, *Classical Music in the German Democratic Republic* (2015, coedited with Kyle Frackman) and *German Television: Historical and Theoretical Perspectives* (2016, coedited with Robert Shandley). He has also published articles in German, French, and Polish on Adorno, film, music, and literature. His book on DEFA director Konrad Wolf was published by Camden House in 2020, and he is preparing a collection of musicology essays. Other teaching and research interests include Scandinavian and Eastern European film, film music, media theory, comparative literature, and philosophical aesthetics.

Jean-Michel Rabaté, Professor of English and Comparative Literature at the University of Pennsylvania, United States, is one of managing editors of the *Journal of Modern Literature*. A co-founder of Slought Foundation, where he curates exhibitions, lectures, and conversations, he is a fellow of the American Academy of Arts and Sciences. He has authored twenty-six books and edited twenty collections of essays. Recent titles include *Rust* (2017) and *Rire au Soleil* (2019), as well as the collections *After Derrida* (2018), *The New Beckett* (2019), *Understanding Derrida, Understanding Modernism* (2019), and *Knots: Post-Lacanian Psychoanalysis, Literature and Film* (2020).

Kenneth J. Saltman is Professor of Educational Policy Studies at University of Illinois at Chicago, United States. His books include *Scripted Bodies: Corporate Power, Smart Technologies, and the Undoing of Public Education* (2016) and *The Swindle of Innovative Educational Finance* (2018).

Heidi Schlipphacke is Associate Professor of Germanic Studies at the University of Illinois at Chicago, United States. Her research focuses broadly on issues of gender, kinship, and aesthetics in the German Enlightenment, in post–Second World War German and Austrian literature and film, and in critical theory. She is the author of *Nostalgia After Nazism: History, Home and Affect in German and Austrian Literature and Film* (2010) and is currently working on a monograph on eighteenth-century German literature and thought entitled *The Aesthetics of Kinship*.

Daniel Steuer is a Research Fellow at the Centre for Applied Philosophy, Politics, and Ethics (CAPPE) at the University of Brighton. Until 2010, he was Senior Lecturer in German at the University of Sussex and a member of the Centre for Social and Political Thought, which he also chaired from 2005-2007. He wrote his PhD on Wittgenstein's reception of Goethe's *Theory of Colours*, and his research straddles the divide between philosophy, literature, and science. His latest publication is *War and Algorithm*, co-authored with Max Liljefors and Gregor Noll (Rowman & Littlefield, 2019).

Christian P. Weber is an Associate Professor and program coordinator of German at Florida State University, United States. His research interests include Goethe, romanticism, aesthetic theory, and biopolitical metaphors of nationalism. He is the author of *Die Logik der Lyrik: Goethes Phänomenologie des Geistes in Gedichten* (Freiburg: Rombach, 2013) and recent articles and book chapters on Kleist's editorship of the "Berliner Abendblätter," Goethe's "Faust" as a critique of posthumanism, Goethe versus ETA Hoffmann on the uncanny, and Anacreontic poetry as a forerunner of Kantian aesthetics.

Sabine Wilke is the Joff Hanauer Distinguished Professor in Western Civilization, Professor of German, and Chair of Germanics at the University of Washington, United States. She is also associated with and teaches in the European Studies program, and the doctoral Theory and Criticism program. Her research and teaching interests include modern German literature and culture, intellectual history and theory, and cultural and visual studies. She has written books and articles on body constructions in modern German literature and culture, German unification, the history of German film and theater, and contemporary German authors and filmmakers, including Christa Wolf, Heiner Müller, Botho Strauss, Ingeborg Bachmann, Elfriede Jelinek, and Monika Treut. Most recently, Wilke was involved in a larger project on German colonialism and postcoloniality and the question of comparative colonialisms, especially how Germany related differently to Africa and the South Pacific. With assistance from the Alexander von Humboldt Foundation, Wilke is now directing a transatlantic research network on the environmental humanities and is working on a new project on environmental criticism, in particular the overlapping concerns of postcolonialism and ecocriticism.

INDEX

4' 33" (Cage)   17
45 r.p.m. record   77 n.14
"1948 Unbound"   136

abstraction   2, 100, 111, 112, 224
abstract labor   221, 223–4, 225, 229
absurdist theater   111, 113–16, 121
absurdity of life   111
Accanto (Lachenmann)   85
The Act of Killing (film)   36–48
Act without Words I: A Mime for One Player   126–7
Adam, Barbara   130
Adamov, Arthur   111
Adaptive Learning Technology   240
Adorno and Performance (Daddario and Gritzner)   126
advertising/advertisements   41, 46–7, 62, 63, 70, 99, 218, 240, 247
aesthetic apparatus   83
aesthetic meaning   23, 33–4 n.4–5
aesthetics   1–2. *See also* art/artwork; Camp aesthetics
  barbarism   169
  lecture on   1, 40, 45–6, 185–6
  moment of resistance in   255–8
  reflective   222
Aesthetic Theory (Adorno)   2, 3, 4, 9, 12, 15, 16, 22, 26–7, 28, 30, 31, 45, 96, 102, 120–2, 160, 161–71, 173, 174, 181, 182–4, 196, 206, 208, 209, 218, 220, 222, 249, 255–8
aesthetic time   173. *See also* empirical time
affect   167
  primordial   66–7
  suffering   162, 165

Agamben, Giorgio   118–19
agency
  conspiracy theory and   241–4
  disembodied telepresence and   236
  expressive   100, 102
  human   128
  inflated and total   243
  montage   105
  social   244
"The Aging of the New Music" (Adorno)   11–12, 24
Ahmed, Sara   162
Air (Lachenmann)   82
Alban Berg: Master of the Smallest Link (Adorno)   60
"Alexandrium Giganteous"   135–6
alienated labor   223
ambiguity, intolerance of   165–6
amusement   61, 62, 252
anarchic noises   84
Anders, Günther   115–16, 117, 123 n.6
Anderson, Benedict   48 n.1
Anif, Haji   42–3
animals   42–3, 195–210
  art/artwork and   181–91, 206–10
  clever   196–201
  human's likeness   184–9
  lack of compassion toward   200
  mimesis   42
The Animal That Therefore I Am (Derrida)   211 n.7
Anthropocene
  cultural expressions   128
  gentle   130
  performances   128–38
  time   130
antinomy   122

INDEX

anti-Semitism 95, 200
Antonioni, Michelangelo 96
arbitrariness 149, 152
Arcades Project (Benjamin) 122–3
art/artwork 2. *See also* music
  absolute freedom in 222
  animals and 181–91, 206–10
  autonomy 214–15, 216
  classicism 25–7
  commodity-character of 218
  contradictory unity of 257
  ephemerality 164, 173
  expression 204–10
  as fait social 255
  immanent analysis of 255
  mimesis 207–8, 256–7
  mode of production 214–15
  power to resist 256
  progressive *vs.* regressive 122
  ridiculousness 185–9
  self-reflexive tendencies 205
  self-reification 221–2
  social content 81–6
  social contradictions in 222
  social labor and 214–29
  social reality and 256
  temporality of 173
  traditional forms 100
  truth-content of 205
  utopian moments of 256
artistic autonomy 2, 105, 228
art object 2
Asian financial crisis 37
"Aspects of Hegel's Philosophy" (Adorno) 221
athematicism 88
atom bombs 136. *See also* nuclear threat
atonality 83, 184, 255
Attali, Jacques 61, 62, 76 n.7
"Attempt to Understand Endgame" (Adorno) 123 n.1
augmented reality 134–6
aura 65, 94–5
auratic 84, 95
Auschwitz 15–18, 108–23, 161, 165, 248–9
authentic art 187

authenticity 65, 66, 172, 252, 257
authoritarianism 37, 38, 39, 48, 234, 241, 245
authoritarian personality 165–6
Authoritarian Personality (Adorno) 166, 259 n.6
autonomous art 10, 19 n.4, 97
  film 102, 103, 105
  labor productivity 217
  music 58
autonomy 86–9
  aesthetic 81
  art/artwork 214–15, 216
  democracy and 254
avant-garde 7, 10, 12, 13, 257–8
  entanglement 257
  French 39
  modernist 145, 158, 255
  music journal 62
  Russian 39

Babuscio, Jack 172
barbarism 169, 249
bare life/mere existence 118–19
Basnett, Caleb J. 212 n.24
Baudelaire, Charles 3, 22, 118, 149, 157
Baum, Vicki 174 n.13
Baxstrom, Richard 49 n.9, 50 n.12, 51 n.17
Beasts of the Modern Imagination: Darwin, Nietzsche, Kafka, Ernst, & Lawrence (Norris) 210 n.3
Beck, Ulrich 138
Beckett, Samuel 3, 12, 15, 89, 98, 108–23, 126, 127, 128, 129, 228, 249, 256
  Endgame 12, 109–19, 121, 122
  Fin de Partie 109
  Krapp's Last Tape 109
  The Unnamable 109, 120, 122
  Waiting for Godot 109, 115, 116
Beethoven 25, 29, 31, 57, 60, 66, 70, 87, 98, 182
Beethoven: The Philosophy of Music (Adorno) 60
Befindlichkeiten 112
Behlil, Melis 40, 46, 51 n.21

Being and Time (Heidegger)   111, 112
Below the Surface   95
Ben-Habib, Seyla   19 n.6
Benjamin, Walter   26, 29, 31, 34 n.8, 38, 42, 65, 77 n.13, 94–5, 105, 113, 114, 117, 118, 122–3, 145–6, 147, 148, 152, 155, 161, 164, 210, 220
Berg, Alban   58, 60, 62, 75
Berger, Peter   9
Berman, Marshall   9, 10
Bernofsky, Susan   210 n.1
Bernstein, J. M.   198
Beuys, Joseph   17–18
Bicycle Thieves   96
binary thought structures   202
binding   252
biology   135, 136
biometric pedagogy   239
birds, song of   182–3
The Bitter Tears of Petra von Kant   173–4
Black and Blur (Moten)   174 n.5
blackbird   182–3
Bloch, Ernst   162
Booth, Mark   175 n.15, 175 n.22
Born Free   43, 48
Boulez, Pierre   60, 83, 84, 87, 88, 91 n.8
Brave New World (Huxley)   38
Brecht, Bertolt   3, 85–6, 101, 120, 215, 220
Bruits: essai sur l'économie de la musique (Attali)   76 n.7
Buchloh, Benjamin   17–18
Buell, Fredrick   137
"Bullwhip Kelp Drones (*Nereocystis volans*) Feeding off of Elliot Avenue Street Signs"   134–5
Bürger, Peter   18
Butler, Judith   161, 163
Butor, Michel   109

Cage, John   17
Calder, Alexander   135
Calinescu, Matei   168
Callois, Roger   42, 43
Cambridge University   241

Camp aesthetics   160–74
  The Bitter Tears of Petra von Kant (film)   173–4
  empathy   172
  experience of distance   171–2
  films and   172–4
  kitsch (*see* kitsch)
  melancholy   171, 172–3
  modernist art   170–1
  as a product of failure   172
  queer culture and   169–70
camps. *See* concentration camps
Capital (Marx)   216
capital accumulation   216–17
capitalism   2
  artistic productivity in   219
  culture industry (*see* culture industry)
  education and (*see* education)
  late   22, 60, 61–2, 87, 98–9, 123, 171, 196
  productive labor in   219–20
Capitalocene   132–3, 135, 138
Cartesian dualism   114
Caruth, Cathy   31
Castorp, Hans   23–4, 25
catastrophe   16, 90, 112, 113, 123, 133, 137, 196, 249, 256, 257
catharsis   161, 167–8
Caudwell, Christopher   82
Celan, Paul   16–17
The Challenge of Surrealism (Gillespie)   52 n.23
chamber music   60
changed humanity   205
Chan Zuckerberg Initiative's Summit   240
Chaplin, Charlie   95
cinema. *See* films
classical music   75, 84, 85, 90
classicism   25–7
climate change   137–8
cognitive utopia   251–2
Cold War   41
Colette   168
collective perception of reality   101
colonialism   133, 200

colonial mirror of production 51–2 n.22
Columbia Gramophone Company 57
commodification 28, 38, 47–8
    films 39
    retroactive 224
    universal 224
commodity 47–8, 247. *See also* culture industry
    aesthetic moment in 39
    capitalist system of 216
    fetishism 52 n.23, 225–6
    industrial production 44, 227–8, 253
    limits to 39
    repetitions 39
    social labor 216
commonality 216
communication 102. *See also* culture industry
    mass media 253
    sphere of 255, 259 n.9
communicative language 151
communism 37
Communist Party 37
complexism in music 86–7
composing 89–90
Composing for the Film (Adorno and Eisler) 38, 49 n.6, 96, 103
"Compositionist Manifesto" (Latour) 129
CompStat 234
compulsive labor 227
concentration camps 118, 121–2
Concept 3–4
concrete labor 223–4, 225
conformism 102
consciousness 228
conspiracy theories 241–5
    antidote to 244–5
    defined 241
    inequality and 242
    as mainstream beliefs 241
    positivism and 242–5
    of replacement 243
    right-wing populists and 242
constellations 3–4, 164, 188, 206, 252, 258

allegorical 150
    films as 104–5
    interlaced 164
    nuclear age as 138
consternation 110
consumer culture 158, 170
consumerism 61–2, 138
consumers 27–8, 43, 62, 64, 74, 95, 228, 252, 254
contrapuntal thinking 251
conventions 27, 45, 202, 227
corporate culture, education and 238
corporeal control 239
"Correspondances" (Baudelaire's poem) 157
Courts-Mahler, Hedwig 174 n.13
critical consciousness 245
critical cultural theory 15–16, 247–58. *See also* culture
critical melancholy 172–3
critical negativity 127
critical pedagogy 236
critique 38, 81–90, 129, 130, 136, 172, 222
    as an aesthetic project 138
    capitalism 132–3, 233
    classicism 25–7
    concept 250
    declinist/elitist 224–5
    as dialectical thought process 249–52
    film production 38
    identity-logic 133
    ideology 132
    intentional exaggeration 250
    interiority 162, 163
    interpretations 250
    masculinity 166
    modern culture 24
    modernism and modern 12–15
    modernist "Sachlichkeit" 169
    political economy 215
    positivism 235–6
    social 102, 162
    television 162
    utopia 162
    Western thought 162

Critique of the Power of Judgement (Kant) 9
Cruising Utopia: The Then and There of Queer Futurity (Muñoz) 162
cubism 83
cultural analysis 166, 247
cultural criticism 247–8, 249. *See also* critical cultural theory
"Cultural Criticism and Society" (Adorno) 247
cultural goods 253
culture
  as an object of sociological knowledge 258–9 n.2
  critical theory of 247–58
  disintegration of 249
  failure of 248–9
  nature and 42
  staging and restaging 253–4
"Culture Critique and Society" (Adorno) 16
culture industry 37, 252–4
  categorical imperative 253
  commercial productions 101
  corruption of 98
  effect of 254
  function of 253
  hegemonic regimes 137
  market-based principles of 98–9
  mass communication media 253
  productive labor and 219–20
  products of 97
  pseudo-realism of 101
  split consciousness and 254
  as a "thought model" 252
"Culture Industry Reconsidered" (Adorno) 98
Current of Music: Elements of a Radio Theory (Adorno) 60, 76 n.6
Curtius, Robert 114
"The Curves of the Needle" (Adorno) 64–9
cynicism 4, 114, 116, 242

Daddario, Will 126
damaged life 171, 251
dandyism 169

D'Annunzio, Gabriele 168
darkness of language 147, 150–1
Darwin's theory of evolution 196
"Das Altern der neuen Musik" (Adorno). *See* "The Aging of the New Music" (Adorno)
Dasein 112
"Das Erbe und die neue Musik" (Adorno) 22, 33–4 n.5
Das Stilgesetz der Poesie (Meyer) 151
data/body privatization
  phase 239–41
  Adaptive Learning Technology 240
  Pay for Success 239
  Social Emotional Learning schemes 240
Debussy, Claude 70
deceleration 129–32
defetishizing 52 n.23
degenerating art 210
dehumanization 195–210
Deleuze, Gilles 87, 88–9, 238
democracy 254
  autonomy and 254
  free expression of opinions 254
Der getreuse Korrepetitor (Adorno) 60
Derrida, Jacques 211 n.7, 211 n.20
Der Schatz des Indianer-Joe (Adorno) 75, 76 n.4
De Sica, Vittorio 96
determinate negation 214
determined negation 120, 162, 171–2, 210, 214, 249, 250, 255
DeVos, Betsy 233
Dialectic of Enlightenment (Adorno) 3, 41, 60, 136, 186, 198, 202, 253, 259–60 n.10
dialectics 249–52
  cognitive utopia 251–2
  negative (*see* negative dialectics)
  oppositional thinking 251
dialectics at a standstill 113, 123
Dialektik der Aufklärung (Adorno and Horkheimer) 16
Die Antiquiertheit des Mesnchen (Anders) 115

Die Autonomie des Klangs (Hindrich) 80
Die flüchtige Wahrheit der Kunst (Lehmann) 80
Die Konstruktion des Ästhetischen bei Kierkegaard (Adorno) 258 n.1
"Die Ursache" (Frank) 117
"Difficulties" (Adorno) 27–8
digital humanities 232
Discipline and Punish (Foucault) 163
disembodied telepresence 236
disposedness 112
dissonance 26, 32, 45, 83, 87, 172, 208–9
Dissonanzen (Adorno) 11, 29, 59
distance/distancing 171–2
division of labor 94, 188, 215–17, 220, 224, 225
"The Doctrine of the Similar" (Benjamin) 42
documentary realism 39
dodecaphony 87–8
drag queen 172
Driscoll, Kári 210–11 n.3

"Eagle" (Calder) 135
Eco, Umberto 10, 18, 19 n.4
ecosystems 134–5
Edelman, Lee 162
Edison, Thomas 57
education
  cultures of democracy in 245
  data/body privatization phase 239–41
  for-profit college industry 233
  industrial scientific management phase 236–7
  neoliberal/accountability phase 237–9
  neoliberal privatization schemes 233
  positivism in 233, 236–41
  voucher schemes 233
Effi Briest (Fondane) 110
ego 199
Eichendorff, Joseph von 141–58
  poetic language 150–7

"Sehnsucht" 155–7
"Zwielicht" 154–5
Einleitung in die Musiksoziologie. See *Introduction to the Sociology of Music* (Adorno)
Eisenstadt, S. N. 10
Eisler, Hanns 38, 95
empirical time 173. See also aesthetic time
empiricism 4, 232, 233
Emrich, Wilhelm 157–8
enactment 48–9 n.4
Endgame (Beckett) 12, 109–19, 121, 122
"Endgames" (Geulen's essay) 175 n.25
end of art 224
enhanced truth content 134–6
Ensslin, Gudrun 82
entanglement 94, 127, 129, 138, 197–8, 200, 257
entartet 210
entertainment 59, 85, 98, 253
entertainment industry 14
The Entire History of the Louisiana Purchase 50 n.11
ephemerality 164, 173
equivalence 27, 166, 199, 200, 223
Erlebniswerte (experiential value) 254
Essays on Music (Adorno) 33 n.2
essence 25, 27, 31, 38, 88, 103, 104, 219
  material 244
  racial 243
Esslin, Martin 111, 120
Ethereal Queer: Television, Historicity, Desire (Villarejo) 162
ethics of camp 160–74
European composers 80–1
Evans, Richard J. 241
Every Student Succeeds Act 240
exchange 38, 39, 41, 51–2 n.22
  positivism 236
  principle of 244
  social exchange 236
exchange society 2

exchange value 98, 99, 219, 223, 224, 225, 236
existentialism 109, 111, 112
existentialist jargon 111
experience
    intellectual 235
    of modernity 9–10
expression 204–10
expressionism 15
extraterrestrial noise 29
extreme weather conditions 134

Facebook 240
facts 234
fascism/fascist 2, 43
    heterosexuality and 167, 174 n.11
    intolerance of ambiguity 167
    rituals of commodity 43
Fassbinder, R. W. 173
"Fassbinder's Debt to Poussin" (Kirby) 175 n.26
Ferneyhough, Brian 81, 86–9
fetishism/fetishization 3, 52 n.23, 218, 225–6, 248
Fifth Symphony (Beethoven) 57
Figaro (Mozart) 73
films 36–48, 94–106
    abstraction in 100
    artistic quality 96
    Camp aesthetics 172–4
    as a collective medium 103–4, 105
    commodification 39
    culture industry 97–100
    foreign 37
    gangster 37, 46, 47
    indexical nature 38
    mimesis 38, 41–6
    as modern art form 38
    montage 39, 103–6
    neutrality of 104
    representational character 100–3
    social antagonism 39
    totalitarian propaganda 101
Fin de Partie (Beckett) 109
First String Quartet (Adorno) 60, 75
First World War 23
Fischer-Lichte, Erika 127–8, 129

The Five Faces of Modernity (Calinescu) 168
Flaubert, Gustave 3
Flodin, Camilla 192 n.7, 212 n.22
Fordist schooling 237
foreign films 37
form 25, 26
    objectivity of 25
    traditional 100
formal subsumption 220
"The Form of the Phonograph Record" 68–9
Forth Worth National Bank 135
Fortwesen 24
Fourneaux, Henri 70
Frank, Leonhard 117
Frankfurt School 226
Frankfurt University 74
free competition 226
French art 168–9
French existentialism 109, 112
French Revolution 142, 147
Freud, Sigmund 14, 29, 30, 42, 44, 51 n.22, 88–9, 166, 169, 210–11 n.3
Freudian death drive 42
"Fugue on Camp" (Pero) 171
Fukushima accident 137
"Futur II" 132–3

gangster(s) 44
gangster film 37, 46, 47
Ganguly, Keya 49 n.5
"Gardens of the Anthropocene" 134, 135, 136
Gasset, Ortega y 247
Gehalt 81, 85, 90, 91 n.10
Genet, Jean 111
genetics 136, 197
geo-logic 132–3
Gerhardt, Christina 211 n.18
German musicology 81
Gershwin, George 70
Gesammelte Schriften 8, 17, 19 n.1
"Gesang einer gefangenen Amsel" 185
Gestalt 26
gesture 88

Getino, Octavio 39
Geulen, Eva 175 n.25
Gillespie, Susan 52 n.23
The Globalization Tapes 39
Goebbels, Heiner 129, 130–1, 138 n.2
Goehr, Lydia 33 n.2, 33 n.4, 183
good society 235
Gracchus, Hunter 118
gramophone. *See* phonograph
Graz production 137
"The Great Acceleration" 136
Greb, Ulrich 132–3
grit pedagogy 238, 240
Gritzner, Karoline 126

Habermas, Jürgen 11, 14, 19 n.6, 87, 259 n.5
Halberstam, Jack 161–2
Halle, Randall 166–7
Hansen, Miriam 38, 49 n.6
happiness 29, 32–3, 47, 61, 156, 189, 249, 256
Haydn 25
Hegel, Georg Wilhelm Friedrich 25, 45, 116, 120, 181, 221, 222–3, 255
Hegelian progression 121
hegemony 95, 133, 204, 207, 208
Heidegger, Martin 109, 111–12, 114, 115, 116, 144
Herzog, Werner 36–7, 49 n.9
heterosexuality 167, 174 n.11
high art 171
Hindemith, Paul 60
Hindrichs, Gunnar 80
History and Freedom (Adorno) 51–2 n.22, 173
Hofstätter, Petra 33 n.1
Holocaust 15, 24, 90, 118, 147, 160, 167
homosexuality. *See also* queer theory
    decriminalization of 166
    effeminacy and 167
    totalitarianism and 166, 167
    trope of 166

Horkheimer, Max 16, 41, 43, 44, 50 n.13, 51–2 n.22, 60, 63, 97, 109, 132, 136, 163, 186, 197, 199, 202, 218, 220, 226, 252, 258 n.1
"How to Look at Television" (Adorno) 162
Huber, Klaus 81
Hulatt, Owen 49 n.7
Hullot-Kentor, Robert 33 n.2, 45, 175 n.24, 192 n.2, 211 n.17
human 195–210. *See also* animals
    as an idea 201–2
    degeneration 202
    Enlightenment model of 199
    likeness to animals 184–9
    mutilation 199
    radical indeterminacy 202
    self-identical image 201
    species and 203
humanity 205
human super-amphibian 202
humor 84, 116–17, 228
Husserl, Edmund 114, 115, 258 n.1
Huxley, Aldous 47–8
hyperobjects 137

identity 67
    commercial culture and 2
    construction 2
    depth model of 163
    mirror stage 67
    modern subject 28
    nonidentical 167
    queer 162–4
    social labor products 222
    traditional music and 31
    universal 183
identity-logic 132–3
identity thinking 196, 199, 204, 206–7
ideology 132
immanent analysis of artwork 255
immanent criticism 248
Impromptus (Adorno) 60
individual 4, 25, 30, 39, 42, 44, 45, 117, 201, 247
    antagonism 188–9

political   133
resilience   240
social labor   217
socioeconomic system and   132
individual art/artworks   224, 258
individual cultural sectors   253
individual experience   127, 158 n.4
individual gesture   89
individual labor   228
individual poem   146
Indonesia   37–48
Indonesian Communist Party (PKI)   37
industrialization   225–6
Industrial Revolution   226
industrial scientific management phase   236–7
Infiltration Homogen für Konzertflügel (Beuys)   17–18
Inhalt   90, 91 n.10
inhumanity   205
"In Memory of Eichendorff" (Adorno)   156
In Search of Wagner (Adorno)   59
insight   250
Institute for Social Research   258 n.1
instrumentalizing artworks   101–2
instrumental techniques   83
intellectual experience   235
interiority   163–4
interlaced constellations   164
intolerance of ambiguity   165–6
Introduction to the Sociology of Music (Adorno)   59, 74–5
Ionesco, Eugene   111
Ireton, Sean   130
irreconcilability   31, 39, 45, 46, 161
Isherwood, Christopher   170

Jameson, Fredric   2, 44
The Jargon of Authenticity (Adorno)   111
Jaspers, Karl   111, 112
Jay, Martin   50 n.16
jazz   60, 63, 66, 137
Jeffries, Stuart   39
Jelinek, Elfriede   136–7
"Jene zwanziger Jahre" (Adorno)   16

Jewish   50 n.16, 117
Joyce, James   3, 11, 108, 111, 120
jukebox   57, 66

Kafka, Franz   3, 12, 108, 110–11, 114, 118, 120, 129, 195, 196, 202, 210
Kagel, Maurizio   82
Kalla, Jusuf   44
Kant, Immanuel   9, 22, 42, 45, 114, 130, 143, 151, 152–3, 158 n.4, 164, 169, 173, 181–2, 214, 248, 255, 257
Kaputt (Malaparte)   112
"Kein Licht"   136–7
Kennedy, Jackie   172
keywords   3
Kierkegaard, Søren   111
killings, reenactments of   37–48. See also *The Art of Killing* (film)
Kirby, Lynne   175 n.26
kitsch   59, 63, 73, 123, 167–71. See also Camp
   culture industry and   161
   defining   167
   as false catharsis   161, 167–8
   queer-phobic sensibility   168–9
   vulgar/vulgarity   168–70
kitschness   169
Klangfiguren (Adorno)   11
"Klassik, Romantik, neue Musik" (Adorno)   25, 30
Klee, Paul   3
Köck, Thomas   132, 133
Kontrakadenz (Lachenmann)   82
Kracauer, Siegfried   38, 49 n.5
Krakauer, Eric L.   98
Krapp's Last Tape (Beckett)   109
"Kriterien der neuen Musik" (Adorno)   11
Kurth, Ernst   83

labor   214–29
   abstract   223–4, 225
   Adorno's equivocation   215–18
   alienated   221, 223
   artistic   222–4
   collective   227–9

compulsive 227
concrete 223–4, 225
culture industry and 219–20
division of 94, 188, 215–17, 220, 224, 225
dual character 221
fetishism 218, 225–6
Hegel's notion of 221
industrial 227–8
objectification 221
private 215, 216
pure means 222
Lacan, Jacques 67
Lachenmann, Helmut 81–6
La condition postmoderne (Lyotard) 13
"Lager, Nach-Welt, Überleben" (Wohlfarth) 34 n.7
Lagerlöf, Selma 174 n.13
La hora de los hornos 39
Lang, Fritz 95
language 11, 129–30, 184, 186, 206
advertising 247
communicative 151
darkness of 147, 150–1
musical 27–8, 82, 89
poetic 142, 143, 147, 149, 150–7
queer 163
theory 151, 153
universal 71–2
La Notte 96
late capitalism 22, 60, 61–2, 87, 98–9, 123, 171, 196
La Terre est un Homme 87
Latour, Bruno 129
Lavery, Carl 130, 131
Lazarsfeld, Paul 258 n.1, 259 n.6
learning analytics 239
lecture(s) (Adorno) 3
on aesthetics 1, 40, 45–6, 185–6
History and Freedom 51–2 n.22, 173
on Marx's materialism 219
on New Music 11–12
Lehmann, Harry 80
Leppert, Richard 62
Limestone, and Other Stories (Stifter) 130

limit-situations 112
listening 33 n.3, 58, 59, 65–9, 72, 74–5, 156, 218
"Listening as the Work of Co-composing" (Weber Nicholsen) 33 n.3
logocentrism 132
long-playing records 72–3
The Look of Silence 40, 41, 46, 47
Love, Heather 162, 174 n.4
Luhmann, Niklas 80, 87
Lukács, Georg 101, 215
Lyotard, Jean-François 9, 13

McClary, Susan 90 n.1
Maeterlink, Maurice 168
The Magic Mountain (Mann) 23, 25, 33 n.1
Mahler, Gustav 32, 59, 89, 191
Mahler: A Musical Physiognomy (Adorno) 59
Mahnkopf, Claus-Steffen 81, 84–5, 89–90
Malaparte, Kurzio 112
man-made art 181, 183
man-made environments 135
man-made structures 134
Mann, Thomas 3, 23
manual labor 218, 225
Marx, Karl 9, 113, 116, 215, 216, 218, 219–20, 221, 223, 224–5, 229 n.6–7
Marxism 109, 113, 120
masculinity 166, 167
massacres in Indonesia 37
mass art 58, 96
mass culture 123, 252. *See also* culture industry
mass media 253
material 18, 45–6, 72
filmic 100–3
fragmentary 12
musical 11–12, 83–90, 188–9
notion of 83
material essence 244
materialism 232
material production *vs.* musical production 218

Mayer, Hans 218
Mazis, Glen 128
mechanical music 61, 69
mechanical musical instruments 71
mechanical reproduction 65, 67–8, 69
media. *See also* culture industry
  consumers of 254
  personalization in 253–4
mediation 2, 25, 26, 102, 104, 217–18, 234, 251
  nature 40, 184, 188, 189
Meinhof, Ulrike 85
melancholy 171, 172–3
"Melencolia" (Dürer) 148
memory 29, 32, 45, 115, 133
  digital 69
  future-oriented 209
  involuntary 115
  of suffering 29
mental labour 218, 221, 225
mere existence. *See* bare life/mere existence
Merton College, Oxford 258 n.1
Metamorphosis (Kafka) 195
Metzger, Heinz-Klaus 85
Meyer, Theodor 151
Meyers, Moe 163
Meyers, Todd 49 n.9, 50 n.12, 51 n.17
Midas and Dionysis 173
Milton, John 219–20
mime 126–7
mimesis 38, 41–6, 160–1
  as an evolutionary strategy 42
  art/artwork 207–8, 256–7
  Camp art 161
  as colonial mirror of production 51–2 n.22
  concept 42, 257
  contemporary subjectivity 44–5
  domination of nature 185–6
  enactment 48–9 n.4
  natural history 45
  organized control of 51–2 n.22
  queer discourse 164–5
  rational 256
  sacrifice 41–3

suffering (*see* suffering)
  theory of 42, 49 n.7, 50 n.16, 51–2 n.22
  as utopian aspect 50 n.16, 161
mimetic behavior/comportment 185–9, 207
"The Mimetic Faculty" (Benjamin) 42
mimetic impulses 207–8, 256
Minima Moralia (Adorno) 3, 26, 29, 102–3, 166, 199–200, 208, 251
mirror stage 67
"The Mirror State as Formative of the I Function as Revealed in Psychoanalytic Experience" 67
model 2, 25, 26, 88, 89, 128, 228–9, 252
modern
  academic usage 8
  imperative of being 22
  modernism and 7–18
modernism 1, 2
  concept of 28
  modern and 7–18
Modernism/Modernity 170
modernity 8, 9
  academic usage 8
  experience of 9–10
  subcutaneous in 30
  as sublime 9
  trauma 24
modernization 10
modern music 23, 61, 189. *See also* music
  traditional music *vs.* 31
  trauma of 27
Molnar, Aleksandar 50 n.16
Molnar, Dragana Jeremic 50 n.16
Moments musicaux (Adorno) 60
Monroe, Marilyn 172
montage 103–6
Moore, Jason 132
Morris, Errol 37, 50 n.12
Moten, Fred 174 n.5
motion pictures. *See* films
Mozart 25, 73, 85, 171–2
multiple serialism 11
Muñoz, José 162

music 11–12, 80–90, 119, 123, 136–137
  classicism 25–7
  commodification of 58
  complexism in 86–7
  content of 188
  dodecaphony 87–8
  Ferneyhough's 86–9
  German-Austrian tradition 23
  giving voice to nature 189
  heroic moment 22, 23
  images and 103
  Lachenmann's 81–6
  Mahnkopf's 89–90
  mass production 57
  parameters 87, 91 n.9
  philosophy of 22
  phonograph/phonographic records 57–75
  retrospective model 89
  Schönberg's 22–3, 28, 29, 30, 31–2, 60, 75, 76 n.3, 82, 83, 84, 86, 87, 110, 123, 142, 188, 189, 190
  Stravinsky's 57–8, 59, 69, 70, 75 n.1, 84, 187–91
  subcutaneous fabric 21–33
  traditional 23, 27–32, 33 n.5
  Wagner's 83, 225, 227
  Webern' 83, 84, 88, 184–5, 187–8
musical formalism 90
musical material 11–12, 83–90, 188–9
musical pedagogy 60, 76 n.3
musical performances 60, 218
musical reproduction 31–2
musical totality 30–1
musicology 80, 81
Musikblätter des Anbruch 62
musique concrète instrumentale 82, 91 n.3
mutilation 199
"My Position on the Phonograph Record" (Stravinsky) 70

National Socialists 210
natural beauty 173, 181–4, 257
nature 41–2
  animated 42
  art and 181–91
  dissonance of 45
  domination of 188–9
  human 195–210
  melancholic representation 172–3
  mutilated 40
  progressive control of 40
  suffering 184–5
nature/culture split 42
nature-dominating rationality 185
Nazism 167
"NB Beckett's criticism of Kafka" (Adorno) 110
Nealon, Christopher 171
negation 2, 12, 249
  determined 120, 162, 171–2, 210, 249, 250, 255
  of future 162
  metaphysical 121
  mimetic 165
  music as critique and 90
  poetic language 153–4
  queer rejection of "the good" 162
  of status quo 257
  of tradition 23, 31–2
negative dialectics 58, 108, 120, 250–1
  positivism *vs.* 234–5
Negative Dialectics (Adorno) 3, 24, 33, 121–2, 162, 198, 251
neoliberalism 44, 61–2, 76 n.7. *See also* capitalism
  education and 236–43
  exploitation practices 133
  political economy 76 n.7
neologism 24
New Complexity 86
New Music 11–12
New Musicology 80, 90 n.1
Nichols, Bill 50 n.10, 50 n.14
Nietzsche, Friedrich 196
Night Music: Essays on Music 1928–1962 (Adorno) 33 n.2
nihilism 122
Nikish, Artur 57
Nixon, Rob 137

No Future: Queer Theory and the Death Drive (Edelman) 162
noise 84, 85, 87, 131, 152
   extraterrestrial 29
nonidentical 3–4, 96, 133, 167, 183, 196, 199, 204, 206, 256, 257
nonidentity 25, 31, 39, 40, 112, 163, 171, 196, 202, 204, 206, 250
Nonnenmann, Rainer 84, 85
Nono, Luigi 82
Norris, Margot 210 n.3
North German Radio 74
"Notes on Camp" (Sontag) 169, 170
Notes to Literature/Noten zur Literatur (Adorno) 144, 158 n.1
nouveaux romanciers 109
nuclear threat 136–8

objectification 48, 221, 248
objective forms 25
obsolete category of taste 169
oil cultures 137
"On Lyric Poetry and Society" (Adorno) 157–8
"On the Fetishism in Music and the Regression of Listening" (Adorno) 218
"On the Mimetic Faculty" (Benjamin) 152, 155
"On the Social Situation of Music" (Adorno) 187–8
ontological essentialism 114
opaque similarities 164
opera 60, 72–3, 74, 82, 85
Oppenheimer, Joshua 36–41, 44, 46, 48, 49–50 n.9, 50 n.11, 50 n.12, 50 n.14
optical unconsciousness 104
optimism 1, 95, 113
orchestral music 60
organized control of mimesis 51–2 n.22
The Origin of German Tragic Drama (Benjamin) 77 n.13, 146

Paddison, Max 33 n.2, 192 n.5, 192 n.6, 192 n.11
pain 160, 161, 163, 165, 199, 204, 206

painting 83
Pancasila Youth Movement 43–4
paradies fluten (Flooding Paradise) 132, 133
Paradise Lost (Milton) 219
Parisian existentialism 111
particular 2, 26, 27, 28, 31
Pay for Success 239
Peirce, Charles 76 n.9
performances 126–38
   augmented reality 134–6
   climate change 132–3, 137–8
   nuclear threat 136–8
permanence 150
Pero, Allan 171
Perroud, Mark 138 n.1
personalization in media 253–4
Personalized Learning movement 240
phenomenology 111, 112, 114, 221, 223
Phenomenology of Spirit (Hegel) 221, 223
Philosophy of Modern Music (Adorno) 59, 76 n.2, 82
Philosophy of New Music (Adorno) 87, 189, 190
The Philosophy of Spirit (Hegel) 223
phonograph 57–75
   mechanical reproduction of sound 67–8
   photography *vs.* 65–6, 68–9
   primordial affect 66–7
   as a status symbol 66
   technological prehistory of 71
phonographic records
   as empty clay pots 68
   enabling possession of music 70
   form of 68–73
   as a form of writing 71–2
   long-playing records 72–3
   modernist perceptions of 75
   photograph *vs.* 65–6, 68–9
   as product of modernity 70–1
   repeated listening 74
   significance of 73
photographic images 100
photography 65–6, 68–9
physiognomy 114–15

280   INDEX

pianista   70
pianola   69–70
piano rolls   57
Picasso, Pablo   3
Pinter, Harold   111
The Places We Learned to Call   50 n.11
Plass, Ulrich   154
player piano   69–70
poetic landscape   144
poetry   122
    Eichendorff's   141–58
    impossibility of   15, 16–17
    language   142, 143, 147, 149, 150–7
The Politics and Poetics of Camp (Meyers)   163
Pollock, Friedrich   229 n.10
polyvinyl chloride   77 n.15. See also phonographic records
pop art   170
Popper, Karl   243
popular music   39, 58, 66, 137
positivism   232–45
    as an ideology   234, 235
    conspiracy theories   241–5
    criticism of   234–6
    education and   235–41
    logic of   236
    negative dialectics *vs.*   234–5
postmodern   13–14
postmodernism   13, 80–1
postmodernity   13
Poussin   173, 175 n.26
power structures   95, 97, 101
preponderance of objects   129–32
Pression (Lachenmann)   82
primordial affect   66–7
Prisms (Adorno)   31
private labor   215, 216
productive labor   219–20
productive worker   219
progress   9, 24, 58, 122–3, 228
    scientific   197
    technological   65–6
progressive cultural productions   248
progressive *vs.* regressive art   122
Proust, Marcel   3, 29, 108, 114, 115

psychasthenia   42
psychasthenia, theory of   42
psychological suppression   199

Quasi una fantasia: Essays on Modern Music (Adorno)   60
queer identity   162–3
queer-phobic sensibility   168–9
Queer Social Philosophy (Halle)   166
queer theory   161–74. See also Camp aesthetics
    ethical agenda   163
    interiority   163–4
    mimesis   164–5

Rabaté, Jean-Michel   127
Rachmaninoff, Sergey   70
racial essence   243
"Radar Camas: Alexandrium Giganteous Spores"   135
radiation   137
radio   76 n.6
rationalization   7
Ray, Satyajit   49 n.5
realism   39, 101
reality
    collective perception of   101
    photographic depiction of   102
real subsumption   220
"Real Time in Oberplan: On Stifters Dinge-A Theatre of Deceleration" (Goebbels)   130
Rebentisch, Juliane   172–3, 175 n.21
reconciliation   25, 26, 28, 31, 32, 38, 41, 48, 153, 171–2, 187, 189, 205, 256
reflection   181
    distance/distancing   171–2
    inhuman   201–4
    self   110, 111, 187, 243
    theory of   101
reflective aesthetics   222
regression   16, 116, 160, 189, 199, 247
reification   10, 11, 13, 14, 16, 21, 42, 46, 71, 191, 201, 208, 209, 221–2
Renaissance   9

representation 100–3
  melancholic 172–3
repression 14–15, 29, 85, 166, 167, 198, 200, 203
reproduction, mechanical 65, 67–8, 69
rescue of semblance 255, 259 n.8
resistance 29, 38, 121, 163, 164
  in aesthetics 255–8
  artistic production 46
  to identity thinking 196
  intellectual 162
  model for 2
  to social unfreedom 215
  to systematic understanding 204
  to totalitarianism 114
"Rewriting Modernity" (Lyotard) 13
Richter, Gerhard 34 n.7
Rickert, Heinrich 114, 115
ridiculousness 185–9
Rimbaud, Arthur 8, 19 n.3, 22
risk 136–8
Robbe-Grillet, Alain 109
Robinson, Geoffrey 37
Rohman, Carrie 210–11 n.3
Romanticism 148, 157
romanticism 15, 117, 145, 146, 184
Rosen, Philip 49 n.6
Ross, Andrew 175 n.15, 175 n.17
Rothe, Matthias 229 n.13
rubber 133
Rubenstein, Artur 70
Ruisdael, Jacob Van 131
Rukun, Adi 40

"Sachlichkeit" 169
sacrifice 38, 41–3
  Enlightenment's version of 42
  ritual 41, 43
Sarraute, Nathalie 109
Sartre, Jean-Paul 109, 111–12
Savage, Robert 211 n.19
Schaeffer, Pierre 91 n.3
Schlipphacke, Heidi 174–5 n.13
Schoenberg, Arnold 3, 22–3, 28, 29, 30, 31–2, 60, 75, 76 n.3, 82, 83, 84, 86, 87, 110, 123, 142, 188, 189, 190

sci-fi B movies 50 n.11
scripted lessons 239
second reflection 203–4
Second Viennese School 76 n.3, 83, 184, 189, 190
Second World War 1, 15, 17, 18, 40, 112, 136, 165, 169, 189–90, 202
secret agents 243
Sedgwick, Eve Kosofsky 161
Seidlin, Oskar 141–4, 148–9, 156–7
Selbstbesinnung 33 n.3
self-preservation 50 n.16
self-reflection 110, 111, 187, 243
self-reification 221–2
semblance 21, 26, 27, 28, 45, 165, 200, 206, 255
serious music 58. *See also* classical music
Shenker, Israel 110
short-playing records 73
shudder 209
Simmel, Georg 236
Smith, Jack 172
social antagonisms 226, 235
social contradictions in art/ artwork 222
social Darwinism 211 n.5
Social Emotional Learning schemes 240
Social Impact Bonds 239. *See also* Pay for Success
social labor 45, 214–29. *See also* labor
societies of control 238
sociocultural conventions 202
sociocultural structures 202
Solanas, Fernando 39
song of birds 182–3
Sontag, Susan 169, 170, 175 n.18–19
Sound Figures (Adorno) 59
sound mass 68
species 203
"Speech on Lyric and Society" (Adorno) 142
Spengler, Oswald 247
sphere of communication 255, 259 n.9
Spitzer, Michael 80

split consciousness   254
Squirrel Hill Pittsburgh synagogue
    shooting   243
Stalking the Subject (Rohman)   210–
    11 n.3
standardized testing   234
star system   253
status symbol, phonograph as   66
Steffen, Will   136
Steuer, Daniel   33 n.1
Steuermann, Eduard   60
Stifter, Adalbert   129–30
"Stifters Dinge"   129–32
Stravinsky, Igor   3, 57–8, 59, 69, 70,
    75 n.1, 84, 187–91
"Stravinsky: A Dialectical Portrait"
    (Adorno)   189–91
structure   84, 88, 99, 156, 257–8
    messianic   163
    opaque similarities   164
structure-sound   84
subcutaneous   21–33
    classicism   25–7
    literal meaning   22
    notion of   22
Subianto, Prabowo   51 n.21
subjectivity   44–5, 48, 198, 208
    camouflage and mimesis   45
    compositional   27, 89
    language and   148, 149, 153
    lyric poetry   144–5
    objectified world of commodity   44
    theory of   158 n.3
    unruly   25
sublimation   14–15
sublime   3, 9, 22, 42, 45, 130, 135,
    182, 227
subtraction   111, 122, 123
suffering   45, 48, 160–1, 189, 257
    affect of   162, 165
    ambivalence   166
    as authentic art   160, 170,
        171, 187
    Camp aesthetics   171, 172,
        173, 174
    capacity for extreme   32–3
    as corporeal   199
    dissonance   208–9

expression of   160–1, 189, 257
externalizing and objectifying   18
memory of   29, 160
nature   184–5
nonidentical identity   167
right to expression   249
Suharto   37, 46, 48 n.1, 51 n.21
surrealism   52 n.23
Swamp (Ruisdael)   131
symphony/symphonic music   57, 70,
    74, 75, 98, 191

taste, obsolete category of   169
Taussig, Michael   51–2 n.22
tautology   250
taxonomies   203
Taylor, Frederick   236
Taylorism   236–7
television   162
telos of knowledge   256–7
temporality of artwork   173
theater
    as epistemological model   129
    performance styles and   126–38
    transformative power of   127–
        8, 129
The Theater of the Absurd
    (Esslin)   111
theatricality   82, 131, 132
theatrical language   131
theatrical model   133
theatrical strategies   138
theoretical formation   252
theory   244
Theory of Musical Reproduction
    (Adorno)   60
theory of psychasthenia   42
Thiel, Tamico   134
Third Cinema   39
Third Symphony (Mahler)   191
time ecology   130
"Todesfuge" (Celan)   16–17
tone mass   68
Ton-Masse   68
totalitarianism and
    homosexuality   166
totalitarian propaganda films   101
totalitarian state   48

totality 113
  musical 30–1
totalization 111
"Tough Baby" (Adorno) 166
tradition 28–9
traditional forms 100
traditional music 23, 27–32, 33 n.5
  modern music vs. 31
  subcutaneous fabric 23
tragedy 118, 146–7, 167
transience 26, 27, 28, 30, 144, 147, 150, 157, 172–3
"Translator's Introduction" (Hullot-Kentor) 45
Transparencies of Film (Adorno) 100
"Transparencies on Film" (Adorno and Eisler) 38, 96–7
trauma 24
Triebleben der Klänge 30
Trump, Donald 233, 241
truth
  of critique/critical thought 250
  enhanced content 134–6
  facts 234
  positivism as an ideology of 234
  taste 169
  of theory 252

Über Jazz (Adorno) 76 n.11
United Kingdom 37
universal 2, 31
  delusive context 165
  false identity with 28
  society and 153
universal atomic annihilation 118
universal commodification 224
universal identity 183
universality 25–6, 221
universalizing of guilt 49 n.9
universal language 71–2
University of Frankfurt 77 n.13
Unmittelbarkeit und Sinndeutung (Rickert) 114
The Unnamable (Beckett) 109, 120, 122
unruly subjectivity 25
utopia 162, 173–4
utopian 257

Verwesen 24
Vienna 60, 62, 76 n.3, 109
Viennese Classicism 25, 30
Villarejo, Amy 162
vinyl 77 n.15. *See also* phonographic records
violence 36–48, 199–200
  intangible forms 199
  physical 199
  psychological 199
volatility and risk 136–8
voucher schemes 233
vulgar/vulgarity 168–70

Wagner, Richard 83, 225, 227
Waiting for Godot (Beckett) 109, 115, 116
Warhol, Andy 172
Weber, Max 10, 91 n.7
Webern, Anton 83, 84, 88, 184–5, 187–8
Weber Nicholsen, Shierry 19 n.5, 33 n.2, 33 n.3, 34 n.9, 48–9 n.4, 164
Wellmer, Albrecht 189
Welsch, Wolfgang 13–14
Widodo, Joko 51 n.21
Wilde, Oscar 168
Wilke, Sabine 174–5 n.13
Williams, Raymond 14
Wirtschaft und Gesellschaft (Weber) 10
Wohlfarth, Irving 34 n.7
Wolin, Richard 52 n.23
works of art. *See* art/artwork
The World in the Evening (Isherwood) 170
"world risk society" 138

x-ray 23–4, 25, 26

Zeitschrift für Sozialforschung (Adorno) 76 n.8, 76 n.11, 258 n.1
"Zur Geschichte der poetischen Literatur Deutschands" (Eichendorff) 151

www.ingramcontent.com/pod-product-compliance
Lightning Source LLC
Chambersburg PA
CBHW072126290426
44111CB00012B/1800